THE
FAMILY
God's Weapon for
VICTORY

ROBERT ANDREWS

Winepress
Publishing
MUKILTEO, WA 98275

To Kathryn and Hugh Andrews,
   who taught me to fight;

To Jill,
   my faithful fellow-warrior;

To my children,
   for whom the battle is just beginning.

Table of Contents

Part Five
"Selecting a Mate"

Part Six
"Building a Heritage"

Appendix

Introduction

God's people are at war. This is clear from even a casual reading of the Bible, and is confirmed by the media every day. We are in a battle-to-the-death with an alien world system, controlled by the enemy of our souls, Satan himself. No prisoners will be taken in this war, and any possibility for compromise is an illusion.

However, many Christians live their lives as though we were at peace. They are able to insulate themselves from the front lines, blissfully unaware of the intensity of the battles that rage on other fronts, in other places. They continue to function on a daily basis in peace-time mode, making no preparation for battle.

Our enemy is an accomplished deceiver, a master of many disguises, who can infiltrate our lives without our knowledge. He piggy-backs into our homes via such things as television, movies, neighborhood friends, recreational activities and innumerable other apparently innocent pursuits, until he is in a position to deliver what is frequently a crushing, disabling blow to our families. Who can defend himself, much less go on the offensive, when he does not recognize that his enemy is all around him?

When Satan attacks overtly, the reality of the war, and the wickedness of our foe, breaks in upon our consciousness like a flood. A Christian husband who had always been a good provider leaves his wife for a female business associate with whom he had frequent "business lunches." A teen-age son, who was a "good kid" as he was growing up in the church, is picked off by the enemy and leaves home to immerse himself in the drug culture. A daughter who was a spiritual leader in high school, is mesmerized by an anti-Christian boy, and runs away and marries him, forsaking her family and all the values she has been taught. The war is now a heart-breaking reality in each of these families.

1

This book is an attempt to help Christians see what is happening around them <u>before</u> they are crippled by the Devil, and rendered ineffectual in battle, and then to equip them to be more effective in the war that is impossible for them to avoid. It grew from the material I taught to seniors over a four year period, at two Christian high schools in Seattle, Washington.

Over the years I have recognized that one of the major battlefields in the cosmic war with Satan and his world system is the family. Sadly, God's people, for the most part, do not have a coherent biblical theology of family life that prepares them to be effective on that front in the battle. Teaching my high school family living class motivated me to organize such a theology. This book is the result.

Much in the book may be found to be controversial, even offensive, to today's reader. While some things that I suggest the Bible prescribes were considered customary, even by non-Christians, only two generations ago, today they are seen as "out-dated," "extreme," or "fanatical," even by Christians. This is a commentary on the enemy's ability to confuse God's people, and to cause us to look to some source other than God's Word for direction.

This book is not a nice, safe book that will help the reader feel good, experience pleasant family life, and live happily ever after. Christian book stores are already filled with books like that. This book is designed to bring discomfort, to challenge basic presuppositions about how a family functions, and to bring readers to a fork in their life's path. Will they continue with "business as usual," or are they ready to be obedient to the One who called them to the battle?

I have tried to omit personal opinions and theories. I'm sure I have not been entirely successful, and there are undoubtedly errors of both commission and ommission. For those I am sorry. The interpretation of the scriptures noted obviously does not carry the infallibility of the scriptures themselves. But my comments represent my best, good-faith attempt to interpret the relevant verses on the family correctly. If there is disagreement on an issue, put it on a back-burner and plow ahead, saving the point of contention for future reflection.

The reader will quickly perceive that I have used the kingdom of God as the touchstone, the frame of reference, by which all family truth is measured. A recovery of an understanding of what it means to walk in the kingdom of God in all areas of life is essential in order for the church to be successful in battle. But that is another book.

This book has indeed been a family effort. My wife Jill, my son Adam and his wife Missy, my other son Jason, and my daughter Ramah have not only been the source of many illustrations, but they have all edited the manuscript, and given invaluable suggestions as to the final form the book has taken. They have also been very willing for their sins and mistakes to be exposed, knowing that others will profit as a result.

Finally, I have not written this book necessarily to sell as many copies as possible. My father died a year before Jill and I were married, so my children never knew their grandfather. I have nothing he ever wrote, so any first-hand knowledge of Hugh Andrews dies with me. I wrote this book primarily to leave for my posterity, so that great grandchildren I will never see will be able to know what their great grandfather believed and taught during his lifetime. Thus they will be better able to understand their heritage.

The truths contained in these pages are not some esoteric theory, gleaned from the Bible by brilliant insight, but still waiting to be applied. As you will see, they have been hammered out in my experience, and in the experience of those faithful brothers and sisters who have walked with me at Tree of Life Christian Church. I have discovered that what God says is worthy of my complete trust and confidence, regardless of current trends and customs. The contents of these pages represent the foundation of my life and ministry over the last 30 years. May God use these truths in your life as He has in mine.

Robert B. Andrews
Seattle, Washington,
July, 1995

Part One
"Laying Foundations"

Chapter 1

Family Shapers

On a recent radio talk show, I heard a noted child psychologist giving a caller advice on what to do when her two year-old had a temper-tantrum. The wisdom from this Ph.D. went something like this:

"Be sure everything that he possibly could break is out of reach, and that the doors are locked so he can't get away, and then lock yourself in your bedroom until he is exhausted and calms down again."

As I listened incredulously I realized that this advice was not given as a joke, but was to be taken seriously. The caller was actually encouraged to "give it a try." The talk-show host then expressed amazement at the wisdom of the guest, and marvelled at his "expert insight." Can't you see the chaos in that home as the little tyke empties the refrigerator on the kitchen floor, dumps the flour canister on the sofa, and swings from the chandelier, all the while reveling in the fact that he has actually driven his mother into hiding. If this "expert insight" is followed, this two-year-old will become a tyrant, ruling over his parents and holding them hostage to his every whim.

This example illustrates a very real problem: If a Ph.D. in child psychology can't be trusted to give you reliable help in raising your children, who can? Just because you can biologically reproduce, does this qualify you to be a successful father or mother? Also, when young people stand before the minister on their wedding day, do they know that they have the tools to build their marriage into a lasting one? No bride or groom expects their marriage to fail, but half of them do. Your family can be a well-spring of love, encouragement, and support, supplying a foundation for a successful and fulfilling life and expressing the reality of the presence of Jesus Christ. It also can be a millstone about your neck, a burden too heavy to bear, a trap from which it seems impossible to escape, and a denial of the legitimacy of the faith you profess. Christians are not immune to such tragic marriages, for the divorce statistics for church members are not significantly different from the general populace.

Your view of what constitutes family is a product of a number of influences, most of which you are probably not even aware. The advice of the "expert" on the talk show is most likely so extreme that it would not shape your idea of how a family should function, but how about more subtle influences? Let's look at several "family shapers" and see if your view of family has indeed been "shaped" by them.

Parents

The strongest influence on your idea of what a family should be is your own family. God designed us to be imprinted by our parents and to learn from them how to function in our own families. Did your father or your mother handle the money in the family? How were final decisions determined? Did your parents bicker and shout? Did they spank the children? Were problems discussed openly, or did everybody ignore them in silence until anger subsided? Was it easy or hard for family members to admit guilt? Your family has been an unconscious model for you, and you will naturally follow that model as an adult yourself.

That is why parents will often say, "I find myself doing to my children the very thing my father did to me, the thing I vowed I would never do." If your home was not a happy, nurturing place where you were prepared well for adulthood, the parental model is a detrimental one. On the other hand, if your home was a genuinely Godly one, you have a good start towards having a successful family yourself.

My parents provided a warm, loving atmosphere for me as a child. I had no brothers and sisters, and my parents had me only after much difficulty. I was the apple of their eye; however, they also understood discipline and ran a very tight ship. I learned early on that respect and obedience were expected of me. I violated the family standards at my peril. The respect and obedience of my own children were thus my top priority as a parent, even before I learned any child training theory, not because I knew that that was important for their sakes, but because that had been modeled for me by my parents.

Let me say up front that a religious family is not necessarily a Godly one. Some of the most unhappy families are also some of the most religious, so don't give up on God because of the damage a religious family has produced in your life.

Movies and Television

Next to parents, nothing impacts us like the visual media. Many children are parked in front of the T.V. from the time they are old enough to sit up alone, absorbing unconsciously all of the ideas flowing out of that powerful little box - ideas about the opposite sex, about marriage and about family. Sexual conquests, promiscuity, marital unfaithfulness, homosexuality, and cohabitation are all portrayed by the media in an acceptable, if not favorable, light. The negative results of lifestyles like these are never mentioned. Sex is used to sell everything from blue-jeans to automobiles, and religious people who might disagree with this view are pictured as narrow-minded bigots, a radical fringe with no compassion.

The traditional family is seldom, if ever, portrayed positively. "Ozzie and Harriet" and "Father Knows Best" are ridiculed as prudish relics of another age. T.V. shows picturing non-traditional families have caused the undiscerning public, many Christians included, to believe that the label "family" can be applied to any living arrangement whatsoever.

The Hollywood idea of love is no less pervasive. Certainly R-rated movies are filled with sex and violence, but a P.G. rating means that the film is O.K., right? Only if you don't care whether you absorb the view that "falling in love" means ringing bells and clashing cymbals, and that there is absolutely nothing you can do when "it" happens to you. It matters not if one happens to be married to someone else, if "it" happens, "it" happens! Certainly, with this perspective, being "in love" has everything to do with hormones and nothing to do with commitment. When the bells and cymbals stop, Hollywood love is over, and one had better begin a search for "it" again.

Many Christians have innocently watched movie after movie, seemingly harmless P.G. or G-rated ones, never realizing that their views of love and marriage were being affected, and even defined, by the images of the media. Our ideas about "being in love," about the seriousness of the marriage commitment, and about the process by which two people come together have been shaped by the "silver screen."

Psychology

There is no lack of books, advice columns, and college courses on the topic of family, for it has been recognized that intact families provide the best defense against drugs, teen-age pregnancy, crime, depression, suicide, and even homelessness.[1] However, as these psychological helps have proliferated, the family continues to struggle.

One nationally-syndicated advice column recently advised an inquirer not to tell her husband about an affair she had had, since "what he doesn't know won't hurt him." Is this the right advice? How do you know?

Trends in psychology change. In the 1950's the parents' bible for raising children was *You and Your Child*, by Benjamin Spock, a famous pediatrician. His word was law, and he was never seriously questioned by the general public. However, in recent years he has altered his previous stands on permissive child training, too late for the generation of children that were parented according to his book. That which is accepted practice in the medical and psychological community today may be in complete disfavor tomorrow. Trendy methods and revolutionary ideas which are hot, new topics for books and talk-shows have a habit of cooling off in the red-hot crucible of experience.

<u>Peers</u>

If you don't know what to do, the natural tendency is to do what everyone around you is doing, particularly an area as inexact as family behavior. Measurable results are so far in the future that no one knows whether or not a particular view of family behavior will produce good fruit.

Take education for instance. If you went to public school as a child, and all your friends are sending their children to public school, the pressure to do the same for your children is significant. It is always difficult to be a pioneer, a trail-blazer. Maybe a Christian school, or home-school, looks really attractive to you, but if no one else is doing it, it will be difficult to be the first in your circles to try.

My wife Jill and I are both products of public education, and we never considered another option for our own children when they were in elementary school back in the 1970's. Most of our Christian friends were doing the same thing we were doing. However, one couple had their children in a tiny Christian school with an enrollment of about 20 students, and we thought they were absolutely crazy. They were true pioneers, willing to follow what they saw to be right, regardless of peer pressure. Now, some 20 years later, we have had a small, co-operative home-school in our church for 11 years, and have seen and adopted the vision for Christian education that my friends had years earlier. Most of us are not strong enough to be able to do what we see to be right regardless of the opinions of those around us.

Teen-agers are particularly susceptible to patterning themselves after their peers. Young people who have always loved their parents, suddenly become sullen and non-communicative at home, because this is the behavior their friends at school are exhibiting. The urge to be a part of a group, to belong, to fit in, is a powerful motivator, and needs to be recognized as a strong "family shaper." The problem arises when no one in the group knows what to do. As Jesus once said, "They are blind leaders of the blind. And if the blind leads the blind, both will fall into a ditch" (Matthew 15:14).

Trial-and-error

A well-defined vision for family life is a crucial part of a successful family. Too many people employ a "trial-and-error" approach instead, making random changes aimed at rectifying previous mistakes. Certainly there is always some mid-course correction, but the problem with this method of administrating a family is that before an error is recognized, many opportunities for positive experiences have been missed. Often tragic damage has been done, damage that may be impossible to undo. Parents have but one try at parenting per child.

Many young people begin marriage with no conception of what will be expected of them, what their role in the relationship will be, or even what obstacles they will face, much less a vision for their family. They become reactors to whatever life brings, rather than initiators who attack life with an overall battle-plan. Their family is shaped by what appear to be almost random choices, some successful and some not. How much better if one can begin marriage with a definite view of family life that has been tested over the years and found to produce the desired results.

Church

If you are a serious church-goer, and pay attention every Sunday, there is a chance that you might have picked up some useful information on how a family should function. However, it is a slim chance, because most churches don't get involved in preaching and teaching on controversial topics that might lead to declining attendance and reduced offerings.

Make no mistake, the topic of family is controversial. Roles of men and women, the place of homosexuals, premarital sex, and child training are all areas of disagreement, not only between Christians and secularists, but also within the church itself. There is no longer a certain sound coming from the trumpet of the people of God as to what constitutes a Christian family. Even if your church does deal with this topic, how can you know for sure that its perspective is the right one when the church down the street presents a different view?

The Minister of Music of a large church was encouraged to come to me for counsel by a mutual friend. He was literally beside himself with frustration. His daughter had been dating a rather unsavory young man for some time, a young man who had initially claimed to be a Christian. She was mesmerized by his charm and, in her father's estimation, was completely controlled by him. She had enrolled in the community college he attended, took a job he had found for her, and accepted a rather expensive automobile from him as a gift. He was also actively involved in the process of turning this 19-year-old girl against her family. The father had just gotten wind of the fact that his daughter planned to marry the young man regardless of whether or not he gave his approval, and felt completely helpless. What should he do? The outcome of this story, including both the counsel I gave him, and the action he took, are related in Chapter 6. This man's church, where he was a staff member, had no answers for him, and had not equipped him to guide his daughter through the perilous waters of mate selection. His church never addressed such crucial family issues.

For too long we have concentrated solely on saving the lost outside the church, and have not learned to preserve the fruit from biological reproduction that God has placed inside the church. If we save the world and lose our own children, we start over again every generation without the strength of a Christian heritage. Equipping the saints for the work of the ministry is one of the tasks of the church (Ephesians 4:11-16), and the most important ministry of the saints is that of training their own families in the ways of the kingdom of God. The question is, "Which church presents the proper vision for Godly families?"

If you think about it, we have all been influenced by these "family shapers" to one degree or another, and yet it can be readily seen that none of them are reliable as a source for truly authoritative information. Where can I turn? Can I do more than just "fly by the seat of my pants?"

I would like to propose to you that the Bible is your only utterly reliable source for information on how to successfully function in your family and be fulfilled in that role. It also tells you how to make your family a source of power and glory as it is used by God to extend His kingdom.

That's not surprising, is it? You knew that's where I was headed. But I want you to know that simply <u>saying</u> the Bible has the answers you need, and really <u>acting</u> on what the Bible says, are two entirely different things. Most of us say we believe the Bible, but when we are faced with a real issue, we look elsewhere for a solution. We rarely think to try to apply biblical principles as best we can to the problems at hand. The Bible becomes, for all practical purposes, a book of salvation only; one that tells me how to get to heaven, but not how to live in every area of life on a daily basis. When the rubber hits the road, we often subconsciously turn to one of the "family shapers" mentioned above, rather than to the only authoritative repository of truth.

We betray our authority source with our conversation. When discussing family issues, I often hear phrases like, "Well, I think...," or, "I believe...," or, "It seems to me that...." When we talk like this, the words that follow these phrases generally express personal opinions formed unconsciously by an influence of which we are probably completely unaware.

When I taught the material in this book in high school family living classes, invariably great controversy arose. There were almost as many differences of opinion as there were students. Some of the students got angry, even to the point, in one instance, of shouting at me in anger in class. The cause of the anger was the agreement we had made at the first of the course to use the Bible as our authority source, our "standard of faith and practice." All agreed that this was right, because, after all, "We're Christians, aren't we, and we believe the Bible, don't we?"

I did not accept personal opinion if it contradicted biblical principles, and I always asked the student who presented an idea where that could be found in the Bible. This proved to be very frustrating to a number of students who soon discovered they didn't believe the Bible as much as they thought they did, but indeed had been captured, in more ways than they knew, by the world's way of thinking.

We have the mind of Christ (1 Cor. 2:16). This is not some mystical possession, hard to understand, that some have and some don't, but is simply the capacity to think God's thoughts after Him, a capacity possessed by every true believer. We find His thoughts in the Bible, and as we learn them and begin to think biblically with the Holy Spirit's illumination, we think with the mind of Christ.

Bringing the Bible, God's thoughts, to bear on every issue, including the family, as the authoritative standard for decision-making is what life in the kingdom of God is all about. It is also a guarantee of conflict, even hatred, from the world, the kingdom of darkness (John 15:18-25). Some of the most violent opposition can even come from worldly Christians who are deceived into believing there can be another standard besides the Word of God. However, we must learn that pleasing God by being obedient to Him is all that really matters, and then determine to do that in our families by faithfully applying biblical truth to every situation. In Chapter 2, we'll see what that means.

"Father, make me aware of the degree to which I have been conformed to the world's thinking in the area of family. Rectify my thoughts to conform to Yours as You have revealed them in Your Word. Amen"

Questions for discussion

1. Which of the "family-shapers" mentioned have influenced your ideas about family? In what ways? What other factors have gone into determining what you think a family involves?

2. What is meant by the "mind of Christ"? Do you have it? What would be necessary for you to do in order to actually experience what that entails?

3. Discuss your view of a family that functions according to the Bible. What would the parents be like? The children? What would people around them think after watching them closely?

[1] "The Family in America," The Rockford Institute, Nov., 1989

Chapter 2

Possible Sources of Ultimate Truth

Before we get into specific family issues, I want to lay a philosophical foundation that will be a great help for you throughout the remainder of the book, so stick with me because this information is important for properly understanding the higher-interest material that follows.

In Chapter 1, I suggested that the Bible was our final authority in all matters of faith <u>and</u> practice. This means that the Bible is our standard in <u>every</u> area of life, including the family. It contains principles that God expects us to follow if we want to be obedient to Him. You may or may not have trouble with that assertion, so I would like to make you aware of what other options you have when it comes to determining a source to which you might look for ultimate truth. In other words, I want you to ask yourself the question, "How do I know what I know?," or, "Whom do I choose to believe?"

What is Your Epistemology?

The process of investigating the origin and limits of knowledge is described by the term *epistemology*. If you want to be intellectually honest, you need to know what epistemology you have adopted, and then be willing to admit it to yourself. This chapter presents **natural law, human law,** and **revealed law** as the only three options you have as possible sources of ultimate truth. Let me make it clear that you already have one of these epistemologies, whether you are aware of it or not.

<u>Natural Law</u>

During the hearings to consider Clarence Thomas's qualifications to serve on the Supreme Court of the United States, you might remember that some of his writings expressing an interest in natural law created quite a stir. Liberal senators were very upset that Thomas might believe in a source of law, or truth, outside of man himself. In writing about natural law, Thomas was simply echoing Thomas Jefferson when he spoke of "the law of nature and nature's God" in the Declaration of Independence.

Historically, most people have understood "natural law" to mean a set of laws, inherent in nature, placed there by God, and universally known by everyone, that tell us how to live. They can be understood by Christians and non-Christians alike, theoretically giving both camps a common ground of agreement. Natural law forms the basis for, as the Declaration states, "the unalienable rights of life, liberty and the pursuit of happiness." The English jurist, William Blackstone, who was the leading legal authority in colonial America, was a firm believer in natural law. His writings were read by all young lawyers in America before they began to practice their profession. The colonists felt they were justified in asserting their independence from England based on natural law theory.

Still, after acknowledging the laws of nature and nature's God in our founding document, God is not welcome in our public arena today. If God has spoken in nature, and everyone can discern what he is saying, why do we ignore His voice?

What's Wrong With Natural Law?

The answer lies in several inherent weaknesses in natural law theory. **First**, nature is not an independent source of law. There is really no such thing as "nature," or "mother nature." Throughout the Bible, God is said to be the Creator and Sustainer of the universe (Col. 1:16,17). He is actively involved every day in sending rain, bringing forth vegetation, providing food for animals, causing volcanoes and earthquakes, sending His Spirit to create life, and withdrawing it from His creatures in death. (Ps. 104). Nature, then, is governed by God's law, and is not an independent source of law itself. Listen to what Professor Archie Jones says:

"The essence of...Natural Law thought is to deny that nature is providentially sustained and directed by the God of Scripture, for such an affirmation would require men to bow to God's revealed word and law. Having denied God's sovereign

16

control over nature, men are left the task of discovering whether there be ethical principles for law inherent in nature, and if so, what these are. If God is not in control of nature, then nature is normative for man, who lives in nature. But does nature contain rules or laws of morality and justice, or not? ...(I)n the absence of God there can be no agreed definition of nature, nor common principles of ethics and law.[1]

Second, nature itself is under God's curse. All of God's creation shows the effects of man's sin, so we cannot get a completely accurate read on what God is saying from looking at nature. Is it right that the strong gobble up the weak? From looking only at nature one could certainly come to this conclusion and then make laws based on this principle. Because animals eat their young, is it normal and therefore right for us to do the same? Because animals are not monogamous sexually, and kill other members of the same species, is that acceptable conduct? Without another standard outside of nature we find ourselves without any firm guidelines to follow.

Third, nature is not specific. Even if we were to assume that we could see past the fallen state of nature and derive principles to guide us in the enactment of our laws, we could never be specific enough to make natural law practical. For instance, how could I distinguish between murder and self defense? Does nature tell me what criminal penalties to assign to certain crimes? I could never derive from nature that it is criminal to lie under oath, nor could I ever get any guidance on a whole range of "moral" issues.

Fourth, men suppress the truth. The Bible teaches that some things can be known from creation, if we had eyes to see. God has left abundant testimony to Himself in His creation, and that testimony is commonly known as "general revelation." God has left His fingerprints on His universe, so that we can't say we haven't heard about Him when He comes to judge us, but we refuse to see the evidence. The Apostle Paul says in Romans 1, that men are without excuse, for creation itself clearly shows the power and divine nature of God (general revelation). Men, however, suppress the truth, become futile in their thoughts, and are therefore fools. Before we become Christians, we are unable to profit from the natural law that God has left in His universe, because our hearts are darkened and unable to see.

If you are a Christian, however, even though creation is fallen, you can see God in His world, but your non-Christian friend can't. The blindness of non-Christians to God's eternal revelation makes a theoretical common ground, or natural law, an illusion. You have new eyes to see (2 Corinthians 5:17), but he does not. There is no basis of agreement based in natural law theory (Matthew 13:13-16). What laws he can know from nature he is blind to, because of his natural rejection of truth. Indeed, "There is none who understands, there is none who seeks after God" (Romans 3:11). Man, then, is left to decide for himself what "nature" is saying, and his fallen humanity is not capable of reasoning its way to correct conclusions.

Natural Law, while appearing to be an answer for those who know intuitively that there must be a source of authority outside of man himself, is riddled with weaknesses that render it nothing more than a religious mirage with no actual substance for practical implementation. This is not to negate in any way the reality of God's general revelation of Himself in nature. But that revelation is totally inadequate to show man how to live, for that is not the purpose of general revelation. Its purpose is "so that they are without excuse" (Romans 1:20).

Human Law

Most of us have grown up with human law, often called *legal positivism*, as our practical source of ultimate truth. This means that autonomous man is his own final authority. The things that seem right in his own eyes become his guiding life principles. The world functions in this manner and makes no apology for this fact, and the church has unconsciously absorbed the same *modus operandi*, using man's wisdom as a basis of truth.

Television and radio talk shows are a classic example of this phenomenon. Phil Donahue will have a panel of people on his show to discuss a certain issue, usually some kinky moral or controversial religious question, or some unconventional approach to life. Ideas will be presented, often with the unstated presupposition that whatever is right for you is right, and one life-style or idea is as good as another. For example, Donahue had a live, homosexual marriage on his show not long ago. Why not? To what authority do you appeal in a "pluralistic society" to say that that is unacceptable? If law originates with man, and our governmental system enacts gay-rights laws permitting such marriages, who can philosophically disagree?

Serious public policy panels use the same approach, but the questions discussed are taxes, relations with other countries, domestic policy, and other issues, with the most persuasive, or best informed panelist able to sway viewers with the logic of his rhetoric. His basis of authority is always his own reasoning (rationalism), what his senses have perceived (empiricism), or what he "feels" inside himself (subjectivism). The appeal is unconsciously to human law.

What's Wrong With Human Law?

Human law, however, has serious problems. If man is the originator of what is right, equitable and proper, **his decisions will always be clouded by self-interest**. I know myself well enough to know that I am self-centered, and, left to my own devices, what I think is right will always reflect that fact. Special-interest groups constantly lobby politicians to promote their agendas and to advance their causes. As the populace discovers that they can elect political candidates who will buy their votes by giving them hand-outs in the form of government entitlements, the tax burden on productive citizens will grow. Laws that originate in the fallen mind of man, like the progressive income tax and other wealth redistribution schemes, are enacted to rob legally those who are America's producers. With human law as a basis for their legislation, our law-makers will invariably lead us down the path to socialism.

This is hard to see, because democracy clothes human law in respectability. After all, if a majority of citizens want a certain thing, doesn't that make it right? Democracy is the rule of the 51%, the rule of a majority of the sinners, the rule of the corporate will. Our politicians are very much aware of what that corporate will is, because most of what they do is predicated on checking the latest polls on the issue, and then acting accordingly. If your senator perceives that a majority of his constituents want abortion on demand, he will vote with that majority. He is lauded for not being an "ideologue," which generally means he has no convictions.

During the 1992 Presidential Campaign, President George Bush removed John Frohnmeyer from his position as head of the National Endowment for the Arts. Frohnmeyer had a record of encouraging government subsidies for pornographic and anti-Christian art. Conservative Christians had been upset with Frohnmeyer for some time, but President Bush did not act until his rival for the Republican

Presidential nomination, Pat Buchanan, began to make an issue of Frohnmeyer's performance. Bush appeared to have no convictions, but simply went where the greatest pressure pushed him.

In my opinion, this lack of conviction was the overriding reason for George Bush's defeat in the 1992 election, not the economy. Bush seldom appeared to be a man of conviction, but always had a "wet finger in the wind." He was always the consummate pragmatist, priding himself in building consensus, in fashioning a "kinder, gentler nation." President Bill Clinton follows much the same tack. I believe the American people subconsciously are looking for a leader with vision and direction who is not afraid to make unpopular decisions if he feels they are right.

Our system of government doesn't often give us those kinds of leaders. Experience tells us that our representatives will generally enact laws that the majority prefers, because they want to be re-elected. How many times have you heard the statement, "I am personally against abortion, but I don't want to impose my morality on others."

Jimmy Carter was a particularly strong proponent of this line of reasoning. As a Baptist, he claimed to be personally against abortion, but as a Democratic president, his administration strongly supported killing babies in the womb. If a politician is particularly principled, he will attempt to legislate what he sees to be right, no matter what the political consequences. After all, all legislation is someone's morality, and others will impose their morality on you if given the opportunity, and all legislation will leave someone dissatisfied. Even so, that legislation originates in the human mind, and reflects human will.

Another problem with human law is its **evolutionary nature**. Proponents of human law see man himself to be evolving, so it logically follows that his source of truth would be evolving as well. In this manner, the Constitution becomes a "living document," changing as man himself changes over the years. Why should we, they say, be hobbled with a static, inflexible system of government, when we can read into the Constitution whatever the era in which we live demands?

Is Human Law the real law of the land?

The Constitution, by the way, is not the comprehensive "law of the land." It gives us broad, general principles, and a track to run on in determining a more detailed "law of the land," which is decided upon by our legislators. The Constitution gives a thoughtful, detailed

20

framework within which laws can be determined. Without a reliable law-source from which legislators can draw, republican government will not work. In the late eighteenth century, the Bible was assumed to be that law source. John Adams, our country's second president said, "Our Constitution was made only for a moral and religious people. It is wholly inadequate for any other."[2]

The framers were men who distrusted centralized power because of the sinfulness of man. They devised a constitution that effectively separated and severely limited federal power. For example, the Tenth Amendment states that all powers not expressly given to the federal government (a very limited number) are reserved for the state governments. Yet today, federal control has crept into almost every area of life, often under the guise of the federal government's stated constitutional power to regulate interstate commerce, or the Fourteenth Amendment's due process clause. Actually, the desire of our courts has been to lead us after the latest politically correct philosophy, rather than insure that the Constitution is adhered to. Those who are determining what is good for you are constantly changing their ideas of what that is.

Evolutionary human law is the self-conscious basis of all our legislation in America today. Some individual law-makers may have another authority-source, but they cannot publicly claim another source and remain politically viable. They will face the same opposition Clarence Thomas did for simply being interested in natural law.

Many in our land have allowed themselves to buy into this relativism as a basis for not only public legislation, but personal morality as well. "It is right if it is right for me," and "Don't shove your morality down my throat," express the attitude of most people in our nation. This fierce individualism without a moral anchor leads to the situational ethics that is very rapidly poisoning the culture in which we live, and in order to survive we must find another source of daily, practical authority outside of ourselves.

By the way, can you see that *natural law* practically becomes *human law* in a religious disguise? Those who historically have claimed natural law epistemology must decide for themselves what phenomena in nature, including their own personal perceptions, constitute natural law to be followed, and what phenomena are irrelevant as a law-source. It is only their human reason, (shaped by our biblical heritage!) that tells them that the perceived "survival of the fittest" in nature does not apply to our society, and therefore, might does not make right. Human

21

law and its reliance on man's mind is unconsciously behind most of our decision-making processes, even though we might claim some natural-law source.

Revealed law

The Bible claims that, outside of man himself and the cosmos in which he lives, there is a source of ultimate truth that is man's final authority. That is the eternal Word of God, as revealed in the Bible itself. It claims to be an absolute, black-and-white standard of righteousness.

The Old Testament is said to be "God-breathed" in II Timothy 3:16; it is said to be "the oracles of God" in Romans 3:2; Hebrews 1:1,2 says that "God...who spoke in times past to the fathers by the prophets, has in these last days spoken to us by His Son," and the Gospels are a record of that Son's life and teaching. Time after time the prophets Isaiah, Jeremiah, Ezekiel, etc., claim divine inspiration, and Peter, in 2 Peter 3:15,16, says that Paul's epistles are also Scripture, on a par with these prophets. Paul, in I Timothy 5:18, quotes from Luke 10:7, placing this Gospel on a par with the Old Testament, calling them both "scripture."

There is no doubt that the Bible claims to be God's word, but what that means might need some clarification. Is the Bible applicable purely as a book dealing with "spiritual" life and conduct, or does it deal with practical, every day life as well? Does it apply to the twentieth century? If so, how much of it? Certainly the Old Testament doesn't, does it? And to whom does the Bible apply, just Christians, or everybody?

Before earnest Christians can apply the Bible to their lives in the area of the family, these are questions that need to be answered. If they are questions in your mind, I have written Appendix A just for you, and you might want to read it now. If not, you are ready for the next chapter.

"Father, show me where I am currently looking to find ultimate truth about family. Don't let me be deceived into thinking my source is Your Word if it is not. Give me divine insight and wisdom. Amen."

Questions for Discussions

1. Discuss the meaning of the word "epistemology." What epistemology do you feel you currently hold?

2. Explain the view of the source of law held by many of our Founding Fathers. Why do you think this view is not supported by many people today?

3. Is there a relationship between human law and humanism? What is it? What do you feel to be the main weakness of human law?

4. Explain how human law and revealed law are different. Analyze the statement, "There are only two kinds of laws, God's Law in the Bible, and man's law (human law). We must choose to follow one or the other."

---

1 Archie Jones, "Natural Law and Christian Resistance to Tyranny," *Christianity and Civilization*, vol. 2, (Geneva Divinity School Press, 1983) p. 123.
2 John Eidsmoe, *Christianity and the Constitution*, (Grand Rapids, MI: Baker Book House, 1987), p. 292.

Part Two
"Getting Started"

Chapter 3

God's Family Business

The Bible tells us that from the beginning the concept of the family has been in the heart of God. He has existed for all eternity in a "family" Himself: Father, Son and Holy Spirit. And while we cannot know fully His motivation for His acts in time, (only what He has chosen to reveal to us), we can speculate that He desired to pattern His creation after that relationship He enjoyed within the Godhead itself. Paul says in Ephesians 1:3 that before creation God was a Father to our Lord Jesus Christ. We can imagine that that relationship was so satisfying, so enjoyable to Him, that He desired the "only begotten Son," (John 3:16), to become "the firstborn among many brethren," (Romans 8:29): a vast family of sons and daughters upon whom He could shower His love and affection, with whom He could share His vision, and through whom He could accomplish His eternal purpose.

What father is there who has not had similar thoughts? If we have found purpose and meaning to our lives, is there not something within us that wants our children and grandchildren, our posterity, to share in that vision?

My grandfather, "Papaw," was a natural-born entrepreneur, the kind of man everyone called a "horse-trader" in early twentieth-century Oklahoma. In 1912 as a young man he started a bank, then traded it for a drugstore in the little rural community of Stratford. The Bayless Drug Company was born. He parlayed that single store into a chain of seven drug stores throughout south-central Oklahoma before he retired at eighty years of age. He lived to be 94 and, before he died, passed that original store on to his daughter, my mother, who owned and managed it for some twenty years.

Papaw's only son died in his twenties of pneumonia, and he saw me, his only grandchild, as the one who would carry on his vision. I really tried to be interested in pharmacy as a profession, get a college degree in that field, and then get involved in one of my grandfather's drugstores, realizing he would undoubtedly leave the whole thing to me as his only heir. Who wouldn't want to inherit a ready-made, productive family business?

However, I had grown up in the city, and I couldn't see myself living in a rural setting. Nor did I see any signs that led me to believe I had a talent for business (that has been borne out over my lifetime as I have continued to demonstrate an amazing ability to buy high and sell low). I can remember how hard it was to tell my grandfather, after my first year in college, that pharmacy didn't really interest me, and I wanted to major in chemical engineering instead. Although he said he understood, and whatever I wanted to do was fine with him, I could see the disappointment written all over his face, because he knew that his life's work, his vision, would not be passed on to his descendants. When my mother finally sold the original drugstore in Stratford, Oklahoma, it had been in the Bayless family continually for over three-quarters of a century. That drugstore was so much a part of our lives that it had become almost a member of the family with a life of its own.

The Eternal Purpose

God too has a vision, a master plan for His vast earthly family. This plan involves every member catching the Father's vision and being involved with Him in the "family business" - the business of extending the righteous rule of His Son Jesus Christ over all the earth. This is the bottom-line purpose, the "eternal purpose," for which you were created; to be a "self-conscious kingdom-extender" for the kingdom of God.

Before God created man, it was decided in the council of the God-head that he would be formed in God's own image, after His likeness (Genesis 1:26). At least a part of that likeness was that man would exist as an individual, but he would also be male and female, alike as generic man, but different sexually, therefore creating the corporate family. Remember, God Himself was one God, but He had a triune personality; Father, Son, and Holy Spirit, making up the Divine family. From the very beginning then, we can see that God had in mind the family to accomplish His work on the earth.

28

The setting into which God placed His first family bears some investigation. Ezekiel 28:11-19 tells us that Satan, one of God's created angels, rebelled against the authority of God Himself. His pride caused him to chafe at the subservient place he held, and caused Him to aspire to be "like the Most High," to want to answer to no one, not even God (Isaiah 14:12-15). He had led one-third of the angels in heaven into rebellion with him (Revelation 12:4), and the earth had become the location of their evil activity.

It was into this battlefield that God placed Adam and Eve, His first human family. Eden was a beachhead that God had established in enemy territory for this newly created family, this "weapon for victory." A part of God's purpose for Adam and Eve and their posterity was to move out from that beachhead over all the earth as God's faithful vice-regents, and to defeat God's rebellious enemy Satan and his demonic hosts in mortal combat. This would then open the way for the rule of God to be established over all the earth.

Why did God give that all-important task to Adam and Eve rather than handling the job Himself with a snap of His own fingers? Why did He involve such obviously fragile and easily-influenced representatives in such a crucial mission? Paul gives us the answer in Ephesians 3:10 when he tells us that God's manifold wisdom is somehow demonstrated to Satan and his demons by using insignificant man to bring His enemy to defeat. He brings glory to His name by succeeding in His mission with such unlikely warriors. God, the creator of the universe, does not need to lower Himself to deal directly with such a rebel as Satan. He can get the job done with us!

During the War for Independence, England's General Charles Cornwallis and 6,000 British troops were defeated at the Battle of Yorktown by George Washington's colonial forces in what proved to be the decisive battle of the war. The formal surrender was set for 2:00 P.M. on the afternoon of October 18 in 1781. I stood on that parade ground a few years ago with tears in my eyes and listened to the recorded recreation of that momentous day. I imagined the lines of British troops, following their mounted officers, marching in columns four abreast to the head of the file, and laying down their muskets - some with defiance, some with tears, but all in defeat. The French and American troops were lined on either side of the file of British as the red-coats marched forward to surrender their weapons. The colonists were outnumbered, and certainly didn't look like victors, as many of them were dressed in buckskins and homespun shirts, but they were the victors nevertheless.

General Cornwallis could not bring himself to surrender his sword to General Washington in person, so he did not attend the ceremonial surrender, claiming to be ill, and sent a deputy to perform that unpleasant task. Significantly, Washington refused to deal with Cornwallis' deputy, but sent his own deputy to accept the sword. Military protocol says that one must deal only with those of equal rank.[1]

God in like manner sent a deputy to deal with Satan. Empowered with the imprimatur of the King Himself, man was sent to the Garden of Eden on a mission to recapture and occupy for the King the piece of real estate called earth. It would not happen overnight, but as Adam and Eve reproduced and filled the earth with their progeny, their army would grow, both in size, and, as they grew to trust and obey the King more and more, in effectiveness as well.

This purpose for the family is summarized clearly in one of the foundational scriptures of the Bible, Genesis 1:26-28, where God speaks into existence man's three-fold purpose:

1. To bear the image of God. This image not only includes the fact that God is a family, but it includes His personality as well. He has a will (He can choose or decide), He has an intellect (He can know or comprehend), and He has emotion (He can love or hate). We have this same three-fold capacity because we are made in His image, and though that image is warped by sin, by looking at man we can get some idea of what God is like. He is like we are, because we were made in His image!

Do you see that God is not some unknowable Deity that we cannot comprehend? Our human nature was meant to be a reflection of our Father's nature, so that we exhibit the family characteristics. God's very character is worked out in our personality. Jesus could say, "He who has seen Me has seen the Father" (John 14:9), not because He was God, though He certainly was, but because He was <u>man</u>, as God intended man to be! He reflected perfectly the character of His Father. God desires that you and I also be a reflection of that Divine nature in <u>our</u> humanity, through <u>our</u> personality, so that when people see us, they see the image of God. That is our birthright. It is a lifelong process, but a goal which He will accomplish in us as we surrender our lives daily to Him and His purpose.

2. To have dominion over God's creation. Man, made in God's image, is the crowning jewel of God's creation, designed to be the steward over God's earth, and to extend His rule from pole to pole.

This is not a popular message today. We hear on every hand that we should live in harmony with nature, realizing that we are nothing more than another rung on the evolutionary ladder, and our concerns are no more important than those of the spotted owl, or the coyote, or the snail-darter. Man is, in fact, said to be the villain for killing those poor cows and pigs who have just as much right to live as we do.

This thinking has its roots in Eastern mysticism and is making serious inroads into our culture through the environmental movement. New Age thinking, which is the driving force for many environmentalists, is nothing more than Eastern Pantheism (God is a part of nature, not transcendent over it), dressed up in Western garb.

Toys for Tots

The scriptures tell another story. They teach that man is far different from the rest of God's creation. He alone bears God's image. He alone can become a child of the living God. He alone is a joint heir with Jesus Christ. He alone can become a partaker of the divine nature as the Holy Spirit takes up residence in his life. He is not simply another part of creation, but the vice-regent appointed to rule over it in God's stead. Adam was given the task in the Garden of Eden to exercise God's rule first over the Garden, and then extending it over all the earth, and since he was to become a child of God and a joint heir with Jesus Christ, the earth and all it contained were for him!

I can still remember distinctly the day Jill and I brought our first child, also named Adam, home from the hospital. We had spent weeks preparing his nursery: new paint job, new drapes, changing table, crib and rocking chair at the ready, toys in place all around the room (as if a new-born would notice). We even had hung a mobile over his crib before he was ever in it! That his room would reflect our love for him and the significance we placed on his arrival was very, very important to us.

However, when we finally brought Adam home and put him in that crib, and saw his little body actually asleep there, the room and all it contained suddenly paled into insignificance. The one for whom the room was created, the one who was made in our image, who bore our likeness, had arrived!

Adam did not live in harmony with his mobile, or his changing table, or his toys, as if they were all somehow equal to him in value. No, they were for him. They were there only because he was there, for without him, they would have absolutely no meaning. What good is a mobile, or a changing table, without a baby?

You can see the application, can't you? We are the climax of God's creative effort. We are His masterpiece, His crowning achievement. Everything that had come before during that week of creation was but a beautiful setting for man, God's ultimate jewel. The trees, the mountains, the fields, the rivers, the plants and animals, are all for us. They are for our use, our enjoyment, and our training, and Genesis 1:26-28 says that we are to rule, to have dominion, over all of them for God.

Make no mistake, ruling for God means proper stewardship of His possessions, the earth and all the resources it contains, for we will answer to God for every stewardship responsibility He has given us. As he grew, we taught Adam not to destroy his toys, to clean up his room, and to take care of all his belongings, but we did not teach him that they were equal to him in value, or that he must live in harmony with them. No, he was superior in every way to his environment, and a part of his training was to be able to rule over, or have responsibility for, all of his possessions.

The logical result of evolutionary thought is to deny this uniqueness of man, and to see him as simply one step in an ever-changing process. Since evolution has been taught almost exclusively in our public schools for the last fifty years, it is easy to see how this biblical view of the uniqueness of man has been lost. Still, we must recover it, for it is a very important concept in the proper functioning of a family.

No Draft Dodging

As I mentioned earlier in this chapter, a part of man's ruling function on the earth from the beginning was to do battle with God's enemy, the Devil. The first skirmish was a disaster. Through trickery and deceit in the Garden of Eden, Satan succeeded in wresting Adam's ruler ship over the earth from him (Genesis 3), and, in the process, captured Adam and Eve and their descendants as his slaves (Romans 6:16). Because of their sin of disobedience in the Garden, Satan could legally hold them and their progeny in bondage with eternal death as their certain future (Hebrews 2:14,15; Romans 5:12).

Jesus, as the Perfect Man, succeeded where Adam failed. Through his obedience to His Father, even unto death (Philippians 2:8), Jesus defeated Satan definitively, stripping him of his power and authority (Colossians 2:15). He restored that legal commission as vice-regent over the earth back to man - this time the New Man, made up of Jesus and His Body, the Church. Satan is no longer "the ruler of this world" (John 16:11), for he has met defeat at the cross. Satan is an illegal usurper, and Jesus is seated in victory at God's right hand in Heaven. His Church, empowered by the Holy Spirit, will actualize his defeat, in time, on the earth (Ephesians 1:15-23).

Too many Christians today do not see this aspect of man's purpose, and therefore cannot pass an understanding of dominion on to their children. We see our salvation as being for ourselves - or what we get; not as being for God - what He gets. We are saved to be about our Father's business; extending the righteous rule of Jesus Christ over the whole earth. We have been told that the gates of Hell will not prevail against our attack (Matthew 16:18); that we are to disciple whole nations and teach them to obey the Law of God (Matthew 28:18-20); that Jesus is now reigning at His Father's right hand; that He will reign there until His enemies are under His feet (1 Corinthians 15:24-28), and that to bring that about is the job of the Church of Jesus Christ. We are to push back those principalities and powers, and extend the rule of the legitimate King, which simply means doing things in obedience to Him in every sphere of activity on this earth. This is extending His dominion.

Not top-down

One thing needs to be very clear. This rule of King Jesus is not extended by force, nor by political power. It is not a top-down rule over unwilling subjects. So, electing Christians to public office to dominate a rebellious populace is not the answer. Political leaders reflect the character of the citizens who elected them, so we invariably get what we are. The election in 1992 of Bill Clinton, recognized by the general populace as a liar and adulterer, was a commentary on the moral state of our land. Only a few years ago, such recognition torpedoed the presidential campaign of Gary Hart.

Political involvement is a necessary activity for God's people, and we must learn to participate in the political process. But to place our confidence in it as the primary way to extend God's kingdom is a serious misunderstanding of spiritual truth. "For though we walk in the flesh, we do not war according to the flesh, for the weapons of our warfare are not carnal but mighty in God for pulling down strongholds,..." (2 Corinthians 10:3,4). Kingdom extension begins with a lost sinner encountering Jesus Christ and surrendering totally to Him as Lord, so that this new relationship affects every aspect of the sinner's life. Old friends, family, business associates, and yes, even political cronies, all are touched by his new life so that one-by-one, they begin to fall to the rule of the King. Slowly, gradually, like leaven in a measure of meal (Matthew 13:33), the kingdom spreads, until the general population begins to desire righteous rule, and God's people are ultimately victorious.

Fortress or field hospital?

Where is this victorious anticipation in the Church today? All too often we have a fortress mentality, holed up behind the stained-glass windows of our churches, not only failing to penetrate society with the gospel, but even losing most of our young people to the war that rages all around us. We are not equipped to preserve our posterity for the kingdom of God.

One pastor told me recently that his denomination estimates that they lose 80% of their youth when they reach high school. We have tried to compete with the world for our young people by entertaining them with Ping-Pong and church socials, and we have lost the competition.

How can we compete with the world in the area of entertainment? Recreation and leisure have become opiates as we have lost our vision, deadening our sense of purpose, and allowing us to endure Monday through Friday. Often our job is nothing more than a means to make money to spend on the weekend, where we sedate ourselves again to endure another week. And so it goes, a vicious circle through life to retirement, working at a job to be able to enjoy leisure time, rather than having leisure time in order to be more productive in God's calling to the family business. Retirement, to most people, is the ultimate drug trip, a Nirvana of endless days with nothing but leisure time. In God's plan, the activity may change at 65, but man has a useful, productive role to play in the family business until the end of his life. This is good news, and the solution to feeling useless in old age.

We have failed to give our children the vision of joining the battle to extend God's kingdom into every area of endeavor. We are "holding hands and sharing precious verses" in our churches to encourage ourselves, which is fine as a preparation for battle in our task of ruling over the earth. But, too often, we are afraid to join the battle. We are simply enjoying the benefits of a man-centered salvation without seeing its God-centered implications.

The world is filled with hurting people, and the church needs to present a gospel that addresses those hurts. The church must be a haven where we can be accepted and loved, a hospital where we can be healed of the wounds inflicted by the world, where God's physical arms can hug us to Himself. But the church is not a rest home where we retire and wait for the "sweet bye and bye," enjoying our salvation. The church is a hospital, yes, but a "field hospital," where we experience the Lord's healing touch, get rehabilitated, and get the vision for the family business - ruling over God's creation, and doing battle with God's enemies.

3. To be fruitful and multiply. The third aspect of God's purpose for man is to fill the earth with descendants, generations of men and women who have been captured by the vision of the task at hand.

Let me ask you, what would you do if you were Satan, and you knew that man had been given the commission and the power to progressively carry out, in time, Jesus Christ's definitive victory over you on the cross, and thereby render you powerless? What if you knew that the more men and women who understood this truth, and acted upon it, the sooner the task would be completed?

We must understand that Satan has been defeated and bound by Jesus Christ (Matthew 12:29; Revelation 20:2), and that his power is severely limited. However, in the wisdom of God, for our training and His glory, God has left the final mop-up duty to us, His Church. As a result, Satan fears those who carry the "name above every name" on their foreheads (Revelation 14:1). We must not be ignorant of Satan's devices (2 Corinthians 2:11). Therefore, we must realize that his main weapon is deception; to trick the Church into believing a lie or not believing the truth. I repeat, if you were Satan, what would you do?

You would deceive man into killing his own offspring! By promoting abortion, you would severely dilute man's power over you by simply reducing his numbers. We don't know how many demons are under

35

Satan's control, but we know that one-third of the angelic host followed him in rebellion against God. By deceit and trickery, this demonic force influences the course of history as it energizes those who either deliberately or ignorantly yield to Satan's will. Every child who is born is a potential powerful enemy of this demonic force, so abortion has proven to be an effective weapon as we continue to blindly slaughter our unborn. In the United States, almost one in three pregnancies ends in abortion; the womb is a dangerous place to be. One and one-half million abortions occur in our nation every year.

The rationalization necessary philosophically to accept abortion is amazing. We have reached the point where, even if it is a human life in the womb, the mother's choice is more important than the baby's life. Satan has blinded men's minds so that they cannot see.

Even if you are against abortion, don't be too smug. Satan is the father of lies and there is no truth in him (John 8:44). He has repeated some of his lies often enough in the media that many unwitting Christians believe him. For instance, have you fallen for this one? "There is a population problem. We are overcrowded and running out of resources and therefore must limit the size of our families." This is conventional wisdom in practically all circles today, even many Christian ones. But how accurate are these assumptions? Let me give you some facts about the world's food supply from economist Dr. Jacqueline Kasun's book, *The War Against Population:*

> [W]orld food production has increased considerably faster than population in recent decades...For example rice and wheat production in India in 1983 was almost three-and-a-half times as great as in 1950. This was considerably more than twice the percentage increase in the population of India in the same period.[2]

Again, Kasun says;

> The massive increases in food production that have occurred in recent decades have barely scratched the surface of the available food-raising resources, according to the best authorities. Farmers use less than half of the earth's arable land and only a minute part of the water available for irrigation. Indeed, three-fourths of the world's available crop-land requires no irrigation.

36

How large a population could the world's agricultural resources support using presently known methods of farming? Colin Clark, former director of the Agricultural Economic Institute at Oxford University, classified world land-types by their food-raising capabilities and found that if all farmers were to use the best methods, enough food could be raised to provide an American-type diet for 35.1 billion people, more than seven times the present population. Since the American diet is a very rich one, Clark found that it would be possible to feed three times as many again, or more than twenty-two times as many as now exist, at a Japanese standard of food intake. Clark's estimate assumed that nearly half of the earth's land area would remain in conservation areas, for recreation and the preservation of wildlife.[3]

Kasun quotes David Hopper, a well-known authority on agriculture, in the Scientific American:

The world's food problem does not arise from any physical limitation on potential output or any danger of unduly stressing the environment. The limitations on abundance are to be found in the social and political structures of nations and in the economic relations among them.[4]

The problem is not a nation's lack of capacity to produce food, but its political and religious structure. Collectivist governments often seize crops and farm animals for the state, severely hindering the farmer's motivation to produce. India is an example of a country hampered by its religion, as rats are often worshipped and fed, rather than exterminated, and cows run loose in the streets, eating precious grain rather than being food themselves.

You can see that this dilemma is a result of not understanding the Christian view of man as the apex of God's creation, with all of creation for his use. If man is nothing more than the material molecules of his body and draws his meaning from an all-powerful state, as is the official view in socialistic countries, or if he is simply a meaningless part of a universe in process as in Eastern religions, then he has no significance as God's image-bearer. This will keep him from developing the technology necessary to continue to increase his food resources. Food shortages generally can be traced to politics and religion. Western plenty is a result of political systems which spring from Christian principles like individual liberty.

Too crowded?

But aren't we literally running out of space? Traveling from coast to coast by car in our country, as I have done several times, will quickly put that misconception to rest. Mile after mile of open spaces greet the eye as the western states are crossed, until one wonders if anyone followed Horace Greeley's admonition to "Go West young man, go West." Our cities are crowded, but only because people tend to cluster together voluntarily due to the greater opportunity for business and commerce in more densely populated areas.

It has been shown that all the people in the world could be put in the state of Texas to form one giant city with a population density less than many of our existing cities, leaving the rest of the world empty! Each man, woman and child would have 1500 square feet of living space. Also the population of the world would have standing room in one-fourth of the area of Jacksonville, Florida.[5]

An overcrowded earth would lead to scarcity, but did you know that there is very little probability of running out of any of our resources in the foreseeable future? Prices, a good indicator of availability, continue to fall for all commodities, indicating increasing supply, and even the Carter administration's gloomy *Global 2000* report admitted as much. Energy resources continue to increase as well. The conclusions of a group of energy experts in 1984 were that "the prospects of running out of energy is a bogeyman. The availability of energy has been increasing, and the meaningful cost has been decreasing over the entire span of humankind's history. We expect this benign trend to continue..."[6]

The same old lie

We have been had. Overpopulation is a myth, but the siren song of the world has been to emphasize the advisability of small families because it is our solemn duty to do our part to preserve the limited resources on "spaceship earth." This is not a new lie. When Satan finds a winner he sticks with it. Plato and Aristotle worried about overpopulation about four centuries before Christ, as did Confucius and other Chinese thinkers. Tertullian and Saint Jerome were early church fathers who wrote of the earth being "full," and, "our numbers...burdensome to the world," and yet we know now that that was a ridiculous misconception.[7]

We will discuss more about having children later, but it is enough to say now that we need to see that our family is for God and His purpose, not primarily for our own pleasure and enjoyment. We certainly will enjoy our family if we build it God's way, but that is not its main purpose. Filling the earth with "self-conscious kingdom-extenders" is.

The concept of the family indeed originated in the mind of God. It was His idea. One man, one woman, and their offspring, bearing the image of their Father, understanding why they are on the earth, giving themselves to the family business of extending the effective rule of Jesus Christ, and passing the vision on to succeeding generations. In the next chapter we will look at how the very first family began.

"Father, open my eyes as to why I am here on the earth. Help me to live my life in light of that great eternal purpose; to willingly join You in the family business. Amen."

Questions for discussion

1. Explain the concept of God being in a family. What verses support this idea?

2. "You were created in God's image." What are the implications of this statement?

3. What do you think God meant by giving man dominion over the earth? Do you see how this concept could be misunderstood? How? Why is it important to understand God's intent?

4. How do you feel about God's command to "be fruitful and multiply?" Give some examples of the world's message about this topic.

---

[1] Peter Marshall, Jr. and David Manuel, *The Light and the Glory* (Old Tappan, New Jersey: Fleming H. Revell Company, 1977), p. 331.

39

[2] Jaqueline Kasun, *The War Against Population*, (San Francisco: Ignatious Press, 1988), p. 33

[3] *Ibid.*, p. 34

[4] W. David Hopper, "The Development of Agriculture in Developing Countries," *Scientific American*, September, 1976, pp. 197-205, in Kasun, *The War Against Population*, p. 35.

[5] Kasun, *The War Against Population*, p. 37,38.

[6] *Ibid.*, p. 41

[7] *Ibid.*, p. 46

Chapter 4

"It is not good that man should be alone"

For the first fifteen years of our marriage, Jill often told me that somehow a part of her was unfulfilled because I didn't "need" her. This became, over the years, the source of a great deal of frustration to her, and while it wasn't a front-burner issue, it was always there just under the surface. We didn't discuss it a lot because, frankly, I didn't know what to do. Yes, I was independent in many ways, and no, I didn't need Jill at my side providing emotional strength to make it through every day. She assured me that that was not what she had in mind anyway. There was a way for me to "need" her that came from strength and not from weakness that wasn't there in our marriage and it left Jill with an unfulfilled hollowness in her heart.

Furthermore, what I did not realize was that I would never reach my full potential as a man until I learned to draw on Jill's womanhood. I think many men don't understand this any more than I did, because they don't understand that God's family business of kingdom extension is a family business. If we have a wife, she is an indispensable part of the management team. God has an inexhaustible supply of ways to help us learn this fact, and if we men are quick learners it will be easier for us. If we are slow-witted or resistant, God will keep pulling more learning-aids out of His bag. God loves us enough to keep at it until we get it. This experience is not always pleasant, so the quicker we learn to see our wives as indispensable, the easier it will be for us.

God's visual aid

Adam was an example of this very thing.[1] God created him on the sixth day of creation, and immediately showed him his role in the family business. I can imagine God taking Adam on a stroll through the Garden of Eden, explaining to him his general job description of ruling there in the Garden, cultivating and tending it, and eventually extending that rule over the whole earth. God gave Adam a vision for his life's work, and then more specifically, He outlined a detailed job-description for him to follow. Being a competent, independent sort, Adam saw no need for any help, either physically or emotionally. He was just eager to get started with his task of ruling over the garden as God's on-sight representative.

God knew better. He knew that Adam had a built-in emptiness, a void, an incompleteness in his life, that God Himself had put there, because He had always had family in mind for man. Notice in Genesis 2:18 God said, "It is not good that man should be alone; I will make a helper comparable to him." In God's plan the helper would not simply wash his clothes (he didn't have any!), or cook his meals (that wasn't necessary either), but would complete him by providing certain strengths in the very make-up of human-nature that he lacked. God created Adam not to function at maximum capacity without this "completer" at his side.

Adam couldn't see it, so God did with him just as He does with us; He gave him an experience to show him his need for a companion. In the very next verse after God's statement concerning Adam's need for a helper, He gave to Adam the task of naming the animals, a Divine "teaching aid" to underscore for Adam his aloneness. As the animals passed by Adam two-by-two and he gave each pair a name, there was awakened in him the thought, "They all have a partner. Why don't I?" He experienced his incompleteness for the first time.

We never learn as quickly as Adam did, because we are sinners and at that point he wasn't. He was very eager to learn everything God had to teach him and his mind was a blank slate, ready to receive new information. Our minds, on the other hand, are warped by sin, and filled with misconceptions that we have accumulated over the years about our mates or future mates. The world has programmed us to think in ways concerning our mates that are diametrically opposed to God's ways. God often must use much more rigorous teaching methods with us.

My mother was a wonderful mom, helping my dad supply Christian discipline, love and nurture for me as a young boy. I was an only child, the apple of my parents' eye, and although that had its advantages, there were some disadvantages too. My mother wanted to be a part of every area of my life, and while that was fine as a child, I felt somewhat smothered as a teenager. She was a very strong, opinionated mother, and as I went through the teen years, I can see now that I began to withdraw and build emotional walls to protect myself from unwanted intrusion, and to preserve my identity as an individual. I was not rebellious nor surly as some teenagers are, but I didn't share any real feelings with my mother either. I became very independent and self-sufficient.

When Jill and I married, I brought into our marriage relationship those same walls which had always protected me from the intrusion of the primary woman in my life, my mother. Now they served to protect me from an intimate relationship with my new "primary woman," my wife. The fact that I was thirty years old when we married only added to my independence. I loved Jill, and wanted to have an intimate relationship with her, but somehow was not able to do that, and after a while, she became frustrated with this husband who would not let her into his life. I really couldn't see what she was talking about, and thought to myself, "Why is she so dissatisfied?"

Adam didn't bring the excess baggage of emotional walls to his marriage that I brought to mine. As the animals paraded by and he gave each pair a name, he was completely free to feel a longing for a companion like each of the animals had, for he had no protective walls or learned misconceptions to overcome. They seemed so content, so satisfied with each other. As he named the last pair and they walked away, I can imagine that Adam was very much aware that he was alone.

"Bone of my bone, and flesh of my flesh"

You know the story of God's provision for that loneliness of Adam's; the creation of woman. Fashioned by God from a rib from Adam's side while he slept, she was brought to Adam as he awakened and presented to him by God Himself. Adam opened his eyes to see, for the first time, the one who was like him but different. Because of his learning experience in God's classroom, he was very much aware of his need for someone like himself to fill that lonely hole in his life. What would be his response to this woman who stood before him? Would she measure up to whatever idea he had for what a helpmate should be?

His response is found in verse 23 of Genesis 2; "This is now bone of my bones and flesh of my flesh; she shall be called Woman, because she was taken out of man."

The English translation of the text does not do justice to the original Hebrew. A rendering that better communicates the emotional content of Adam's words would be, "Wow! This is what I have been waiting for. This woman will be a part of my very life. I am totally committed to her."

Granted, to awaken with a beautiful woman in her altogether standing before him is enough to excite any man, but Adam's enthusiastic acceptance of the one whom he would later name Eve goes deeper than that. Adam had never seen a woman before so he had nothing with which to compare Eve. How did he know she would fill the void in his heart? Could he tell if she measured up to his standard of what a good wife should be by inspecting her, or interviewing her?

No, the reason Adam accepted Eve so enthusiastically was that **he trusted God to provide for him just exactly what he needed!** He was already convinced that God had his best interest in mind when he created Eve for him, and he accepted her as just the right provision for his needs because God gave her to him.

So Eve was designed to complete Adam emotionally; someone to love who would love in return, a companion with whom he could commune on the deepest level, someone to whom he would "belong," who cared if he lived or died. However, there was more to God's intent for Eve than simply to meet Adam's emotional needs.

Adam's business partner

Some men tend to see their wives as nothing more than an attractive play-pretty; someone to keep around to meet physical and emotional needs, but certainly not as having the mental capacity to make a contribution to a life's calling.

I believe God intended something more. He gave Eve to Adam to help him in his administration of the garden, which was no small task. We don't know how big the Garden of Eden was, but it was evidently of considerable size, as four rivers are mentioned as flowing from the garden in Genesis 2:10-14. Adam and Eve must have possessed incredible powers and abilities in their unfallen human souls to be able to handle such a job description.

Can't you see Adam giving Eve a detailed tour of the garden, relating to her exactly what their job responsibilities to cultivate and tend it entailed, just as God had instructed him? He would need her help, her insights, her feminine abilities that he was already noticing that he lacked. She indeed was like him, but oh, so distinctively different! He could see that she would indeed make a huge contribution to the mission they had before them.

The world, for the past 20 years, has told us that the only difference between men and women is physical; other than some very obvious external differences, men and women are just alike. Whatever a man can do, a woman can do just as well and, even more importantly, be completely satisfied doing it. We will discuss roles of men and women in marriage in great detail in later chapters, but it is enough to say here that it was Adam who initially had the vision, the mandate from God, for his family's direction, their life's work (he got that mandate even before Eve was on the scene), and then shared it with Eve. She was to be his "helper" in carrying out that vision.

Different fulfillment for men and women

God has made men to be fulfilled by their life's work, their calling or vocation. The sense of satisfaction that comes from completing a task and knowing that it was done well is God's reinforcement of His vocational call. Men tend naturally to throw themselves into their jobs. If they understand that their vocation is a calling from God, as spiritual a calling as being a pastor, and if they see it as only one of the responsibilities that God has given them to accomplish, along with caring for their families, then this total vocational commitment is a good thing. One of the fruits of the Reformation was an understanding of this fact; any job, done as unto the Lord, is a holy calling.

Men are more apt than women to be "big picture" people. They tend to see the long-range effects of certain actions, and they are better able to make hard decisions concerning children, finances and family philosophy that will achieve desired outcomes. They are equipped to handle the temporary emotional pressures that always threaten to dissuade them from their vision.

Women, on the other hand, are wired much differently. God brought Eve to Adam after his mission had already been given to him. Adam already had received his calling; Eve was to help him in the accomplishment of it. She adapted herself to his vision. She completed what he lacked in his own person to accomplish what God had given him to do.

Because of this God-ordained difference, a wife finds fulfillment by identifying herself completely with her husband; with his plans, his dreams, his direction. As she adapts her unique abilities and contributions to his vision for the family, she realizes the destiny for which she was created, and her husband likewise is provided with essentials that he cannot provide himself. This is all a part of the wonder of God's provision in a mate. "Oh, the depth of the riches both of the wisdom and knowledge of God! How unsearchable are His judgments and His ways past finding out!" (Romans 11:33).

By taking her husband's name, a woman is signifying that she is taking on his future, whatever it might hold, and giving up her right to be independent from him and his direction. The refusal of many modern women to take their husband's name (or retaining their maiden name with a hyphen), implies that they are reserving the right to continue to set the course of their own lives; to have a separate vision, direction, or calling.

There is a spiritual principle at work here. Jesus said, "For whoever desires to save his life will lose it, but whoever loses his life for my sake and the gospels will save it" (Mark 8:35). For the husband, fulfillment comes from losing his personal, selfish motivation in the area of his vocation, realizing that his efforts in his work-place are to extend God's kingdom, not to glorify himself with money, prestige or power. For his wife, fulfillment comes from losing her life in her husband's by giving herself completely to him.

I am firmly convinced that we would have much more prudent marriages in the Christian community if these things were understood. Is this the man I really want to give my future to? Can I trust him not to use me for his own selfish purposes?

Can you see why it is imperative that husbands recognize their need for their wives, and not only intimately share their hearts with them, but also allow them to be vitally involved in their vision as well? The purpose of the wife's life is to help her husband in his life's work. If he does not understand this, and fails to open his whole life to her and allow her to complete him, not only will he miss her contribution, but she will spend her life searching for fulfillment, never experiencing it to the degree that God intended.

Maximizing family potential for the kingdom

Many men fail to utilize their wife's resources, and therefore never maximize the potential that God has built into their marriage. While the husband is the head of the relationship, implying direction and decision-making, she is the heart, signifying sensitivity and compassion. He must be open to her input because God made her to see and understand many things that he cannot, and he is a fool if he does not take advantage of her insights. He must not be threatened if she has superior intelligence or abilities, for he can use them to increase the impact of the family for the kingdom of God. He must see the two of them as a unit, "one-flesh" (Genesis 2:24), not in competition, but with each partner contributing something the other lacks for the glory of God.

On the other hand, he must not surrender his leadership of the family. God will hold him responsible for giving that leadership, just as he will hold the wife responsible for following it. The New Testament makes it clear that "...in Adam all die" (1 Corinthians 15:22), not "in Eve." Adam was responsible for the disobedience of his family. He surrendered his family leadership to his deceived wife (1 Timothy 2:14), followed her foolish directive (Genesis 3:6,17), and led the human race into sin.

I believe if Adam had said to Eve, "Drop that fruit right now. You know God said we are not to eat it," even after she had eaten, sin would not have been imputed to the whole human race. Adam was not only the head of his family representing Eve, but he also represented all of us. His unwillingness to confront his wife and exercise strong leadership for her, and Eve's desire to act independently of her husband, were at the heart of the fall of man.

A recognition of not only natural gifts and abilities, but also of divinely ordained roles for husband and wife does much to eliminate destructive competition and maximize all the potential God has built into a marriage for His kingdom.

A "made-to-order" spouse

As Adam would soon discover, life with Eve was not always a picnic. He discovered that she had her limitations as a woman, just as he had his limitations as a man, but through all the difficulties they would encounter, a sovereign God was working "all things according to the counsel of His will" (Ephesians 1:11).

For those of us who are married, God has designed each of our spouses just for us. They are "made to order;" made to His divine specifications with our individual needs in mind. He wants us first of all to recognize our need for them, and then to see that they are His perfect match, His perfect fit, for meeting those needs, though it might take some years of adjustment together to see clearly!

God's idea about what we need in a mate is very seldom the same as ours after a few years of marriage. A typical attitude after about 8-10 years together is, "She seemed so perfect for me before we were married; how could I have been so blind. How could I have missed her self-absorption and self-centeredness?" Or, "He seemed so suave and virile. Why didn't I notice his anger and lack of self-control?"

Yes, you married a sinner, and there is nothing like marriage to spotlight all of your mate's sins. But let me let you in on a little secret that very few Christians understand. God is not primarily concerned about your pleasure in your marriage, if that pleasure is derived from possessing a perfect mate that never makes a wave. No, He's not! Marriage is not for you and your enjoyment, but marriage is for God! Remember, He wants you and your family to be involved with Him in His family business, in His great eternal purpose. Your mate is one of the tools, probably the main tool, that He has in His hand to accomplish His work in your life, to get you ready to be in business with Him.

It's hard to see our spouses, who sometimes seem so impossible to live with, as just what we need to help conform us to God's image. We want to run, to get away, because it's too painful to have to look at ourselves when there are seemingly unresolvable difficulties with our husband or our wife. It's too painful to ask the question, "Oh Lord, is it I who is at fault in this matter?" We all find blaming our spouse for our conflicts to be very natural. Didn't Adam say, "The woman You gave to me made me do it," and didn't Eve say, "The serpent tricked me and I ate"? Yes, blaming someone else for our own sin is as old as time and a very natural reaction. We have to learn a new way. Marriage is an excellent laboratory in which to conduct the experiments that will lead us to new discoveries about our own shortcomings, and then help us to turn from those things.

Personal marriage test #1

My natural independence, plus an interest in basketball, led Jill and me into our first crisis in the early days of our marriage. I was coaching at the high school where I taught, along with working for the Associated Press as a "stringer" at the home games of the local professional team, the Seattle Supersonics. I was gone an average of three or four nights a week, leaving Jill at home alone with two small boys. I knew nothing about really caring for my wife and being concerned with her needs as her husband, and I was blind to the warning signs she was desperately flashing. How could she be a helper to this man she had given herself to if he was never there?

We lived in the University District at the time, and rented spare bedrooms to college students in the big three-story house we owned. One of those roomers was Alex, a husky, blonde, bearded, sensitive, poetry-loving graduate student whom we had known for some time.

Alex was very different from me. At that time, my main literary interest was the sports page, and any poetry past "Casey at the Bat" was lost on me. Needless to say, Jill saw in Alex something she didn't see in me and was very attracted to him.

After I left for work each morning, Alex would come down and have coffee with Jill and they would discuss whatever two sensitive, poetry-lovers discuss. I was oblivious to what was beginning to develop, still ignorantly bouncing my basketball, being gone most of the time doing what made me happy. I was so blind that I even sent Alex skiing with Jill one night as my substitute in a ski school where Jill and I acted as chaperons.

Jill and Alex were both committed Christians with the best of intentions; a lonely young wife whose husband took her for granted, and an immature young man who was flattered that a slightly older woman was attracted to him. They certainly didn't start out, either of them, to try to develop a relationship with each other, but before either realized it, they were emotionally involved.

Jill knew, even if I didn't, that she was heading for trouble, and she had to tell me before it was too late. "Alex likes me," she blurted out one day, and even then the truth didn't penetrate my dense skull.

"Of course he does. You're a super girl," was my reply as I left for another basketball game. My blindness and stupidity could only be matched by my utter self-centeredness. Jill was crying out for me to help her extricate herself from a situation she knew was wrong, but she felt powerless to do anything about it.

Finally what was happening became so obvious that even I couldn't miss it. As Alex walked into the room one day I saw Jill's face come alive, and I realized then for the first time that my wife had a strong emotional attraction for another man.

My first reaction was to see myself as a victim of an incredible lack of character on Jill's part. "How could she do this to me? We're married! She is supposed to have left all others. How can she look at another man?" When I confronted her with those words, her reaction was certainly not what I wanted to hear.

"Alex is different from you. He has qualities that you don't have that I really respond to. I still love you very much, but Alex meets needs I have that you can't meet."

There was no repentance; not even any sorrow over what she was doing. I couldn't believe it. Didn't she understand what it meant to be married? I hadn't let myself get involved emotionally with other women. Was it too much to ask that she do the same? My pharisaic self-righteousness that had always been there was laid bare, but as yet I couldn't see it. At that point, acknowledging any wrongdoing on my part was unthinkable. I had been wronged, plain and simple.

When I confronted Alex, he played dumb, claiming to be completely ignorant of any emotional involvement with Jill, leaving her to take full responsibility. He was truly a descendant of his original ancestor, Adam, who said to God, "The woman that you gave to be with me, she gave me of the tree and I ate." His total unwillingness to admit any attraction to Jill was later the thing that broke the spell and freed her.

I left for work every morning knowing that Alex would probably be down for coffee, and even though I did not fear the development of any physical relationship at this point, I knew that the feelings Jill had for him would not die as long as she saw him daily. Should I ask him to move out and make him a martyr to Jill? I didn't know what to do.

Jill still stubbornly refused to admit that she had wronged me, and I wanted her to admit as much. However, the more I pushed her to do that, the more she dug in her heels. I can remember very vividly leaning up against the refrigerator in the kitchen as Jill did the dishes one evening, badgering and berating her, trying to get her to admit she had sinned against me, with only a cold, stony silence as a response.

Suddenly, right there in the kitchen, the truth came in a flash of revelation. "It's your fault, Robert. Your lack of love and care for Jill has done this. It's all your fault."

I saw it clearly. The nights away selfishly pursuing my own interests at her expense, ignoring her emotional needs, and not letting her into my life had left her unprotected and vulnerable. I was reaping what I had sown.

Right in the middle of my tirade, my words suddenly became, "Oh Sugar, I'm so sorry for what I have done to you. It's my fault. Will you please forgive me?," as tears filled my eyes. Jill looked at me incredulously. Was I being sarcastic? When she realized my confession was genuine, she slowly began to cry too, and out of her mouth tumbled all the words I had wanted to hear for so long. "No, it's my fault. I don't know what came over me. Please forgive me. I didn't mean to hurt you."

I asked Alex to leave the next day, and he did, with never a word of repentance or apology to Jill or to me. We saw him in social situations a couple of times in the years that followed. He married, had a family, and eventually moved to Africa as a director in an international, well-known mission organization. I wonder if he ever was able to face his own sin and take responsibility for his actions?

Painful lessons

I found God's classroom to be somewhat painful. As I said, God loves us too much to let us continue on the course we are on without some very vivid visual aids to help us learn the lessons He wants to teach us. The situation I have just described was one of those visual aids.

What did I learn? Let me say that mastery learning is God's goal, so we can expect other lessons on the same subject until we catch the concept. I haven't mastered these concepts yet, but I'm pressing on toward that goal, hoping to show enough progress that my Heavenly Father won't have to apply too much more pressure before I learn the lessons to His satisfaction.

1. In my "one-flesh" relationship with Jill, there are deep emotional needs that only she can meet. She has become a part of me, and the thought of her responding to another man was more than I could bear. No matter how independent I might seem, I need my wife. God has designed me, as a married man, to be incomplete emotionally, and in my calling, without my wife intimately involved with me.

2. She needs me. In order to be fulfilled, Jill needs to be a vital part of every area of my life. I didn't try to include her in my basketball coaching (I did that later with much better results). She needs me to protect, nurture and cherish her. If I do not do that, she will be vulnerable to attacks from the enemy that could come in every

conceivable form, from materialism and an obsession with "things," to a desire for honor and glory in the world, to an attraction to the opposite sex. If I am giving my wife the attention she needs, I and my vision will fill her eyes. As a married woman, she will look elsewhere for fulfillment if I don't bring her into my life.

3. "I was wrong" are the hardest words in the English language to push out of my mouth. They stick on my tongue as if it were Velcro! I want to find every way possible to blame my wife for all of our relational difficulties, and not to look at myself. I need God to help me be ruthless in the evaluation of myself, and gracious and forgiving in my evaluation of my wife. Unfortunately, I am a master in reversing that order.

After twenty years of counseling couples, I have found that the single most prevalent source of relational problems between family members (husbands and wives or parents and children), is an inability of one or both to look clearly at themselves and to admit their own lack of conformity to God's divine order as revealed in the Bible. Remember, God's Word is our standard! Each of us is much more eager to see the sins of the one with whom we are struggling than we are to see our own. May God give each of us the grace to look clearly at ourselves and ask, "Is there any wicked way in me"? (Psalm 139:24).

"Oh Lord, take the scales from my eyes and allow me to see where I really am. In every relational difficulty, help me to sincerely ask the question, 'Is it I?,' and then help me to really want to hear the answer. Give me the grace to understand that I can face my sin because you have died for it on the cross, and you do not hold it against me. Amen"

Questions for discussion

1. What are the sources of some "walls" in your life that might hinder you from giving yourself to your present or future mate?

2. In what ways have you protected yourself from having to "need" your mate? Why do you think you have found it necessary to do this?

3. Think about a difficult relationship you are having right now. Can you see what you have done or an attitude that you have had that is not according to God's Word? Ask God to help you.

4. If you are married, thank God for providing just the right husband or wife for you (Because He has!). If you are not married, thank Him that His plan and His timing is perfect, and tell Him that you want to learn, as quickly as possible, everything He has for you to learn before you are married.

---

[1] For the ideas in the following material concerning Adam's acceptance of his helpmate, I am indebted to Don Meredith, *Becoming One*, (Nashville, TN: Thomas Nelson Publishers).

Chapter 5

Who is in charge?

No question is more basic to family life, and indeed to life in general, than "Who is in charge?" Satan questioned the authority structure of the universe when he rebelled against God by challenging His place as the "most high" (Isaiah 14:12-14), and there has been an intense battle on the earth over that question ever since.

Wars are waged as nations fight over who has authority over a piece of real estate and those who live on it. Individuals disagree about authority over possessions, and families and churches struggle with the question of who makes decisions, which is, at its root, an authority issue. Conflicts, from the most minute personal disagreement, to the largest world war, are generally conflicts in some way over authority.

God claims to have all authority as the rightful King over all the earth, and He tells us that He has delegated His authority to His representatives who are to exercise it according to God's law, thereby establishing a divinely-ordained hierarchical structure called the kingdom of God. However, Satan resists that delegated authority with all the rebellion he can incite by using the main weapon at his disposal, deception. He tricks his unwitting human accomplices into either exercising their authority improperly by using some means other than the law of God, or rebelling against God's properly instituted authority.

To those with spiritual eyes, it's easy to see that history is the out-working of this invisible spiritual battle. What a tragedy that history, as taught in our schools, is often such a boring subject. History is generally presented as a random series of events, with no meaning or purpose, when in reality it is a cosmic war for ultimate authority, raging on the earth between the kingdom of light and the kingdom of darkness. The definitive victory was won by Jesus Christ at Calvary, but Satan, with fierce determination, continues to try to put off the inevitable outcome as we work to implement Christ's victory in time.

A major portion of this satanic attack against God's delegated authority today is within the family. The family, along with the church and civil government, are the three institutions God has ordained to be the primary vehicles to extend His victory over the earth. However, Satan has used the feminist movement, which hates the authority structure of the family as taught in the Bible, to neutralize the effectiveness of many families by attacking and ridiculing God's design for family rule.

Churches that should be teaching God's family authority structure have been intimidated by the world into compromising the clear, biblical pattern for family life. Not wanting to be called "chauvinistic," or seeming to subjugate women and hold them back from realizing their "full potential," churches have not taught their men what the Bible says about how to be husbands and fathers, or their women how to be wives and mothers.

If it is the teaching of the Bible, will it keep women from maximizing all that God has given them? Of course not, but we have been deceived into thinking as the world thinks by the enemy of our souls, and not as the Word of God instructs us.

If churches have not taught compromise, they have often omitted any teaching at all about the authority structure in the family for fear of offending their members, whose only input then comes from the media and other sources in the world that Satan controls and uses. He knows that if he can wage a successful propaganda campaign and shape the views of God's people in this all-important area of authority in the family, he will be able to disable them as an effective fighting force, for we saw in Chapter 3 that the family is the normal battle formation God uses to deploy His troops. Satan has been very successful in working out this plan.

Family authority structure

I Corinthians 11:3 gives the divine authority structure of the family. "But I want you to know that the head of every man is Christ, the head of woman is man, and the head of Christ is God." Figure 1 puts this family authority structure in diagram form.

I have made two changes in the diagram. First, I have changed the word "woman" from the New King James to "wife," as the Greek word is *gune*, which can be translated either "woman" or "wife."[1] Since there is no biblical evidence that God intends every man to have authority over every woman, I believe the correct translation here is "wife." The other change is the addition of children under the authority of both man and wife. This is taught clearly in Colossians 3:23 and Ephesians 6:1-3, where children are instructed both to honor their parents and to obey them in all things.

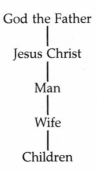

God the Father
|
Jesus Christ
|
Man
|
Wife
|
Children

Figure 1

The submission of Jesus Christ

You might not have realized that God has had a family for all eternity. Before He was a Creator, a Savior or a King, He was a Father, the "God and Father of our Lord Jesus Christ" (Ephesians 1:3). As a matter of fact, His primary nature is that of a father, and that divine family, the God-head, is the pattern for all earthly families. God the Father is the namesake, or the identity, of all fathers, in heaven and on earth (Ephesians 3:14,15). This means that fatherhood had its origin in God and that all fathers are to be replicas of Him.

Notice in the diagram that God the Father is the head of Jesus Christ, who is God the Son. What does this mean? The Greek word for "head" here, *kephale*, signifies "authority or direction."[2] Aren't Jesus and God the Father both co-equal members of the Trinity, with equal worth, equal holiness, and equal power? Aren't we to worship each, along with the Holy Spirit, as members of the Triune Godhead? Without doubt that is true. But in the divine family, as in the human one, there is an authority structure that relates to *function*, not to value or worth.

Jesus said that He taught His Father's doctrine (John 7:16,17), He spoke His Father's words (John 12:49,50; 8:26-28; 17:8), He gave His Father's commands (John 10:18), He worked His Father's works (John 5:19,20; 10:32; 17:4). He said His Father was greater than He (John

14:28), and He sought His Father's glory and honor (John 7:18; 8:49,50). He said that He always did His Father's will (John 5:30; 6:38), and His authority was delegated to Him by His Father (John 17:2; 5:27; Matthew 28:18), indicating His perfect submission in all things to His Father's decisions. He always pleased His Father in all He did (John 8:29). In summary, Jesus was the least original Man who ever lived! He never thought, spoke or acted *independently* of God the Father.

Jesus' subordinate <u>functional</u> position as Son in no way lessened His deity nor His worthiness as an object of worship during His ministry on earth. He simply did not function independently, out from His deity, but "emptied Himself of His privileges."[3] He was "very God of very God," but lived for thirty years as the Son of Man. (That title, Son of Man, by the way, was Jesus's favorite name for Himself). He lived in complete submission to the will of God the Father. His life was a demonstration of how God intends for <u>man</u> to live in His kingdom. Of course, the humanity of Jesus was sinless, and ours is not, but can you see how He could say, "The works that I do shall you do also, and greater works than these shall you do, because I go to the Father" (John 14:12)?

He was living as man, in the power of the Holy Spirit, under the authority of His Father, just as we are to live. When He "went to the Father," He sent back the Holy Spirit, that third family member, on the Day of Pentecost. The Holy Spirit was under the Son's authority (therefore ultimately the Father's), because He was sent by Jesus (and also the Father). The Holy Spirit had confined his activities to the earthly, fleshly body of Jesus while Jesus was on earth, but now the Spirit was released to dwell in His new body, the Church, in fullness of power.

For Jesus, submission to the authority structure in Figure 1 meant being reviled and hated by the religious leaders of His day; being falsely accused and going through the mockery of a trial; being deserted by His friends in His hour of need; and then suffering the penalty for the sins of mankind as He died on a Roman cross outside Jerusalem. All this was the will of His Father. Jesus adapted Himself perfectly to His Father's vision and purpose by learning His Father's heart, and then doing what His Father wanted Him to do.

Those in the world who do not understand spiritual truth associate submission like this with weakness. Achieving recognition and a place of prominence by being "captain of my fate and in control of my own destiny" is generally associated with strength. But for Jesus, the willingness to do His Father's will was the way to power and authority, the avenue to exaltation. For "God also has highly exalted Him and given Him the name which is above every name, that at the name of Jesus every knee should bow..." (Philippians 2:9,10). The cross came before the crown.

Jesus as the "head of every man"

Just as Jesus yielded to the will of His Father in the divine family, the man, as the head of the earthly family, is to yield to Jesus. Notice in Figure 1 that no one else comes between a man and Jesus Christ. No church, no elder, no personal pastor, no spiritual guru; Jesus is the "head of every man."

One of the characteristics of cults is the tendency to control the lives of those involved in the cult. Permission from the leadership is often necessary to make major decisions, sometimes even minor ones. Even Christian churches with orthodox doctrine and sincere motives can fall into the trap of usurping the place of the Lord in a man's life because of a desire to see him grow in Christ. Understanding Jesus as the head of every man, and teaching men to learn to hear from the Lord themselves in their decision-making, guards against church leadership overstepping its bounds.

The church certainly has input concerning the lives of its members. It must exercise its biblical authority to excommunicate in the case of blatant sin committed by unrepentant members. However, it is its teaching from the Word of God, not its coercion, that points men to the Lord.

At one point in my spiritual pilgrimage, I was a part of a church with a strong "discipleship" emphasis. I was being "discipled" by my personal pastor while at the same time pastoring others myself. We took this seemingly endless hierarchy very seriously, with all kinds of biblical rationale for our actions.

While "discipleship" itself is a biblical concept, and young believers especially need personal care, we did not understand the absolute necessity of allowing Jesus to always remain the head of every man, and encouraging him to make his own decisions. No other man ever becomes his "head." Yes, a man must receive input from church elders, submitting himself to their leadership and teaching. Certainly listening to other wise council can be very helpful. But in the final analysis, each

59

must make the decision that he feels the Lord, through the Holy Spirit, is asking him to make. We didn't understand this principle of Jesus being the head of every man, and often usurped the Holy Spirit's role in people's lives with much pain resulting.

The king over his domain

Figure 1 sheds some light on one of the ideas discussed in chapter 3; a part of God's commission for man was to "rule" for Him on the earth. God has given us specific stewardship responsibilities, and He expects us to rule over them for Him, and in this way, His rule is effectively extended. In the parable of the talents in Matthew 25:14-30, Jesus explains that we will one day give an account of how we have ruled over His possessions. All that we have belongs to Him (Psalm 24:1), and we are but stewards, or caretakers.

One of those responsibilities that God has given to a man, over which he must learn to rule well, is his wife and children, his family. Most men do not think of themselves as rulers, or kings, over their families, but they are. Each man is a king over his domain and carries God's divine authority into his home as its head. He must learn to rule over it as Jesus Christ's representative, first to his wife and then to his children.

At this point I can almost feel the resistance. "What do you mean, 'rule?' That sounds heavy-handed and tyrannical to me. I don't like that word." I can understand that reaction, and it expresses a legitimate concern that I want to address very carefully.

The rulership of Jesus Christ

Was Jesus heavy-handed and tyrannical? Did those to whom He ministered feel put down, dominated and suppressed? Does He not currently rule over all the earth? He does (Acts 2:33, 1 Corinthians 15:25), and He has delegated this gracious servant-rulership to men in the family to exercise for Him. In His prayer in John 17:18, He says that He is sending the disciples into the world just as His Father had sent Him into the world; to extend the rule of the kingdom of God. Properly administered, that rule will produce peace and freedom.

In John 17, Jesus gives an accounting to His Father for His rulership over the disciples, His "family," while He was on the earth as the Son of Man. Let's see how Jesus ruled over His family, and we will see how in turn we, as men, are to rule over ours.

First, as I have already said, Jesus ruled as a **steward**. It's important to see that at least six times in this chapter Jesus refers to His disciples as "the men you have given Me" (vs. 2,6,9,11,12,24). He understood that He was but a steward, not the "owner" of those under His authority. As a steward, He never magnified Himself but constantly reminded the disciples that he represented His Father. He was quick to give credit or glory to His Father (vs. 4), revealing by His words and deeds what His Father was like, always letting His disciples know that everything He said and did originated with His Father (vs. 6,7).

Second, Jesus ruled as a **servant**. To rule should inherently connote service. Because our politicians (our "public servants" in civil government), tyrannical church leaders, and domineering husbands, have often used their power selfishly for their own ends, they have given us a warped concept of "ruling." Jesus was indeed a servant-ruler, saying in Matthew 20:28, "the Son of Man did not come to be served but to serve, and to give His life as a ransom for many," leaving an example of the attitude of a servant-ruler for His disciples by washing their feet at the Last Supper.

Third, Jesus ruled as **king**. He taught His disciples to be obedient to God's Law as He expressed it (vs. 6). He expected to be obeyed by the disciples, and He equated their obedience as evidence of their love for Him (John 14:15,21,23,24). He did not hesitate to act and speak with authority, because He knew He carried the authority of His Father. His leadership was decisive, and when that leadership was challenged by a "family" member, He was willing to confront that resistance head on, because He knew He led according to God's Word, and to refuse to follow His leadership was to resist the plan of God (Matthew 16:21-23).

Fourth, Jesus ruled as **lover**. Jesus was confident that His Father loved Him, and the love relationship He had with His Father was reproduced in His love for His disciples (vs. 23,24,26). His Father's love flowed through Him to His "family," as He nurtured and cherished them, literally giving His life for them.

Finally, everything He did was bathed in prayer for His disciples (vs. 9), and for us as their spiritual descendants (vs. 20) that they and we would not be captured by Satan (vs.15).

This is the report Jesus gives His Father in John 17. He does not shrink from being held accountable for what He has done during His ministry, and opens Himself up to evaluation by the One under whose authority He resides. His report is the specifics on how He had ruled over those God had given Him. His rule doesn't sound very oppressive to me, but it was rulership nonetheless, because responsibility for them had been given to Jesus, and Jesus is giving an account of that rule here in John 17.

The result of Godly rule in the lives of the disciples

The result of Christ's rulership over the disciples is also given in His report to His Father in this chapter. Godly rule in their lives produced fruit, as it always will in the lives of those who want to live in the kingdom.

First, they recognized His authority over them as from God and willingly received it and submitted to it (vs. 7,8). They did not resist His leadership, because if they had, they knew that they would be resisting God. They knew Jesus was sent by His Father (vs. 8).

Obedience to Jesus was not something the disciples ought to do, needed to do, and should do, but really didn't want to do. His rule caused them to <u>want</u> to obey Him, for they knew that obedience to Him and His teaching brought life (John 6:68), so obeying was something that was not difficult for them to do. When given the opportunity to leave Him, and reject His rule, Peter spoke for the twelve as he said, "Lord, to whom shall we go? You have the words of eternal life" (John 6:68).

Second, the Godly rule of Jesus Christ set His disciples apart from the world and its attractions (vs. 13-19). They gave themselves to Jesus' vision of the kingdom, and saw in that vision a reason for living. They were no longer permeated with worldly thought patterns, but they had had their philosophy of life rectified so completely that they could be sent back into the world to effect change without being "picked off" by the enemy. They were truly "in the world but not of it," and the destiny of their Savior became their eternal destiny as well.

Because they were no longer "of the world," their presence caused those who hated Jesus and His message to also hate them, just as Jesus had predicted (John 15:18,19). He even went so far as to say that if the world spoke well of them they should beware (Luke 6:26), because those truly under His rule would suffer the same fate He suffered - hatred and persecution from the world. The disciples were actually to rejoice in the midst of that persecution, because they were following in the train of a long line of kingdom men (Matthew 5:11,12).

Third, the Godly rule of Jesus Christ produced unity among those over whom that rule was exercised (vs. 11,20,21). The petty squabbling and divisive jealousies so prevalent among the disciples dissolved as their vision of Jesus was clarified and made operative by the Holy Spirit after Pentecost. On that day they were all together *"with one accord* in one place" (Acts 2:1), and Peter stood to preach *"with the eleven"* (Acts 2:14). After some three thousand were saved and added to the church there in Jerusalem that day, they were *"together,* and had all things in common" (Acts 2:44), and they continued "daily *with one accord* in the Temple and breaking bread from house to house" (Acts 2:46). As the disciples submitted themselves to His rule, they experienced peace among themselves.

Fourth, I want to mention one more result of faithful ruling here in John 17 that is very exciting. When Satan tempted Jesus in the wilderness, his final temptation, his supreme attempt to pull Jesus away from submission to His Father's will, was to offer Him rulership over the kingdoms of the world with all their glory, if He would but fall down and worship Satan (Matthew 4:8,9). Authority is the issue here. Who will be Jesus' head in Figure 1? You know the story of Adam facing that same decision and choosing Satan, and Satan became "the head of every man." Jesus, however, chose to submit Himself to His Father's will, and the humbling, life-long obedience that that entailed, ending in the obedience of the cross (Philippians 2:7,8). He rejected the visible, glorious ruling over the kingdoms of the world for the seemingly insignificant rulership over a motley band of twelve very simple, unimportant nobodies, *because that was His Father's will, and there can be but one will in the family!* He ruled faithfully, even perfectly, completing what He had been given to do, always seeking to glorify His Father in that rulership (John 17:4).

What was the result of this submission by Jesus to His "Head"? Because of His long-range vision ("for the joy that was set before Him" [Hebrews 12:2]), He was able to endure the hardship, the pain, and the shame of the cross, and now has been glorified before all His enemies, being elevated to the right hand of God the Father with all power and authority!

To glorify means to magnify, honor, praise, and extol.[4] Jesus glorified His Father while He was on the earth by submitting to His will (John 17;4), and then the Father glorified His Son by exalting Him and giving Him a name "which is above every name" (Philippians 2:9). He is now the ruler over all the earth, the King over all other kings and the Lord over all other lords. All authority in heaven and on earth has been given to Him, and His rule will never pass away. What Satan promised Jesus when he tempted Him in the wilderness, the "kingdoms of the world," Jesus has now acquired legitimately by submission to His divine Head!

In John 17:22, Jesus prays to His Father, "And the glory which You gave Me I have given them." His rule in the lives of twelve common, uneducated fisherman would produce such radiant glory in what they said and did that their message would transform the world. Jesus did not spend His disciples on Himself. He did not use them to make a name for Himself, to build His own independent empire, but discipled them in such a way that they realized all their potential for extending His Father's kingdom His Father's way.

"As My Father has sent Me, I also send you"

We have seen in this chapter that God the Father sent His Son into the world, first, under His (the Father's) divine authority, His rule, and then to exercise that rule over those the Father had given Him. We have seen the characteristics of that Godly rule and the results it produced in the lives of the disciples. That is the kingdom of God; where the rule of God is observed. Now Jesus says an amazing thing, first in His prayer to His Father in John 17, and then to the disciples: "As You have sent me into the world, *I also have sent them into the world*" (John 17:18), and, "As My Father has sent Me, *I also send you*" (John 20:21).

Do you see how divine authority is delegated by the Father? Nothing is more crucial for an understanding of the operation of the kingdom, including the family, than this! All authority originates in God (Romans 13:1), and flows first to Jesus ("All authority has been given to Me in heaven and on earth" [Matthew 28:18]). He learned to live under it in the divine family, the Godhead, then He exercised it over the "family" God had given Him (His disciples). Finally, He sent that "family" into the world, just as God had sent Him. How? To live under God's delegated authority, to exercise that authority over the family (both natural and spiritual) that God has given them, and then finally to send their own family into the world. So God intends to extend this divine chain until the end of time!

That is how the kingdom grows; Jesus' disciples yielding to God's authority where they find it, wielding it over specific stewardship responsibilities, and sending out, or fielding, those over whom they have ruled, to continue the divinely-ordained chain of authority; all men living under the immediate headship of Jesus Christ! All kingdom activities, including family life, are built upon this foundation.

Rulership in human families

When a man rules in his family according to Figure 1, he must learn to rule as Jesus has demonstrated, if he indeed is sent as Jesus was sent. **First**, he must see himself as a **steward** of that family, viewing them as a precious treasure whom God has given to him for a season, and over whom he is to rule well, for he is accountable to God for what he does with the Master's possessions. Men, we do not "own" our wives and children, They belong to God, and they must know that we rule for Him, by His Law, with His wisdom and love, in His power, and for His purpose, helping them to develop all the gifts and abilities that they have been given. They must see that we are not trying to control them, or have power over them in any way for our own benefit.

Second, fathers are also called to be **servants**. Just as stewardship is for God, service is for those under our care. To rule well means that our authority and power as heads of our homes must never be used to subjugate family members for our personal convenience, our selfish purposes, or our own honor and recognition, but always for their benefit. Our decisions will often represent a personal sacrifice for the well-being of all the rest of the family members.

Third, a man must see himself as the **king** over his domain, ruling in his home. Our families must learn to obey the law of God as it comes through us as fathers. We must learn how to teach our children (Ephesians 6:1) and our wives (Titus 2:5) to be obedient to us as kings in the home because we represent Jesus Christ to them. We must be sure, as Jesus did, that the law we administer is not capricious, laid on our families out of our own minds, but that it is from God's law, the Bible.

This concept is very difficult for many men to grasp, particularly in today's society where men have been denigrated, put down and figuratively castrated. The Bible, however, is our standard, and we must not be distracted from our mission of ruling by cries of "chauvinist," "tyrant," "woman-hater," or accusations of trying to subjugate women.

We **must** see ourselves as kings, for "as a man thinks in his heart, so is he" (Proverbs 23:7). We cannot rule until we see that God has indeed called us as men to rule in His kingdom for the benefit of our wives and children, for they will not realize all that God has for them if we do not. Our wives will have a much more difficult time developing a "gentle and quiet spirit" (1 Peter 3:4), and thereby becoming Godly older women able to teach the younger women (Titus 2:4), if we are not ruling as kings in our home. Our children will have difficulty obeying and honoring us and our wives, as they are told to do in the Bible, if we do not demand it and rule with authority as kings. They will miss the long-term benefits associated with honoring mother and father, and instead experience the curses associated with rebellion and disobedience for the rest of their lives. This very unfortunate scenario could be avoided if we as fathers demand that they honor and obey us as children.

Fourth, we rule as **lovers**. All that is wrapped up in the love of God is to flow through us as fathers to our families. "The love of God is shed abroad in our hearts through the Holy Spirit" (Romans 5:5). How that happens is the topic of chapter 7.

Finally, following the example of our pattern-man, all that we do as rulers is bathed in prayer for our families; for them specifically, and then for our descendants, both spiritual and physical, that will come from them. Our prayer is that God will capture them all for His kingdom, that none of our heritage will be lost to the enemy.

The results of Godly rule in human families

Men, if we rule over our families in the power of the Holy Spirit (who is available to us as Christians), as the Son of Man ruled over His, can we not expect the same results that He saw, and that He reports to His Father in John 17?

First, if we are functioning properly as husbands, we can expect our wives to recognize the divine order illustrated in Figure 1, and then to submit to our headship. God has built into every woman a desire to be ruled by a Godly man who will exercise his rule in the same manner that Jesus did. That desire is a part of her, and even though she may not recognize it, and even initially battle her husband's leadership with every pressure she can exert, she wants desperately for him to succeed in capturing her heart and will. If we rule well, we can expect our wives and our children to embrace our rule, not obeying because they "ought to, need to, or should," but because they want to, realizing that life results from proper order in the home. They will come to understand that by resisting us they are in effect resisting God.

My daughter, Ramah, is currently a junior in college, and, like many 20-year-old girls, enjoys the opposite sex. I have been very protective of her and have not allowed her to date, which has been a struggle for her at times, but she has just recently come to a new willingness to fully embrace our family method of biblical courtship.

In discussing this on the phone not long ago, she said something that let me know that my fun-loving, anything-for-a-good-time little girl was growing up. "Dad, I know you won't let me marry anyone that is not right for me. I trust you."

She did not feel this way in high school when all of her friends had boy-friends, were dating and getting physically involved. She did not even necessarily agree when those same girls were then breaking up with those boys, with only a broken heart and varying degrees of sexual experience to show for their involvement. Now, however, she has come to understand the principle of my rule in her life, and has yielded to it, recognizing the protection it affords her. She is secure in the knowledge that life and health will result. I'll discuss courtship in detail later.

Second, just as Jesus' rule sanctified, or set apart, his disciples from the world, our leadership as fathers in our homes will do the same thing. If a man has ruled well, he does not have to worry about losing his children to the world when they leave home. He doesn't have to wonder if they will be picked off by the enemy at college as they are exposed to all the ideologies that are contrary to Scripture. He doesn't have to be concerned about drugs, AIDS, atheism, evolution and all the other boogie-men that cause Christian fathers to grow cold with fear. If he has ruled well, his children will adopt his world-view, embrace his value-system, and love his Lord.

My daughter recently told me of a group of professors at her Christian college who pride themselves in their rather liberal ideas. Some of the students, including one of Ramah's good friends, are enamored with the brilliance of these professors, and a number of these students have been captivated by a philosophy I'm sure their parents felt would never reach them at a Christian school. A father who has ruled well has set his children apart from the grasp of hostile ideas that would destroy his heritage. His children are free to go into the world to influence the world rather than to be influenced by it.

Third, Godly rule in the home will produce unity, or peac all in the family have come under the one will of the father. S at peace with one-another, supporting and encouraging

67

They obey and respect their mother because they know that she represents their father. In his absence she faithfully and diligently carries out his policies. As a result, when he comes home he supports all of her decisions that were made while he was away. The children know that it is impossible to play one against the other, and therefore they are much quicker to obey their mother, who does not naturally carry as much authority with her children as her husband. They understand that to disobey her is to disobey him, and they know that they will be held accountable for that disobedience. There is security and peace in the home. The whole family is a reflection of the kingdom of God, and as a result of this oneness "the world will believe that You (God the Father) have sent Me (Jesus Christ)" (John 17:21).

Fourth, just as Jesus was glorified by His Father as a result of submitting to His will, and He in turn passed that glory, God's very glory, on to His disciples (John 17:22), proper rule in the family will cause that glory to shine in the faces of those who willingly yield to the father's rule. 1 Corinthians 11:7 says that "woman (*gune*) is the glory of man."

After being around a woman, even briefly, I can often discern what kind of a relationship she has with her husband. She is a reflection of the care that she receives, unknowingly radiating the glory of God when her husband rules over her properly, and, just as surely, demonstrating by her attitude, actions and personal demeanor the absence of that rule.

A servant-ruler is not threatened by his wife's gifts and abilities, for he knows that she will be invaluable to him as he makes decisions for the family, once she has come under his authority. She can make him "look good," as the glory that his leadership produces in her radiates forth. He is responsible to see that all her potential in God is realized, that she is doing all that God created her to do. Proverbs 31 is a summary of some of those things she can accomplish as a biblical wife and mother under her husband's authority.

Some women have become impatient, chafing under the headship of a husband who is either threatened by his wife's abilities and keeps her down, or is just ignorant of his responsibility to release his wife into the fullness of her talents and abilities. For whatever reason, she has struck out on her own, becoming involved in some "women's ministry," or some other independent activity. Invariably, a hardness or independent spirit develops, and the glory that comes from submission to her husband as a helpmate disappears.

Even if that husband doesn't understand how to rule well, or even if he is not a Christian, yielding to his rule is God's way for his wife. For the past three years Ann has come relatively regularly to Tree Of Life on Sunday morning. She is married to a non-Christian who has never cared if she came to church or not because he was doing his own thing on Sunday anyway. So, Ann would come with her children, always praying for her husband, that he would become a Christian.

We began to notice recently that Ann had not been in attendance for several weeks and asked one of her friends where she was. She told us that Ann's husband is beginning to read the Bible and wants Ann to stay home with him on Sunday morning and watch church on TV with him. He is even asking her questions about Christianity.

During the 8 years Ann has been a Christian she has never badgered her husband or preached at him, but silently continued to submit to his leadership. Her face has been filled with the glory of the Lord, or as Peter says, "the incorruptible ornament of a gentle and quiet spirit" (1 Peter 3:4), and her husband is being won without a word as he observes Ann's continued submission and respect for him.

Some women have blind-spots in their lives that hinder the glory from shining. Maybe she talks too much, or brags excessively about herself and her children. Maybe she holds grudges and can't forgive, or gossips, and is not warm and hospitable. Maybe she can't look at herself and admit she's wrong. All of these things cut off the shining of the glory of God in her life.

A part of a husband's task is to lovingly confront her over these character faults, helping her to seek the Lord's power to overcome them. His evaluation will be invaluable to her, and, properly done, will help her to maximize the gifts and abilities God has given her.

Unlike Jesus, a husband is not a perfect leader, and it is imperative that he be open to his wife's input into his life as well, as long as she does not challenge his position of authority in the home. Jill will frequently see mistakes I have made in dealing with people, insights I have missed, or just plain dumb things I have done that I have not seen. When she tells me about it, I don't always like it and often don't respond really well initially, because my pride is wounded. "Surely if that is true, I would have seen it," is often my first reaction. Generally, upon reflection, I realize she is right, and, in my "bull-in-a-china-shop" method of operation, I have said or done something inappropriate. I need her to do that for me. No one is as lonely as the "emperor who

69

has no clothes;" the person everyone is afraid to be honest with because of his unwillingness to look at himself. Jill can be very, very honest, but in the very act of confronting me, she does not challenge my leadership.

"Arrows in the hand of a warrior"

Just as God the Father sent a representative, Jesus Christ, who thought, spoke and acted in accordance with the heart of His Father, Jesus in turn sent His disciples out in the same manner. Now the chain of growth in the kingdom continues as we <u>yield</u> to the authority under which we find ourselves, <u>wield</u> the authority properly that God has given us, and then finally <u>field</u>, or send out, those who have learned our hearts.

This is the message of Psalm 127:3,4. "Behold, children are a heritage from the Lord; the fruit of the womb is his reward. Like arrows in the hand of a warrior, so are the children of one's youth." The final step in ruling well in the family is sending out, or "shooting the arrows" that God has given as a heritage, armed with the message of the kingdom, to strike a blow at Satan's heart.

Nothing is more satisfying, more fulfilling to a man than to have those in his family, over whom he has ruled, reflect in their thoughts, words and deeds what he has given his very life to build into them. His influence for the kingdom is extended into the next generation, and will indeed live on through the ages as his children perpetuate the chain.

It is crucial that a man's wife see this kingdom vision as well, if indeed the children are to be effective arrows. It will be difficult to point those arrows if there is an uncertain, or divided vision in the home. Make no mistake, a wife can either be a tremendous asset, fleshing out her husband's vision and helping to implement it, or a millstone around his neck, resisting his leadership and direction.

For the first 15 years of our marriage, Jill was unable to give herself completely to my vision for the direction of our family. Because of her very modest upbringing (she grew up in the country in rural Georgia without a father), she needed to be "somebody," to "make it" in her own eyes. On the other hand, coming from basically a loving, secure family, I didn't feel the pressure to prove myself, and our direction was not toward fame and fortune, but toward exploring the frontiers of New-Testament church life - not always a popular direction. Although she agreed with me in theory, when opposition to what we were doing would surface, she found herself, by her own admission, often whining and complaining and wanting to find a more acceptable line of work.

By the grace of God I somehow stood firm over those years, not really understanding at the time what I was doing and making a lot of leadership blunders, but knowing that God had pointed me in a direction that I must go. I eventually began to learn how to better love Jill, which was what she really needed, and to communicate to her my vision for the kingdom of God in a more understandable manner. Wonder of wonders, she gradually responded, finally learning to adapt herself to me, until now I know that what she says and does represents our vision, for that vision has now become hers.

She, however, doesn't hesitate to tell me what she thinks, both positive and negative, and, as a result, we will often disagree. That very disagreement leads to very profitable discussions, and, even though I must ultimately set our course, her input adjusts and completes our direction.

Jill can now be an invaluable helpmate for me. She is very insightful and sensitive, and has a wonderful, warm, friendly way about her, making her an older woman to whom the young women in our church naturally gravitate. She continually amazes me with her wise, well-thought-out counsel. As an elder in the church, responsible for the spiritual well-being of the people, I know that Jill is telling these young wives and mothers solid, biblical truth. I am confident she has the same vision for the family I do, that what she is communicating reflects my emphasis and direction. I can truly "send her out," so to speak, to represent me with supreme confidence.

The greatest joy I have ever experienced has come to me through my three children. Each one of them is totally unique, completely different from the other two, making his/her own distinctive contribution to the family and the kingdom of God. They absorbed my vision and learned my heart as children. My two sons are now young adults and they are on their own (the married one officially), arrows flying true to the mark. My daughter is 21 years old, a junior in college, and still under my authority, but the major work of preparation for life has been done. The vision of the kingdom has been transmitted. Fine-tuning is all that remains of her parent's job.

Do you see why the kingdom of God is like a stone that crushes all other kingdoms and eventually grows into a mountain that fills the whole earth (Daniel 2:35)? Do you see that the kingdom of God is the "big picture," the defining framework into which all aspects of the Christian faith must fit? As we understand the principle of authority upon which the kingdom of God successfully functions, learn to apply it properly in our families, and then teach it to those non-Christians who enter the kingdom through our evangelistic efforts, truly the enemy <u>will</u> become a footstool for His feet (Psalm 110:1).

"Father, help me to see the authority under which you have placed me as **Your** authority, straight from You. If I resist it, I am resisting You. Give me the grace to yield to that authority, and to learn from it the lessons you have for me. Empower me by your Spirit to then wield the authority you have given me as Jesus would, and finally, to transmit my heart to those under my care, sending them out as kingdom-extenders. Amen."

Questions for discussion

1. Discuss the statement, "All conflicts arise over the issue of authority." Do you agree or disagree? Why or why not?

2. Under what authority has God placed you? What is your attitude toward it? What can you do that you are not doing to please that one?

3. What has God given you to rule over? Evaluate yourself as to how you are exercising that responsibility under God. How are you doing?

4. Who can you invision "sending out" at some time in the future? What message will they carry? What obstacles do you see that will have to be overcome in order for them to reproduce your heart?

5. In what way is the kingdom of God "the framework into which all aspects of the Christian faith must fit." Do you agree or disagree? Why or why not?

---

[1] W.E. Vine, *An Expository Dictionary of New Testament Words*, (Old Tappan, New Jersey: Fleming H. Revell Company, 1966), Vol. IV, p. 215.
[2] *Ibid.*, Vol. II, p. 202. Also see Wayne Grudem's study on the meaning of *Kephale* published as an appendix in *Recovering Biblical Manhood and Womanhood*, co-edited by John Piper and Wayne Grudem (Wheaton: Crossway Books, 1991).
[3] NKJ, Philippians 2:7, margin.
[4] Vine, Vol. II, p. 152.

Chapter 6

"Leave...cleave...become one flesh"

When God presented Eve to Adam, he saw her as "bone of my bones, and flesh of my flesh," because she actually came from his body. She was fashioned from one of his ribs, so she was "one flesh" with her husband in a unique way that we can't duplicate, being literally one flesh with him physically.

But the next verse in the biblical account, Genesis 2:24, applies that same concept, "one-fleshness," to all marriages down through the ages, implying that there is a mysterious union between a man and a woman that occurs on a deep, soul level. "Therefore a man shall leave his father and mother and be joined to his wife, and they shall become one flesh."

This verse is quoted by Jesus in His discussion with the Pharisees on the subject of divorce. Paul then quotes it twice in His epistles, once when discussing the one-flesh relationship of a husband and wife as parallel to Christ's relationship to the Church, and once, surprisingly enough, as a reason to abstain from sex with a prostitute.

The beginning of a family

We will discuss what becoming "one-flesh" entails in great detail later, but, for now, we want to investigate how that most intimate of all human relationships begins.

Some of what I'm going to say might seem impossible in today's world. I know many of our children have grown up in a world where a family begins in a totally different manner, but I'm convinced that this biblical approach can be captured again by God's people, and it will help make our families powerful centers in which God's family business will flourish. (Keep in mind I'm not dealing with the selection of a mate here, only the beginning of a new family.)

Genesis 2:24 says that becoming one flesh begins with two very important steps for the man. First, leaving mother and father, which involves leaving not only their physical household, but also the parent's authority, provision and protection. Second, being joined to, or, as the King James Bible puts it, cleaving to his wife. The man is specifically mentioned here and not the woman, not because she doesn't do these two things also, but because he represents the family as its head, just as Adam represented the whole human race when he fell. The woman indeed also leaves parents, and is joined to her husband in that distinctive one-flesh bond.

"You're on your own"

Figure 1 in Chapter 5 demonstrates that the children in a family are under the authority of their parents. They are to obey them "in all things" (Colossians 3:20) and they are to honor, or respect them (Ephesians 6:1-3). Obedience deals with external actions, while honor involves internal attitudes. A child's parents represent God to him, and they must teach him to obey and honor them for his sake, because if he learns to obey and honor them, he will find it much easier to obey and honor God when he has his own family. Nothing is more crucial to a child than this, and the biblical method of training a child to comply with these admonitions will be covered in detail later in the book.

When do a young man and a young woman "leave home," come out from under this parental authority, and take responsibility for themselves? Some would say that upon graduation from high school parental responsibility is over and the child is now an adult and on his own. He pays for his own college, and, if he stays home and has a job, he pays room and board. Others would say that a certain age is the time of independence, or when the son or daughter is able to support himself or herself. But the question should be, "What does the Bible say?," and indeed the Bible does have a clear position on this question.

Genesis 2:24, the verse that speaks of leaving mother and father and cleaving to a wife, is quoted by Jesus in Matthew 19:5, where His statement begins with the Greek words *heneken toutou*, which mean, "for the sake of this."[1] In Genesis 2, this phrase connects verse 24, with verse 23, which is Adam's statement about his one-flesh relationship with his new wife. The phrase would read, "for the sake of this (the husband and wife one-flesh relationship), a man shall leave his father and mother..." In other words, the cause, or reason, for leaving and cleaving is marriage, and until that occurs, the son or daughter is still under the authority, protection, and provision of his or her parents.

This brings up a whole bag of questions, and I want to consider each of them carefully, because this truth is a very important one that the Church needs to recapture. First I will deal with sons and then with daughters, because, due to their different roles in a biblical marriage, a father will treat them somewhat differently. However, though I address sons specifically at first, the material is general and applies to both.

How does a son "leave home?"

On the wedding day, there is a dramatic change in the relationship between a son and his parents. Figure 1 from the last chapter changes and becomes Figure 2.

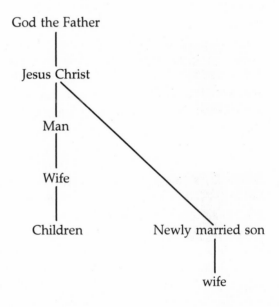

Figure 2

A clean break

Notice that the newly married son is no longer a "child," under the umbrella of authority of his mother and father, but is now directly under the authority of Jesus Christ as he begins a new family.

The lines in Figure 2 between the mother and father and their newly married son are no longer there. The son is now directly accountable to Jesus Christ. This truth has some very significant practical implications.

Although there will continue to be respect for the father's wisdom and experience, and certainly a wise son will avail himself of that resource, there is no longer any God-ordained authority there. A wise father will be very careful not to offer advice unless he is asked by his married son. He will even let his son make mistakes (at least what the father might think to be mistakes). If the father exercises this care, and the son and his new wife see right away that he is not trying to continue to be an authority in their lives, they will often seek his input into major decisions.

However, a wise father will not always give it, because he realizes that his son now needs the experience and the freedom of going alone with his wife before God and hearing His voice for Himself. Remember, "Jesus is the head of every man" (I Corinthians 11:3), and although the son hopefully has experienced a personal walk with the Lord, in matters of <u>authority</u> his father has been the Lord to him. His voice has been God's voice, and even though the father has been teaching his son to hear God all along, now he is on his own for real.

This can be a very difficult time for parents, particularly mothers. The son who has always needed them is no longer a child, and he doesn't need them in the same way anymore. That one whom the parents have given their lives for, who has been the very focus of their attention for years, is now focused on someone else. The relationship is going through a dramatic change, and the parents' ability to hold their son in an open hand and let him change to become a man will determine the depth of their continuing relationship. It is a bitter-sweet time, as the parents are proud of the maturity they see in their son, but miss the little boy they loved so much.

Getting ready to drive solo

It should be the purpose of every father to prepare his son for that day, his wedding day, when he will be out from under his father's authority and become directly responsible to Jesus Christ. Of course, he hasn't been a "child" for a long time, and ideally his father has allowed him to take more and more responsibility as he has prepared his son for this day. Probably the father has not given a great deal of explicit direction to his son's life for some time, allowing him to make more and more of his own decisions as he has gotten older. This is a very important phase that a father must take his son through, or he will be unprepared for being the head of his home on his wedding day.

When my oldest son, Adam, turned sixteen and got his driver's license, he was just like all sixteen-year-olds who love their new freedom to take out the car without Mom and Dad. He had just met some new friends at Warm Beach Conference Center, where he had been attending a Christian camp. Since he was the only one with access to a car, he wanted to drive up to Warm Beach (about an hour's drive from our house); pick up his friends; drive back past our house to an ice cream store he had located about thirty minutes the other way; take them back past our house to Warm Beach; and then come home!

Again, like all sixteen-year-olds who are just beginning to drive, he didn't have a real good grip on distance, or how long it takes to get from place to place. I asked him if he was sure he wanted to drive that much.

"Sure, Dad, no problem." The excitement of his new friends, and his opportunity to be alone with them in the car, overshadowed any grain of common sense a sixteen-year-old might have had time to develop.

As I evaluated whether or not to let him go, I determined that the trip was not dangerous - at least not any more dangerous than any other car trip. Adam was a good driver, and Jill and I both felt that he understood the importance of really concentrating on his driving when his friends were in the car. We knew the kids to be from the families of the Conference Directors, and we weren't worried about them. The only question was the wisdom of doing all that driving to get an ice cream cone!

A technique that I liked to follow with my children as they were growing up was to always let them do what they wanted to do unless there was a reason not to do it. (In my estimation, not their's!). A loving father, who derives his identity from God the Father, enjoys blessing his children. I could have told Adam,

"No, you can't do all that driving. That's foolish." He would have been disappointed, but that would have been that.

However, I decided to bless him and let him go, realizing that a lesson on counting the cost was about to be learned.

When he dragged himself home, well after mid-night, he had deposited all the kids at their homes, spent over five hours driving, and not had any volunteers to chip in on gas. He had learned a lesson that was indelibly imprinted on his mind, and that went toward making him the man he is today. Adam now has a wife and two children of his own, and we still laugh about that incident, but I believe he learned something that night that he will one day be able to pass on to his own son.

In preparing a son for leadership, a good father knows when his son is ready to make more and more of his own decisions. For instance, when my two sons were in the little cooperative home-school in our small church during junior high, they learned to be responsible for achieving the goals we set for their educational program. Then, when they went to high school at a large traditional Christian high school, they continued that practice. I set the broad, overall parameters for them ("Take all the courses that will get you ready for college. Leave all your options open"). They then did all the details themselves.

Unless a son's rebellion has been broken and he wants to please his father, allowing him to make his own decisions is madness. If he wants to just get by in school, take the easiest courses possible, and do as little work as he can, the father must obviously still supervise his education. If he has not done this task when his son was still in elementary school and then tries to do it in high school, it will be a good deal harder, but still doable. If left to himself, the son's poor decisions will be destructive to his own character, and to the direction a Christian father wants his son to go. The fences need to be brought in, and the freedom to make decisions limited until there is a desire to do the father's will.

Pushing that bird out of the nest at the right time

Another point needs to be made here. The mother and father birds are the ones who literally push the baby bird out of the nest as the baby learns to fly. We're dealing with children and not birds, but the principle is the same. The father decides what the son is able to handle, not the son himself. Young men are not very adept at evaluating themselves, and remember, evaluation is one of the responsibilities of the one in authority in a relationship in the kingdom of God. Some sons think they are ready for more than they can handle well, and some sons can handle more than they think they can. The father knows his son, and his honest evaluation, with his wife's insights, must be the one that is followed, as he is the one accountable to God.

God the Father evaluated His Son ("You are my beloved Son in Whom I am well pleased" [Mark 1:11]). Jesus in turn evaluated His "family," His disciples ("they have kept Your word," "they have received your words," "they have believed that You sent Me" [John 17:6-8]).

A son must understand that his father will evaluate him as long as he is under his father's authority, and the father must not shrink from that task. His approach should be encouraging and up-building, always trying to begin with the positives in the evaluation, but addressing the negatives nonetheless. What a tragedy for a son to learn of his weaknesses from those in the world who do not love him, rather than from his father who did not love him enough to be honest with him.

The father also must evaluate his son's readiness for marriage. It is important that the son get his father's blessing or approval, not only with regard to the girl he is marrying, but also his own readiness to begin his own family. He needs to be ready to take on the full responsibilities for a wife and children physically, spiritually, and emotionally, and his father will know when he is ready better than he will. If a son marries without his father's blessing, he is coming out from under his father's protective umbrella of authority. We will discuss that situation later.

When the son is ready to marry, the father will not have had to make any large course-corrections in the path his son is on for quite a while, and he should be confident as he sends his son out to start a new family that he has fulfilled his responsibility before God to bring him up in the "training and admonition of the Lord" (Ephesians 6:4). He has pointed his "arrow" straight (Psalm 127:4), and his son will "seek first the kingdom of God" (Matthew 6:33) his whole life. This job of preparation begins when a child is first born, and it's a full-time job, but with his wife's faithful assistance, and an understanding of biblical principles, a father can be assured of success (Proverbs 22:6).

Knowing his father's heart

Up until the wedding day, the father has been the authority in his son's life. As I have suggested, the father should have given more and more freedom to his son as he has seen that the son is able to make wise decisions. The fences have been extended gradually as the son has proven himself to be faithful. The son has learned his father's heart, and is making the same decisions the father would make. Remember Jesus saying, "I always do my Father's will" (John 5:30)? That is the father's goal for his son; to inculcate his will, which should be the will of his head, Jesus Christ, into the heart of his son.

When my second son, Jason, was playing on the golf team at the Christian high school he attended, he came back from a trip one night after dark. He and a fellow team-mate decided to play a trick on the night watchman before they came home. They went down the hill from the school and made a commotion in the bushes, attracting the attention of the watchman, who came to investigate with his flashlight. Jason and his friend doubled back to the school, unnoticed by the watchman, who was looking everywhere for what he believed to be trespassers up to no good.

Jason and his friend had a good laugh, and started to head home in the friend's car, when his friend had another idea. Why not release the parking brake on the watchman's truck that he had left on campus, and roll it a block away so he can't find it, turn the radio way up so he'll get blasted when he turns on the ignition, and wrap this toilet-paper that's under the seat all around it?

At this point, a little bell went off in Jason's brain. As he told me later, when we were discussing the adventure,

"Dad, I knew you wouldn't mind if I played a little trick on the watchman by making a racket (He was right), but I knew when Eric started to push his truck down the street and wanted to sabotage it, you wouldn't want me to do that" (He was right again!). He left Eric, who carried out the plan, and found a pay phone to call Jill to come pick him up.

Eric was caught, and he and Jason both had to muck out the bottom of a pond as punishment, but I didn't care, because my son, at age 17, had demonstrated that he was learning his father's heart.

What confidence there is, when a father has been faithful to train his son, to stand before the minister on his wedding day, knowing that his son's direction is set, and he has learned his father's heart, which is the same heart as his son's new head, Jesus Christ.

Absentee fathers

Let me digress for just a quick minute. You might be reading this and thinking to yourself,

"Why didn't my father give me this kind of preparation for my marriage?" or,

"Why isn't my dad helping me right now to get ready for marriage?" What should a son do if his father does not know about this truth and does not attempt to give his son the kind of input the son might genuinely desire?

He should go to his dad and confess any bitterness he might have toward him, and ask his father to forgive him for any difficulty he caused him that made it difficult for the father to rule well over him. Some fathers would like to be this kind of a father, but they haven't known enough truth to be able to move into ruling well with confidence, and any resistance from their son reduced them to shouting, anger, and finally retreat.

Other fathers are too selfish, lazy, or fearful, and don't care enough to expend the effort to be servant-leaders. The son should go to that father and explain his need for a protective umbrella of authority, and ask his father if he will be that covering, assuring him that he will do as the father directs.

In either instance, the son should realize that any harbored bitterness he has toward his father will be very destructive in his own life, and cause difficulties in his own family later on that don't even seem to be related (Hebrews 12:15). That bitterness is sin, and needs to be repented of and forsaken. Cry out to God for help in giving you the power to forgive your father.

This approach is honoring to your father, and God is pleased when you do that. The principle in healing damaged family relationships is always to walk in the light with one another, repenting of anything that you have done to hurt the other person, then forgiving them for hurting you (Ephesians 4:32), and releasing any residual bitterness that might remain. 1 John 1:7 says that the result of that willingness to walk in the light and repent of exposed sin brings fellowship with one another and with God.

The older, unmarried son

If a son is older and not married does he remain under his father's authority? I believe he does, because he, as yet, has no family himself over which to rule. All of us need to be in a family somewhere, either ruling or being ruled over. To be independent, out from under the family authority structure, and not feel the weight of the responsibility for others is a "freedom" that we were not designed to experience.

This, of course, does not mean that a father tells his thirty-year-old single son what to do. The son has been on his own for years, maybe even living in another part of the country. It means that he still honors his father's <u>authority</u> in his life, something his married brother no longer does. He lives in the light of a mental awareness of a protection and provision that his father still provides. He is still there for the son to lean on if necessary.

As I write this, Jason is 25, in graduate school, unmarried, and living at home. I have not made a decision for him in years; he is free to disagree with me, and he certainly can catalog my faults. However, he understands that he is still under my authority.

Jason worked for one year full-time, and works part-time now that he is back in school. I do not charge him room and board, since I see that provision as my responsibility for all those who are under my authority. As a result he was able to save several thousand dollars toward the time when he will be married. He has one more year in a three year program, and will continue to live at home, until he "leaves his mother and father and is joined unto his wife."

I understand the freedom that Jason needs to hear from God himself at this point. He has proven his ability to do that, and for me to routinely intervene would be detrimental to his maturity as a man. However, if it were to become necessary to do so to save him from what I perceive to be a serious mistake, I would not hesitate. I love him too much to abdicate my responsibility.

How does a daughter leave home?

Much of what I have said applies to daughters as well as sons, but there are some distinctives that apply only to daughters that bear mentioning. The goal in raising a son is to prepare him to be *in* authority, while the goal in raising a daughter is to prepare her to be *under* authority. When a woman marries (again, we will deal with the process of mate-selection later), the authority in her life is transferred from her father to her husband. When the minister asks in the marriage ceremony, "Who gives this woman to be married to this man?," the answer is very significant, for at that point, if the answer is in the affirmative her parents have surrendered their daughter to another; to his authority, care, and protection; to his vision and life-direction. She will take on his name, meaning she will be identified wholly with him; with his failures as well as his successes. He will be the father of her children, and he will have primary responsibility for their training, their education, and their spiritual growth, and they will also carry his name. She will go where he goes geographically. She will, in a real sense, lose her life in his, that they may become "one flesh."

Did you know that all that was involved? Most of us didn't when we got married. If we had, we might not have done it. But that's what the Bible says. As a matter of fact, it says even more. In Ephesians 5, we are told that wives are to reverence their husbands as if they were Jesus Christ, submitting to them in all things. Don't react to that yet! We will talk about what that means in another chapter.

A young man who marries a girl who does not seek first the kingdom of God will have difficult times, but he still is the leader; the one who puts his stamp on the children; the one who sets the direction for the family. If he remains strong in the Lord, fulfilling his ordained role, his wife will most likely eventually follow.

For a young woman to marry a man who does not seek first the kingdom of God presents a much tougher scenario. He is the leader, the one who leaves his imprint on the children, the one who sets the direction for the family, and the direction will be away from the Lord. The wife must follow the admonition in 1 Peter 3:1-6 to continue to submit to him, to even call him "lord" as Sarah did Abraham, and trust the Lord that he will eventually be won as he experiences the power of his wife's submission to him.

This is a much more difficult road. That's why the scriptures make it clear not to marry unbelievers. That doesn't mean all you have to do is get the prospective bridegroom to say, "I'm a Christian," and every thing is all right. Many who claim to be Christians are practical unbelievers as far as investing their lives in light of Christ's call to discipleship. Can you be a Christian and not be a disciple who wants to obey His Lord? That is a topic of much controversy and beyond the scope of our discussion. A father needs to do all he can to give his daughter to a man who wants to be a spiritual warrior in the Lord's army.

The father's job; protection

It's important for a father to see that it is his prerogative to decide which man his daughter will marry. He even has the authority to prevent her from marrying at all if he feels the time is not right (1 Corinthians 7:34-38).

I have counselled several times with parents who let their daughters date young men that they did not approve of, and then when they wanted to get married, threw up their hands and said. "What can we do?," and went ahead with the wedding. What a tragedy to spend twenty years raising a young woman to be a woman of God, and then give the rest of her life to a man who is not interested in the kingdom of God, or who does not understand how to love her as a servant-ruler.

Remember, the father has absolute authority over his sons and his daughters. Maybe he has not recognized this because he has not had a theology of marriage and therefore has not understood his role, and has just gone along with the world's pattern. Nevertheless, authority in the lives of his unmarried sons and daughters has been given to him by God.

A father must protect his daughter; that is one of his <u>main</u> responsibilities. He must protect her from giving her heart away to a young man whom he would not want her to marry. He needs to do everything he can to help her save her heart for the one she marries. He cannot leave that to her, because she is young and emotional and has no experience, and does not understand that character is much more important than a cute smile or a great physique. The father must realize that the man to whom he gives his daughter must be his choice, with his daughter's concurrence, because the stakes are too high.

Let me finish the story I began in Chapter 1. Some time ago I got a call from a friend who wanted me to meet with a Minister of Music from a large, nearby church. As we met for lunch, he told me a tragic story of a wonderful daughter he was about to lose. Mary had been dating what her father perceived to be a rather unsavory young man for some time. Bill, the young man, had gotten Mary a job, given her a several-thousand dollar car, and enrolled her in the community college that he attended.

In the father's estimation, Bill was turning his daughter against her family, because he knew that the father did not approve of him. He had cast a spell of control over Mary, and she was deceived and helpless to see what was occurring. The last straw, that caused the father to seek help, was some very good information from a friend that Mary and Bill were planning to get married with or without his permission, and our mutual friend suggested that he meet with me.

After listening to his story, I went over with him the biblical principles of authority I have covered in this chapter, and suggested a course of action consistent with those principles. The father swallowed hard and said he wanted to run everything by the other leadership in his church, and he would get back to me.

We met a week later with his senior pastor, who supported everything I had told the father, and concurred with me that it was a biblical solution. I told the father that there was a chance he would lose his daughter, but if she married Bill, he would lose her anyway. Better to do the right thing and trust the Lord with the results.

I could see both the resolve and the fear on his face as we left the luncheon.

He and his wife took their daughter away for the weekend for a time alone as he presented to her what he had determined to do. These are the main ideas that he presented to her, in his own words and his own way:

1. "I want to apologize to you for not being a biblical father to you. I have not been as involved in your life as I should have been; I have not protected you; I have not loved you enough to confront you when you needed me to; I have not exercised biblical authority in your life by erecting clear parameters as I should have. Will you please forgive me? From this day forth, I will attempt to be the kind of father you need."

2. "You are not to see Bill ever again. You will quit your job, drop out of school, and I'll return the car to Bill as I tell him what we are doing."

3. "You will accompany me on a business trip I'm taking this next week. We'll be gone for two weeks."

4. "I know this is a shock to you and you are feeling resistant right now. I want you to know that I am not threatening you. I am clearly telling you what I want you to do so there will be no misunderstanding. If you choose to disobey me, I want you to know that you will be rebelling against God, as I am His authority in your life as your father."

5. "If you should disobey me, and run away and marry Bill, though I pray you won't, your mother and I will no longer consider you to be an active part of our family. We will still love you and you will still be our daughter, and we will miss you more than you will know, but you will not be welcome at family functions. We will treat you as other young women we know and care for. Furthermore, I will remove you from my will, for the wealth of the righteous is not laid up for the wicked, but the reverse."

6. "I love you more than life itself, and as the head of our home, I take full responsibility for where we are today. Again I hope you can find it in your heart to forgive me."

The father called me about a month later for coffee. Mary was with him as we met. Her face was radiant. She wanted to thank me personally for my counsel to her father. She told me how she didn't understand what was happening during that weekend away with her parents, and that she was very angry, but she obeyed her father because he was so strong. Then about a week later, while they were on their trip, she saw it all as if a curtain had been lifted. She couldn't believe she had been so duped, and she couldn't thank her father enough for saving her. She was already talking to her friends with similar boy-friend problems, explaining that the answer was the strength and protection of their fathers. The father had decided to rule in his home and protect his daughter and peace was the result.

A new family

A daughter comes out from under her parents authority on her wedding day, just as does a son. However, she comes under the authority of her new husband, or, in Figure 2, under the authority of a "newly married son" of another family. There is no favored set of parents in God's plan. One set of parents do not have more authority or influence than the other. A brand new family under Christ is born.

Sometimes it is more difficult for parents to release a daughter than a son, but release her they must. The time for input and evaluation is before the commitment and during courtship. After the wedding it is too late. The parents must bite their lips unless they are asked for input.

Often the groom will not be able to support his bride "in the manner to which she has become accustomed." The bride's father and the groom's father must resist the temptation to help the new couple overly-much, because providing for his new family is the sole role of the husband, and being robbed of this privilege by well-meaning parents, robs him of a portion of his manhood. Certainly gifts, even nice ones, appropriately spaced, are in order, but the everyday expenses of the family must be the responsibility of the husband (1 Timothy 5:8).

Care of the unmarried

A man's daughter continues to be under his care until she marries, and if she doesn't ever marry, she remains there. As in the case of a son, she will, for all practical purposes, be on her own as a mature adult, but her father needs to continue to protect her, both emotionally and physically. A woman should never be out from under a man's care. When her husband is dead, or her father, if she has remained unmarried, she is covered by another male member of the family; a son or brother, etc., and if there is no family remaining and she still lives, the church will care for her if she has lived a Godly life (1 Timothy 5:3-10).

As you can see, there are many more factors that go into the beginning of a family in a biblical fashion than at first meet the eye. I have tried to present the "leaving" aspect, along with the necessary preparations, in this chapter; "cleaving" and "becoming one flesh" will be covered later.

Most of us did not have the benefit of this kind of protection and preparation. Our sons and daughters can! The end will be that they will not carry all the excess baggage that we have had to unload to become equipped to do battle for the kingdom.

As you see the biblical standard, resist the temptation to dwell on the hurts of the past. Place them behind you and say with the Apostle Paul, "Forgetting those things which are behind...I press toward the goal for the prize of the upward call of God in Christ Jesus" (Philippians 3:13,14).

"Father, help me to yield to your authority in my life. As a young person, use this authority to prepare me for my wedding day. As a parent, help me to then be faithful in the preparation of my children for full, rich lives given to the extension of your kingdom."

Questions for discussion

1. Compare how a son leaves the authority of his parents with how a daughter leaves. How are they similar? How are they different?

2. How can a father prepare his son for the day he leaves his authority? His daughter?

3. Discuss potential problems that you can foresee in this biblical process. In what ways would the world consider this approach silly?

4. What advantages do you see in following this pattern? What problems would be alleviated?

---

[1] W.E. Vine, *An Expository Dictionary of New Testament Words,* (Old Tappan, New Jersey: Fleming H. Revell Company, 1966), Vol. I, p. 175.

Part Three
"Fulfilling Roles"

Chapter 7

"As Christ Loved the Church"

"He saw her across a crowded room. Her long, blonde hair sparkled in the sunlight streaming in the window, and her smile radiated warmth and friendliness as she talked with her friends. He drank in her perfect features - high cheek-bones, full lips, and huge blue eyes. As she rose to leave, her body was momentarily outlined by the movement of her dress. He gasped involuntarily. He was drawn by an overwhelming force to go meet her. As he walked up to her, and introduced himself, his hands were trembling and his knees were weak. He knew at that moment that they would spend the rest of their lives together."

Most of us have grown up on a steady diet of some variation of the above theme in movies, books, and stories. We are told that "falling in love" is a delicious, all-consuming emotion that just happens; there's nothing that one can do to stop it, and until it happens to you, you surely don't want to get married. Hollywood has conditioned us to believe that love is some irresistible, emotional force that sweeps over us and leaves us powerless.

Our children expect their love for their future spouses to be like that. They have been set up for failure in their marriages, for, if love is an emotion that they will "fall" into, then they will think they have "fallen out" of it when the inevitable happens and the emotions cool. They certainly wouldn't want to stay married to someone they don't "love." The divorce rate in America is mute testimony to the fact that Hollywood has failed to teach us what we need to know to handle successfully a relationship with the opposite sex.

The Bible pictures marriage in a totally different light. We are concerned primarily with "falling in love" so we can get married; the focus is on marrying the one we love. The Bible, on the other hand, focuses on our attitude and behavior <u>after</u> we are married, or, <u>loving the one we marry</u>! Very little instruction is given in the Bible on the selection of a mate; it's almost as if who you marry is not important if certain basic requirements are met, and if both husband and wife understand and fulfill their biblical roles. If they do that, God will fill their hearts with feelings for their spouses. This is the message of the Song of Solomon, the book in the Bible that shows us not only the sanctity of married love, but that God wants us to have spice and excitement as well!

God has made us *male and female*, and there is a natural, God-given chemistry between the sexes. When both husband and wife understand their biblical roles and function in them within the context of a committed, permanent marriage relationship, that chemistry releases wonderful emotions for one another that God intended for us to enjoy.

The game of love?

The world teaches young people very different behavioral patterns for men and women in marriage than does the Bible. Competition, game-playing and manipulation are the methods by which the world teaches that the sexes relate, with both spouses trying to win a battle and secure for themselves what they see is necessary to meet their own personal needs. That is not God's plan, and, since marriage was invented by Him and intended for His glory and honor, we need to see what rules He has given us for its successful practice.

Ephesians 5:18-21 gives the prerequisite spiritual foundation that will make walking in God's design for marriage possible:

"And do not be drunk with wine, ..., but be filled with the Spirit, ..., submitting to one another in the fear of God."

This passage is the foundation for the verses that follow which outline the roles of both men and women in marriage. Without the power of the Holy Spirit it will be impossible to do what each partner is asked to do. The instructions will seem unfair, impossible, and outdated. In actuality the following verses, Ephesians 5:22-33, are the specifics for each partner as they "submit to one another in the fear of God."

For the next two chapters I want to look at the man. There are two major responsibilities that will make him a Godly ruler in his home. In chapter 5 we saw that he is to rule and generally what that means. Now we will look in detail at the first of these two responsibilities of his rulership - loving his wife, and the out-working of that task.

Doing the impossible

The Apostle Paul begins his instructions to men in Ephesians 5 with a command in verse 25:

"Husbands, love your wives, just as Christ also loved the church, and gave Himself for it..."

The greek word for "love" in this verse is the word *agape*, which is a word that is used in the Bible to define God Himself. "God is love (*agape*), and he who abides in love (*agape*) abides in God, and God in him" (1 John 4:16b). *Agape* has its source in God, and husbands can love their wives in this way only if that love is produced in them supernaturally by the Holy Spirit.

Notice it is a command: "Husbands, love your wives..." How can we as men be commanded to do something only God can do? This is the paradox of the Christian life; God commands us to obey His Law, and we find ourselves powerless to do so until we trust Him completely to produce that obedience in us by His Holy Spirit (Romans 8:4).

A wife is to be the object of the strongest, most creative force in the universe, *agape* love, the love that Jesus Christ has for His Bride, the Church. It can melt the coldest heart, change the most intransigent will, and heal the most damaged soul. There is a boundless supply of this love that has been poured out in our hearts by the Holy Spirit (Romans 5:5), and when God created man both male and female, he intended that the male would unleash that powerful love upon his wife. He is to love her "as Christ loved the Church!"

Love without reason

Agape love is unconditional. This means that it is a "love without reason," not conditioned on any behavior or quality of the loved-one. Did not Jesus show His love for His church by dying for us while we were still lost (Romans 5:8)? Were we not dead in trespasses and sins (Ephesians 2:1), totally depraved, with nothing to commend us, no reason for God to love us within ourselves, and with no salvage value whatsoever (Romans 7:18)? And yet because of God's great love for us,

93

He saved us by His grace (Ephesians 2:4-8). That is the way Christ loved the church, and that is the way men are to love their wives.

This love is not, "I love you if...(if you are sweet, if you are nice to me, if you are responsive to my attention, if you are faithful to me, if you do what I say)," nor is it, "I love you because...(because you are pretty, because you are intelligent, because you are thin, because you are pure)." Those types of love are not love at all, but indicate a selfishness that is really saying, not, "I love you," but, "I <u>want</u> you and love me!"

No, *agape* love is "I love you in spite of...(in spite of your selfishness, in spite of your deceit, in spite of your manipulations, in spite of your resistance to my leadership, in spite of your independence, in spite of your unfaithfulness, in spite of your lack of love for me). I love you, and my love is so strong that you cannot resist it, nor can you do anything to cause me to withdraw it, and it will capture your heart!"

"But you don't know my wife!"

"All this sounds so sweet, but let's get practical," you say. "You don't know my wife. You don't know how hard, aggressive and competitive she can be. She can put me down at every turn and make me feel like a nobody. She can be a class A bitch."

Or maybe this is your response. "My wife is so manipulative you can't believe it. She always manages to get her way by pouting or whining, and I feel guilty if I don't give in. She acts so sweet that I was taken in before we were married, but she is really very selfish and controlling."

Could this be you? "My wife doesn't respond to me sexually. She was a hot potato before we were married, but now she's like a cold fish. She makes me feel really unattractive sexually."

All of us as husbands face situations similar to these after the new wears off in our marriages, because our wives are sinners, just like we are. It's easy to love someone who is lovely, but sinners are not always lovely. *Agape* loves right through the sin. It loves her when she seems to be unlovely, with nothing to commend her. It does not pout, or get its feelings hurt when the loved-one does not respond in a way the husband feels she should, when she does not seem to appreciate all of the wonderful qualities her husband possesses. It does not even seem to notice whether there is a response or not, because it doesn't matter. *Agape* is selfless. It never changes, no matter what.

That is the love God commands a man to extend to his wife. Most of us feel we deserve better, don't we? We certainly deserve at least a wife who appreciates all we're doing to try to be biblical husbands. But let me remind you that Jesus loved you when you cared nothing about Him, when you shoved His love right back in His face and wanted nothing to do with Him. He loved you through that rebellion, and He commands you to do the same toward your wife.

You say, "That's impossible!," and it is. You can only do it as you cry out to God to fill your heart with a supply of that supernatural love.

First things first

Agape love is initial. Jesus committed Himself to us on the cross, in His humanity, before He knew if anyone would respond. Didn't his disciples all flee in fear, and didn't Jesus die alone? Jesus came after us when we wanted nothing to do with Him. "There is none who seeks after God (Romans 3:11)." He pursued us, tracked us down with His "Hound of Heaven," the Holy Spirit, until He trapped us in a corner, and then He stepped on our necks with His love until we shouted, "I give up, Jesus, I give you my life!"

In like manner, the man is the pursuer, the aggressor, the lover. He is the initiator, committing himself first in his love relationship with his wife.

Today, Satan is doing His very best to destroy marriages by reversing God's divine order. Even as children, little girls are learning to be pursuers as their parents allow them to call boys on the telephone. As they enter puberty, the aggression intensifies, as girls actually pester boys for dates and then practically attack them sexually. All this time the boy is learning to be passive, to be cool, and let the girls come to him. He is learning to be a responder to a girl's advances rather than an initiator. He is learning to play the girl's role, while the girl is learning to play his!

The amazing thing about this is, that when a woman has succeeded in capturing a man in this way, and he carries over this passive attitude into their marriage, she will eventually despise him. In every woman's heart there is a desire to be ruled over with *agape* love by her man. She longs for an aggressive, strong, initiating lover, to whom she can give her life. God made her that way, and she, unknowingly, helped to create the passive, weak man whom she married, and for whom she now has no respect.

"What do you mean, 'Lay down my life?' "

Finally, *agape* love is <u>sacrificial</u>. Jesus is our perfect pattern for our task as servant-rulers in our families. "The Son of Man did not come to be served, but to serve, and to give His life a ransom for many" (Matthew 20:28). Jesus did not please Himself, but continually gave His life away for others, culminating in that final great act of service, literally laying down His life voluntarily on the cross for His church. Men, this is our pattern of sacrificial love for our wives!

Often, there are conflicts between what a man always did as a single man, and what he will be called upon to do as a husband. Getting married means much more than simply having a new roommate, for his wife has now become one-flesh with him, and has needs as a wife that her husband is designed by God to meet. His time is no longer only his, to spend upon himself, but to be invested wisely on his family.

My family was always very involved in athletics when I was a boy. Both my mother and grandmother were avid University of Oklahoma football fans, to say nothing of all the men in the family. Mom could discourse at some length on the intricacies of the Split-T formation, and talk intelligently about the weaknesses of next year's team and the possibility of another national championship. We had season tickets to the games from the time I was a third-grader until I went off to college there as a freshman, making the 250 mile round trip on each game-day. We also loved going to the baseball games of the local Tulsa Oilers, and followed the Tulsa Golden Hurricane basketball team.

On top of all that spectating I was a mediocre high school basketball player, and a seldom-used pitcher on the University of Oklahoma baseball team, and from age 10 up, I spent a great deal of time playing golf, up to three times a week in the summers. I mention all this to communicate the idea that sport played a rather large part in my life as I was growing up.

Jill, on the other hand, came from a totally non-athletic family, with absolutely no interest in athletics, except social. The extent of her involvement was four years of cheer-leading and four years of bench-sitting with the basketball team in high school that she, to this day, remembers absolutely nothing about.

You can see that when we got married there was a conflict. I have already related in chapter 4 how my lack of understanding of my responsibility as a husband to sacrifice my own interests for the welfare of my family got us in trouble. I was doing what I wanted, and not considering the needs of my family.

That first crisis in our marriage was a wake-up call, and for the first time I began to realize the implications of being married. I put my golf clubs away, to pull them out again only after my boys were old enough to play. The only day I could play, Saturday, was also the only day I had to be with my family. A game of golf in Seattle takes at least six hours on Saturday, considering going and coming, and as a young married man with two little children, I just didn't have that kind of time. Some Saturdays Jill would leave for the day with her friends for a shopping trip, desperate for adult conversation, while I stayed home with the kids. I can still remember the new appreciation I had for her on those Saturdays, for all the hours she put in each week caring for and nurturing our children, and also the immense relief I felt when she came in the door on Saturday evening.

Harder to do for me was to limit my TV time on weekends to one game. If the University of Oklahoma, or the University of Washington, was playing on the tube on Saturday, and the home-town pro team, the Seattle Seahawks on Sunday, I determined to watch only one. I made myself choose, because no one else in the family was interested and they all needed their daddy's attention. I can still remember the agony of some of those choices. From my vantage point now it seems silly that it was such a big deal, but I remember the huge sacrifice it appeared to be at that time. Many men spend all weekend in front of the TV, week after week, while their children grow up without them and their wives grow more and more bitter, until they finally give up and begin an independent life that does not include their husbands.

Some men refuse to let their families encroach upon their own personal habits. Rather than doing things their wives can do with them, they continue to do only their own individual activities. Their night out with the boys to play basketball, or their all-male two-week hunting or fishing trip is much more important than taking their wife out to dinner to bless her just for her pleasure. This of course does not mean that a man never plays ball, or goes hunting, or does anything by himself, but he does those things only after his wife and children are cared for and secured in his love.

Beginnings

The unconditional, initial, sacrificial, *agape* love I have described was all theory to the zealous, young campus evangelist who saw a beautiful dark-haired new recruit standing in a registration line at the Institute of Biblical Studies in San Bernardino, California (a ministry of Campus Crusade for Christ). I was 26, had been on the Crusade staff for three years, thoroughly enjoying working 16-hour days speaking in fraternities, sororities and dormitories, holding late-night Bible studies, and having evangelistic appointments each hour during the day. If you think I was too busy to think about girls, you are right, but summers were a more leisurely time of training at the organization's headquarters, and it was there that I met Jill, who had come to California to join the staff of Campus Crusade for Christ.

When I first noticed her waiting in the registration line, I dusted off one of my best lines, walked up to her, introduced myself, and asked her if she believed in love-at-first-sight! Jill laughed, and as we talked and got acquainted, I made a date with her to go to Disneyland that next weekend with several other couples. The beginning of a fairy-tale, Hollywood love story, right? Wrong! We had no idea that four long years of lessons in the Lord's schoolroom lay ahead of us.

After a couple of weeks of constant companionship that first summer, including long hours of deep discussion, I was convinced that I truly did love Jill, and I wanted to spend the rest of my life with her. There was one small problem. She was not convinced.

As we talked, I learned that Jill had grown up in a tar-paper shack with no running water in rural Georgia with an irresponsible father, who, because of his drinking, continually embarrassed and hurt her emotionally as a child. Conflicts between her parents over his problems left her feeling very vulnerable, and when he was killed by a hit-and-run driver when she was twelve, she saw it as the ultimate abandonment, and she unconsciously shut down her emotions to keep from ever being hurt by a man again. As a result, she found it impossible to respond to me. Add to that the fact that, at 6'4" and 165 lbs., I was not the image of the handsome, dashing prince-charming the movies had conditioned her to expect. She told me that she really liked me, that we had wonderful times together, and we had much in common, but she did not "love" me. She did not have the feelings that she would surely have if she were "in love."

I, of course, was crushed, but as the summer wore on and we continued to be together, my love for her did not fade, but only grew. She enjoyed being with me, loved to talk to me for hours at a time, even appreciated the way I made her feel special, but was convinced she could not marry me, because she had no romantic feelings for me. Thus began a stormy, four-year relationship, during which time I learned that, indeed, she had never had feelings for any boy, as she continued to protect herself from experiencing again the pain her father had caused her.

I didn't understand this clearly at the time. I only knew that she said she didn't love me, even though she often acted like she did. I still wanted to marry her, and even almost talked her into it once, only to have her call and tell me she just couldn't do it, because she just didn't have any feelings for me.

"That's it!," I told her. "It's over." After three years of disappointment I had finally had it.

My thinking, clouded by the emotion of the rejection I felt, went something like this: "She won't have this faithful hound to kick around any more. She has given me just enough of a bone to keep me interested, but no longer! I deserve better. The most eligible bachelor on the Campus Crusade staff, and she treats me like this!"

We didn't communicate for almost a year, and during that time I began to learn about God's *agape* love for His Bride, the church. As I saw the "width and length and depth and height" of that love (Ephesians 3:18), I began to see my love for Jill in that same light. The issue had been whether or not she loved me, but now I saw that the only issue was, "Robert, do you love *(agape)* her?," and the answer, even after a year apart, I knew was an unqualified "yes!" I saw, for the first time, that her inability to respond to me was a tragedy for her and not for me. I knew, also for the first time, that the opportunity to love her far out-weighed anything I might miss if she never did have feelings for me. True joy and fulfillment comes from loving, and not from being loved. Furthermore, I began to see that her only chance to experience the joy of loving would be in response to a love that absolutely would not quit, would not be discouraged, would not make any demands upon her to respond whatsoever!

The following are excerpts from the letter I wrote her in March of 1968:

"Probably the hardest thing I've done in a while is not phone you today. My pocketbook just won't allow it. Besides, I can write what I want to say much better than I can say it on the phone."

"I have remembered something in the last two days that I have forgotten for almost 2 years; something I have known intellectually but

99

have never really applied, and it is this: The issue in our relationship is not even remotely whether or not you love me. The issue, my dear one, is that I so love you. I always have and I always will. I remember saying that to you some two years ago and really meaning it, but somehow over the last two years I began to believe that I deserved more; that somehow you ought to love me too. That is no more the issue than is our love for God. It's not that we have to love Him, but that He loves us!"

"Dearest one, I want you to know that whether or not you ever love me just doesn't matter. I couldn't say that two days ago, but I want you to know that I really mean it. J.J., love for you has been in my heart for four years. After not seeing you for five months, it's there; after being apart and broken-up, it's there. It's just there. I love you. No matter what you do or say, or don't do or don't say, I love you. Could God speak any clearer?...As long as God is sovereign I never need to look back and worry over some supposed miss-step, but simply let out the love God has put in my heart for you."

"So, my darling one, I don't care if you ever tell me you love me; don't care if God ever changes your heart. I want to love you for the rest of your life, take care of you, forsaking all others, with no strings attached, with no demands that you love me back."

"I'm expecting you to get cold feet before the wedding, maybe even cry and try to talk me out of it, show me all kinds of lists that show you don't have any feelings for me, but Jill, I don't care! Spring is the time, and May 18 is the date, if that day is O.K. with you."

Her response to my letter was pretty much what I expected; she wasn't affected. I had made bold and blustery noises before, but always folded when she didn't respond. My attempts at loving her with God's love had not brought her running before because she knew in her heart that they were not genuine, and she wasn't about to suddenly fall into my arms now. She had heard me cry "wolf!" too many times. But this time, somehow it really didn't matter. I wrote her again, and again, and after each negative answer from Jill claiming "it won't work," I would respond with a positive, strong, affirmation of my love. I couldn't believe that it really didn't matter if she ever loved me or not, for I was intoxicated with the love of God flowing through me to Jill.

I understand now that Jill was unconsciously testing me, attempting to run me off if she could; trying me to see if indeed she could trust me with her life, trust me to still love her when she was not lovely. Would I leave her as her father had done? The following is an excerpt from her letter of March 21:

"I'm finding it so unbelievable what's happening; I'm afraid to trust that it's real. But I might as well tell you because if it flops it'll kill both of us anyway! Ever since your second letter, and progressively as the others have come, I've seen an unbelievable change in my attitude. I am really looking forward to talking about getting married. I can't wait to see you and hear everything that you will say to me. I'm excited about what is happening in your heart. I really am responding like crazy and it's so new I'm afraid it will go away. But that sick feeling, the lump in my stomach, is completely gone."

"I've told everybody about your love letters and how they are affecting me, and they are all so thrilled! Can you believe I'm telling everybody?"

"You've convinced me (almost completely) that this thing is all settled. I love the way you're talking. It's not arrogantly telling me what's what...it's the confident boldness that you know where you're going and that it's God's will. That's exactly what I've wanted. It's so different than before. There is so much more depth, certainty and authority. It seems too good to be true. I want so much to trust and believe that it's real this time. I'm not looking for verses or praying desperately or anything. I'm just waiting impatiently for all this time to pass so I can be with you and see what happens."

When we were married two months later, Jill had still never told me that she loved me, for indeed at that time she could not. I have kidded her over the years that I was afraid that when the minister said, "Will you take this man to be your lawfully wedded husband?," that she would say, "No!" But it no longer mattered. The joy, the fulfillment, the satisfaction for me was in loving her.

I was not a perfect lover by any means, and the lesson I had learned would need relearning several times again, and indeed is being more fully learned even as I write, but the foundation was laid and the truth of *agape* love had been "seen" with spiritual eyes.

It is interesting that when women are instructed to love their husbands in Titus 2:4, a different word than *agape* is used. It is a form of the verb *phileo*, which means "tender affection."[1] This is more of a response love, a response to qualities that are observed in the loved one. Women are never commanded to *agape* their husbands. That commitment, which is the glue that holds the marriage together, is the

101

responsibility of the husband. That makes sense, doesn't it, because it is Jesus' love for His bride, the church, that holds us to Him (John 10:28,29).

The Savior of the Body

In Ephesians 5, as Paul discusses marriage, he equates that one-flesh relationship with the relationship Christ has with His Church. Jesus is like the husband, and the Church is like the wife. Furthermore, he moves very easily from one union to the other, and, in fact, it isn't always clear which one he means. That is by design, for marriage is to be a picture, for human eyes to see, of that spiritual union between Christ and His Bride.

With this in mind, we can see that as Paul portrays the results of Christ's love for us, He intends for us to understand that those same results occur, on a human level, as men love their wives with that same love. In verse 22, in the middle of the section on the wife's role, which we will cover later, Christ is said to be "the Savior of the body." There is, of course, a unique way in which only Christ is our Savior. He "saves" us from sin, gives us eternal life, brings us into His family, and assures us of Heaven. However, Paul means for us to see something more in this passage.

Learning to love my wife with the love of Jesus Christ has been, as I have said, a life-long process for me, only beginning during those tumultuous days before we were married. I frequently have congratulated myself for learning a tremendous spiritual lesson concerning some aspect of this truth, and while I was patting myself on the back, either forget the principle I had just learned when I had to apply it in another situation, or fail miserably in some other area.

Some time ago, Jill and I were going through one of those times. We were lying in bed at about 3:00 A.M. very emotionally discussing our relationship, and we were at what appeared to be an impasse. Jill was not responding to me in the fashion that I deemed she should. The life-changing lessons I had learned about love before we were married had been totally forgotten as the day-in and day-out tedium of life dulled my memory.

As we talked, not without some tears being shed on both sides, I suddenly was aware of another presence in the room. As a matter of fact, Jill remembers me saying something like, "Who's there?," as I rolled over on the bed and looked behind me. No one was there of course, but the presence of the Lord was almost overwhelming. This very rarely happens to me, certainly no more than a half-dozen times in my life, but I almost audibly heard the Lord say to me, "You will be her savior."

Twelve years later we can look back and see that that night was a significant turning point for us. As the days went by, and I noticed Ephesians 5:23 in a new light ("He is the Savior of the Body"), the significance of that emotional night became very clear to me. Just as Jesus was our Savior because of the strength of His love that took Him to the cross, I would "save" Jill from a lifetime of insecurity, fear and bound-up emotions with the strength of my *agape* love for her, a new facet to the diamond of truth the Lord had taught me that brought us together - a truth that had grown dim. The Lord would use me to actualize, or make experiential, the salvation He had indeed won for her on the cross. There are continual times of struggle for me, and my love for her is never perfect, but I see my task clearly: to be an agent of salvation for her. As a result, our relationship continues to grow, and she becomes more and more the woman God desires her to be.

Helping his wife to unload emotional baggage is only one way that a man's love can "save" her. Women need to be protected from situations they were not designed to have to face. Salesmen, bill-collectors, and necessary unpleasant confrontations with the world are all examples of things a husband needs to handle. A woman longs to know that her man will take care of all such problems, that he will be "in charge." The pressure of supporting the family, and decisions about money should rest squarely on the man's shoulders, for biblically that is his responsibility. Training and educating the children is another load he should carry. We'll talk a lot about that later.

Committed to obey

To understand that God expects anything more from them than to just do what comes naturally in their marriages and try to get along as well as possible with their wives, is a brand new idea to many men. They have not realized that God expects them to love their wives with an *agape* love that is unconditional, initial, and sacrificial. However, understanding what God tells us to do in the Bible is one thing; doing it is something else. Is it possible to actually achieve a measure of success in loving my wife in the way I have described when I have no passion to do so; no "fire" any more for the one I once loved so much?

103

When I saw the truth of being Jill's "savior," my heart was dead toward her. After 14 years of marriage the red-hot lover of a few paragraphs ago had become cold and distant. No feelings, no emotion, no more "love." I could barely remember the excitement of our courtship - the way I longed to spend every minute with her, the thrill of getting her letters, and the way time flew as we talked for hours. The excitement of those first few years of our marriage with a young family, the feeling of going after God together with reckless abandon (Once throwing everything up in the air and then moving to California to be a part of a Christian community!), was all a distant memory.

Jill's inability to respond to me emotionally was unconsciously wearing on me, and the understanding of a husband's love for his wife that I had begun to see when we got married, and any concern I once had for Jill's spiritual and emotional health, was long forgotten. We unknowingly settled into living separate lives. Divorce was not an option for us, so I think we both resigned ourselves to living out the rest of our lives with a huge emptiness in our marriage.

The crisis I described above was the turning point. I saw that to be a "savior" involved <u>commitment</u>. Maybe there would never again be "feelings" for my wife, and I really didn't think there would be, but by the grace of God, the determination grew over a matter of months to obey God and love my wife with *agape* love. When we married, I had come to grips with <u>her lack of feelings for me.</u> Now, I faced a new challenge: <u>my lack of feelings for her.</u>

I can remember driving home at the end of the day (by that time I was a full-time elder in the church), knowing that I felt no love for Jill, and sometimes I even felt hostile toward her, but asking God to give me the power to love her. My prayer was,

"Father, you have commanded me to love Jill, and I am committed to obeying you. You would not ask me to do something that you would not give me the power to do. I can not love her in my own strength, so fill me with your Holy Spirit, your power, your love."

When a husband makes a <u>commitment</u> to love his wife in this way, and then very honestly and openly repents when he fails (if necessary to his wife), God will prove Himself to be faithful to make His strength perfect in that husband's weakness (1 Corinthians 12:9).

As I write, this happened eleven years ago. After about three years of gradually understanding and implementing what I have related, the feelings began to return, and after five years I could honestly say that I loved my wife with a deeper, richer emotion than ever.

Changes occurred in Jill that I can only see from an eleven-year vantage point. For years I saw nothing, nor did I expect to. My mission was to love her; God would have to do in His own time what He said He would do when He met me on that night in our bed-room.

Jill has given herself to me in a new way by fully adopting my vision of our life-purpose. I feel, for the first time, that she is truly my "helper," and is as committed to extending the kingdom of God in the way that God has shown me as I am. Whereas before I often had to resist her input because we did not agree on our basic direction, now I am fully free to have her as a full partner in our mission, profiting from all her insights and wisdom, because I know we are one in the vision of our life-purpose. I no longer feel as though I am dragging an anchor in the sand.

I can see that Jill is more free to let down her walls of protection emotionally, because she is more confident that my love is permanent. She can see more clearly with each passing day that I am in for the duration; not just to stick it out together, but to actively love her. She still struggles with the concept of being loved for no reason; not because of any quality in her, but because of the quality of God's love. I believe salvation is a life-long process, and we are both grateful for the progress the Lord has allowed us to see so far.

The promise

"What if there is never a change in my wife? What if I love her in this way and she stays like she is now?" Most men fear that their love will go down some black hole deep within their wife somewhere, never to make a difference. Remember, genuine *agape* doesn't worry about the response of the loved one. It keeps its focus steady because of its intrinsic nature.

However, the Apostle Paul does promise all husbands that there will be results if we are faithful. Those results are not so much changes in her as they are changes for her. They are changes that reflect her progressive, ongoing salvation.

In verse 26, Paul says that Jesus' sacrificial love for the Church sanctified and cleansed it with the washing of water by the word. To sanctify means to set apart. We have been set apart from the world by our eternal Bridegroom for Himself alone.

The application to a marriage is obvious. A woman who is loved in this way does not have a roving eye. She is not susceptible to advances by other men, for the powerful love of her husband has sanctified her, or set her apart from all others, just for himself alone. That love has literally built a spiritual fence around her, and she is secure in her husbands love, and all other men hold no attraction for her. Women who have affairs are generally women who are not loved by their husbands, and are unknowingly searching to fulfill an emotional need to be loved as Christ loved the church.

She is also cleansed by his love. He makes her feel important, though she may have always felt insignificant; beautiful, though she may have thought herself ugly; worthy, though she may have felt worthless; and clean, though because of her past, she may have felt dirty. If she has a promiscuous past, and if the blood of Jesus has washed her whiter than snow, then her husband makes that cleansing real in her experience as his flesh and blood arms enfold her and envelope her in his love.

Spotless and Wrinkle-free

The third result of a husband's love for his wife is given in verse 27:

"...that He might present it to Himself a glorious church, not having spot or wrinkle or any such thing, but that it should be holy and without blemish."

When Jesus returns for His Bride, she will not be old and wrinkled, or dressed in dirty, ragged clothing, as if to say, "No one loves me," but she will be "dressed in fine linen, clean and bright" (Revelation 20:8). She will be a beautiful Bride, having made herself ready for her Bridegroom by overcoming all her enemies, and accomplishing all that God has given her to do as she has responded to the love and leadership of her Head in heaven. On that awesome day her Lover will come bodily in power to present her to Himself to spend eternity in His glorious presence.

In like manner, when a man loves his wife as Christ loved the Church he earns the privilege of presenting her to himself as a wife that is full of glory. The miracle of *agape* love is that the spots, wrinkles and blemishes, both emotional and physical, that were so important are gone. Maybe she won't change the habits that you find so unattractive. Maybe an outside observer will not be able to tell any difference in her character or how she acts, but it will no longer matter! If God supplies you with the power to love her with *agape* love, you will change, and you will see her as holy!

When I was young, I always wondered how married couples, no matter how old, continued to be physically attracted to each other when the vitality and attractiveness of their bodies were gone. I vastly underestimated the limitless power of God's love. They don't even see the wrinkled faces, the lumpy bodies or the double chins, because by their love, those husbands have presented their spouses to themselves "without spot or wrinkle or any such thing."

Jill was a beautiful woman when I married her by all objective standards, but when we were struggling in our relationship I could have cared less. That physical attractiveness that seems so important to immature young men and women means nothing if there is no oneness in the relationship. Now Jill and I are both in our mid-fifties, we have both gained more than a few pounds, and again, using objective standards, the bloom is definitely off the rose. But, you guessed it, we could care less! Jill is more beautiful to me than ever before. I have presented her to myself as a glorious bride.

The world knows nothing of this kind of love, and men who reach my age with enough money to make young women interested, dump their wives of 25 years for young bodies that they fool themselves into thinking are interested in them. Affairs are rampant, even in the church, because men are not committed to loving their wives with God's love. Because of a lack of understanding of this truth, Satan has been able to shipwreck countless church leaders, who throw away their ministries for the brief, fleeting pleasure of sin.

I love my body

Paul concludes this passage on husbands and wives in Ephesians 5 in verses 28-33 with a reversal of the parallel examples he has used. The Body of Christ has been pictured as a Bride, but now a man's bride (wife) is said to be as his own body. Notice the flowing transition from the divine (Christ and the Church) to the human (man and his wife).

"So husbands ought to love their own wives as their own bodies; he who loves his wife loves himself. For no one ever hated his own flesh, but nourishes and cherishes it, just as the Lord does the church. For we are members of His body, of His flesh and of His bones. 'For this reason a man shall leave his father and mother and be joined to his

107

wife, and the two shall become one flesh.' This is a great mystery, but I speak concerning Christ and the church. Nevertheless, let each one of you in particular so love his own wife as himself, and let the wife see that she respects her husband."

I must admit that for as long as I can remember I have been interested in my body. In high school, I was an extremely skinny, pimply-faced bean-pole, standing 6'2" and weighing 135 pounds as a senior. I can remember the pain of comparing myself to the fully-developed football players, and wondering what it would be like to have an attractive body. I was not socially adept with girls, and didn't have the confidence to be any kind of a leader. I have always said that at that time in my life I couldn't even lead in silent prayer!

After graduation, I took up weight-lifting in the hope that I could at least look normal. Several years, and many high-protein milk shakes later, I was much stronger, and, at 6'4", had ballooned to 165 pounds, where I remained for 25 years. I was the world's strongest zipper!

I share this with you to illustrate what we all feel. Paul is right when he says that no one ever hated his own body. When I was young, if you had asked me, I would have told you that I hated my body, but in actuality I loved my body and I would have given anything to be able to remake it, because it was so important to me. I certainly didn't love or accept the way it looked, but I loved the body itself. Down through the years, I have spent massive amounts of time on my body; feeding, clothing, housing, exercising, cutting, clipping, shaving, tanning, and resting it. I knew it was the only one I would ever have, and so it was precious to me. As Paul says, I "nourished and cherished" it.

Men, we are to see our wives as we do our bodies; not perfect, nor always as we would like them to be, but the only ones we will ever have, and worthy of our nourishing and cherishing, an important part of *agape* love.

Most wives do not feel as though their husbands cherish them, because we seldom do things that we don't enjoy just to bless our wives. For example, Jill loves to have me go shopping with her, sit and watch her try on clothes and comment interestedly, and then take her out to lunch. I hate shopping, and I am exhausted after about an hour of just sitting and watching. She knows I feel this way, so to take her shopping and out to lunch communicates that I cherish her.

Nurturing is an equally important part of loving. God has given each man a supply of sustenance for his wife, and only he, as her husband, knows what she needs. However, if he is not concerned with her condition enough to expend energy to nurture her, she will shrivel and "die."

My mother was an expert at growing African violets. I can remember five or six rows of plants in a window with a northern exposure under a tree, each plant displaying a gorgeous profusion of fragile, deep purple blossoms. Many people cannot get these delicate plants to bloom because they need just the right amount of filtered sunshine, water and food, with too much or too little of any one of these components fatal to the blooms. Without the expert touch of the grower, there will be rich, lush green leaves, but no beautiful blossoms.

Wives are like those delicate African violets; they bloom beautifully under the expert hand of a loving gardener. But a husband's inattention causes the light in his wife's eyes to go out, testimony to his neglect, selfishness or lack of skill. Nourishing and cherishing his wife are indispensable aspects of the *agape* love a man is commanded to have for her.

Theory or life?

What I have shared with you in this chapter has formed the foundation for basically everything I have been able to share with others over 25 years of ministry. Marriage has proven to be a wonderful training school for me, my "seminary." Jill and I have not tried to hide our difficulties as we have experienced them, and pretend that everything has always been wonderful. We have learned that others profit more from hearing of our failures than our successes. To talk only of our success communicates our spiritual pride, discourages those who hear, and causes them to feel they cannot measure up.

We have also learned that real ministry in the lives of others generally occurs naturally, or unconsciously, without us trying to be the experts. By being real and honest with others about who we really are, warts and all, allows the Lord to use those experiences in their lives, often without our knowledge.

Every heart-ache can be turned into a blessing if we see it as from the hand of a God who loves us with *agape* love. He is teaching us exactly the lesson that we need to learn, and will use that lesson, when we learn it well, to affect those all around us, to the end that the rule of

His kingdom will be extended. Paul said, "So then death is working in us, but life in you" (2 Corinthians 4:12).

By the way, rarely does a day go by that Jill does not tell me how much she loves me, and how much she appreciates the salvation that has come through my love. She too has been able to experience, particularly in the last five years, the fulfillment that comes from loving.

"Father, make me a man who loves my wife as you loved the church. May this be to me not a theory, but a real-life experience. Do whatever you need to do to bring me to a full understanding of this truth. Amen"

Questions for Discussion

1. Discuss how *agape* love would appear to you if you were able to exercise it (men), or if it were exercised toward you (women).

2. What do you see, as a man, to be the main obstacle for you in loving in this way?

3. As a woman, how do you see yourself responding to this kind of love? In what ways are you loved like this? In what ways are you not?

4. How can an understanding of the sovereignty of God make a difference in your attempts to love (men) or be loved (women)?

---

[1] W.E. Vine, *An Expository Dictionary of New Testament Words* (Old Tappan, NJ: Fleming H. Revel Company, 1966), Vol. III, p. 21.

Chapter 8

Leadership - A Certain Sound

The influence of the feminist movement has left much of the church hesitant to address some of the topics we have been discussing for fear of being misunderstood and accused of being "sexist," or for fear of having truth twisted and used as an excuse for sin.

There certainly are men who have heard the message that they are to rule in their homes and have used that truth as an excuse to be abusive and tyrannical toward their wives and children. Because of their own needs and insecurities, they do not understand servant-leadership, nor the reality of the Day of Judgment when they will give an account for the stewardship they have been given over the lives of those in their families who are so cherished by God. Men who mistreat those precious ones for whom God intends for them to care do so at their own peril, both in this life and the one to come.

However, that is not an excuse for ignoring such a vital, spiritual truth. Was not Paul's message of the grace of God misunderstood and misapplied (Romans 3:8, 6:1,15)? We must be as careful as possible to guard against misunderstanding, exaggeration and lack of proper balance, and we can attempt to make the Kingdom message as palatable as possible, but in the final analysis the presentation of truth must not be conditioned on whether or not those who hear it appreciate it. If it is God's truth, it probably won't win any popularity contests, but it will bear fruit.

We saw in the last chapter that rulership begins with genuine, *agape* love. However, that is not where it ends. The other main component of effective rule is leadership. Both of these aspects of ruling are absolutely necessary in order for a man to see the kingdom of God expressed in his home. Leadership in the family without selfless love is oppressive and despotic, but love without authoritative, Godly leadership causes a

111

lack of respect and even contempt, as a wife and her children unconsciously seek the strength that the man, as head of his home, is not providing.

Strong family leadership from the father also gives security and purpose. Without it, family members generally have no clear direction toward biblical life goals, for the father is the one God designed to provide that, and he is the one naturally equipped to do so. His wife does not as readily think in terms of long-range, ultimate issues, nor can she provide the firmness and discipline necessary for stable family life as intuitively as can her husband. Yes, contrary to what the world would have us believe, there are inherent differences in the sexes that go much deeper than simply physiological characteristics, and these effect their respective roles in family life.

Pre-fall leadership

This was certainly the case with Adam and Eve. We discussed in Chapter 4 how God gave Adam the task of cultivating and tending the Garden of Eden before Eve was on the scene. Then, after God presented to Adam his "completer," he undoubtedly took her on her first tour of the Garden, explaining to her their mission in life, just as God had previously done with him.

His leadership was natural and not contrived, because he was the one equipped with the knowledge from God as to what their task in life would be. It flowed naturally from the unique characteristics God had given him, and Eve's response to his leadership was equally as spontaneous. There was no controversy, no "battle of the sexes." Adam was the leader because he was the one whom God had chosen to create first, and he was the one who had received specific instructions from God, including the prohibition on eating from the fruit of the tree of the knowledge of good and evil.

He shared all of God's words with an eager and receptive helpmate. The name he gave her at this point, Woman ("because she was taken out of man" [Genesis 2:23]), signified her natural subservience to her husband.

Eve's "better idea"

When Eve (then known as "Woman") succumbed to Satan's temptation (Genesis 3:1-7), this divine order for the family was violated. She ignored Adam's vision as to their mission in life (to take dominion over the garden for God, as His representative, by tending and cultivating it, and then, eventually, to spread that dominion over the whole earth [Genesis 1:28]). She disobeyed Adam's instructions pertaining to the tree of the knowledge of good and evil, and acted independently of his leadership. She was deceived as Satan attacked her by appealing to her short-range appetites (the fruit was "good for food"), her feminine desire for beautiful things (it was "pleasant to the eyes"), and her ambition ("desirable to make one wise").

There is certainly nothing inherently evil with any of the attitudes that Eve displayed. God has given women appetites, an appreciation of beauty, and ambition. All these things, properly channeled for the Kingdom of God, are good things. But to satisfy physical appetites apart from God's plan, to indulge in attractive "things" without moderation and wisdom, or to be driven by ambition for one's own recognition and honor, were aberrations of God's intent for Eve, and plunged the whole human race into sin. Those same distortions of God-given drives continue to be destructive to us today.

Satan began his attack on Eve by insinuating that God was unfair ("Has God indeed said, 'You shall not eat of every tree of the garden?' "). His question was an overstatement of what God had actually said, and with it he planted the idea in Eve's mind that God was unreasonable to tell them to abstain from eating of the fruit of even one of the trees in the garden. Her answer, ascribing to God the prohibition of even touching the forbidden tree, was also an overstatement, and opened the door to Satan's direct attack on the veracity of God ("You will not surely die"). Satan concluded his temptation by enticing Eve with the same illusion he himself was living; to be like God, independent of Him, existing autonomously from Him, living by one's own standards rather than God's.

Eve bit, and we, her descendants, continue to bite today. We also think we can live apart from God's Law. Our pride tells us we too can decide right and wrong for ourselves. We too can be our own god. The fruit of that thinking is mushrooming all around us, as we think we know better than God does about how men and women should relate, and how children should be raised. Today, collective man, the state, sees itself as God, and decides what is right and wrong totally apart from God's Law.

A basic difference between men and women

Whether or not Adam was present as Satan tempted Eve is conjecture. If he was, he watched without intervening as Eve fell for Satan's deception, and then sinned with her by eating of the fruit also. If Satan waited to approach Eve when Adam was not present, Adam must have listened to her rendition of the encounter, and then meekly followed her leadership into disobedience. In either case, the Bible is clear that Eve was deceived and Adam was not (1 Timothy 2:14). He knew very well what he was doing - rebelling against the clear instructions of God. Eve, on the other hand, let her emotions about the things we have discussed cloud her thinking.

Let me say here that the way women are put together makes them susceptible to temptations like this. Their strength in the marriage relationship is to deal with tasks that necessitate sensitivity to emotional issues. They are generally much better at empathizing with emotional hurts, extending care during illness, and noticing and filling needs of family members and others. Women can often more easily talk about themselves and how they feel about relationships, therefore tending to be more people-oriented than men, and they usually have closer and more intimate friendships. These characteristics are absolutely necessary and vital to a complete family unit. However, when important decisions with long-range implications must be made, it is generally not wise to base them on how one feels at that particular time, because feelings change very rapidly. Women often have more of a tendency to act based on current feelings than do their husbands.

Adam, along with most men, tended to be more cognitive. That is generally the male orientation, equipping us for our role of family leadership. We are not as moved by emotional appeal as we are by "the facts." Decisions are not made as often on the spur of the moment based on how people feel, but on an evaluation of the evidence. Men are therefore better equipped to make the decisions that are necessary for a leader to make, though they often need their wives to help them temper those decisions with compassion.

When my daughter Ramah was in the third grade, she received a cowboy hat from her grandmother that was a most prized possession. She wore it to school one day to show it off to her classmates. One friend was Cindy, a little girl who enjoyed being in charge as much as Ramah did, thereby causing untold relational difficulties. I had told Ramah very clearly that I did not want her reacting to Cindy, and she was to refuse to get into any more disagreements with her, which were increasing in both number and intensity. She understood that any more fracases would bring dire consequences.

The cowboy hat proved too tempting to Cindy. As the girls were loading into their respective car-pools after school was over, she knocked it off Ramah's head, and then proceeded to "accidently" step on it. Ramah was furious, and belted Cindy as hard as she could with her full book-bag, knocking her down and into a thorny bush just outside their classroom.

I was the school administrator at the time, and hearing the commotion, went outside and found a sobbing Cindy and a defiant Ramah, who was sure Cindy had gotten exactly what she deserved. I sent Ramah home with the promise that I would be home shortly to handle the matter.

When I got home about an hour later, I found Ramah moaning in bed with a thermometer in her mouth, and the back of her hand on her forehead, milking the onset of the flu for all it was worth, with Jill as the concerned mother hovering over her. Ramah did have a fever of 102, but as I told her, sickness is no excuse for disobedience. Jill, as the nurturer and nurse, did not want to spank Ramah, but in order to be consistent, I felt I had to enforce the standard I had set with biblical discipline, so I did. (In the unit on children we will cover how that is done). The point here is that I, as a man, was able to make a decision based on what I saw to be the right thing to do, apart from feelings of compassion I had for my sick daughter. Jill could not have brought herself to discipline Ramah, and we would not have done it if she had been the decision-maker.

We have laughed together many times over the years, remembering Cindy sprawled out in the sticker bush. Ramah remembers, along with the fact that Cindy didn't get disciplined at all, a growing awareness of the sure consequences of disobedience. This awareness has stood her in good stead as she has grown into a young woman and has come to realize that obeying God is very crucial.

You might say, "That's overkill. You didn't need to spank her when she was sick. There were extenuating circumstances." That's true, and certainly not spanking her would not have hurt a thing in that instance, but going ahead with the discipline reflects an attitude of trying to do the right thing every time, even if it's hard, and keeping all the bolts tight on the good ship "family." Men are better equipped to be consistent in making the hard decisions than are their wives.

Adam's leadership vacuum

Whereas Eve did not see clearly what was happening in the garden as Satan tempted her, when she offered the fruit to Adam, he knew perfectly well what was occurring. He knew, and yet seems to have made a deliberate decision to disobey anyway. That is the thrust of 1 Timothy 2:14, "And Adam was not deceived, but the woman being deceived, fell into transgression."

If Adam knew what he was doing, then why did he do it? It was not as though he actively, aggressively disobeyed God, or that the fruit was so attractive to him he could not resist. No, he simply did what so many of us do as husbands; he just "went with the flow," letting his wife do whatever she wanted, even though he knew at the time that she had been tricked by Satan into disobedience. He avoided confronting her and abdicated his role as leader in the family with disastrous results; a curse from God on each of them, and banishment from the Garden of Eden for life.

It's so much easier to not be involved, particularly if the wife is competent and independent like Eve was. Training the children, managing the finances, setting the family social calendar, deciding on piano lessons for the kids, and overseeing church involvement, are all responsibilities that are easy to ignore after a long day at work. But, by ignoring those responsibilities, and others equally as important to family life, a man creates a leadership vacuum that a conscientious wife must fill in order to preserve the family. Gradually a woman becomes a safety net for the family, stepping into the breach that her husband has vacated. The result of her efforts to do her husband's job is often either excessive stress, or a hardness that comes from a woman trying to fill the man's role in the family. The gentle and quiet spirit so precious to God (1 Peter 3:4) has been unconsciously lost as she tries to do a job she was not designed to do.

Certainly this is not to say that women make no decisions, or have no influence on final results. Of course they do. But the final decision, on major, course-determining issues, must be the husband's, if the divine order of the family is to be followed.

As men have abdicated their roles as lovers, and then as leaders in their families, women have become bitter, sometimes even rejecting men as unnecessary and useless, and in reaction have turned to feminist ideology. They have not clearly understood that emotional abandonment has caused the hostile feelings they find springing up

116

within them. Behind practically every militant feminist is a tragic story of rejection, abuse, or abdication of responsibility by some man, either a father or husband. Their God-given desire to respond to a man has been buried under piles of mistreatment, weakness, or neglect.

This same scenario is repeated more subtly in the Christian community as women whose husbands have refused to lead find spiritual outlets in "women's ministries," women's Bible studies without any oversight, and a whole range of other autonomous activities. Men then wonder why their wives develop independent, resistant attitudes. The problem invariably lies at the foot of a passive husband who does not understand the natural consequences of his abdication.

Man's fear of confrontation

Why do men abdicate their responsibility as leaders in the family today? Certainly being ignorant of their biblical responsibility is a major reason. Laziness and selfishness are two other big factors, along with a feeling of inadequacy due to past failures and today's antagonistic culture. A church that recognizes the centrality of the family, and that will encourage and equip fathers in their leadership role, is an invaluable resource if men are to be successful family leaders. However, there is another aspect of male abdication that is more subtle and that we must consider.

Eating of the forbidden fruit was easier for Adam than going through the unpleasantness of telling Eve, "No!" She had just made a major decision that was contradictory to Adam's direction for the family, and yet he meekly surrendered his leadership authority to her because he was afraid to confront her and incur her displeasure. She, being deceived, subconsciously challenged his leadership and "won."

Man fell, not because he ate an apple that God said not to eat, but because Adam failed to carry God's delegated authority, and exercise it properly. Satan attacked the order of God's Kingdom, and Adam yielded.

Another interesting observation here is that the same thing happened during the life of the "last Adam," as a beloved member of Jesus' "family," Peter, was deceived by Satan into resisting Jesus' plan to go to Jerusalem in Matthew 16. However, Jesus recognized Satan's voice in the voice of Peter, and resisted the temptation to abdicate His leadership, and rebuked Peter. Adam did not resist Satan's voice in the voice of Eve, but obeyed her, rather than rebuking her, and He became Satan's slave (Romans 6:16).

117

God's curse on Adam was based on this failure to lead: "Because you have heeded the voice of your wife..." (Genesis 3:17). Certainly a man must listen to his helpmate, profiting from her input and insights, and we will talk about that more in just a minute. But when a wife contests the direction for the family that the husband has set, he must learn to lovingly, but firmly, resist her challenges and manipulations in order to maintain the integrity of his position as head of the family. He cannot give her a voice in the family direction until she yields to his leadership.

God's curse on women: the desire to control

God's curse on Eve is an interesting study. After telling her she will have pain in childbirth, He says, "Your desire shall be for your husband, and he shall rule over you" (Genesis 3:16). Commentators have generally thought that this has some sexual connotation; that even though they will have pain in childbirth, women will still want to engage in the act that produces children. However, the Hebrew word for "desire," teshuqah, is used only one other time by Moses in the Pentateuch, and that is in the next chapter as God warns Cain before he kills his brother Abel, "And, if you do not do well, sin lies at the door, and its desire is for you, but you should rule over it" (Genesis 4:7).

Sin's desire was to control, or capture, Cain, and indeed it did. In the same way, as a result of God's curse, a woman's natural way is now to try to control her husband, to contest his leadership, to run the family if she can. It is almost as if God said to Eve after the fiasco in the garden, "If you really want to run things I'm going to let you. I'll give you a built-in propensity to do so and show you by experience that My plan is the way the family works best." His Kingdom only functions His way.

Biblical history records several instances of this feminine penchant for control; Sarah's attempt to use Hagar to "help" God fulfill His promise to Abraham (Genesis 16); Rebekah's deceit in tricking Isaac into giving his blessing to Jacob instead of Esau (Genesis 27); Rachel and Leah's manipulations of Jacob and Laban (Genesis 30, 31); and Jezebel, the wife of King Ahab, who led her husband into idolatry, and in essence ruled Israel through him (1 Kings 16:29-34,19,21). In Revelation 2, Jezebel is again mentioned, this time as a feminine religious spirit who has gained control, and who has led astray the church in Thyatira.

This desire to control their husbands is very much observable in today's "daughters of Eve." The passivity and irresponsibility men have

118

inherited from Adam fit together with it like a hand in a glove. Fallen men tend to want someone else to take the responsibility for the leadership of the family, and their wives step right up to do so. Neither understand that the pattern they are following is a result of sin, and God wants to reverse that curse in Jesus Christ, restoring His divine order.

God's curse on Eve does not always result in passive men, though that is the spirit of this age in America. The last part of the curse, "...and He shall rule over you," has meant, down through the ages, that women would be little more than property, subjugated and tyrannized by sinful men. That is the case in Muslim countries today. However, wherever the gospel has gone, the curse has been reversed, with the status of women dramatically improved as they are seen as equal to men in every way. Certainly there are men with this distorted view of women in America today, who lord it over their wives. But by far the predominant problem in our culture is the weak, passive man, who, for one reason or another, refuses to lead.

Only in Jesus Christ can the curse be reversed in family life, with loving, Godly rule being instituted by Christian husbands, and wive's natural desire to control overcome by a desire to submit to their husbands as unto the Lord (Ephesians 5:22). In Jesus Christ the divine order of the family can be reestablished.

All horses are gray

Jill and I counselled some time ago with a Christian couple who had been married for some twenty-five years. The husband, Dale, was from a tragic family where there was sexual confusion and no training in being a man. He had never been able to grow up emotionally, and was still a little boy in his own mind, though he had developed the skills that made him attractive socially. His wife, Donna, was a very competent, talented woman, who had taken all family responsibilities for years. She was a good mother to their children and had taken that role for her husband as well. Dale, feeling absolutely no responsibility for his family, had been sexually promiscuous over the years, always being forgiven and taken back by his wife. He genuinely wanted to be a good husband and father, and was a leader in his church during many of the affairs. His distorted image of himself as a naughty little boy being spanked by his "mother," and a lack of understanding as to his responsibility in his family, did not allow him to change.

119

His most recent escapade was the last straw for Donna, who desperately cried out for help. Jill and I, as we met with them both, tried to communicate God's family order to them, and that Dale's sin was a symptom of his failure to commit himself to rule in his home by loving and leading his wife. She did not want to hear that there was anything any deeper than his sexual unfaithfulness. "Just get him to quit having these girls and be faithful to me and everything will be alright." She wouldn't listen as Dale shared how he felt useless in his home as Donna made every decision and fulfilled the role of family matriarch perfectly. His picture of himself as a little boy, incapable of responsibility, was reinforced every day.

I laid out for Dale a strategy of first genuinely repenting and turning from his sin (He had done that many times), and then committing himself to rule in his family, beginning to take the responsibility for direction and decisions (He had never done that!). We would hold him accountable to being in church for every meeting, allowing himself to be encouraged by other men who were going through similar situations. He was greatly encouraged, and determined to do as I had suggested.

Donna, however, was not as eager to implement new family leadership. After 25 years of living with a little boy, she had no faith that he would be able to rule in their home. Jill and I tried to explain the role of the church in equipping Dale for his job, but she was unable, or unwilling, to surrender her authority. She just wanted him to quit having affairs, and in essence remain a little boy under her rule. She could not see that she had unconsciously figuratively castrated him, and his affairs were the only way he could prove to himself that he was a man.

Dale, in the final analysis, was unable, or unwilling, to confront his wife and assume his rightful place as ruler in his home, just as Adam had been unwilling to confront Eve in the garden. He called one day, and rather sadly told me they would not be meeting with us any more. Donna was unwilling to see her part in the untenable situation in which she found herself. She could only ride the "white horse," while Dale felt very comfortable on the "black horse."

In reality, all marriage horses are grey. Until both husband and wife realize this fact, there can be no real solutions to marriage problems.

Not one option among many

It is important to realize that leadership for the husband in the family is not simply one option among many family life-styles. It is God's way, and any other way will have consequences that are destructive to the Kingdom of God, particularly in the lives of the children. Children intuitively know that their father should be in charge, and resentment, even bitterness, toward one or both parents is often the result if he isn't. Insecure or domineering girls, and irresponsible or passive boys, are often the product of matriarchal families. The model before the children as they have grown up is the model they will naturally follow as they start families of their own.

Regaining family leadership is not an easy task for a man who hasn't exercised it, because years of functioning a certain way has programmed everyone's "personal computer" in the family. It takes time and a genuine desire to be obedient to God, to begin to function properly. Children are in the habit of looking to Mom for decisions and ignoring Dad, and wives get used to making independent judgments on a whole range of issues from finances to child training apart from their husbands. These men have generally been too lazy, selfish, or fearful to take any leadership responsibility.

It is much easier for a man to know about loving and leading his family before he marries than to have to jack up years of family structure and slide under a new foundation. If you are unmarried, be sure any potential spouse understands the biblical model for marriage and desires to walk in that way. We will talk more about that in the chapter on selecting a mate.

If you are already married, remember that God can redeem and restore to their proper place those who cry out to Him. The following is a suggestion for beginning again in the correct manner.

Starting again

If you are the man in the family, and you have realized that you are not currently in the position of leadership that God has ordained, sit down with your wife and repent to her. Go through something like the following: "I have come to realize that I have not provided the leadership for you God has ordained that I provide as the head of the home. I want to repent of that right now, and ask you to please forgive me. By the grace of God and with His power, I'm going to make leading my family top priority." Tell your wife that you have allowed

121

her to carry things on her shoulders that you should have carried; left her to make decisions you should have made; not loved her as Christ loved the church. Promise her that from this day forward you are going to do your very best, by the power of God, to take your God-given responsibility to lead your family.

You might be thinking, "Why should I repent? She has been only too eager to run the show. The idea of submitting to my leadership has never crossed her mind."

If that is your attitude, let me say that she has only taken the leadership that you have been willing to give up. If she runs your family today, it is your fault because you have let her. Men have not seen the importance of being the head of their families and sometimes even joke about checking with "The Boss," and have all too often gone down without a fight. That, in itself, is a reason to repent. Whether or not a wife submits to her husband is her job; providing clear direction is her husband's. He must stick to his job; she to her's. Her role is the topic of Chapter 9.

Even if your wife agrees with the biblical model for family, and wants you to be the head of your home, do not expect her to do cart-wheels over your announcement of your repentance and desire to do it right, particularly if you have been married for some time. "The proof of the pudding is in the eating," and talk is certainly cheap in this situation. Before she lays down the reins, she wants to be sure that you have picked them up. Here are some habits for you to develop that will confirm in her mind that you indeed have those reins firmly in hand.

Characteristics of family leadership

1. Decision-making. Leadership, in the final analysis, is decision-making. Regardless of what is said, regardless of how things might appear, the one who makes the final decision is the leader. Decision-making in the family must not happen by consensus, or by majority vote. It is the duty and prerogative of the husband, for God will hold him responsible for his family, and for all the decisions that effect it, even if those decisions were made by the wife. Adam was accountable before God for the momentous decision Eve made to eat the forbidden fruit. "For as in Adam all die..." (I Corinthians 15:22), "Therefore, just as through one man sin entered the world, and death through sin..." (Romans 5:12), "For if by the one man's offence, many died..." (Romans 5:15), "Therefore, as through the one man's offence, judgment came to all men..." (Romans 5:18).

Adam tried to pass the buck to Eve for that fateful decision in the garden when God confronted him and held him accountable; "The woman You gave to be with me" (It's also a little bit Your fault, God!), "she gave me of the tree, and I ate." God did not buy Adam's story; "Because you have heeded the voice of your wife...(and did not make the right decision yourself!)," God's curse came upon mankind. As I suggested in Chapter 4, if Adam had overruled Eve's decision, even after she had eaten of the fruit, man would not have fallen, and sin would not have entered the human race. God would have honored Adam's headship.

Can you see why the husband must make his will known to his family members and expect them to carry it out? He will be responsible before God. Once his family members adopt that will, and desire to please the father by endeavoring to carry it out, they can be given great responsibilities with great freedom as they mature enough to be able to perform them. We will discuss how children are brought to that point in the section on child training.

I have seen many older married couples who have settled into such a deep rut that the perpetual word proceeding from the husband's mouth is, "Yes, dear." He has been unknowingly stripped of his self-respect and any confidence he might have as a man because of years of compliance to his wife's leadership. To disagree with her is unthinkable, and he has settled into life as a drone, filling his capacity as one who works, and makes reproduction possible, but little else, certainly not leading the family by making hard decisions. A man like this will need an extremely large dose of courage from the Lord to withstand the pressure that will come from confronting his wife. It is possible, however, and necessary, if he is to realize the divine order in his home.

A husband needs big ears

2. Listening. After a day with the kids, every woman desires some adult conversation with her husband. Too often we come home, give our wife a cursory kiss, turn on the T.V. or pick up the paper, and do not provide the opportunity for her to share about her day, and in turn tell her about ours. We communicate unintentionally to her that we are not interested in her, or in what she does, and that what she does is unimportant. Trying to lead a wife without listening to her, and then communicating back to her, is an impossibility, and will cause her to resist our leadership.

It took me years to understand this principle, and I still have a hard time implementing it. To sit down and spend a block of time with Jill, sharing real feelings with her, and listening to her fears and problems, and renewing her vision for our direction as a family, was totally foreign to me when we married. Eventually, we set aside the first hour after I got home in the afternoon to be alone together. The kids knew that was our time, and left us alone (That takes some training but it is doable). Jill would get me a snack and we talked over the day together. I looked forward to those times as much as she did. Our irregular schedules make that more difficult now, but I try to take her out to breakfast on Monday mornings for an unhurried time together.

Listening to a wife's suggestions as to family decisions and direction is another facet of this leadership quality. Any good leader takes advantage of the insights and wisdom of those he leads, and leading a family is no exception. By listening to our wives and giving them the opportunity for input, we increase the chance of making a proper decision. The same is true for our children as they grow older.

Keep in mind that listening to our wives and children is not the same as doing what they say. Remember Adam's problem was "because you have listened to the voice of your wife" (and have done what she said!), which, in that instance, was wrong. The decision is still the husband's, and must remain so, but a good leader is not threatened by suggestions from his family, and can give them credit for good input.

Maybe your wife is smarter than you are. You would be a fool to not take advantage of her intelligence. Maybe she is more perceptive and more thoughtful. You should let those gifts enhance your understanding. Maybe she is even naturally stronger-willed than you. You must realize that leadership does not go to the smartest, most insightful, the loudest, or the most insistent family member. The leader is the father, who listens to all input, and then makes the final decision himself, because he is the man. The final decision could well be the wife's suggestion, but it is the final decision because the father decided that it is the right thing to do.

Reading between the lines

3. Understanding. Every woman needs a man who can, "...dwell with them with understanding, giving honor to the wife, as to the weaker vessel..." (1 Peter 3:7). This means that it is possible to understand your wife, contrary to popular opinion. A man needs to be

aware of his wife's emotional needs; to know when the African violet needs fertilizer and when it needs water, when it needs sunshine and when it needs shade. Women often don't know what they need, and in fact often think they need one thing, when in reality they need something far different, because their emotions affect their logic. A woman was designed to be cared for by a man - first by her father, then by her husband. Because of this, God has given men the insight to know what their daughters and wives need, and then the ability to supply it.

The "honor" mentioned in the above verse includes the investment of time, energy, and care necessary to really understand our wives. A husband must be able to recognize that his wife has certain needs that sometimes are the opposite of what she says she wants. When she lashes out at him, he must be able to discern what is the real cause of the outburst. Has he hurt her in some way, is she really crying out for help because of some other problem, or is she being selfish and demanding her way? He must know, because each of those root causes demand a different response. We will run ourselves ragged and not be able to rule well if we don't ask God to help us understand our wives, see beneath the surface, and then meet their real needs.

How often I have seen men who key their own attitude and behavior off their wives because they don't understand them. They will react to them by pouting, or ranting and raving themselves, rather than trying to calmly look beneath the surface for the real problem. Jill has often said to me, "When I'm emotional and out of control, please don't believe me and let me have my way. Stand firm like a rock, and let me be an egg and break all over you." Of course, she never says that in the heat of the moment; only when she is "clothed and in her right mind." If I believed everything she said we would have divorced long ago, and many couples do, because men do not understand their wives.

Getting his hands dirty

4. Serving. The concept of servant-leadership was introduced in Chapter Five, but I would like to emphasize it here, because it is very important to understand that this is the only kind of leadership that is valid in family life. A man must look for ways to serve his family from a position of strength, as the decision-maker. He does the unpleasant things instead of ordering others to do them; he inconveniences himself; he tries to lighten the load of those under his care without

robbing them of the opportunity to do a hard job and succeed. To serve a wife and children properly takes wisdom from God, which He will give if we ask Him.

Children learn to serve, not only by being made to serve, but by watching their mother and father serve as well. If they have to do chores around the house, as they should, and their parents are simply using them to keep from having to do anything themselves, the children's attitude will be, "I can't wait until I'm an adult and in charge so I won't have to do anything either." We must teach them by example.

We were in a home not long ago where the father worked long hours every day as a construction worker. When he came home he often prepared dinner for his family, and then cleaned up the kitchen. On the one hand, this arrangement seemed to suit the couple and they were proud of the fact that they were "androgynous in the kitchen," with no clearly-assigned roles. On the other hand, this lack of definition caused an underlying tension in the family.

This is not what being a servant-leader means. The husband should have calmly and clearly defined the role he expected his wife to fill, whatever that might be. If he felt that she should be responsible for the meals, he should let her know that clearly, and then expect her to prepare them. If he wanted to fix them himself, that too should be clearly stated.

There are definite responsibilities in the Kingdom, and a good ruler encourages those over whom he rules to discharge their own well, bringing a sense of fulfillment that will not come if he relieves them of their obligations. There are times, of course, when all might pitch in to help do a certain task. A ruler must know when to serve by lightening the load, and when to require performance of duties.

An example of the former occurred when our two little boys were in diapers. Jill prepared dinner each night, and after we ate, she gave the boys their baths and got them ready for bed while I cleaned up the kitchen. We had decided when we married that the kitchen was her domain, and I gave her complete freedom to buy the groceries (keeping within our budget), and cook whatever she wanted. She told me, in so many words, to stay out of her area, which I was only too happy to do, until the children came. Then we followed the above procedure for several years. When the children were old enough, they became the helpers, and I thankfully stepped aside, though I still come out of retirement occasionally when the kitchen is a mess and Jill is gone, or when we have a large dinner-party. She knows the kitchen is hers, and is blessed when I help. In the same way, yard maintenance is mine, and I'm blessed when she helps me weed the flower beds every summer. She doesn't expect me to cook and wash dishes, and I don't expect her to weed.

A leader who takes the biggest piece of meat at the dinner-table, who demands that the family watch his preference on T.V., who is too protective of his free time to help other families move, or who is selfish in any number of other ways, will raise children who will never learn to be servants, no matter what he tries to teach them, and the Kingdom of God will suffer loss.

Shouldering the load

5. Providing. God designed that the responsibility for providing the financial support for the family rest squarely on the shoulders of the husband. "But if anyone does not provide for his own, and especially those of his household, he has denied the faith, and is worse than an unbeliever" (1 Timothy 5:8). This is not a popular message today, as our economy is based on two incomes, thereby militating against mothers remaining home with their children. But in order for a man to see himself as the leader in his home, with the members of his family dependent on that leadership as they should be, he must provide for their physical needs.

Most Christian women, (unless they have been influenced by the siren song of the feminist movement and have bought the lie that their potential will not be realized if they are "only" a wife and mother), long to fix up a home for their husbands, and provide the security in it during the day for their children. We will talk about that extensively in chapters 10 and 11. Surprisingly, many men are pressing their wives to work in order to bring in the extra dollars to provide a somewhat higher life-style. In so doing, men are placing their most precious ones in the jungle that is the work-place, a jungle women were never intended to enter, where predators abound.

This does not mean that a woman never can work outside of the home. Sometimes there are extenuating circumstances that will necessitate doing so: temporary crises, sickness, divorce, or the death of a spouse. There may be other situations as well. But God's norm is for a man to support his family, and for his wife to be a "worker at home" (Titus 2:5). When this normal life style is possible and followed, it brings great blessing.

When leadership is challenged

What does a man do when his decisions are challenged, as they inevitably will be? He must realize that he is gaining ground for the kingdom of God, and his leadership of his family is an important part of the extension of that kingdom. Because that is true, Satan will do everything possible to thwart his attempts to lead, just as He did with Adam.

If your wife is resistant to your leadership, first be sure you are committed to loving her with *agape* love, and that you are demonstrating the five characteristics of leadership we have just discussed. Be sure that your decision does not violate biblical principles, and that it comes after much prayer. Remember, Jesus is your head and you are attempting to do what He wants you to do. If you have met these requirements, and your wife still disagrees with you, you must make your decision anyway, against her wishes. You must learn to make what you perceive to be the right decision, not the expedient one to simply relieve pressure. Remember, your wife has a propensity to resist you until you demonstrate that you are strong enough to lead her.

Shootout at O.K. Corral

The above scenario happens in most marriage relationships, either before the wedding or after it. Every woman wants to know that her man will be strong enough to care for her if she gives him her life, so she will test him, albeit unconsciously. She will try all the wiles at her disposal to get her way, all the while hoping against hope that her man will stand firm against her and not give in. Every woman needs the security that comes from a husband who can care for her in this way, even when she is resistant to that care, and will only really respect him if she cannot manipulate him to do her wishes.

When Jill and I were on the staff of Campus Crusade for Christ before we were married, I was the Western Regional Director, traveling over a ten-state area, speaking and giving leadership to the staff members on the various campuses in that region. Each of the four regions in the U.S. also had a Regional Woman's Representative, who worked with the various women staff members in that region, speaking in sororities, dormitories and to various women's functions, such as teas, women's retreats, etc. Each Regional Director appointed his own Regional Women's Representative, and mine had just gotten married and left the region, leaving an opening for one of the four top jobs for women on the Campus Crusade Staff. Jill was on the campus at the University of British Colombia at the time, and it appeared that she was the natural woman to fill the vacancy, due to ability, gifts and experience.

Because of her background, and her need to prove to herself that she was worthwhile by being successful in other's eyes, she desperately wanted the job that I had the power to give her. I was right in the middle of trying to get her to marry me at the time, and certainly wanted to do everything possible to facilitate that, but I somehow knew that this position was not what Jill needed; this was not what was best for her at that particular time in her life. It would simply exacerbate a problem I knew the Lord wanted to deal with. I wanted her motivation to be clean and free from self-seeking, and even though I loved her desperately, I had to tell her that I was not going to appoint her as the Western Regional Women's Representative.

Jill knew that by looking only at externals she was the logical choice. She also was aware of her impure motivation and did not disagree with my reasoning. But she still desperately wanted that job. She begged, cajoled, pouted, got angry, cried, and basically tried every manipulative trick in the book to get what she wanted, but to no avail. I somehow held firm and did not give in, even though I did not at all understand the principle I'm relating to you now.

I can remember one particular instance where Jill, in exasperation, said, "Do you mean to say that I'm qualified to be your wife, but not to be the Women's Regional Representative?" I told her that the qualifications for the two jobs were totally different!

We both look back over almost thirty years and know that this instance was our "Mexican showdown" where it was established who would ultimately run our family. Jill learned that I would stand firm and not let her manipulate me to get what she wants. I believe in every marriage there will be jockeying or sparring to see who will be in charge, and at some point every man must establish his leadership through a crisis with his wife, standing firm against the result of the fall in his wife's life. He must not surrender that leadership if he desires be obedient to God's biblical pattern.

What if a wife still refuses to yield to her husband's leadership, even after he is "doing everything right;" loving her, trying to make good decisions, listening to her, trying to understand her, serving her, and providing for her? Maybe she undermines his discipline with the children, or refuses to follow his wishes with the finances, or rebels against any other of his directives.

At some point he must ask her if she really wants to be married to him. He cannot surrender his leadership, for that is an indispensable part of a biblical marriage. He must, through many tears, and with much love, tell her that he desperately wants her to be with him, to be his help-mate, to labor with him in the vision God has given him, but it cannot be on her terms. If she refuses to do as he says, she will have to leave in order to preserve the integrity of his family. His covering of protection and provision is for those who submit to his rule.

Does this sound too hard? I am convinced that there are very few women who will come to this point without yielding to the leadership of a husband who is loving her as Christ loved the church, but every husband who determines to lead his family must be prepared for this possibility.

In John 6:66-68, after delivering a particularly straightforward message, many of Jesus' followers "went back and walked with Him no more" (vs. 66). Rather than beg these "disciples" to stay, reinterpret His message so it would be more palatable, or soften His words so as to not offend, Jesus turned to the twelve and asked them if they too wanted to leave. The door was always open if they did not want to submit to His rule in their lives. A wife must know that this same consequence is the result of her refusal to yield to the rule of her husband.

Some men say, "We never fight or have any disagreements whatsoever." This is not always a good sign. Peace in the home is an indication of one will, but whose? In many homes the wife is never crossed by her husband, so there is no reason for her to be resistant. If the husband says, "I want you to go buy three new outfits for yourself," or, "We are going to eat out every night this week," her obedience to his wishes tells him absolutely nothing about her submission to his leadership. Submission to authority is only a theory until a woman is asked by her husband to do something she really doesn't want to do. His willingness to give her that directive, and her willingness to carry it out, is the true test of biblical leadership in their family.

The results of responsible leadership

Leading properly is not an easy job, and it can be a real temptation to want to throw in the towel when there is resistance from the family.

However, the rewards are definitely worth the fight. Let me enumerate five of them.

First, the family members will bear the stamp of the father. They will adopt his vision, his values, his world-view. He can see his influence extended into the next generation. Without his strong leadership, those in his family are open to other philosophies and life-styles, often antagonistic to his.

Second, strong leadership makes for secure family members. If a man's wife and children know that no one is really in charge, fear and insecurity will grow because they know intuitively that they are not qualified or equipped for family leadership. Nothing is more frightening to a little child than to push on his father in an attempt to find strong boundaries, and find none there.

Third, there will be a respect for all authority. Weak leadership at home often means that the family member has not learned how to submit to authority anywhere, whether it be teachers, coaches, employers, or the civil government. Strong leadership prepares children to function successfully in the world.

Fourth, leadership, with concurrent accountability, makes for family members who can accept responsibility, because they can govern themselves. They can be called up to realize their full potential.

Fifth, and finally, the whole family, under the decisive leadership of a strong father, will be a healthy, functioning unit that can experience together the blessings of God, and fulfill the purpose God created the family to accomplish.

"Father, open my eyes to see how I am fulfilling my role as leader in my family, and give me the grace to lovingly and firmly take the reins of leadership in areas where I have abdicated. Help me to adjust myself to your thoughts in this matter, rather than praying that You will adjust to mine."

Questions for discussion

1. Discuss how you feel about the concept of leadership in the family being the responsibility of the man. Do you agree or disagree? Does your experience bear out this scriptural principle?

2. Can you see the results of the fall in the relationships between men and women that you have observed? What are some examples? How do men shirk responsibility and women assume it?

3. If you are married, what are the issues that have been "Mexican showdowns" with your spouse? Who has "won?" If you are single, what have been some issues that your parents have faced? What was the result?

4. To what lengths should a man go to establish his leadership? How should he handle family members who will not follow?

5. Explain how proper family leadership establishes the Kingdom of God.

Chapter 9

Imperishable Beauty - A Gentle and Quiet Spirit

"Do not let your beauty be that outward adorning or arranging the hair, of wearing gold, or of putting on fine apparel; but let it be the hidden person of the heart, with the incorruptible ornament of a gentle and quiet spirit, which is very precious in the sight of God." I Peter 3:4,5.

In today's culture in America, a woman with a gentle spirit as described by Peter in these verses is becoming more and more of an anachronism. Whereas the Bible says that that spirit is precious to God, and therefore much to be desired, society subtly, and sometimes overtly, tells a woman, "stick up for your rights." "Don't let anyone take advantage of you." "You can do anything a man can do." Women are taught that sexist men have subjugated them, and kept them in bondage, by forcing them to stay home and bear children, and that they must fight their way into the aggressive, competitive, business and professional world. Only by reaching the highest positions of power and influence in that area of endeavor can they find true fulfillment and meaning in life.

So goes the conventional wisdom of our day. This "wisdom" does not make radiating a gentle and quiet spirit an easy task.

Is this assertive, confrontive attitude (so often necessary to be successful in the world) the attitude a Christian woman should have? It is obvious that many women have been greatly influenced by this kind of thinking. They have not realized that the real issue is not "What can I do?," but rather, "What does God say I should do?" A woman's capability to do anything a man can do does not dictate the necessity of her doing so. Because she can develop toughness and competitiveness, should she? As in every other area of life, we must look to the Bible to

133

see what God says about the character traits women should seek to display, and the role they play in society and the family. We must bring our ideas about the subject into conformity with His, not expecting Him to put His stamp of approval on our "creative" ideas about how we can be fulfilled.

By the way, a gentle and quiet spirit has nothing to do with personality. A woman may well have a bubbly, outgoing demeanor, but an attitude of submissiveness and peace that radiates from deep within and expresses itself through her unique personality. On the other hand, a woman may be quiet and seemingly very sweet, and yet be hard and rebellious in spirit, like a brick hidden in a paper bag. All women are equally capable of exhibiting the spirit that God seeks.

The ministry of older women

In Titus 2:3-5, Paul gives directions to older women, first pertaining to their own personal conduct. He then instructs them in a very vital ministry that is often neglected in the church today: the ministry of teaching the younger women.

I believe one of the major reasons for weak and ineffectual churches today is a profound neglect of the role of the "older woman." When children are raised and gone, many women without a vision for this role use their new "free time" to get a job outside of the home, or even to begin a new career in the work place, taking with them all the experience and knowledge they have acquired over the years about being a wife and mother. This experience could be shared with young mothers who are struggling with learning how to successfully perform their role in their family.

Imparting personal life experiences, both successes and failures, from this reservoir of knowledge is real, get-your-hands-dirty ministry, and it is desperately needed in the church. Dissatisfied, frustrated wives make it difficult for husbands to lead their families effectively, and ineffective families make weak churches. Weak churches hinder the work of the Kingdom. Older women have a very, very crucial role to play in seeing the family become a weapon for the ultimate, experiential victory of the Kingdom of God.

In these verses in Titus 2, Paul tells us what the older women have learned and are to share with the younger women:

"(T)he older women likewise that they be reverent in behavior, not slanderers, not given to much wine, teachers of good things- that they admonish the young women to love their husbands, to love their children, to be discreet, chaste, homemakers, good, obedient to their own husbands, that the word of God may not be blasphemed." Titus 2:3-5

These verses are crammed full of enough content for several year's worth of women's Bible studies. Rather than teach theology, which is the elder's job, women need to be focusing on the material presented here when they teach the younger women. Who better to do this than Godly older women who have successfully developed these qualities and have gone through all the difficulties young wives must face? (Certainly not the elders!)

Three of the qualities Paul enumerates here that older women are to build into their proteges pertain specifically to family life, so I would like to use them to form an outline to investigate the wife's role in the family. We will discuss wives loving and obeying their husbands in this chapter, being homemakers in chapters 10 and 11, and then loving their children in the section on child training.

The ideas we will explore here are extremely controversial today. That fact in itself is a commentary on the influence the feminist movement has had on the church. Forty years ago these ideas were commonplace and universally accepted. Remember, the Bible is our standard, and we must anchor our view of marriage roles there and not to the accepted practices of the day.

Love their husbands

Why does a young bride need to learn to love her husband? Doesn't she already love him? Why would she marry a man she didn't already love? We're talking here about learning to love your husband when the romantic feelings fade, as they inevitably will, in the day-to-day reality of living with a man who is a sinner.

The word for "love" here is a different word from the one used for a husband's love for his wife in Ephesians 5. As I pointed out in chapter 7, this word is from the root *phileo*, which means a tender affection. It signifies a more responding type of love, while *agape*, the love a husband has for his wife, is an initiating love. Ideally, the husband's strong, *agape* love will call forth the wife's love in response. Since all husbands are sinners, and we are not perfect lovers, this is not always the case. We will deal with what a wife does in an imperfect situation later.

Practically, how does a wife "love her husband?" We know that if she is to learn how to do that from an older woman, this love must not be an irresistible force she cannot control, anymore than is her husband's love for her. No, loving her husband is something she can learn how to do, then decide to do, and finally, with practice, get better and better at. What should the older women teach her to do?

Love him "positionally"

She can love her husband "positionally" by embracing his headship in her life. Paul says,

> "Wives, submit to your own husbands, as to the Lord. For the husband is the head of the wife, as Christ is the head of the church; and He is the Savior of the body. Therefore, just as the church is subject to Christ, so let the wives be to their own husbands in everything." Ephesians 5:22-24

This is a command, not a suggestion, and the rationale for it is the pattern relationship that Jesus has with His church. As you know, marriage is a picture of that relationship, and, just as the church submits to Christ in everything, so does a wife to her husband.

Notice the word "head" again. It is the same Greek word, *kephale*, that we discussed in chapter 5, meaning authority or direction. The wife is to "submit" to that authority just as if it were to Jesus Christ Himself. That is what the Bible says, so it is not surprising to learn that the Greek word for "submit" is *hupotosso*, which is a military term meaning to rank under, or to put in subjection.[1] Paul goes on to say that not only is a wife to be subject to her husband just as if he were Jesus Christ, but that she is to do so, not just when she thinks he is right, but in everything!

We saw in chapter 5 that Jesus demonstrated this principle very clearly. As the second person of the Trinity, He showed us how to be under authority in the kingdom of God by submitting to His Father, the first person of the Trinity, in everything even though He was equal to His Father in every way. In the same way, wives are equal "heirs together of the grace of life" (1 Peter 3:7) with their husbands. "There is neither male nor female; for you are all one in Christ Jesus" (Galatians 3:28).

This means that a wife's <u>relationship</u> to God is identical in every way with her husband's. However, they have a different <u>function</u> in His kingdom. Just as God the Son functioned completely under the authority of God the Father, a wife is to function completely under the authority of her husband. This brings harmony to the home as all members of the family yield to the will of its head, and extends the kingdom of God into that home as its members operate as God intended them to operate. There is always a clear line of authority in the kingdom, for it represents the delegated rule of God. Without that clear authority structure, the rule of Jesus Christ, or the Kingdom, is not realized.

The whole story

Why does this concept of a wife's submission to her husband evoke such a violent reaction today, even from the church? I believe teaching on the subject has often been incomplete. Much of the emphasis on a wife's submission has neglected the husband's responsibility to love and lead his wife, as we discussed in chapters 7 and 8. As a result, there are men in our churches who bludgeon their wives into submission without having a clue about their own responsibility in their families. Just as we respond to Christ's love for us, a wife who wants to obey God will respond to her husband if he is ruling properly. Built in to her by God is a desire to give herself to a strong, decisive man who is laying down his life for her.

At this point, if you are struggling with the concepts presented here, you might want to reread Chapters 7 and 8 to remind you of the pattern for headship God sets before each husband. Is submission to a man like that difficult? I know we as husbands are not like that yet, but we are trusting God to make us so. Our wive's submission only hastens the time when we will be as you want us to be!

Many Christian women read the Bible and see what they are theoretically to do - submit to their husbands in all things - but find it very difficult to actually do this in today's culture. There are some very real hindrances these earnest women face who sincerely want to obey God in their marriages.

Correcting some misconceptions

First, she will often have misconceptions as to what submitting to her husband means. It does not mean being a doormat for a physically or verbally abusive man who is using his wife for himself. Sometimes it is imperative that a wife flee from a husband like that. Paul intimates as much in 1 Corinthians 7:10,11 when he instructs wives to not leave their husbands, but if they do, either to remain unmarried or to be reconciled. He implies that there will be times when leaving is necessary.

If the situation at home becomes unbearable, or there is reason to fear for the safety of family members, the wife should say to her husband, "I love you and want to be your wife, but not under these conditions. When you have gotten some help and can rule well in our family, I will return." Leaving is often the only thing that will get the attention of the abusive husband, and properly done is far more biblical and effective than verbally badgering him. Obviously, the details of how this will work vary in every situation. Still, the principle is that a woman does not have to remain in an untenable situation because of some ill-conceived notion of "submission."

"I win - you lose"

Another misconception many women have is that submission is a contest, and "If he is stronger than I am, I will submit to him. If he is not, I won't."

Strength of will is not exclusively a male characteristic. Women are often stronger than their husbands. However, they can establish their husbands as heads over them by their willing submission to them. They can make it easy for their husbands to rule, or they can make it extremely difficult, depending on their understanding of their biblical role. Submission is not a contest, with leadership going to the strongest marriage partner.

Jill and I did not understand this when we were married. After some ten years of marriage she gave me a very small, beautifully wrapped Christmas present. Inside I found a bright red heart with the following note: "When we were married, we battled for leadership in our family and you won. However, I never willingly, as a conscious decision, gave you my heart. Today, as an act of my will, I give my heart to you. I yield to your leadership and direction in my life."

We had come to understand the principle, though walking that relationship out in experience has not always been easy. We are still learning what that means in experience.

138

"Only if you're right"

A final misconception is that submission is dependent on right decision-making. "I will submit to him as long as he is right, but if he makes a stupid decision, I reserve the right to make the final one." Submission is not a matter of right and wrong. His decisions are the ones that God has decreed should determine the direction of the family, right or wrong. If he is wrong, God will hold him accountable, and his wife can trust the Lord to protect her.

A woman must realize that a man who is learning for the first time to lead his family will make some mistakes. But the support of his wife will encourage him to seek her input in order to help him in the process. On the other hand, if he is locked in a struggle with his wife for the right to make the final decision, he must reject her input until he knows she is submitted to his headship and is not trying to run his family. He cannot compromise his position as the decision-maker. The kingdom is not expressed according to our ideas of what works, but according to God's design, and that is male leadership. Any other pattern will have adverse affects on all family members. Once she yields to him, he can take advantage of all her wisdom, but not before.

"Wrestling with an alligator?"

This concept is hard for many women to understand. They often say, "He's just being stubborn. I know what's right, and he knows I know, but he just refuses to do it. Shouldn't he do what I say if we both know it's right?"

In the short run, that's probably true, but a man who is just learning how to lead feels that competing with a strong wife for the decision-making position in the family is like wrestling with an alligator. He will sometimes refuse suggestions he should take because of past lost wrestling matches he knows he should have won. The sooner he feels secure in his place of leadership, the sooner he will be able to receive her input. She, on the other hand, must see that by being the "safety net" for her husband, she has helped to create the situation in which she finds herself, and that some transition time will be necessary before he can receive her input.

Against the tide

The second hindrance a wife must face as she attempts to obey God and submit herself to her husband is the prevailing feminist culture of our day. Every day she is bombarded with voices from every quarter telling her to be her own person, seek her own life, have her own career, and be independent of her husband. Examples of successful career women who answer to no man are held up as the only women who are being fulfilled as persons. Young Christian women are made to feel that only those who are incompetent and not capable of running their own lives are under the authority of their husbands, and that they had better throw off that archaic authority structure or they will miss true fulfillment. Those who preach this message fail to understand that being under functioning authority actually frees a woman to develop all the gifts and abilities God has given her in a way that will preserve her feminine uniqueness as a woman of God.

In the August 4, 1994 issue of USA Today, the *Money* section's lead article was about a woman who is the CEO of the third largest maker of intimate apparel in the country, and the only woman CEO of a member of *Fortune* magazine's famous list of the top 500 companies in the country. USA Today writes, "She made $3.1 million last year, and she's happy to argue why she is worth it. She landed on *Fortune*'s list of the Seven Toughest Bosses In America for calling her salesmen eunuchs. She works 16 hour days."

I'm sure many women read that article and said to themselves, "She's made it. That's what I want for myself." However, what does God think of her "success?" Does she have a "gentle and quiet spirit?" Did she learn to "submit to her husband in all things as unto the Lord?" Those are questions the Bible teaches she will one day be asked as she stands before the Judge of all the earth and is held accountable for her every thought, word, and deed.

The Power behind the throne

A third hindrance to biblical submission is fear; a fear that might be expressed in this way. "I don't think my husband can be trusted with my life, the lives of my children, and the future of our family. I am afraid he cannot handle the responsibility if I really submit to him and help to establish him as the head of our home."

Many competent women have been safety nets for families with husbands who, for one reason or another, have not assumed their proper role as head. The thought of surrendering their prerogative to make final decisions to husbands who have proven their incompetence, at least to their wives, is a very scary concept.

1 Peter 3:1-6 speaks directly to this situation. Here Peter teaches that when a man does not "obey the word," a wife is to submit herself to him nonetheless, "without a word," or without badgering and complaining, and he will "be won," or begin to obey the word, as he observes his wife's chaste and respectful behavior. If he won't obey God's Word, what makes a wife think he will obey her's? Her gentle and quiet submission is a much more powerful force for change, and represents more beautiful "adorning" than "arranging the hair, or wearing gold, or putting on fine apparel." Peter then uses Sarah as a biblical example of one who "adorned" herself in this way. She submitted herself to Abraham, calling him "lord," even when he abandoned her to be in the harems of two different kings (Genesis 12:10-20; 20:1-18). This is a beautiful example of doing the right thing, the "good" thing, without any fear or terror, as Peter says, and then trusting God to protect and provide. For, in submitting to her husband, a woman recognizes that she is submitting to God and trusting Him as the power behind her husband.

This is an extreme example, and one that occurred in an age when women had no choice but to do as their husbands said, so trusting in God was Sarah's <u>attitude</u>. Peter says that this <u>attitude</u> is one we are to emulate, even though we may have other options available to us physically.

Obeying God rather than man

As I mentioned earlier, I believe there is a time when a woman may find it necessary to disobey or even leave her husband, but those times are very rare and that option must be exercised with great caution. Whenever his directive is directly contrary to a clear and obvious command of God, disobedience is warranted. Peter and John's disobedience to the Sanhedrin in Acts 4:13-22, and Rahab's lie and disobedience to the King of Jericho (Joshua 2:1-7) are classic examples of obeying a higher authority. Ordering his wife to become a prostitute, to be an accomplice in a crime, or to become involved in the occult would be instances that would warrant a wife disobeying her husband. However, even in the act of disobedience, there can be an attitude of submission, as the wife tells her husband clearly that to obey him would unquestionably be disobedience to God and she cannot do that.

This is not an excuse for women to look for loopholes so they can do their own thing. It is a last resort, a final step after appeals to the husband to change his demands have been rejected.

Some examples of situations where obedience is appropriate include not going to church because the non-Christian husband wants his wife to stay home with him; working outside the home because the husband wants her to do so even though the wife wants to stay home and care for the children; and not tithing even though the wife knows it is the right thing to do. As a wife attempts to please her husband by obeying him in these areas, Peter argues in 1 Peter 3;1,2 that he will notice her obedience, and God will eventually change his heart.

Each of these examples is "spiritual" in nature, and the temptation is to go ahead and do the religious thing with or without the husband's approval. However, this is a denial of the principle of headship in the family, and of the truth of Proverbs 21:1. "The king's heart is in the hand of the Lord, like the rivers of water, He turns it wherever He wishes."

"Lose your life to find it"

Another fear might be expressed like this: "I am afraid if I really yield myself to my husband in all things before he loves me unconditionally, that that submission will go down a black hole somewhere and be forever lost. He will never change, and I will have lost my life." Losing our lives is never easy, but is it not a spiritual principle that to do so means receiving it back again (Matthew 16:25)? That is the pattern Jesus set for us as He submitted Himself to death of His own volition (John 10:17,18), and He was ultimately vindicated and exalted to God's right hand (Philippians 2:5-9)!

Right now, submitting yourself to your husband might seem like death to you, and in a sense it is. Losing yourself in a man who does not know how to love or lead you seems impossible to do, but there are no qualifiers in the command in Ephesians 5: "Wives submit to your own husbands, as to the Lord,...just as the church is subject to Christ, so let wives be to their own husbands in everything." It does not say, "if he loves you," or, "if he is worthy," or, "if he is hearing from God." This is your chance to go to the cross. No one can force you to do so. No one "takes your life from you." Can you see that this is the path to life and exaltation? Desperately holding on to your life by refusing to submit to your husband means missing the life and glory God has for you.

You can see that following the Lord in the area of submission without fear is not an exact science. Much prayer and counsel with Godly, more mature, older women and elders, and encouragement from others in the church, is necessary to walk successfully through the difficult situations that will often arise.

"I just want to be me"

God created each of His children as individuals. We are all gloriously unique, with unique gifts and abilities, strengths and weaknesses, and each of us has a unique purpose in God's Kingdom. However, there is a huge difference between the words *individual,* and *individualism.* Individualism implies independence, an attitude of "I don't need you. I'm going to do what I want to do, no matter what you might say."

This spirit of individualism, or independence, is everywhere in the world today, and many Christian women have imbibed of it. This spirit is the fourth hindrance to biblical submission. It is a very subtle thing, and can be seen in a woman's desire for a career apart from her husband, or her desire to keep her maiden name after marriage, and can even masquerade as a personal "call" to a particular ministry.

When a woman marries, her call is to her husband as his "helpmate," not to Africa as a missionary, or to some "women's ministry." Those ministries may exist in the context of the church, but not apart from the covering of her husband. How many times have family needs been neglected and husbands and children suffered because a wife's first priority was her "ministry?" Those "ministries" often draw women away from the church and lead to spiritual pride as they now are "more spiritual" than their husbands, and "know more Bible" than they do. The key to evaluating a women's ministry is this - does it conform to the standard set in Titus 2 for what the older women should teach the younger ones?

If a man is a banker, his wife's call is to be a Godly banker's wife, doing all that that position demands in order for her husband to be a successful banker in the Kingdom of God. Her ministry is never apart from her husband or out from under his covering, but to always supplement him and his call. Is not that what a "helpmate" does? A feminine spirit of independence, no matter how religious, has no place in marriage.

The "pride of life" to which Eve succumbed in the Garden of Eden was really nothing more than this spirit of independence, this desire to be something apart from God and His divine order, to be wise, to know all that God knows. Its fruit is a delusion, for the promised independence is nothing more than submission to a different head. We are all "that one's slaves whom [we] obey, whether of sin to death, or of obedience to righteousness" (Romans 6:16). Eve discovered slavery to sin (independence) much more demanding than obedience to God and His law.

Reversing the curse

In the last chapter, we discussed God's curse on the woman in Genesis 3:16: "Your desire shall be for your husband, and he shall rule over you." This is the fifth and final hindrance to biblical submission that I want to consider.

As a result of this curse from God, there is something in every woman that fights against the concept of submission. The very idea of allowing men to rule over them in marriage is odious to many women, even Christian women. Some will even go to great lengths to try and explain how Paul didn't mean what he said, or suggest that the passages on submission are for another era and no longer apply today.

When a woman who has not been trained in biblical submission and does not recognize her natural propensity to control her husband marries, she subconsciously begins to attempt to be the decision-maker, the leader in the family. Often she is not aware of what she is doing, and would even deny it if confronted with the idea. Combine that with man's inclination to evade responsibility, and you have a relationship headed for trouble.

When a woman discovers that she can control her passive husband (who by the way may be a strong leader in his business and other areas where he is not trying to lead a controlling wife), she soon loses respect for him, and even despises him, for she knows intuitively that God's original design, and His present plan in Jesus Christ, is for her husband to rule over her. This often is most obvious in their sex life, for no woman wants to make love to a weak man whom she can control.

As the husband senses his wife is dissatisfied with him and tries to please her by doing what he thinks she wants, she despises him even more, and sees his attempts to please her as weakness, for he does not understand the distinction between blessing and pleasing his wife. He is helpless to know what to do. Both marriage partners are ripe for affairs; he, needing to prove his manhood again, and she, looking for a strong man who will rule over her.

Genevieve had been married to Bob for 25 years. They had both become Christians as a young married couple, and had begun sincerely to try to follow the Lord. They had gone to several churches over the years and had been involved in Bible studies and outreach groups. When Genevieve came for counsel, she was very distraught and got right to the point. Bob had suddenly left her and moved to an apartment at the opposite end of town. What could she do to get him back?

As we talked, I could sense that she was a very strong woman who had recently had a new experience with the Lord, and she was ready for the first time to look at herself. From the information she gave me, I pictured her husband as a Christian man who knew divorce was wrong, but was so tired of his wife's domineering manner, that he finally, after 25 years, got up the courage to leave, and did so. He had no understanding of his responsibility to rule in his home, and peace in his personal life was more important than continuing to struggle with his wife's controlling nature.

I was very straight with Genevieve about the control she had probably exercised over her husband over the years. I encouraged her to go to Bob and confess her domination and her unwillingness in times past to submit to him, but that with God's help, she wanted with all her heart to do so now. She agreed with my analysis, and eagerly went to talk to her husband.

He heard her repentance without comment. I'm sure he felt, after 25 years, it was simply a ploy to get him back. I believe Genevieve sincerely wants to change, but at this point Bob only wants freedom from a marriage that has made him feel like less than a man. He has not known how to rule, and without that knowledge, she has made it impossible for him to do so.

A matriarchal relationship like this so often fails because God has purposely affected marriage with His curse. He has designed this most intimate and important of all human relationships to be practically impossible apart from the restoration and the reversal of the curse that is in Jesus Christ. A woman was not created ever to be out from under the authority of a man; her father before marriage, and her husband after the wedding day. If she rejects (or loses) the authority in her life that is designed to produce a gentle and quiet spirit, the results will often be tragic. It is interesting to note that in the book of Revelation two women are used to illustrate spiritual truth; a beautiful Bride, the Church, in submission to her Bridegroom, Jesus Christ, and the rebellious whore of Babylon, out of control and in submission to no one.

When a woman recognizes within herself this penchant to want to control her husband, she should go to him and tell him that she knows she has resisted his authority and that she no longer wants to do so, asking for forgiveness. She should tell him that she needs him to give her direction and leadership, and she wants to do all she can do to establish him as her head.

There is tremendous power in submission like this; power that will make a strong man out of a husband who has been weak and vacillating; power that can give confidence to a husband who has felt inadequate and insecure; power that can make a man of God out of an immature, responsibility-shirker.

"Have you considered..."

Any discussion of submission is incomplete without a look at the process of appeal to authority. Certainly there are many times when a man has failed to consider all the factors before making his decision. Maybe his information has been incomplete, or possibly he has not considered all the ramifications of his decision, and therefore his determination may be flawed in a way he does not realize. It is important for the good of the family that his wife, and even his children, feel completely free to come to him with their disagreements, and that he be open to hear them.

A woman can say, "You're not listening to me," to her husband, and sometimes be right, but often those are code words for, "You're not doing what I want." Once her case has been presented clearly, a wife must leave the decision to her husband, and trust "the Power behind the throne," the Lord Himself, with the outcome.

Jill has learned over the years how to make appeals masterfully, as well as give me constructive criticism. She presents what she thinks and perceives about a certain situation when she has a different opinion of what should be done than I do, and then will quite often say, "I'm really glad I don't have to make this decision," reinforcing my concept of her confidence in my decision-making ability. I find myself being extremely careful before I make a decision counter to her opinion.

She criticizes me equally well. As I mentioned in Chapter 5, she will often see something I have done, or something I have said in a sermon, that is inappropriate or unwise, and will tell me so, always in a respectful way that does not denigrate me or make me feel stupid. My reaction is often, initially, to be defensive, and to try to explain why I said what I did. Jill then says very calmly, without trying to convince me that she is right, "What you do with this is up to you. I just wanted to point out to you what I noticed." More often than not, after thinking about the instance for a while, I realize that she is right. I need her to be honest with me and help me with my blind spots.

A woman will not be able to be a help-mate in this way unless she is free to disagree, to appeal and to give constructive criticism. But in that freedom she must disagree properly and preserve the integrity of her husband's leadership.

Love him personally

This brings us to the second way a wife can love her husband. After loving him "positionally," by submitting to his headship, she is to love him personally. Paul says in Ephesians 5:33: "...and let the wife see that she respects her husband." In the same way that men are told to dwell with their wives in an understanding way (1 Peter 3:7), wives need to understand their husbands as men. Men are different from women in some fundamental ways that are good, contrary to what feminism would have us believe.

Men have egos! Women commonly see this as a negative thing. But a man's ego is given to him by God for the work he has to do. A wise wife will respect her husband's manhood. A man has to lead his family, provide for them, protect them. All these things require ego strength to accomplish. It is necessary for him to go out into the world and compete, confront, conquer, to "stand in front" of whatever obstacles there are to his family's welfare. This requires personal confidence and strength.

Men are task and goal oriented from an early age. It is in the relationship with his wife that a man learns valuable lessons in how to have personal relationships. Have you noticed how little girls giggle (relate) and little boys tussle (compete)! A wise woman will affirm her husband's ego, not deflate it, because she will understand that it strengthens him for his vital work of taking his responsibilities as a husband. Nothing is more debilitating to a man than having his wife be disparaging about his manhood.

The characteristic that women dislike in some men is egotism, not ego. Egotism is an inordinate concern with one's self to the exclusion of others, whereas ego is the element of being that enables a person to have the capacity to think, feel and act. Egotism is a sin, which is better left for God to deal with through a wife's prayer. A wife's part is to continue to encourage her husband's person and manhood in healthy ways through love.

Worlds to conquer

Men need work. The Dominion Covenant found in Genesis 1:26-28 gives man his job description for life. God made man in His image to subdue the earth and have dominion over it. A man needs to conquer his world, whatever it might be, to fulfill his portion of that mandate. For some men this world is lands.

My brother-in-law is master of his lands. His home sits on 100 acres upon which he has built a beautiful little lake. He is always working on his property, adding buildings, improving others, thinking about how he can increase his holdings or make things better. Another friend, whose world is his lands, has said jokingly that his ambition is to buy every piece of property that lies next to his. Of course if that were possible, he would then own the whole world! He is a very successful land developer.

Other men see their job as their world to conquer. They do so by improving their skills or getting promotions. One of our church elders is a fireman. He has advanced from a beginning fireman at age 20, to one of a small group of battalion chiefs in the Seattle Fire Department by retirement age. Another man is in city government and has to weather the political storms that come with every election in order to keep his job and advance. It is a real challenge, requiring great personal skills. These men are conquering their worlds, all for the kingdom of God!

Owning a business or company is another kind of world to conquer. These men shoulder all the responsibility and risk involved in

148

that world. As a teacher, or pastor, the world to conquer is the world of ideas. My son Adam is working on a PhD in History and plans to be a college professor. His office is stacked with books; his energy goes toward reading and thinking about ideas; his life goals have to do with changing the intellectual world through the power of ideas taught in the classroom.

A wise wife will understand this fundamental need that a man has, and will encourage her husband in his work and try to be a helpmate for him in it. She will not require him to have to choose between her and his work. She will not demand time or money that he cannot provide, but will, instead, be a good steward of the resources he provides her. It will help her tremendously to remember that this is the man that God gave her, with all his strengths, abilities, and weaknesses as well, and to love him as he is.

It is this fundamental need in men that explains why it is necessary for a wife to be sure that she does not usurp her husband's place as provider and conquerer. It is difficult for a man to cherish a wife who is competing with him in the area where God has given him responsibility and where God intends for him to express his manhood.

Are men sex-crazed fiends?

Men need sex. The second part of the Dominion Covenant is to be fruitful and multiply and fill the earth. It is God's plan for men to be the agressors sexually for the purpose of filling the earth! However, His plan was for that drive, which He has put into man, to be satisfied with "the wife of his youth." The filling of the earth was to be accomplished in an exponential way as each man did his part in his own family.

A Godly wife will understand that her husband has a God-given drive for sex that she does not have, and that he will generally want sex more that she does. She will not allow the prevailing ideas about the traditional male as a selfish, domineering brute, to infiltrate her thinking. The terrible sin and crime that results from the sexual drive inherent in men is the result of the fall and our departure from God's law. All men are not living a lawless, self-gratifying life. A normal, healthy, Godly man has a strong sex drive.

It is so like our all-wise heavenly Father to have a complete and perfect plan for this area of our lives. The purpose for sex is procreation, but in fulfilling God's purpose in God's way is great reward. It is the sexual union of a man and a woman that causes them to become one

149

and have the greatest intimacy that is possible on earth. It is the human relationship that God uses to show our relationship with Him. There is a plan for the protection of this sexual union called marriage.

The idea of marriage is a "theological" idea, not a "logical" one. This will be explained in more detail in another chapter. For our purposes here, a loving wife will know that, as she fulfills God's plan for her life through sex with her husband, she is bonding with him and forming a spiritual, one-flesh relationship.

Independence, the spirit of the age

A man needs a wife who knows how to love him personally. The Bible is full of evidence for this beginning with Gensis 2:18 where the Lord said that it is not good for man to be alone. At this time in our history, men go out to work and have to deal with the women of the age every day. Show him another kind of woman when he comes home. Ask God to help you be a good wife, one who is a crown to her husband (Proverbs 12:4).

Are you willing to contribute to his success and see it as yours, too, without having to be a success on your own? Are you willing to be one with him; identified with him? We cannot be autonomous. It is an illusion; a deception of Satan. 1 Corinthians 11:11 says, "Nevertheless, neither is man independent of woman, nor woman independent of man, in the Lord." To be a biblical wife, a woman must be vigilant against the spirit of this age which pits women against men, and encourages women to be independent of their husbands. The war between the sexes is suicide. In Proverbs 8:32-36 the Bible discusses the wisdom of following God's ways and the foolishness of rejecting them. The passage ends with these words: "All those who hate me (and My law) love death."

God's way is that a woman love her husband in his person as we have discussed, and she will discover God's way to be a path to life for her.

A true helpmate

The final way a wife is to love her husband, after positionally, and personally, is practically. As I suggested in Chapter 4, a man is called to a task, while a married woman is called to her man. She is his helpmate, designed by God to assist him in his mission, whatever that may be.

Sometimes it is very easy to see how a wife can love her husband in this way. My friend Ron is an excellent optometrist, but always struggled to find the right office manager to run his office. Finally, in near desperation, his wife Linda, whose children were in high school, agreed to fill in on a temporary basis. Suddenly there was peace and harmony in the office. Linda, who has excellent people skills, was able to take from Ron the burden of hiring assistants and dealing with personnel, and he was able to do what he does best, take care of his patients. Linda loves working with her husband every day, and she soon found that she became an "older woman" spiritually to the young girls who work there as assistants. This "experiment" started some ten years ago and is still running smoothly.

My son Jason's basketball coach in high school always did the little extras that make for a well-planned, well-organized program. Pizza and ice cream feeds at his house, meetings with moms and dads, slick-paper game programs with player biographies and statistics, and dinner together with all the parents and players before tournament games made playing for Larry a real experience. Going 22-3 didn't hurt either! The person who made a lot of it happen was Linda, Larry's wife. She was always behind the scenes, doing many of the extras, helping to give a small-school basketball program a big-school feel. She was just as emotionally involved as Larry was, even though she didn't teach pressure team defense.

If your husband is in a vocation that does not allow you to actually work with him, your assistance will be more subtle. Do you make his home as pleasant and enjoyable for him as possible? To find peace there instead of strife is a blessing to any man, and your recognition of the primacy of his will in the home brings that peace. Do you discipline the children faithfully in his absence as he desires, or do you make excuses for them? Do you carry out his wishes in the area of money to the very best of your ability or do you follow your own guidelines? These are areas that a woman's practical obedience demonstrates the degree to which she has learned to love her husband in a practical way. Jesus said, "If you love me, keep my commandments" (John 14:15). Talk of love without obedience is just that - talk.

Who is whose helpmate?

As a young man, Jim was self-employed, working out of the home as an author. He was able to be with his young family much of the day, often helping his wife Lisa with household chores and the care of their pre-school children. As his reputation grew, so did his responsibilities, including a visiting professorship at a Christian college, and he was not able to do what he had done previously at home. Lisa relates how his absence was initially irritating to her, because, in his absence, her responsibilities grew as well, and they were not as glamorous and exciting as Jim's. Another source of frustration was that, as an accomplished artist, she had not been able to pursue her painting as actively as she would have liked because of their growing family.

One day she realized that she was called to be Jim's helpmate; to be of assistance in any way possible to him, as he pursued his call, which was not to make her homemaking easier. When he could, he did, but that was not his call! When she saw this, there was a release into a new freedom.

As she told Jill and me this story, she was radiant with her understanding of this truth; the truth of losing her life in her husband's. She marveled at the opportunities the Lord was providing for her to paint in the midst of her responsibilities as a homemaker, even to the possibility of a commission portrait of a national leader.

What if a woman feels called to the mission field? What should she do? She should pursue that call, under the authority of her father, as a single woman, until God brings along a young man to be her husband with a similar desire. If He does not, she should remain single. She should not expect to have her husband go with her to the mission field if that is not his calling in life. He is not her helpmate. She is his, and when she marries him, his name, his vision, and his calling, all become hers.

A message from Mars

I know that if this is the first time you have heard these ideas, they are probably so foreign to you that you may have trouble seeing any possible application of them to your life. Even if you are a Christian and a regular church-goer, our culture has so successfully pressed us into its mold that the concepts presented in this chapter seem ancient and outdated, and even a little foolish. However, as I point out in Appendix A, God is an unchanging God with unchanging standards ("The entirety of Your word is truth, and every one of Your righteous judgments endures forever" [Psalm 119:160]), and even though times have changed, human nature has not. Relational problems remain the same.

As a woman gives herself to learning to love her husband by making God's word "a lamp unto [her] feet and a light unto [her] path" (Psalm 119:105), she will experience the blessings God gives to those who obey Him. By submitting to her husband's headship, by reverencing or respecting him personally, and by offering to him all her gifts and abilities to help fulfill his calling, she will experience freedom (Psalm 119:45), peace (Psalm 119:65), and "great reward" (Psalm 19:11). I believe that reward of which the Psalmist speaks is at least two-fold.

First, she will radiate that gentle and quiet spirit so precious to God that becomes to her an imperishable beauty that does not fade away with age. Every woman wants to be beautiful, and she does all she can, with what she has, to appear as physically attractive as possible, but she knows that physical beauty is very, very temporary, and will one day be completely gone. "We do not look at the things which are seen, but at the things which are not seen. For the things which are seen are temporary, but the things which are not seen are eternal" (2 Corinthians 4:18). Happy is the woman who has realized this great truth in her youth, and has spent her early years, while she is still physically attractive, developing imperishable beauty.

Second, she will experience the joy and satisfaction that only comes from fulfilling God's purpose for her life. She was made for such a time as this, for such a task as this. She is a woman of destiny, for as she gives herself to God's great purpose, out of her life will come a heritage of men and women who will become weapons for God to use as his kingdom covers the earth.

"Father, as a woman, I want to have a gentle and quiet spirit. I know this is not a function of personality, but an inner spiritual dimension that only women of God can possess. Show me how I fall short, and by Your Holy Spirit, smooth off my rough edges. Use my husband (or my mother and father) to help me. Amen."

Questions for discussion

1. Do you have an "older woman" in your life? How has she helped you? In what ways could you be helped by her ministry? Discuss ways that this ministry in the church can be made to be more effective?

2. How does an understanding of the woman's role in the family change your perspective on getting married? What precautions should be taken? What are the qualifications you would look for in a future husband?

3. How do you feel about the idea of submitting to your husband in everything? What if he "does not obey the word?"

4. What do you think about being your husband's support and helper, even to the extent of losing your own dreams and ambitions in his? Can you do this with joy? Why or why not?

5. Discuss the relationship between submission and a gentle and quiet spirit. Can you have one without the other? Why or why not?

[1] W.E. Vine, *An Expository Dictionary of New Testament Words* (Old Tappan, NJ: Fleming H. Revell Company, 1966), Vol. IV, p. 86.

Chapter 10

Homemaker - A Multi-talented Professional

At my daughter Ramah's Christian high school, the seniors took a career-survey class in which all the students, girls included, were encouraged to think in terms of independent career choices. The only girls who volunteered that they wanted careers as wives and homemakers were Ramah and a few other girls from our church. The idea was perfectly acceptable to the teacher, and was not ridiculed or made light of by the students, but it was interesting that there were only a handful of these Christian girls who would admit to such a desire. I suspect there were many more who harbored a similar ambition in their hearts, but somehow had been made to feel that doctor, lawyer, or engineer were more challenging professions. There is absolutely no reinforcement in the culture today of the idea that a full-time homemaker is a desirable, first-choice profession. The subliminal message is that homemakers must not have been capable of landing any other job, because homemaking is generally never mentioned as a legitimate career option, and is even ridiculed by the militant, gender feminists.

This Christian school was completely neutral, and, as a matter of fact, the teacher asked Jill to come and present the option of homemaking as a career to the students.

Is that what homemaking is? Only one career option among many for our Christian young women? Or should we be actively encouraging them in that direction? Before the watershed years of the 1960s, when our culture still bore a semblance of our Christian heritage, vast numbers of female college students still majored in "Home Economics," not to pursue a career as a professional dietitian, interior decorator, or fashion designer, but in anticipation of homemaking as a career. Does God have an opinion on the matter?

Every woman will be a homemaker. The question is, what will she make her home to be? If she is also an engineer or a lawyer, or holds down some other full-time job outside the home, home will be a place to sleep and catch a few hasty meals, a place to refuel for the real race that is occurring somewhere else. It will be a place for a mother to try to have "quality time" with the children on weekends after five days of sending them to day-care, or seeing them for a few fleeting minutes each evening after giving the cream of her energy to her job.

Home as the hub of ministry

On the other hand, a full time homemaker can see her home as a destination stop, not a place to eat and sleep on the way to somewhere else. As she creates her "work-place" to be an expression of herself, rather than a house with furniture in it, it can become the hub of a potentially powerful ministry, first to her family and then to the world around her.

House-husbands?

Before we go any further, I have assumed something I need to try to support with some Biblical evidence, and that is that the wife is the homemaker and not the husband. In this day of unconventional relationships, what is wrong with a "house-husband" who stays home while the wife goes out to make the living?

As I mentioned in Chapter 5, a part of leadership as the head of the family is provision. In 1 Timothy 5:8, Paul very clearly places that burden on the shoulders of the husband, for at least two reasons. **First**, a woman is not designed by God to carry the weight of that responsibility, and when she must, for whatever reason, there is an emotional, and even a physical price that is paid. We do not change God's design with impunity. **Second**, if a woman is providing for the family, it is much more difficult for her to remain in her role of submission to her husband. "He who pays the piper calls the tune," is not scriptural, but it is an old English proverb that I believe is most often true. The one who is the breadwinner will naturally gravitate to a leadership position in the home, and will tend to be the policy-setter.

In Titus 2:5 women are actively admonished to be homemakers, and nowhere do the scriptures advocate that men should do so. In Proverbs 31, the chapter that delineates all the activities available to a "virtuous wife," the home is called "her household" four times, indicating an area of specific responsibility given to the wife. Her husband, who generally functions outside the home in his capacity as provider (though not always, i.e., the author in the last chapter), has delegated the area of the home to her, and, as we will see shortly, that includes authority over a rather wide range of responsibilities.

The Biblical pattern, then, is that the wife be the homemaker and not the husband. Any other pattern will have adverse affects on the home as a functioning hub of ministry.

Home as a ministry to husbands

We saw in the last chapter that one of the ways a woman can love her husband practically is to create a home for him that is a pleasant haven where he can be refreshed and recharged for the task to which God has called him. Well-decorated and clean, peaceful and orderly, home can not only be a place of physical blessing, but a source of life and encouragement when a wife sees the home as a spiritual oasis for her husband. Her vibrant spiritual life can be like water in a desert to him, particularly when being "in the world but not of it" has been particularly exhausting. As a wife matures in the Lord, she will become more and more of a helpmate in this way, producing more spiritual capital than she consumes.

Nothing is more satisfying to a man than to come home to his kingdom, his home, and find that in his absence it has been well maintained. His policies have been carried out carefully, and his wishes have been anticipated, because his wife knew his heart and wanted to please him in all things. She has followed his directives even in areas where she might not totally agree with him, because she has accepted his rule in the home and in her life. A woman who has learned to do this is the one whose "worth is far above rubies. The heart of her husband safely trusts in her" (Proverbs 31:10,11). She has discovered the key to using the home in ministry to her husband.

This might seem idealistic and unattainable to women who are already married and in a situation unlike this, and, in a sense it is, but so are all the standards God lays out for us in Scripture. However, we do not ignore them and go our own way because they are idealistic, but acknowledge that they are the goals toward which we reach, and embrace them, recognizing them as "the upward call of God in Christ Jesus" (Philippians 3:12-14). In this passage, Paul sees his imperfections

("Not that I have already attained, or am already perfected"), but is not discouraged because of his failures ("forgetting those things which are behind"), because he is confident of his forgiveness for those shortcomings and his standing with God ("Christ has also laid hold of me"). In the same way God is calling us "to press toward the goal" God has set for us as husbands and wives.

Home as a ministry to children

Children, warriors for the Kingdom of God in the next generation, are most effectively trained in the home by the parents. Line upon line, precept upon precept, this training constitutes potentially the most far-reaching ministry those parents will ever have, because their influence, their deposit in the lives of their children, can reach down through the generations in their posterity.

Modern technological society, with its emphasis on impersonal function rather than personal relationship, has subtly communicated the perception that a day-care worker, or some other surrogate parent can do as good a job of caring for a child as the parent can. Maybe even better if they are "trained professionals." Someone else can take the kids to Little League, or dance rehearsal. Somebody else's mother can be a teacher's aid at school. They will do just as good a job as you would, or so the reasoning goes.

That may be true, if parenting requires only the function of meeting physical needs. However, there is much more to parenting than this. Children who have grown up knowing that they are more important to their parents than anything else (and to a child, this is communicated by "being there") are eager to adopt their parents values and philosophy of life. They do so very naturally, because God has built into them a desire to be like their parents. On the other hand, those who know in their hearts that they were not at the top of their parent's priority list will often look elsewhere for direction for their lives, and even sometimes actively reject their parent's lifestyle. There were needs other than physical ones that were not met for them because the home was not utilized fully as a place of ministry.

Home as a center of life and service to others

The Bible has a great deal to say about the ministry of hospitality. Being hospitable is one of the qualifications to serve as an elder, and it is mentioned in both 1 Timothy 3 and Titus 1. The word is *philoxenos*, and means "love of guests."[1] We are to be hospitable to other Christians (1 Peter 4:9), and also to strangers (Matthew 25:34-36).

As believers and unbelievers alike enter a home to partake of the hospitality of a family functioning as God designed it to function, they cannot escape the powerful witness of the presence of the life of the Lord. Jesus Christ is expressed in a living model of God's plan for family life.

When the home is seen as a full-time ministry hub with the wife as residing homemaker, opportunities for service to the needy are everywhere. Temporary house-guests are an excellent way to extend the love of the Lord.

Within one two-year period our home was "home" to a newly married couple with a baby who were starting a new business and could not afford rent (5 months), a single young man who came into our church as a new Christian, with no Christian background, and no understanding of the Christian life or what a Christian family could be (3 months), some old friends (our age) who had recently moved to Seattle and needed a place to stay while going through the transition to a new location (6 months), and their son and his wife and three young girls, all under 6, who have just moved here as well (2 months). Currently a single man who is estranged from his wife resides with us as he pursues the healing necessary to restore his marriage.

Each of these instances represents ministry to the needy in some way or other, that would have been very difficult if Jill had not been a full-time homemaker.

Not everyone can open their home in this way because of space limitations, or because of family needs. We have the room, and our children are either grown and gone, or almost grown, and the need for private family time is not so great. The issue is not to do what we do, because every family is different, but to grasp the vision of the home as a dynamic source of ministry where the life and vision of the Kingdom is shared with others.

Exceptions to the rule

So far in this chapter I have tried to show that the biblical standard for the career of a married woman is homemaker, and this is the ideal we should work to attain. However, let me be very clear in saying that this is not meant to imply that a married woman should <u>never</u> work outside the home. Obviously there are circumstances that arise that might necessitate a wife entering the work-place.

In the last chapter, I mentioned the optometrist whose wife works in the office with him every day, and serves him in a way no one else could. For her, the office has become a hub of ministry, while her home, even though she is not there every day, is still effective, particularly as a temporary home for the needy.

Another man at Tree of Life has been without a permanent job for two years. He is very talented, with a wide range of skills. But with four boys, two in college, and two in high school, his sporadic, temporary employment has not covered the family's expenses. His boys have worked, and his wife has held down a very responsible position at a university during this time. Her salary has covered their house payment each month. Still, her testimony, as well as her husband's, is that as soon as possible, she wants to return home as a full-time homemaker.

The most difficult situation of all is that of the single mother who must work to support herself and her children. Sexual liberation and no-fault divorce have dealt a tragic blow to women, the very ones whose self-proclaimed feminist leadership has fought so hard to "free them from their husband's domination." "Being free" has included being free from a husband's obligation to stay with his family as a means of economic support. Most of these single mothers must now be the only family breadwinner and find child care for their children, even though they would like nothing better than to stay home with them. What can they do? In today's society, even if the single mothers are church members, their church is often not patterned after the New Testament community, with intimate, caring relationships with people who would do everything in their power to help. Many churches have become nothing more than religious organizations to attend on Sunday. The single mother is basically on her own, with only the ever-present state to offer assistance. The biblical model is for the church and family to meet her needs.

The Bible teaches in Deuteronomy 24 that God cares for women and children who are without the protective covering and provision of a man. In the Old Testament, land owners were not allowed to reap their harvest a second time because what remained after the inefficient first harvest was to be gathered by widows and orphans. It was necessary for the women to work; there were no handouts, but God provided for their needs. I believe God has a special provision for those single mothers who find themselves in the position of having to spend all day away from their children. He will strengthen them and multiply the effectiveness of their time with their children. As they walk in obedience to Him, trusting Him to provide, He will put them in a church with elders who take seriously their charge to care for the sheep that God has given them, and who, along with other church members, will help with child training and other tasks that are very difficult for a woman to do alone.

A homemaker's job description

As we drive by road construction crews and notice the inevitable woman holding the "Slow-Stop" sign, Jill and I often comment on how challenged she must be in her career. We have determined, after much observation, that she must master three hand motions, with several possible variations, before she can really be a success at her job. First, the wrist-rotation motion to turn the sign from "stop" to "slow," and the reverse-wrist-rotation motion to turn it from "slow" to "stop." Second, there is the arm-pointed-downward-at-45-degrees-with-index-finger-extended motion, indicating the path approaching cars must take. Finally, there is the up-and-down-flattened-palm-open-to-the-ground motion, indicating "Slow down!" This hand motion demands coordinating rapidity of motion with speed of oncoming car, communicating a sense of urgency. The career(!) sign-holder must be able to do all these motions with either hand, and also have mastered the infinite number of combination hand motions that it might be necessary to perform, i.e., "oncoming car, in wrong lane, going too fast." How much more challenging and fulfilling this career must be than just being a homemaker!

This is a humorous example of a phenomenon occurring everywhere in our culture; women leaving the career to which God has called them, which is homemaking, and entering areas traditionally, for good reason, reserved for men. My intention is not to belittle a sign-holder who is a single mom who would rather be home with her children, but she has to work, and she has found a lucrative job. I'm simply saying that God's first call to His daughters is to be homemakers, and it is there that the greatest fulfillment lies.

There are a wide range of job possibilities open to women today that were not available to them 30 years ago. How can being a homemaker possibly compare to some of these exciting, challenging opportunities? Is it possible for a talented, intelligent young wife to really be stretched to the limits of her abilities if she stays home and manages her household? In Proverbs 31:10-31, the Bible paints a rather interesting picture of what the term "homemaker" entails, by relating a composite woman who embodies the spirit of a biblical homemaker. I want to go through that section and pick out some significant details that shed new light on the term, "homemaker."

"What am I worth?"

Proverbs 31:10-12. Here the groundwork is laid for the homemaker's job description, as her relationship with her husband is emphasized. She is said to be a "virtuous wife," whose "worth is far above rubies" (vs 10).

The estimation of the worth of a diligent homemaker was far different when these words were penned than it is today. Homemakers are often asked, "Don't you work?," and are jokingly accused of always being "barefoot and pregnant." Upon meeting new acquaintances in today's society, homemakers know they will face the inevitable question, "And what do you do?" They also know the uncomfortable feeling they experience as they search for an answer. They feel compelled to say something besides, "I'm a homemaker," because in today's society that's not really acceptable. Our culture says to women who choose homemaking as a career, "You don't do anything really worthwhile. You are just a homemaker."

The Bible views homemaking, as presented in this chapter, as an honorable role, both demanding and fulfilling. As a woman performs it diligently, it qualifies her for praise and honor from God, her husband, her children, and the whole community.

Her husband trusts her

Her "husband safely trusts her" (vs.11) for two reasons. **First**, he has confidence in his wife to manage his household competently, as a good steward, and actually increase the value of their estate ("He will have no lack of gain"). **Second**, "she does him good and not evil all the days of her life" (vs. 12). He trusts that in his absence she will carry out all his policies just as if he were there. She understands Kingdom living to such a degree that she represents her husband and his will in all that she does. He knows this, and "safely" trusts her with all he has, because she has rejected the "right" to act autonomously and desires to please him in all she does.

Just like Nordstrom

Proverbs 31:13,18-25. In these verses, the virtuous woman is portrayed as going through all the necessary steps to insure that her family is properly clothed, and in the process of simply caring for them, she discovers a ministry to the needy, and a profitable home business as well.

In verse 13 she finds the raw materials (wool and flax) from which she makes cloth with her hands (scarlet and purple from the wool, and linen from the flax) in verse 19.

In verse 20, her hands (mentioned five times in these 3 verses), that have worked so diligently to clothe her family, now reach out in compassion to clothe the poor with some of the fruit of the labors of those hands. The homemaker sees her home, and what she has created there, as not only for herself and her household, but for the needy as well.

Verses 21 and 22 describe for us the clothing the virtuous woman has made. Because of her diligence and perseverance in providing for her family, she has become very accomplished in fashion design (vs. 18). She is concerned that she, as well as other family members, are presented attractively, and her clothing is now of such quality and style that she can start a home business of designing and marketing what she has made, both wholesale and retail (vs. 24).

Her husband, who, in this case, is well known in the community as an elder, has high visibility as he sits in the gates, and has been a very effective model for her creations, so that the word of her skill has spread (vs. 23). She has made him "look good" to those he meets during the course of his day.

Notice that this has all been accomplished while the virtuous woman remained in the home, simply doing what had been given her to do in an excellent fashion. An outreach ministry, and a profitable business, were both spin-offs of caring for the clothing needs of her family.

Verse 25 is a reminder to us, that, just as real beauty is not external, but is a gentle and quiet spirit, the virtuous woman's real clothing is "strength and honor," not what she has made with her hands, and will cause her to "rejoice in time to come."

A chef in the Kingdom

Proverbs 31:14-15. These two verses communicate some very interesting ideas about how this virtuous woman views her responsibility to feed her family, one of the main tasks of a homemaker.

She definitely was not the kind of cook who looks at the clock at 6:00 P.M. and says to herself, "What shall we have for dinner?" Verse 14 says that she "brings her food from afar," or, she has interesting and unusual meals that have variety, demand planning and creativity, and sometimes require special ingredients that are not available at the corner convenience store. That does not stop her from preparing the meal. She does what is necessary to get the ingredients, for she is an accomplished chef, not a short-order cook. She not only prepares excellent meals for guests, but for her family as well, because she sees that as a very important part of her ministry to her husband and her children.

Her meal preparation often demands an irregular schedule, so she must, on occasion, arise before dawn (vs. 15a). She understands the importance of mealtime, and the stability it can give to a family, so she does whatever is necessary to be ready, and to make it special.

There is always enough food for guests who might be in the home, and all who enter her home feel welcome to "stay for dinner." and there is certainly also enough for the young girls who help her run her household (vs. 15b)

There's still more to be done!

Proverbs 31:16,17,26,27. Clothing and feeding her family, and the activities that resulted from those tasks, were the basic functions that a virtuous wife performed. However, Proverbs 31 includes a number of other opportunities for her to display her abilities. In verse 16a she is seen to purchase a piece of real estate, and her deliberations before the sale are mentioned as if to let us know that she was not simply acting as her husband's agent. He must have recognized her proficiency in this area and given her free reign to make real estate decisions herself, probably using his family capital. This must be the source of "he will have no lack of gain" in verse 11. By her purchases their estate is growing.

From her profits from her home business (Her clothes are selling well!), she plants a vineyard, probably on the land she has just purchased (vs 16b). This means the land will be productive and justify its acquisition. She did not spend all of the profits from her home business on herself and her own desires, but is wise enough to plow a portion of it back into a producing investment, the vineyard, and uses its harvest either for the family, or to continue to build the family estate with the sale of the grapes.

This homemaker somehow finds the time to "gird herself with strength," and to "strengthen her arms," in verse 17. These terms are redundant if they both refer to the same thing, exercise sufficient to keep the virtuous wife in physical shape. The second phrase refers to just that, but the first phrase, I believe, is a reference to the supply of spiritual strength she draws from God to accomplish all she must do as a homemaker.

"She opens her mouth with wisdom," in verse 26a, implies some form of teaching, either the instruction of her own children at home, or teaching, both formally and informally, in her capacity as an older woman in the community. She is certainly qualified, because "on her tongue is the law of kindness" (vs. 26b), not malicious gossip. She is an example for the younger women in this regard, for the area of the tongue is the most difficult area of life for us to master (James 3:8).

The final task mentioned in the job description of this ideal homemaker is in verse 27a: "She watches over the ways of her household." This indicates her administrative ability to coordinate the efforts of all who help her; her children as well as her servants. They are all responsible to her, and she leads them with grace and kindness. She does not use her children and servants to evade work herself, for she "does not eat the bread of idleness" (vs. 27b). Her leadership is by example.

That is the job description of the virtuous women as described in Proverbs 31. It would take Wonder Woman to actually work all of that activity into a day! God is communicating to us, not that all of that must be done by all homemakers, but that when one of His daughters goes to work for Him, in His family business, He has real work for her to do that is demanding and challenging.

In the next chapter we will apply this portion of Scripture to today, and look at what happens to the woman who decides to take God up on His challenge.

"Father, give me eyes to see my home as a hub of ministry, to my husband, my children, and the world. Help me to see all the tasks that I must do there the way you see them, and then give me vision for the results that you will bring out of my efforts. Amen"

Questions for discussion

1. Discuss some ideas you might have to make your present or future home a "hub of ministry" to your husband. What difficulties do you see in doing that?

2. Repeat question 1 for your children, and then for the world.

3. Which of the activities performed by the homemaker in Proverbs 31 do you feel are not applicable today? Why not? What other activities should be there in today's society? Why?

---

[1] W.E. Vine, *An Expository Dictionary of New Testament Words*, (Old Tappan, NJ: Fleming H. Revel Company, 1966), Vol. II, p. 235.

Chapter 11

The Application of Proverbs 31 Today

Proverbs 31 was written several hundred years before Christ to people living in a culture far different from 20th century America. Much of what this composite, ideal homemaker did is not necessary today because of our modern technology. Her servants have, of course, been replaced by electrical appliances, so her administration and organizational skills are necessary only for herself and her children, as she trains them to take responsibility, and organizes her own activities.

However, the spiritual principles presented in this chapter are timeless, and are as applicable today as when they were written. The foundational unit in the kingdom of God, and in society, is still the family, and in order for the family to function as an expression of the kingdom, its divinely-ordained authority structure must be observed, with all family members operating within God's prescribed parameters. This chapter's concepts allow women to do just that; live life within the boundaries that God says will produce the very maximum degree of fulfillment. As in every other situation in life, if we think we have a better idea of how married women should function than God does, we do so to our peril.

Dressed for the '90s

All the work required to clothe a family in biblical times is thankfully unnecessary today. Finding raw materials, making cloth from them, and then sewing the actual clothing by hand as the Proverbs 31 woman did, has been replaced by merely going to the store and purchasing the needed items. While probably not demanding as much time or skilled labor, this is not as easy as it sounds to most men.

Women are often the butt of jokes because they always seem to be shopping, as if shopping were a pleasurable event that everyone loves to experience. But that is the case only if money is no object. For most women, it is necessary to shop, not simply buy, and shopping is very difficult. It means finding the very best clothes available, in terms of quality and attractiveness, at the best possible price, considering family budget restraints.

Remember, the virtuous woman outfitted her whole family. I believe that a woman is generally more concerned with dress than a man, and needs to take the responsibility to see that all her family is as well dressed as possible. That does not mean that other family members do not have an interest in their clothes, or do not go shopping on their own, but the wife needs to make it happen if necessary. If the husband is not interested in clothes, or has no feel for dressing appropriately, his wife must help him.

As our family was growing up, Jill would periodically take each of us shopping, determine what we needed to fill out our wardrobes, and help us with selections. The children always loved those shopping trips, and I always hated them, as I still do. I like to be dressed well, but I detest the process. I know spending money on clothes is necessary, but I hate it. I always enjoy wearing the new clothes, but Jill generally has to badger and cajole me until I finally give in and go. When I realized that Jill is just doing her God-ordained job, my attitude improved immensely.

Some women are masters at dressing their families on a shoestring. They never buy any items not on sale, and know all the best stores for bargains. Value Village can be a gold mine, but demands a lot of shopping to find the best deals. These women have taken seriously their charge to clothe their families in the best possible way, and still stay within their clothing budget.

I believe a husband should give his wife a certain amount of money each month that she must manage in order to meet household needs, including clothes for the family, if she is willing and able to follow his economic policy. He must trust her with that money, allowing her to spend it as she deems appropriate, and not try to micro-manage her expenditures. Remember, "The heart of her husband safely trusts her."

However, if she still struggles with submitting to her husband and wanting to please him in the area of money, micro-management is mandatory. If the husband did not learn to handle money properly as a child, and cannot budget his income successfully, the church needs to be available to help him in this crucial area, with financial seminars, or personal counselling if necessary.

Before we leave the realm of clothing, let me make one more comment. The virtuous woman herself, not just her family, was well clothed. A homemaker, in order to get done all she must do, needs a degree of self-discipline. She, in a sense, is her own boss in the short term, accountable to her husband ultimately. A part of that discipline is getting dressed each day just as if she were going out of the home to a job. She will not wear a business suit, but she needs to dress with pride. In God's eternal plan, the profession she represents is the most important profession a woman can enter.

One of the cliches about homemakers is that they are lazy, sloppily dressed, and lie around watching soaps and eating bon-bons all day. Dressing as well as possible, considering the tasks at hand for the day, communicates a belief that homemaking is God's first calling for wives.

The evening meal as family ministry

In another age, the evening family meal around the table was the climax of the day. It represented the one time of the day the whole family could be together. The experiences of the day were shared, the children received correction and instruction, and the Lord was honored after the meal. It was a bonding time where family unity was built, and direction and purpose for the family was communicated.

T.V. trays, Little League, school activities, and irregular work schedules, to say nothing of fast food restaurants, have made this time as rare as the Edsel. It is almost impossible to reserve this time for all family members to be at home around the table every night. But making it top priority, and accepting very few reasons for missing an evening meal, communicate its importance and improve attendance dramatically. This time can be one of the main weapons in the father's arsenal for imparting his vision to his family.

The meal itself is a critical part of the effectiveness of the event. If it is hastily thrown together with little thought, or if mealtime is habitually late, or not served at any particular schedule, the importance of the occasion is not communicated. On the other hand, if the homemaker has given herself to the planning and preparation of a substantial meal, well presented, at the announced time, the stage is set for the family to be built up and strengthened.

When Adam, Jason, and Ramah were young, our ritual around the table at night included a report from each child on important events of the day, including what was learned of significance at school. All listened as each child had the stage for his turn. I can remember many times explaining more fully some idea that had arisen, or going off on some tangent, following the questions of three young, inquisitive minds. "L..L..L..Let me show you on a napkin," uttered with my slight stutter, was a phrase I used often that we all remember with fondness today. Those times were crucial in imparting the idea that learning is important, and I believe they promoted a thirst for it as well.

Young children, particularly, need the structure this meal provides. Being dragged from pillar to post every evening, with no set schedule, and no regular meal, does not contribute to growing into secure young adults. Mother's meal preparation is foundational to everything else that can happen during this time.

"Are there two six o'clocks in the day?"

Breakfast is important too. I watched the young couple who were living with us at the time begin the day. The husband generally left for work shortly after 6:00 A.M. His wife got up with him while their girls were sleeping and prepared a light breakfast while he was getting ready, and then they had a brief time alone together. When he left, she went back to bed. She then fixed breakfast for her children when they got up. She was literally "arising while it is yet night" to "provide food for her household," fitting her schedule to her husband's.

Jill hates mornings, but she got up for years to make breakfast and school lunches for our children. She understood that children need a good, hot breakfast before they begin the day. This is a vital part of the homemaking profession. Eventually, as the children reach teen years, having them fix their own lunches is good training in taking responsibility.

The meal as ministry to those outside the home

The final aspect of food preparation that I want to consider is the impact it can have as a ministry to others outside the family, both believers and unbelievers. I believe the message communicated to guests invited into the home for dinner is more significant than is generally recognized.

In the Bible, providing a meal for a guest was a way of showing honor to that guest. In Genesis 19, Abraham was visited by three heavenly visitors, a physical, pre-incarnation appearance of Jesus, along with two angels, probably Michael and Gabriel. Abraham recognized them as, at least, being from God, and immediately, after bowing himself to the ground in greeting, went to Sarah his wife and told her to quickly begin preparation of a rather elaborate meal, including freshly baked cakes, butter, milk, and a freshly killed calf. This was Abraham's way of honoring such important visitors.

In the next chapter, the two angels visited Lot in Sodom to warn him of its coming destruction. Upon entering Lot's house, "he made them a feast, and baked unleavened bread, and they ate" (Genesis 20:3).

In the New Testament we see the same pattern. Jesus, as a distinguished teacher, was the honored guest at meals, or feasts (Luke 5:29-32; 7:36-39), he used the concept of bestowing honor at feasts in His parables (Luke 14:18-24; Matthew 22:1-14), and at the Last Supper He inaugurated His New Covenant with the first New Covenant meal, with His disciples as His honored guests, with the bread and wine representing His own body and blood. Each Sunday, as we renew that Covenant with Him at Communion, we are in places of honor at His table, as He provides the ultimate meal for His people.

We need to recognize the importance of honoring others, and recapture this biblical custom by regularly inviting guests into our homes and providing a meal for them. In turn, as we partake of the hospitality of others, we should realize the honor that has been extended to us.

Using all her gifts

I love the virtuous wife's involvement in this next venture, because it must be so shocking to the reader who thinks a homemaker's only activities are "housework," and tasks that have to do with the children. She actually purchased a piece of property, and, as I mentioned in the previous chapter, she was not simply carrying out her husbands orders, but making the decision to buy herself!

Any talent, ability or gift a homemaker has should be used by her husband to further his goals for his family. I can imagine a scenario where a man marries a woman who has grown up with a father who was particularly adept at buying and selling property, either his own, or as an agent. She took an interest in his activities as a girl, and found she had a knack for evaluating real estate and anticipating the optimum time to buy or sell. Because of her interest, she even took some real estate courses in college, and when she married her husband, she already had a portfolio of several rental houses, which she was able to manage herself.

Her husband, on the other hand, had no real estate experience, and even though he was interested in acquiring some property, didn't have the time, nor the ability (he eventually would learn from his wife) to be successful. He would be a fool not to release his wife to exercise her ability to the fullest.

There are several things to notice here. **First**, she is not working outside the home as a real estate saleswoman. She is buying and selling her own property from her own home. She is on her own time, setting her own schedule, still able to care for sick children and other family emergencies. She does not have a career apart from her husband. **Second**, she continues under her husbands authority. He has delegated this job to her, and she does it at his discretion, though he wisely has given her complete authority. **Third**, her husband must still be responsible for the overall family finances, though he has given her a budget to manage.

Some men, who are not naturally gifted with money, and who have wives who are, use that as an excuse to give her the financial responsibility for the family. As the head of the family he must have that responsibility, and make overall financial decisions, though he has given his wife money to manage herself to carry out her own tasks, in this instance, to buy land.

The husband must help his wife to be sure that she is able to keep her many obligations in balance, not ignoring some tasks while overemphasizing others. As we saw, the ideal homemaker is an excellent manager and can do this, but that is a goal that all have not as yet attained.

The sky is the limit

The example in Proverbs 31 is real estate, but the principles are the same, no matter what the endeavor. The homemaker can pursue whatever her mind can conceive, if it meets the three criteria mentioned above. God is eager to see her employ all the abilities He has given her, because he gave them to her to be used. One can see that the problem feminists have with homemaking is not really that it limits women in any way. It is rebellion, a problem with the authority structure of the kingdom of God. They do not want to acknowledge that a wife must remain under the rule of her husband.

Let's stay in shape

Staying in shape is probably not as easy as it was in Bible times. Without electrical appliances, many of the tasks of the virtuous wife demanded more physical exertion than they might today. So, to remain physically fit in the 1990's often requires some kind of an exercise program. Jill hates to hear this, and has been known to say she would rather die young than exercise (I told her it was too late!), but the virtuous woman is concerned with both her physical and spiritual condition.

Physically, aerobics, swimming, biking, walking and any number of other activities will do the job, but the key is regularity. This is where good organization comes in handy again. To exercise hard for a week, and then do nothing for two, does little good, and only makes you sore.

Spiritually, fitness is 100% a function of faith. Bible reading, prayer, fellowship, and sharing one's faith with others are all good works, results of being spiritually fit, and of no value in getting you there. The most important truth a homemaker can grasp is that her personal, intimate relationship with her Savior is based on who she is to Him, not on what she does. The press of the day's activities will never quench the peace and joy of a woman who is resting in the arms of a sovereign Father who does not allow anything into the life of His beloved but those things He desires to be there. They are for her best interest, no matter how terrible they might seem. Discouragement, doubt, and fear give way to spiritual fitness in the face of this kind of faith.

Wisdom comes with years

One of the characteristics of youth is a feeling of invincibility. The young feel as though they will live forever. The reality of the transitory nature of life has not dawned upon them as yet. "As for man, his days are like grass;...For the wind passes over it and it is gone." (Psalm 103:15,16). An understanding of the certainty that each of us has but a finite number of days to live, in a way that affects one's life, is truth that is hard for the young to grasp just because they are young.

The Bible places a great deal of value on age ("elder," "older woman," etc.), because wisdom, the practical application of spiritual knowledge, is generally directly proportional to number of years lived. One of the tragedies of youth is often ignorance of this fact, and henceforth, along with the sense of invincibility, is a cockiness somewhat akin to the 16 year-old car-driver; just enough experience no longer to be properly afraid.

173

As a young man of thirty, I was convinced that I knew most of what was really important to know. I had been an enthusiastic evangelist on the college campus for seven years, and had learned to answer the objections and excuses college students had about the Christian faith so well that I was confident that I would never embarass myself as I talked to students about the Lord.

I had presented the gospel at meetings in fraternity and sorority houses and other living groups on campus, and had seen numbers of students respond. I was somewhat scornful of older pastors who did the "dirty work" of caring for a flock in a church, because they were not "on the front lines," and even though I didn't say as much, I didn't think there was anything much they could have taught me. I desired to serve the Lord with all my heart, but I was too ignorant, because of my youth, to have learned to appreciate the value of the full-orbed ministry of the body of Christ. He hadn't taught me that lesson yet.

Looking back today, from a twenty-five year vantage point, I am amazed at my ignorance at that time. I didn't even know enough to know what I didn't know! As a relatively young Christian in my twenties, I didn't understand the value of experience that only comes with age, and I was often too busy talking to be quiet at the appropriate time to listen with respect to those with more experience than I. During my thirties God gave me that opportunity, for which I am eternally grateful.

Paul's instruction to Timothy in 1 Timothy 4:12 to "let no man despise your youth," has been taken to mean, probably mostly by young people themselves, "don't let anyone hold you back just because you're young." In context, yes, he was to teach as Paul's apostolic representative, not neglecting his gift (vs.13), but in so doing he was to be careful to be an example by his conduct (vs. 12), including respect for older men and women (5:1), so that no one would feel he was arrogant, and not mature enough for the job Paul had given him to do. In other words, don't let anyone despise your youth because you are too arrogant to see that you don't know as much as you think you do!

Character flaws like arrogance are a part of all of our lives when we are young, and the Lord spends a life-time smoothing off those rough edges. With the young, He hasn't had much time yet for that process.

Words of wisdom

The homemaker in Proverbs 31 is obviously an older woman, because "She opens her mouth with wisdom, and the law of kindness is on her tongue" (vs. 26). She has lived long enough to have overcome the self-centeredness and brashness of youth, and has acquired wisdom, with its companion character quality, kindness. She has something to say. She is ready to "open her mouth."

Years ago, in getting acquainted with a member of the church we were attending, Jill was relating a bit of what her job in Campus Crusade for Christ had involved; speaking to girls in their living groups on college campuses. The response was perceptive, if indeed somewhat rude. "What did you think you had to say?" Jill realizes now that at that time in her life she probably didn't have a lot to say, but her new friend was not yet ready for the role of older woman herself, because the law of kindness was definitely not on her tongue!

Our society does not appreciate age as did the Hebrews, and as a result we often ignore those who have the most to tell us. Older women who have pursued the Lord and his Kingdom diligently throughout their lives, have had the time to have gone through the pressures and difficulties that make their experiences valuable to younger women. They should be valued as treasures in the church, and the younger women should honor and respect them, seeking them out as those with genuine life and wisdom to share. They are the women's Bible teachers, as they teach the format Paul sets out for older women to teach in Titus 2.

We need each other

To be organized is a wonderful gift to have as a homemaker. Completing the host of tasks she faces each day is certainly much easier if it comes naturally, as it does to many women. It is said of the Proverbs 31 woman that "She watches over the ways of her household (administrates her home in such a way that it runs smoothly), and does not eat the bread of idleness." As one woman said, after reading this chapter, "How does she have time to eat anything!"

A woman who is not naturally gifted in organization can feel very discouraged by the standards set here. She must realize that this is a composite woman, a fictitious woman, whom God is using as a standard, a standard that no one actually meets perfectly. Much of what this virtuous wife does are tasks that demand organization and the ability to push a job through to completion, and the organizationally gifted will shine here. Those who are not must be as disciplined as possible, and through hard work, achieve a measure of success in the task-oriented portion of her job.

However, God does not make mistakes in the giving of gifts and abilities. He does not give anyone all of them. The organizers do not need to feel too proud of being able to do well what God gave them naturally the ability to do, because often they have difficulty in relating to people. And, by the same token, frequently those without natural organization excel in the area of personal relationships. They are excellent with people, and find they have the younger women's ready ears because of their relationships with them. Often, more gifted organizers see the task as primary, and people get in the way of tasks. As one woman actually said to Jill, "Tuesday is my day to shake out the scatter rugs, and I don't want anyone to come by so I'll have to talk to them." This is a task-oriented woman who undoubtedly keeps a beautiful home with everything in order, but it is doubtful that she needs to worry about younger women coming by and interupting her cleaning to ask any questions, thereby profiting from her experience.

This is God's way of showing us that we need one another. We need each other's gifts to spur us to excel still more in areas in which we might not be naturally gifted. The highly-organized often need to learn to relate better with people, and need to learn from the relaters how to do so, while the relaters need to learn from their more task-oriented sisters how to better execute the jobs they must perform.

When women must work outside the home

We have taken a rather detailed look in this chapter at God's divine call to married women to be workers at home, and what that entails. What about those single women who as yet are not married, or who will never marry? What about widowed or divorced women? Of necessity, there must be a place in the work force outside the home for them, for it is often necessary for them to work to support themselves and their children. In Biblical times, fathers either continued that support, or picked it up again, but that is often not the case today.

It is important to see that God's norm for women is marriage, and this book's topic is the family. I am not attempting to deal with those atypical situations mentioned above, although I realize there are many women who find themselves in one of those circumstances. However, let me say just a brief word that might be helpful as a guide for single women who must work.

It is important to remember the quality that God prizes so highly in a woman; a gentle and quiet spirit. Employment should be in a position that does not hinder, or if possible, even enhances that spirit, though what a woman does will not guarantee that she will demonstrate this quality (A homemaker can certainly be contentious and ill-tempered). Confrontation or competition with men, or any type of corporate decision-making responsibility, does not reinforce the character God is looking for. On the other hand, the caring, nurturing professions can be a way for that to be expressed and encouraged. The medical profession (doctor or nurse) and the teaching profession are two of those avenues, and I'm sure there are others that would qualify as well.

Another consideration that bears brief mention is the susceptibility of women in the work-place to sexual advances, be they intentional or unintentional. Women are attractive to men, and sexual relationships generally don't start out intentionally. A lonesome woman is noticed by a man who is having trouble in his relationship with his wife, she gives him an open ear as he shares his problems, and an affair is born. This tragedy is replayed over and over again daily among Christians, and must be carefully guarded against when a woman goes to work outside the home.

The reward

We have now come to the last four verses of this famous chapter, and in them we see the reward that God promises to the faithful homemaker who is obedient to the Lord's word by determining to be the virtuous wife portrayed here. Salvation and God's gifts, talents and abilities are by grace, completely free and totally unmerited. However, the message of the Bible, from cover to cover, is that God's <u>blessings</u> and <u>rewards</u> are based on our faithfulness to do what He has asked us to do (Deuteronomy 28, Galatians 6:7-10, Matthew 25:14-30, Psalm 19:11, Proverbs 13:13 etc.). The reward promised here is consistent with the purpose for which God created woman, as we saw in Genesis 2, and makes all other rewards pale into insignificance.

In today's world of unlimited "opportunities" for women, they are free to pursue any glamorous, powerful, lucrative occupation they desire, and whenever possible, by government mandate, they are even given actual preference over men in entering those fields. What would make an enthusiastic, competent, intelligent woman choose to stay home, far from the spotlight, and be a homemaker?

Many non-Christians are discovering by trial and error that God's design for woman is the only one that works in the long term, and are coming back home, in some cases, because of physical or emotional necessity. But why would a young Christian wife start out her married life with the intent of being a homemaker?

The answer is in verse 30: "...But a woman who fears the Lord, she shall be praised." The fear of God is said to be the beginning of wisdom (Proverbs 9:10), and it is wise to do one's very best to please the awesome, all powerful, creator God (Jeremiah 32:17,27), from whom you cannot hide (Psalm 139:7-12), and who knows your every thought (1 Corinthians 3;19,20). It has been said, and rightfully so, that the Christian life can be boiled down to two things, and two things only; discovering what God wants me to do, and then doing it. When I understand the fear of the Lord, my life is given to that end.

The Proverbs 31 woman has done that very thing. She has discovered what God wants her to do (yes, He does have a vocational opinion for wives), and she is doing it, and the reward is, "...she shall be praised" (vs. 30b), a foretaste of the praise she will receive directly from God on "that Day," when He says, "Well done, good and faithful servant."

We saw in chapter 5 the kingdom principle of the one under authority living his life to please, and therefore bring praise and glory to, that one under whose authority he lives ("I have glorified you on the earth. I have finished the work which You have given Me to do" [John 17:4]). The one in authority then, in turn, honors and glorifies that one he has loved and led ("And now, O Father, glorify me together with yourself..." [John 17:5], "Therefore God also has highly exalted Him...[Philippians 2:9]).

Just as God the Father heaped glory and honor on His Son, who was obedient unto death, God showers praise upon that daughter who seeks to honor Him through her faithful obedience as a worker at home, praise that is more deeply satisfying than any other reward she could receive. His praise comes to her through three channels, according to the final four verses in this chapter.

Praise from three sources

First, "Her children rise up and call her blessed" (vs. 28). Those little ones who never seemed to notice or appreciate their mother's selfless giving, her unceasing encouragement, her tireless labors, her willingness to be inconvenienced, and her seemingly endless time for them and their activities, have now, in their adulthood, and in their mother's old age, given her the recognition she has earned. They remember!

I don't believe a mother could possibly have a better, more satisfying reward. My mother was in a nursing home for a few months before she died, and I watched the adult children of many of the elderly women who lived there. Some exuded love and care, and by their very actions, brought glory to their mothers, demonstrating what kind of mother she must have been. On the other hand, some came out of a sense of only duty or obligation, as infrequently as possible, probably reflecting the lack of time and energy their mother had given them as children. Faithfulness brings reward.

Second, "Her husband also, and he praises her, 'Many daughters have done well, but you excel them all'" (vs. 28b,29). This praise is from the one directly in authority over her, her husband, the one she is called to please, the one who has evaluated her work, and has found her praiseworthy. He is echoing God the Father's evaluation of His thirty-year-old Son at His baptism, that is today a model evaluation to be used by all who are in authority; "You are my beloved Son (wife, child, employee, etc.), in Whom I am well-pleased" (Mark 1:11). "Beloved," is a key word, because it is the husband's love for his wife that has called forth her outstanding performance as a homemaker.

The husband recognizes that there were other options open to his wife, if not other occupations in his day (there certainly are in ours!), certainly other attitudes besides the desire to please him, namely the independent attitude of seeking to please herself. His evaluation is not just of her external performance, but of her heart toward him, and therefore toward God.

Those around her may have thought that she was wasting her talents, not fulfilling her potential, or not being realistic by trying to live in another era. Even other homemakers may not have liked the way she ran her household, and unconsciously tried to make her feel guilty because she didn't keep house like they did, or didn't discipline her children right, or a thousand and one other ways she might not have measured up to their standard. She refused to listen to any of them, for it didn't matter to her what they said. She focused on pleasing only one person, God's delegated authority in her life, her husband, and now His public praise is her reward, an earnest toward God's praise on "that Day."

Third, even though there has been opposition and pressure on this homemaker to go another way, in the final analysis, even those in the world, when they see the "fruit of her hands," will have to praise her as well, though I believe sometimes grudgingly. They cannot argue with what they see; her marriage, her home, her children. Isaiah 2 says that the world, when faced with its own miserable failures, will one day come to the church and say, "...teach us His ways, and we shall walk in His paths" (Isaiah 2:3). I believe a great factor in that turning to the Lord will be Godly homemakers who have determined to be Proverbs 31 women.

The "big picture"

We saw in chapter 5 that our enemy, Satan, has stolen the excitement of history from our students by robbing it of its underlying purpose and meaning, a cosmic battle between two kingdoms. He has caused us to look through a microscope at the details and dates, and forget the telescope, through which we see the "big picture."

He has done the same thing with being a homemaker. He has caused us to focus on the individual tasks without the overall vision of the framework in which they fit. This is like a carpenter trying to build a house without a blueprint. He can saw boards and hammer nails very well; he can both frame and finish, even roof and install siding with masterful skill, but without a plan, and the ability to read that plan, the result will be very questionable, no matter how talented the carpenter.

The blueprint, the master plan, is the kingdom of God. Unless the homemaker can read the plan, and see how her calling fits into the kingdom, she is simply grinding out obediently a series of rather difficult tasks. She is focusing on the individual trees and missing the beautiful evergreen forest. She will miss the peace and joy that accompanies life lived self-consciously in light of the kingdom of God (Romans 14:17).

Two laborers were working side-by-side, diligently digging a ditch. The first man was grumbling unhappily, and looking at his watch every five minutes, while the second man, with a smile on his face, was singing joyfully as he worked.

"What are you men doing?" a passer-by asked, noticing the strikingly different demeanor of the two men. "I'm just digging a ditch," muttered the first man. The second man looked up, his face beaming. "I'm building a cathedral!"

What are you doing today? Are you just wiping noses, sweeping floors, washing clothes, and cooking meals, or are you building the kingdom of God, a cathedral made of living stones where God in all His fullness comes to dwell. That is your calling.

"Father, illumine my eyes to first <u>see</u> your kingdom in the calling of homemaker. Help me to see past the antagonism and ridicule all around me, the negative input, even from well-meaning Christians, to the glory of your calling. Then, give me the grace to <u>enter</u>. Amen."

Questions for discussion

1. In the application of the job description of the virtuous wife, which tasks do (will) you find easy to do and which ones are difficult? Are you an organized task-oriented person, or are you a "relater?" How do you know? Which one do others think you are?

2. Which activities in Proverbs 31 do you enjoy? Which ones do you dislike? Do you have to do them? What would make them more palatable?

3. What things does a homemaker miss that she could have as a woman working in the world? What things does a woman working in the world miss that a homemaker has?

4. Do you see how homemaking fits into the overall vision of the kingdom of God? How? Why not? Can you really see yourself as "building a cathedral?" How? Why not?

Part Four
"Experiencing Oneness"

Chapter 12

Know the Enemy

Practically every magazine, every billboard, every T.V. commercial pictures scantily clad young women selling everything from automobiles to cough syrup. Television and movies picture pre- and extra-marital sex as exciting and normal, and try to convince you that everyone who is not completely repressed or personally repulsive is "doing it." For example, the T.V. show *N.Y.P.D. Blue*, the big hit of 1993-94, featuring scenes with nudity, is said to want to "push the envelope" of on-screen sexual acceptability, in the words of the show's producer, Steven Bochco.

What has happened to the Christian moral fiber of our country? It seems that in only a few short years we have lost our moral bearings completely. Dr. Joycelyn Elders, former Surgeon General in President Bill Clinton's administration, in promoting condom distribution in high schools, was quoted as saying that we have taught our children what to do in the front seat of automobiles; now it's time we taught them what to do in the back seat.[1] Her advice to young girls; "I tell every girl when she goes out on a date - put a condom in her purse."[2]

Our nation's leadership is actually promoting immorality. What chance do we and our children have to remain sexually pure in what has become a "wicked and perverse generation"? I believe we have a good chance, if we understand that we are facing a very organized and well-defined enemy, and if we have a basic understanding of the nature of the "culture war" in which we find ourselves. In the next four chapters, I will attempt to equip the reader with the necessary information to be armed and ready; first, to be successful in standing personally against Satan's sex disinformation campaign; and then, to help in the battle to recapture our culture from one who is, to most

Christians, a shadowy, undefinable enemy. The purpose of this chapter is to expose our enemy.

Armed for war

We are to "occupy," or "do business," until Jesus Christ returns (Luke 19:13). We are to make disciples of all the nations (Matthew 28:19), and the gates of Hell will not prevail against our attack (Matthew 16:18). We are commissioned to capture the culture for the Kingdom of God by the power of the gospel, and to do that, we must be equipped with the proper knowledge of the battle and our available resources as God's people.

Many Christians are unaware that we are in a battle for the minds and hearts of our children, who are the next generation. They know nothing about the enemy's battle plan. Paul says that he is not ignorant of the Devil's devices (2 Corinthians 2:11). We too should be able to discern spiritually what is happening in the world, as were the "men of Issachar" (1 Chronicles 12:32), to chart a plan of action, and then be able to communicate that plan clearly to our children.

We have too often told them, "Don't get involved sexually," without giving any reason or explanation except, "The Bible says not to." The Bible tells us why not to as well, and we must give our children the "full counsel of God" if they are to be fully armed. The Lord said, "My people are destroyed for lack of knowledge" (Hosea 4:6). Our young people cannot be fully armed for the conflict today if they do not know why God says what He does about sexual purity and marital faithfulness. When all about them are going another way, an understanding of the reasons for keeping God's Law, and the consequences of breaking it, are an invaluable protection.

Know your enemy

In order to understand why our society is in a moral abyss, we must realize that we have gone through a religious paradigm shift since the tumultuous days of the late 1960s. Until that time there was a Christian consensus in America, a recognition of the validity of Christian moral values. We expected our political leaders at least to attend Christian churches, to be faithful husbands, and any hint of moral scandal generally meant the end of a political career. You didn't have to be a Christian personally to believe that sex outside of marriage was wrong, and pregnancy out of wedlock was a source of shame throughout society. The residual culture resulting from our Christian roots, with its moral absolutes, was still very evident, although the vital faith of our beginnings as a nation was but a memory. Without the root, the tree will eventually wither and die. Our nation's tree lasted over a century without much national root, but in the 1960's the leaves began to fall off in earnest. That decline has continued to the present.

Education of the young is crucial to the perpetuation of any ideology, because the ideas today's children adopt will be tomorrow's public policy. In the early 19th century, Robert Owen and Horace Mann, two educators who were very antagonistic to Trinitarian Christianity, understood this truth. Owen's ideas fueled the public school movement in Boston as Unitarians began in earnest to attempt to free future generations from what they saw as the repressive, guilt-inducing Christian religion.

Until this time, education in America had been primarily the responsibility of home and church, with a high degree of literacy as a result.[3] However, under the direction of Mann, as Secretary of the newly-created Massachusetts Board of Education, education gradually shifted from its libertarian, free-market base, to a centralized, government controlled bureaucracy, financed by property taxes.[4] As tax-supported government schools grew gradually in popularity, they soon came to a place of educational dominance in America.

In the early 1900's, John Dewey, often called the father of modern education, espoused the idea of socialization, rather than that of learning established truth, as the first goal of education. He felt that learning to read must be secondary to becoming a perfectly integrated and socialized "world citizen." He believed that literacy was even an obstacle to the socialist society he desired to build because it fostered the ability to acquire knowledge independently.[5] Dewey's thought has had a tremendous impact on education, and today's public schools are, to a great extent, a product of his work. He was an avowed Secular Humanist, strongly anti-Christian, and a signer of the first Humanist Manifesto. His influence in colleges and universities, particularly teacher's colleges which train teachers for government schools, has been profound. Secular Humanism has become the dominant world view in our nation, supplanting Christianity, largely because of his ideas.

It has taken almost 200 years for the vision of Owen, Mann and Dewey to come to fruition, but Humanism has finally become our unofficial national religion, with the public school system our state church, where Humanist doctrine is officially taught.

Subverting America

How has Humanism come to this position of dominance in our land? Satan has orchestrated a brilliant plan to subvert Christian faith in America. He has used a number of accomplices, who, if they had been acting alone, would not have been able to succeed.

First, Charles Darwin's theory of evolution surprised an intellectually flabby church, and drove God's people out of the marketplace of ideas into a "stained-glass ghetto" behind the four walls of the church. The concept of constant change with no absolutes has effected much more than biology, as evolution has been applied to law, ethics, politics, economics, and even history and literature, changing a fixed "original intent" in all of these disciplines, to a flexible adaptability in order to fit the Humanist agenda of the day.

Second, a liberal Supreme Court, sympathetic to Humanist goals, has eliminated any hint of Christianity from public life, relying on a fallacious interpretation of the First Amendment. The framer's original intent was never to separate God from state, but to keep state control out of the church. With Christianity gone from the public square, Humanism, with its situational ethics and moral relativism, now has complete free reign.

As a nation we tend unconsciously to follow our leaders. When the Supreme Court struck down all the state laws against abortion in 1973, the vast majority of Americans were against abortion. Now, polls show an equal number on each side of the issue. The courts have been a powerful influence for Humanism.

Third, Christians in great droves adopted a theology that made it easy to justify surrendering this world to the Devil, and only look ahead to the next world. Since these Christians felt incapable of competing intellectually against evolution, naturalism, socialism, ethical relativism, self-actualization, and other Humanist dogma, they adopted a brand of neo-platonism that allowed them to withdraw. They taught that "This world is evil and belongs to the devil. It is only the next world that is really important." "Don't get involved in politics, law, or the media, or any other position of influence, because that's dirty business. You can't do that and really be spiritual." Our young people were told that the ministry or the mission field, or some other "full-time work," is what you do if you are really committed to Jesus Christ. As a result, those positions of influence in our country are now occupied almost exclusively by Humanists. They set the legal agenda by which we must live in America.

Humanism as a religion

Religion is an inescapable concept. All cultures, all societies, and all nations spring from the worship of the religion of that particular nation. Buddhist culture in Tibet is a reflection of the thought and practice of the pursuit of Nirvana. Indian culture, with its aimlessness, mirrors Hinduism, Iranian militancy is the outworking of Islam. Likewise, Western Civilization, with its free enterprise and technological progress, of which the United States has been a part, is the product of Christianity. However, we are in the process of embracing, as a nation, the non-theistic religion of Humanism, the worship of man and his potential. Be assured that Humanist culture, with its attendant moral standards, or lack thereof, is sure to follow. Western civilization is now constantly attacked on our college and university campuses and in the media, and is presented as only one of many equivalent world cultures.

In *Torcaso vs. Watkins* in 1961, the Supreme Court said:

"Among religions in this country which do not teach what would generally be considered a belief in the existence of God are Buddhism, Taoism, Ethical Culture, Secular Humanism and others."[6]

Humanism was recognized as a religion by the courts. In the preface to the *Humanist Manifestoes I & II*, Paul Kurtz says:

"Humanism is a philosophical, religious, and moral point of view."[7]

John Dewey, who signed the 1933 *Manifesto* said:

"Here are all the elements for a religious faith that shall not be confined to sect, class or race...It remains to make it explicit and militant."[8]

Humanism is a secular, atheistic religion that is not recognized as such by most Americans. We are accustomed to only thinking of religion in terms of God, because of our Christian background. Therefore, we do not recognize Humanism as a religion. That is why the doctrine of separation of religion and government (or "church and state"), as interpreted by our present court system, is so vehemently insisted upon by Humanists. It has allowed them access to the public arena, while eliminating Christianity.

Humanist morality

All religions embrace some form of morality, or ethics. Our new national religion of Humanism is no exception. David Noebel, in his exhaustive analysis of today's competing world views, <u>Understanding the Times</u>, quotes from *Humanist Manifesto II:*

> "We believe that intolerant attitudes, often cultivated by orthodox religions and puritanical cultures, unduly repress sexual conduct....The many varieties of sexual exploration should not in themselves be considered 'evil'...individuals should be permitted to express their sexual proclivities and pursue their life-styles as they desire."[9]

Planned Parenthood has done much to further this philosophy and the "sexual revolution" which the Humanist cause champions. Faye Wattleton, one of the organization's recent presidents, was chosen as "Humanist of the Year" in 1986. She states that the organization's aim is not to stop teenage sexual activity through education, but to prevent teenage pregnancy.[10] One staff member of the organization stated that the goal of Planned Parenthood was to help "young people obtain sex satisfaction before marriage. By sanctioning sex before marriage, we will prevent fear and guilt."[11]

This is the morality that is being carefully promoted in our public schools through Sex Education classes. The Sex Information and Education Council (SEICUS) publishes literature that is used in classes throughout the nation. Listen to this quote from SEICUS Study Guide 5.

> "The choice of a premarital sex standard is a personal moral choice, and no amount of facts or trends can 'prove' scientifically that one ought to choose a particular standard."[12]

Study Guide 9 states,

> "The strict Judeo Christian codes inherited from the past, in which chastity is prescribed, are being challenged. Rational inquiry is replacing blind faith. A so-called "new morality" is being ushered in."[13]

190

Beginning in elementary school, students are bombarded daily with this type of moral relativism. It takes a very knowledgeable child to withstand the attack.

A battle to the death

Most Americans think "pluralism" is a wonderful foundation for our way of life. "We accept all faiths. You can believe whatever you want to believe and be accepted here. We have complete freedom of religion." However, to the founding fathers of our country, that meant freedom within the bounds of Trinitarian Christianity. The intent of the First Amendment was to guarantee freedom from federal interference in each state's **Christian church**, never to put Christianity on a par with every other religion! Humanism has used this misunderstanding of the original intent of "pluralism" to infiltrate our country, and eventually to take over the levers of power in our nation.

It is impossible for competing religions to dwell together in "peaceful coexistence," for an indefinite period of time. The God of Christianity is locked in mortal combat with the god of all other religions, Satan, with each side taking no prisoners. A "pluralistic society" is a myth. We have been able to talk about pluralism in America, but until this century we have not really lived it. Previously, Christianity, with its culture and value system, had no real rival. It was the *de facto* religion in America. Since the 60's, that has all changed dramatically. We now have pluralism, with Humanism currently in the ascendancy, but with no clear winner as yet.

More and more Christians are waking up to realize that the enemy has infiltrated the camp and has gained control. At the same time, the Humanists, who have been supremely confident because of their successful takeover of the positions of power in America, are resisting this awakening of the "religious far-right" with increasing alarm. "Hate-monger," "bigot," "homophobe," and "fundamentalist," are favorite terms used by the media and many of our nation's leaders to describe Christians who only want to see Christian morality return to our land.

Make no mistake, Humanism is a religion that will allow no rivals, and Humanists are panicked as they see the sleeping Christian giant beginning to stir. Our nation's leadership hasn't forgotten God, as some claim. They have tried to forget Him, but how do you forget a 400 lb. gorilla?!

What the Humanists understand and we don't, is that pluralism is but a transition state, existing while competing religions battle to an eventual victor. Marxism, Humanism's revolutionary first cousin, gained control of Russia in 1917, and proceeded to eliminate its rivals physically. That religion lasted 75 years in Russia. It finally collapsed under the weight of its own inadequacy, and the internal weakness that came from the hidden, unreported, advance of the gospel in thousands of illegal home churches. This is how Christianity will ultimately win the religious battle: By the power of the two-edged sword that comes from the mouth of Jesus - the Word of God (Revelation 1:16) - spread over the earth by His Body, the Church (Habakkuk 2:14). Whether our nation will succumb first as Russia did, is still unknown. Vital Christianity is our only defense.

Humanism is after our heritage. Humanists have used their educational disinformation campaign very successfully so far. We must educate our children in the truths of these next four chapters.

"Father, help me to see the enemy in the area of sex. I know that he is trying to capture me through ignorance, disinformation, and deceit. Open my mind to new truths, and make me ready to be obedient to you."

Questions for discussion

1. Give a brief history of how we got to where we are today, with Christianity banned from public life. Who played significant roles?

2. Explain how Satan's three "accomplices" mentioned in the chapter contributed to Humanist takeover in America.

3. Why is Humanism a religion? Why are the Humanists so enthusiastic about separation of church and state?

4. Explain what pluralism is, and why it will not be a long-lasting philosophy. What do you think would be the governmental structure God would want us to have as a nation?

---

[1] *New York Times*, September 14, 1993, p. C-9.
[2] *Ibid.*

3 Samuel L. Blumenfeld, *Is Public Education Necessary?*, (Boise, ID: The Paradigm Company, 1981), p. 42-47.

4 *Ibid.*, p. 184.

5 Samuel L. Blumenfeld, *N.E.A. - Trojan Horse in American Education*, (Boise, ID: The Paradigm Company), p. 53-71, 104-108.

6 David A. Noebel, *Understanding The Times*, (Manitou Springs CO: Summit Press, 1991), p. 33.

7 Paul Kurtz, ed., *Humanist Manifest I&II* (Buffalo: Prometheus, 1980), p. 3. Quoted in Noebel, p. 32.

8 John Dewey, *A Common Faith*, (New Haven: Yale University Press, 1934), p. 87. Quoted in Noebel, p. 33.

9 *Humanist Manifesto II*, p. 18, as quoted in Noebel, p.211.

10 Faye Wattleton, "Reproductive Rights for a More Humane World," *The Humanist*, July/August, 1986, p. 7. Quoted in Noebel, p. 211.

11 Lena Levine, "Psycho-sexual Development," *Planned Parenthood News*, Summer, 1953, p. 10. Quoted in Noebel, p. 211.

12 Ira L. Reiss, *SEICUS Study Guide 5: Pre-marital Sexual Standards*, October, 1967. Quoted in Noebel, p. 212.

13 Harold T. Christensen, *SEICUS Study Guide 9: Sex, Science and Values*, February, 1969. Quoted in Noebel, p. 212.

Chapter 13

The Place For Sex

I had been in this place many times over the years, but it never seemed to get repetitive. I knew the young couple who stood before me very well. I had watched the girl grow up with my daughter in our church, Tree of Life. Her fiance had joined with us about three years earlier as a college student, and I knew he wanted his future family, that was beginning on this day, to be a weapon God would use to extend His kingdom.

They both thoroughly understood the material in this book, and they had indicated during pre-marital counselling that they were eager to put it into practice. The sexual experience they would have later that night, and would continue to have as man and wife, would occur in the context that God intended. As they walked down the aisle after my announcement that they were now "husband and wife," I knew that God was putting together a new "one-flesh fighting unit." Publicly, that process was beginning here at the ceremony as they made public their covenant with one another, and their one-flesh bond would actually be formed that night as they went to bed together.

Sex was God's idea, and He invented it for a reason. It is a powerful engine that He uses to run His family business, and as with any motor, the operator must know how to use it before turning it on. God has left us an owner's manual, the Bible, and we need to follow its instructions carefully in order to achieve maximum results from this powerful engine that we find within our bodies.

The last thing most of us want to do is read the manual starting a new engine. We are so eager to begin the task at hand that we think we will learn as we go. But in the case of sex, if we don't follow the manual, serious injury to the operator will invariably occur! The instructions include the "where" for sex, which is the topic of this chapter, and the "why," which is covered in Chapter 14. "How" and "when" to turn on the engine is critical, because once it is running, it is almost impossible to turn it off! That is Chapter 15.

The marriage covenant

When the young couple mentioned above were married, they entered into a covenant with each other, and with God. They promised to do certain things, before all the witnesses who were in attendance that day. Today, marriage vows are often just a formality, but in this instance, I made it clear to this young couple that entering into covenant with God and each other was very serious, for God would hear their vows, and hold them accountable for keeping them. Covenant always has sanctions; blessings for keeping the terms of the covenant, and curses for breaking them. When God is invited to participate in a marriage covenant, it is a very serious matter.

This understanding of marriage is the context for a sexual relationship that can be all that God intended. Marriage and sex are inseparably linked together in Hebrews 13:4, and then given God's blessing. But sex outside of marriage is condemned:

"Marriage is honorable among all, and the bed undefiled, but fornicators and adulterers God will judge."

1 Corinthians 6:9,10 says that those who practice fornication, adultery, homosexuality, and sodomy, among other sins, will not "inherit the Kingdom of God." From these two portions of scripture we can see that God looks with favor on sex, but only within the bonds of marriage. There are eternal consequences, as well as temporal repercussions, when His restrictions are ignored. There are several other scriptures that say basically the same thing (including Exodus 20:14; Leviticus 18; Deuteronomy 5:18; 22:13-30; Matthew 19:9; Galatians 5:19-21; Colossians 3:5,6; etc.). God is adamant about the fact that sex is to be exclusively within the context of marriage.

Is God just an old meany who doesn't want his children to have any fun? No, sexual purity, meaning sex only within marriage, is very important to God for a very good reason.

One-flesh through sex

Sex plays a unique role in the eternal purpose of God. If you will remember from Chapter 3, we saw that God gave man a helper to become one-flesh with him, to be his "completer," to help him as he entered the family business of extending God's Kingdom. Genesis 2:24, in speaking of marriage, says:

> *"Therefore a man shall leave his father and mother and be joined to his wife, and they shall become one-flesh."*

Paul gives us some insight in 1 Corinthians 6:15,16 as to what "one-flesh" means, and how it happens. He quotes Genesis 2:24, and then applies it to sex with a prostitute:

> *"Do you not know that your bodies are members of Christ? Shall I then take the members of Christ, and make them members of a harlot? Certainly not! Or do you not know that he who is joined to a harlot is one body with her? 'For the two,' He says, 'shall become one flesh.' "*

Sex with a prostitute has nothing to do with becoming one by having the same life goals, the same interests, the same personality, or all the other ways becoming one, or one-flesh, with your wife might happen. If you become one-flesh with a prostitute, as Paul argues here, then that must occur through purely physical sex, because that is all that happens with a prostitute.

However, the result of sex is much more far-reaching than simply a physical experience. That is why sex is so important. It forms the one-flesh relationship between husband and wife in marriage, and is the basis for oneness in all the other areas of a marriage that are so crucial. Sex is not simply physical, like any other bodily function, but it is a **total-person act**, where two people are tied together by an invisible chord, a soul-tie, that hooks them to each other. Paul says that that even happens when a man has sex with a prostitute!

This is what the Humanists cannot accept about sex. If man is purely an animal, the product of evolution, without a soul, then sex is just a pleasurable, physical act, with no consequences. Why not have sex whenever you feel like it, with whomever attracts you? That is what the Humanists advocate, and that humanistic reasoning is why the Christian must not unconsciously buy into their life-style.

Man is much more than just an animal. He is a creature made in God's very image, who was designed as a sexual being to become a two-person, male-female, "one-flesh fighting unit" through sex. That one-flesh unit is the primary way God deploys His troops to accomplish

His purpose on the earth, and to tamper with the way God designed the units and put them together is to seriously hinder His business of extending His Kingdom.

Can you see that sex is intended by God to be the foundation of marital oneness? Without it, two people might live together, be good friends, and agree on any number of issues, but they would not be "one-flesh." We will look at the ramifications of using sex in a way that God did not intend in the next chapter.

Marriage as a "moral fence"

Marriage is like an oyster; the marriage covenant, entered into in a public ceremony, is the shell that protects the oyster. The real animal is the unseen, one-flesh, sexual relationship, that is safely protected inside the shell.

Another illustration pictures the marriage covenant as a moral, protective fence around the one-flesh relationship between a husband and wife. Society has historically recognized the importance of protecting that relationship and has enacted civil laws to do so. Until this generation, divorces were hard to obtain, as there had to be "grounds," usually some reason for the divorce that had a biblical base. "No-fault" divorce has changed that, and getting in and out of marriage is extremely easy now. It's as though marriage is little more than a living arrangement.

The marital union is receiving less and less economic protection as well. Our tax laws are no longer structured to favor families, and medical benefits that used to be only for families are now often available to "domestic partners" (read: live-in lovers, homosexual or otherwise). These changes are occurring as we are allowing Humanism to gain more and more of a foothold in America.

The marriage fence, a public declaration of covenant between two people, has the **first** purpose, then, of providing protection for the one-flesh, sexual relationship. It keeps intruders "out." The rings on the fingers of both man and woman signify that they are both "taken," are already one-flesh with another, and are off-limits to outside advances.

Also, the marriage fence keeps each partner "in." The vows they took were very serious, and, whether understood or not, they were heard by God, and if broken, will call down sanctions on the head of the one who broke them. A proper understanding of those vows goes a long way toward keeping a Christian faithful in times of temptation.

Naked and unashamed

The **second** thing the marriage covenant does, is to provide a secure, permanent atmosphere that allows the development of true intimacy. The fence engenders confidence in each marriage partner that the other will still be there tomorrow, and therefore it is safe for them to open their hearts and be vulnerable. Sex becomes an expression of true intimacy, protected by the fence, rather than a substitute for it.

Women who agree to a sexual relationship outside the fence of the marriage covenant are looking for this intimacy, and hope to find it through sex. However, the physical act itself, without the commitment of marriage, while creating a one-flesh bond, is not the same as the personal intimacy that she longs for. She could well establish a soul-tie to one with whom she has no intimate relationship. They are obviously not synonymous, as there is no personal intimacy with a prostitute, while Paul says there is a soul-tie.

Marriage is no guarantee of intimacy, but the commitment is there to give the couple enough time to establish it, if they both are desirous of doing so. The bond established through sex, the soul-tie, is the basis; personal intimacy is a growing experience built on that basis.

One factor which is very important in establishing intimacy is found in Genesis 2:25: "They were both naked, the man and his wife, and were not ashamed." In the Garden of Eden, this nakedness was certainly physical, but I believe in the context of Genesis 2, there is a deeper meaning. 1 John 1:7 is the same idea, "But if we walk in the light, as He is in the light, we have fellowship with one another..." "Walking in the light" is another way of saying "naked," and is a prerequisite of intimate fellowship, and means openness, honesty, and vulnerability.

For example, as a man and woman enter marriage, it is important that they are completely transparent with one-another about any past indiscretions, "naked" with each other, for if there is a covering and hiding of previous sexual sin because of shame, personal intimacy will be impossible. The advice given in the syndicated column that I referred to in Chapter 1, "What he doesn't know won't hurt him," if followed, would keep the inquirer from experiencing what God has for her in her marriage.

Any pretence, any deception, any deceit, or any lying between marriage partners, will destroy the oneness God intends for His "one-flesh fighting units," and thereby hamper their effectiveness.

Principles of marital sex

In 1 Corinthians 7:3-5, Paul outlines three principles for married couples to follow in their sex life together. They are all three related to each other, though there is a slightly different shade of meaning in each. Paul concludes by saying in verse 6 that "I say this as a concession, and not as a commandment." In other words, it is not mandatory to marry, for in fact, Paul says, that in view of "the present distress," (persecution of the church by the Jews, and by the Romans under Nero) it would be better for a man to "remain as he is" (vs. 26). However, to the married, he gives these instructions:

The principle of giving.

"Let the husband render to his wife the affection due her, and likewise also the wife to her husband" (vs. 3).

"Affection" here means sexual affection, and the implication is that affection is a mandatory responsibility if one is married. It is incumbent upon the wife to be ready to "give" to her husband the sexual affection that he needs, because it is "due" him. It is likewise obligatory that the husband be ready to "give" sexual affection to the wife. The emphasis in this verse is on the giving of sex to one's spouse, based on the fact that the sex-drive God built in to both men and women is designed to be satisfied in marriage.

The principle of authority

"The wife does not have authority over her own body, but the husband does. And likewise the husband does not have authority over his own body, but the wife does" (vs. 4).

Whereas in verses 3, the emphasis is on giving what is due, the emphasis in verse 4 is on taking what is needed, just in case the spouse neglects his/her responsibility to give. One cannot say consistently, "I'm too tired" (generally the woman), or, "I'm not interested" (often the man), because God says your body is no longer your own. A man's body belongs to his wife, and she can use it for her own sexual satisfaction. The same is true of the woman's body; it belongs to her husband for his satisfaction. If the woman is genuinely tired, the husband needs to find a better time when his wife is fresh, and when the wife can make herself as attractive as possible for her husband, but each spouse should remember that having sex is a responsibility they took when they married.

The principle of consistency

"Do not deprive one another except with consent for a time, that you may give yourself to fasting and prayer; and come together again so that Satan does not tempt you because of your lack of self control" (vs.5).

There are times when abstinence is good, just as are fasting (abstaining from food), and watching (abstaining from sleep), two other disciplines mentioned in the Scripture. These disciplines do not earn favor with God, but Paul did say "I discipline my body and bring it into subjection" (1 Corinthians 9:27). Any time we are able to deny bodily appetites, though they be good in themselves, we demonstrate that we are not controlled by our bodies, but we indeed control them. Paul says abstinence from sex, by mutual consent, only for a season, is one of those disciplines. This must not be a lengthy abstinence, for Satan is walking about "like a roaring lion, seeking whom he may devour" (1 Peter 5:8). Lack of sexual affection at home opens both husband and wife to temptation.

Sex, with the above exception, must be consistent between husband and wife. One can see how extremely important God views sex in marriage. He has eliminated all the avenues of escape from sexual responsibility with the first two principles, and now emphasizes the regularity of physical intimacy with the third. It is difficult, if not impossible to share regular sexual affection with someone toward whom you have hostility, or someone you do not respect. This makes it mandatory to walk in the light with each other so those problems can be dealt with. Each time a husband and wife come together sexually, the one-flesh bond is strengthened, and an avenue is provided for personal intimacy as well.

We have seen that within the marriage covenant is the only place for sex to occur because of its power to make two people one-flesh. Then we looked at three principles of married sex that demonstrate how important God sees a sexual relationship in marriage to be. In the next chapter, we will explore some other purposes God has in mind for this wonderful gift that He has given us.

"Father, help me to hold my "vessel" in honor until I am married, and then show me how to use this wonderful, powerful tool you have given me to create a "one-flesh fighting unit" for the accomplishment of Your task. Amen."

Questions for discussion

1. What do you see as the significance of marriage being a covenant with the marriage partners and with God? How would that understanding change the practice of marriage today in America?

2. Based on the oyster and the fence illustrations, what makes two people "married," or "husband and wife?" What does the ceremony do? Why are the guests there?

3. Explain the difference between being "one-flesh" with someone, and being personally intimate.

4. Paul's three principles of married sex occur right in the middle of a very practical chapter in 1 Corinthians where he is encouraging the Corinthians not to marry if possible. Does that mean marriage is a less spiritual path to take? Why or why not?

Chapter 14

God's Purpose for Sex

We saw in the last chapter that sex accomplishes one of God's objectives for a married couple; becoming one-flesh together through the creation of a "soul-tie." I want to continue to look at that phenomenon in this chapter, as well as discuss two other objectives God has built into sex; procreation and pleasure. These three aspects of a sexual relationship are all clearly revealed to us in the Bible, and an understanding of them is crucial for anyone who is married, or who one day will be. Ignorance or disobedience to the law of God in any one of these areas hinders the work of God, and leads to much unhappiness and heart-ache that could be avoided.

The passage in 1 Corinthians 6:9-11 mentioned in Chapter 13 begins with one of Paul's favorite expressions, "Do not be deceived." Sexual sin always has consequences, even though the world says to go ahead and violate those "outdated, repressive, puritanical taboos." God does not appear to us in person, jump up and down, and wave red flags to get us to see the gravity of living a life in violation of His Law. Because He "only" tells us in the Bible, we often ignore His clear instructions, having no fear of the results of our disobedience. If that is true, then we truly <u>are</u> deceived.

<u>Purpose #1 - The Creation of a One-flesh Bond</u>

An unwanted soul-tie

The couple who came for counsel had been happily married for 15 years and had four children. They were active Christians, pillars in the community, and, by all appearances, very happy. However, as they shared their story, I could see that their ignorance of spiritual truth in the area of sex had robbed them of what God desires for His people.

As a girl, Sandra was very attractive, and had always dated a number of boys throughout high school and college. She was a Christian, and had been taught to not get involved sexually, but there was never any reason given to her, other than "nice girls don't." She wanted to be a nice girl, so she didn't, at least not for a long time.

She resisted all sexual advances until her junior year in college, when her high school sweetheart finally broke down her defenses and had sex with her. They continued a sexual relationship, off and on, for several years, and then they went their separate ways. Sandra actually was glad the relationship was over. Her feeling was, "That's over with. I can get on with my life." She did not understand that a soul-tie had been formed.

She met Jim some five years later, a committed Christian who had managed to keep himself sexually pure. They fell in love and married, and then set out to build a life together. However, there was something missing in their sex life, and in their ability to be intimate with one another. It was only a nagging, subconscious feeling that they could see later as they looked back, but in the press of life, they ignored the warning signals.

Then came the bombshell. On a trip back to her hometown by herself to see an ailing parent, Sandra ran into her high school boyfriend. She was amazed at her response when she saw him, her first sexual partner. He had gained well over fifty pounds, was bald, and bore absolutely no resemblance to the dashing, athletic young man she had known twenty years earlier. Yet as they talked, she felt a tremendous sexual attraction to him, an attraction she had never felt for Jim. He came by to see her several times, and they again got involved sexually, although she was able to resist his attempts to have intercourse with her. She was doing everything she could to be faithful to her husband.

Sandra came home and told Jim what had happened, somehow knowing that that was something she must do. He was devastated. She had told him nothing about her earlier sexual experiences, feeling that they were in the past, before she was married, and they didn't matter. She had confessed them to God, and she was forgiven, so she saw no need to expose her indiscretions to her husband. She hadn't understood the long-term effects of sex, nor the importance of being "naked and unashamed" with her husband. Jim suddenly felt that he was married to a stranger he didn't know.

As Jill and I counseled with Sandra and Jim, we explained the non-physical dimension of sex, and its purpose; to create a one-flesh bond that would "brand" two people for each other. Sandra had been "branded" by her first sexual encounter with her high school boy friend, and that brand was still there after twenty years, making Jim's brand unclear, or diluted. That dilution, and Sandra's unwillingness to "walk in the light" with Jim, was a big reason for their inability to be personally intimate.

Unwanted soul-tie #2

Bob was an old friend I met when I first came to Seattle in 1964. We were both single, eager young Christians who were very serious about God. We spent a lot of time together jogging, hiking, and evangelizing, and commiserating together about our singleness. We finally got married about the same time, he to a young girl whom he had met on a trip to California where she was staying with some mutual friends.

Patty had gotten pregnant by a married Los Angeles policeman, her first sexual partner. She was staying with friends of Bob's until she had the baby, and when Bob came for a visit, they hit it off immediately. She had the baby, gave it up for adoption (which was almost universally done then), and she and Bob were married.

Jill and I saw them periodically for the next few years, staying with them as we passed through the area of California where they lived. They had one child, and then after about ten years, they divorced. As I talked to Bob, he told me a tragic story which, again, could have been prevented with an understanding of the power and purpose of sex.

"I never felt like she was mine. As we drove on the freeway, every time we passed an L.A.P.D. motorcycle patrolman, she would turn her head to see if it was her lover." The soul-tie was there, doing what God had designed it to do, keeping two people for each other. Tragically, they were both married to somebody else.

These two stories are tragic, but they illustrate the wonder and wisdom of God's plan, if God's law is followed, and sex is confined to marriage. When a man and woman marry, and have not had previous sexual experience, the soul-tie that forms as they develop their sexual relationship keeps them for each other. They are not attracted to others because their complete sexual experience has been with each other. There are no memories, no thoughts of previous sexual experiences, and little, if any fantasizing of other sexual partners. Their strong soul-tie, formed by sex, is God's way of protecting them for each other, and from Satan's attacks on their oneness. He wants desperately to destroy this "one-flesh fighting unit" that is such a threat to him, by attacking them at the very point of their oneness, through sexual sin. When God's law is followed, the soul-tie offers real security.

All sin is not the same

You can readily see why Paul teaches that sexual sin is different from any other sin. All sin has the same effect on God. It is against His character, and He abhors it. Any sin, without the blood of Jesus, will send the sinner to hell. But in this life, all sin does not have the same effect on the sinner! Listen to Paul in 1 Corinthians 6:18:

"Every sin that a man does is outside the body, but he who commits sexual immorality sins against his own body."

If a man lies, he can repent of his deceit, and he is personally not affected, though there will be results of his sin, i.e., his reputation may be destroyed. Gossip can be acknowledged and forsaken, and others may be hurt, but the gossiper can do his best to repair the damage, and is not effected in his own person. A thief can repent of his old ways after he becomes a Christian, and make restitution, and there is no residual effect in himself. But sexual immorality can be genuinely confessed and forsaken, and sincere repentance can occur, but the soul-tie remains, because God invented sex to bind two people together! It happens when two people who are not married have sex, just as it does when they are married. Just as babies come from having sex, married or not, so does a one-flesh bond.

One who forms a one-flesh bond with someone other than wife or husband, Paul says, sins against himself, or does himself evil, because he is hindering his own present or future marital relationship. He is adulterating, or diluting, his capacity to form a marital bond, because he is attaching himself to someone else. That's what adultery is; adulterating, or diluting a one-flesh, marital bond by having sex with someone other than husband or wife.

Nothing left to give

That brings up one more facet of this powerful tool that needs to be considered. If a man or woman has had multiple sexual partners before they marry, one can see that they have been joined in one-flesh relationships with all those people. They have given themselves, maybe even while trying not to, and then tried to "take themselves back," by forgetting that partner and going on to another one. But in each instance, there is a joining of souls in a supernatural way, and complete retrieval is impossible. As the relationship is torn apart, a bit of them remains with each partner. Finally, when the man or woman marries, there is little left for the one to whom they now desire to give themselves wholly.

Ted was very much a sinner before he became a Christian, engaging in many sexual affairs. He was very soundly saved, and immediately went into campus evangelism, eventually meeting a young, Christian girl with similar interests. Soon they were married.

I remember riding up a ski-lift with Ted as he told me that his new wife, Mary, who was a virgin when they married, had had no trouble enthusiastically adjusting to sex, but that he, the old experienced one, was having some real problems. He had already given himself away.

The world says, "Sexual experience before marriage is good. Then you'll know what to do on your wedding night." To be beginners together as you learn to give yourself to each other is far better than having nothing left to give. Truly, "My people are destroyed for lack of knowledge" (Hosea 4:6).

Sowing and reaping

These first pages in this chapter are, I'm sure, very discouraging to those who have been involved in sexual immorality. When we see what God intends for us when we keep His law, and what we have done just because we didn't understand the consequences of disobedience, we can see the wickedness of Satan's deception. However, the Bible teaches that there is real hope. I'll cover that in a moment.

Some might say, "What we did when we were non-Christians is all under the blood. The slate is wiped clean. We start fresh."

Certainly, as far as our sin before God is concerned, that is very true. He has forgiven all our sins, no matter what they are, placed them as far from us "as the East is from the West" (Psalm 103:12), and our sin He remembers no more (Jeremiah 31:34), because we have trusted Jesus as our Savior. But being forgiven for our sin, and being unaffected by our sin are two very different things. We never sin with impunity; every sin has its result, and as we have seen, sexual sin has much more far-reaching effects, personally, than any other sin.

Paul says, again, "Do not be deceived, God is not mocked; for whatever a man sows, that he will also reap." It is not that God is out to get those who are sexually immoral. It is that He has placed in His universe the law of sowing and reaping, just as surely as He has placed the law of gravity. Sowing obedience to God's moral law reaps a blessing; sowing disobedience reaps a curse, in this instance, the curse of a soul tie with someone other than one's marriage partner. Do not be deceived into thinking there will be no residual effect of breaking God's law.

Walking in the light

There are several portions of scripture that give the Christian who has been sexually impure some very real hope that God can restore what Satan has tried to steal through his deception. Obviously, the joy of giving the gift of one's virginity to husband or wife on one's wedding night is not possible, and there will be other problems that must be faced. Sinning and being forgiven always has consequences that not sinning doesn't have. But, I believe previous soul ties can be broken, allowing the establishment of a new one-flesh bond with one's spouse.

In James 5:16, we are admonished to "Confess your sins to one another, and pray for one another, that you may be healed." In reaction to Roman Catholicism, Protestants have focused entirely on confessing sins only to God, with no intermediary. They have forgotten this aspect James mentions of confessing sins to one another for healing and restoration, both physically and emotionally. The guilt and shame involved in sexual sin often makes this very hard, but I am convinced that this is the way to freedom from unwanted soul-ties.

In the example at the beginning of this chapter, Sandra had confessed and repented before God, but had hidden her "secret" from her husband, and the soul tie remained. As she opened herself up to Jill and me, and confessed to us and to her husband her sin, we were able to pray with her, and the soul-tie was broken. There is tremendous power in "walking in the light" with one another, not hiding from the light of God, nor pretending to be someone you are not.

Binding and loosing

Jesus said to Peter, "And I will give you the keys of the Kingdom of Heaven, and whatever you bind on earth will be bound in heaven, and whatever you loose on earth will be loosed in heaven" (Matthew 16:19). A proper understanding of this verse includes the fact that this is not just authority given to church officials, but to the church itself, the Body of Christ. The priesthood of the individual believer is a tremendously powerful truth which was recovered during the Reformation, and which we must not ignore. It is not just the "professionals" that do the work of the ministry, but individual saints, the people of God. As we confess our sins to one another, and pray for one another, that ministry, including "binding and loosing," is carried out.

Jill and I prayed for Sandra, and asked God to break the soul-tie she had established with her high school boy friend. As members of the Body of Christ, with the authority that Jesus gave us in Matthew 16:19, we loosed her from her one-flesh relationship with him that was a result of the sin that she had confessed to us. God has ordained that our prayers, undoing the results of that specific sin, did something her private prayers to God could not do. They set her free.

A plan of action

If you are young, single, and sexually pure, it is difficult to understand the gravity of the topic we have been discussing. I covered this material with four classes of graduating seniors from two different Christian high schools. Many of the students who took the class learned the material, agreed with it, and even made A's, but many of them continued their previous sexual practices, with several pregnancies resulting.

"How could they fall into that trap after what they heard?" was my reaction. Still, I know that young people do not have the experience to know themselves the importance of purity, and obedience to God. If they really don't see the importance of that obedience, and they have not learned to respect and obey their parent's instructions, it is very hard to then obey God, particularly in the area of sex.

If you are young and still sexually pure, the problems you will avoid by obeying God may be difficult for you to understand. Talk with someone who has had to reap what they have sown because of not understanding these truths, and then determine to follow the principles of purity we will cover in Chapter 15. Understanding God's purpose for sex while you are young, and then obeying Him, will minimize the excess baggage you will have to unload to be effective for the Kingdom of God.

Purity by the grace of God

The second class of reader is the married man or woman who was a virgin on their wedding day. Your purity is because of the grace of God and His inscrutable plan that brought you safely through the pitfalls of pre-marital youth. The temptation to pride is almost inevitable, unless one really believes that "The steps of a good man are ordered by the Lord" (Psalm 37:23), and "A man's heart plans his way, but the Lord directs his steps" (Proverbs 16:9). Thank Him that He has delivered you from a difficult path that some of His children must walk. Give Him glory for your purity, and not yourself, and reject the temptation to look at others with the intolerance that comes from a proud heart. Your pride will negate the impact your life could have for the Kingdom.

Your experience of waiting for sex until marriage is the norm for God's children, though today it is not typical. However, the Lord says that He will not rest, for the church's sake, "until her righteousness goes forth as brightness, and her salvation as a lamp that burns. The Gentiles shall see your righteousness, and all kings your glory" (Isaiah 62:1,2). As we acquire a vision for the Kingdom of God and His righteousness (sexual purity), and impart that vision to the next generation, the world will see the glory of God in our families!

Parents as God's representatives

The third category of reader is the single man or woman who has not remained sexually pure, for whatever reason, and has established one or more soul-ties with others.

If you are in this category, the first step is to recognize your sin, to face it squarely, and to be sure you have repented before God. You have disobeyed His Law, and there are consequences. It does not matter whether the sin occurred before or after you became a Christian, the results of sexual sin remain, though you are forgiven by God.

Once you have repented to the Lord, go to your parents and confess to them what you have done. Make use of the principle in James 5:16, confessing your sin to them very honestly, and then ask them to pray for you, exercising the authority of Matthew 16:19. Have them pray to break the soul-tie that binds you to your previous sexual partner, and then release you to be joined to your future mate.

Some parents are not Christians and therefore they do not have the power to "bind and loose" as members of the Body of Christ. Others may not care about the sexual purity of their children. In those cases, confessing to them what you have done is still appropriate since they are in authority over you, representing the Lord. Then find an older Christian of the same sex whom you trust to pray for you. If you are a man, it could be an elder in your church. If you are a woman, find an older woman whom you respect.

Some people say, "Why do I have to have someone else, particularly my parents, pray for me? Why can't I break the soul-tie in prayer myself?" As I said above, God has ordained that in the Body of Christ, we need each other, and there are some things that only our brothers and sisters can do for us. Also, being open about your sin with your parents is crucial, because of their position of authority over you. If you do not confess to them, in essence you haven't confessed to God, because they are His representatives in your life. You have disobeyed them, and "walking in the light" with them restores fellowship in your family. Placing yourself in a position to need them, and their authority in your life, requires the humility that will then allow true ministry to flow as they pray for you.

Satan will use fear and shame in an attempt to keep you in bondage. He does not want you to "walk in the light" with your parents, for that is the way to freedom. You might be extremely afraid of what they will do when they find out about your sin. Whatever the consequences you must suffer as a result of your disobedience, it is most important to be free from the guilt of hidden sin, and the soul-tie that would hinder your future marriage. Your parents are the ones who are in authority over you, and it is important that you go to them.

Obviously, there may be extenuating circumstances where confessing to parents is not appropriate, i.e., a daughter who has been molested by her father. Counsel with mature Christians as to a plan of action is then necessary. However, in a normal situation, following these principles is God's way to spiritual health.

Naked and unashamed with your spouse

Finally, there is the reader who is married, and who was not a virgin when he/she married. If that describes you, honesty with your spouse, and repentance to him/her for diluting your one-flesh bond, represents the only way to experience the depth in your marriage relationship that God desires. The way to wholeness is the same as that of the one who is unmarried, except your spouse, rather than parents, can be the one that prays for you to break the soul-tie and loose you from past sexual bondage.

211

Some feel that their marriage partner can not handle this information, and they will be emotionally destroyed. Remember, you are telling them, not to hurt them, but to clear the way for a new dimension in your marriage. Through the initial pain of full disclosure will come the strength of a much stronger one-flesh bond. In Genesis 2:25 it is said of Adam and Eve that they were "naked and unashamed." The application to us is more than simply physical. It also means that there is nothing hidden, no untold secrets, no hidden strings that Satan can pull in blackmail. "He knows everything about me and still loves me." "She knows all my worst secrets and still wants to be my wife." What a wonderful place to be! "Naked and unashamed" is God's formula for powerful marriages.

No wasted experiences

"Why didn't I know this when I was young? Why did God let me make the mistakes I made?" are representative of the thoughts many of us have when we realize the beauty of God's plan. As we learn God's ways, to ask "Why?" of God becomes less and less necessary, and accepting His plan, even though we may not understand, becomes easier as we come to know His heart of love.

God "works all things according to the counsel of His will" (Ephesians 1:11), even our sin. Somehow, His kindness extended to us as sinners is a demonstration of His grace and wisdom to "principalities and powers" (Ephesians 2:7, 3:10). If He used Pharaoh's hard heart and eventual destruction "that My name might be declared in all the earth " (Romans 9:17), He can somehow use your sin to accomplish the same end.

Your restoration to wholeness, and the health of your marriage can be a dynamic testimony to God's power to heal. As Paul says of the nation Israel and their eventual restoration, "Now if their fall is riches for the world....how much more their fullness!" (Romans 11:12). Sharing the difficulties, even the heartaches, you have experienced along the path God has taken you, can be a source of life to a new believer. Paul says, "So then death is working in us, but life in you" (2 Corinthians 4:12). Your experience will prepare you to help others walk a path of holiness.

It took a divine mind to think of creating sex to achieve the objective of making two people into a one-flesh unit to better accomplish God's purpose. When we see it clearly, our response is the same as Paul's in Romans 11:33-36:

"Oh, the depth of the riches both of the wisdom and knowledge of God! How unsearchable are His judgments and His ways past finding out!
'For who has known the mind of the Lord?
Or who has become His counselor?...'
For of Him and through Him and to Him are all things, to whom be glory forever. Amen."

Purpose #2 - Procreation

"Be fruitful and multiply"
The second objective for sex, after oneness, is procreation. "Be fruitful and multiply; fill the earth...." (Genesis 1:28), was God's command to Adam and Eve, repeated again to Noah in Genesis 9:1 and Genesis 9:7. Only a little more than a generation ago, this command was still unconsciously a part of the fabric of our society, because a large family was a badge of honor.

Today, however, we have listened to the strident voices of the radical environmentalists as they have convinced us that the world is over-populated and we must reduce the size of our families. We saw in Chapter 3 the fallacy of that argument. There is an extensive body of scientific literature supporting the thesis in Chapter 3 that over-population is a myth.[1] However, the general public never hears about it because the media generally has adopted the radical environmentalist's agenda.

There are several other factors besides environmental concerns that have contributed to the great reduction in family size over the last few decades. The government has encroached upon traditional family responsibilities with seemingly helpful entitlement programs such as Social Security. It has partially relieved the burden of caring for parents in old age, making a large family less of a necessity. The urbanization of the population has eliminated the requirement of having children to work on the family farm. As we have strayed from the Bible's teaching concerning how to train children, they have become more unruly, disrespectful, and very hard to handle, causing parents to shy away from having more than a very few. Children are also expensive, and the government provides no real tax incentive to encourage having them. Add to these factors the general, overall selfishness of a culture that sees children as a huge inconvenience, particularly to women who want careers outside of the home, and it's no wonder the size of families has plummeted.

In an issue of *Parade* magazine in the Sunday Seattle Times several years ago, the cover was a large picture of Joe Montana, the famous NFL quarterback, in a football pose. Around the edge of the page were face shots of various famous people, in completely unrelated fields. What did they all have in common? They were all the only child of their parents. The inside article extolled the virtues of only children, pointing out that they were generally smarter and more successful than those who had siblings as they grew up. The article debunked the myth that only children were spoiled, and basically painted a glorious picture of having but one child. This is an example of how our society has been duped by Satan, the enemy of our souls, to ignore God's command to reproduce and fill the earth with Godly Kingdom warriors.

The Bible's view of children

The Scriptures paint a far different picture of children. They are invariably portrayed as blessings from God (Genesis 33:5; 48:9; Deuteronomy 28:11; Psalm 128). As He opens and shuts the womb (Genesis 30:22, 1 Samuel 1:6), the more children, the more blessings (Psalm 127:3-5). Parents are given the responsibility to train them (Ephesians 6:4; Proverbs 22:6), and are told that if they do, their children will give them rest and delight (Proverbs 29:17), but if they don't, shame and grief will result (Proverbs 10:1; 29:15). Grandchildren are said to be the crown of old men (Proverbs 17:6). In the unit on children, we will explore this topic in great detail.

A big mistake

Some married friends who live in another part of the country used to come through Seattle periodically to visit their families. They always stopped to see us on their visits, and it seemed that each time they came to town they had a new baby. Their children were always very well behaved, and they had a very happy family, but as the number of children climbed to seven, Jill and I wondered what in the world they were doing. They never said anything to us about why they had so many children, and we never asked. I don't know to this day if they understood the family as a weapon for God, or if they just liked kids. I do know, if they did understand, and they had told us, we would have responded very eagerly to the concept.

214

Because we did not understand, after our third child, Ramah, was born, Jill and I decided we didn't want any more children. We now had our daughter we wanted so much, and <u>we</u> felt our family was complete, our quiver was full, with three children. We prayed, and asked the Lord what we should do. Since all our Christian friends who were serious about the Lord were limiting their families to two or three children, and then getting vasectomies, we saw no red flags. At age 36, I made what I feel today was the greatest mistake of my life. I had a vasectomy, too.

Some twelve years later, as I began to learn the biblical perspective on family, I said to Jill:

"What has been the greatest blessing of your life?"

"Without doubt, my three children," she answered.

"Do you see what we have done?" I said. "We have looked up at God and said to Him, 'Thanks for your wonderful blessings, but we don't want any more of them. You can keep any more that You would like to give us. Thanks, but no thanks.' "

We did not understand that children are not for us, if we want them, but for God, and His great purpose of extending His kingdom. They are like arrows (Psalm 127:3-5), instruments of war, by which our influence can be extended into the next generation. Well-trained, with a vision for the kingdom, they will fly straight and true, into the heart of the Devil. The more arrows we have, the more effective we become as warriors in the battle.

I went to a urologist, and told him I wanted a reversal.

"Do you want more children?" he said.

"Not necessarily, but I want God to be God again in our family, and if He wants to bless us in that way, we want to receive that blessing."

He performed the surgery, and although God did not send any more children (He had about a two year window when He could have), we felt we had been obedient to what we had seen.

A violent reaction

This message often brings a violent reaction from those who hear it. Why is that? My intent is not to make people feel guilty for decisions they have made concerning family size, but only to present the very biblical view of an open womb as a blessing from God, and a closed womb as a curse. Jill and I know that there are many who will respond to this message when they hear it, just as we would have if our out-of-town friends had told us. We have determined never to keep

215

quiet but to always "be ready" if we have an opportunity to share "a reason for the hope that is within you" (1 Peter 3:15). Several babies are alive today because God used our readiness to speak. The message of children as weapons of war is a very large part of why there is a hope within me.

This is a very controversial message in the church today, and if you do not respond, don't let it spoil the usefulness of the rest of the book. Simply ask the Lord to show you if it is right. Don't be threatened, but resolve to be obedient to what the Lord shows you, not what you read in a book. Compare what I have said with Scripture, your "standard of faith and practice." That is what you must obey.

Purpose #3 - Pleasure

God's endorsement of pleasure in married sex

Some consider the Song of Solomon to be a book about the relationship of Christ and the Church, rather than an actual, historical story. They read it as an allegory picturing God's relationship with His wife Israel in the Old Testament, and then Christ's love for His Church in the New. However, while there certainly can be these applications made, there is no reason to believe that this is the primary interpretation. Only if sex is viewed as unspiritual, and a necessary but base activity, is this interpretation employed as the primary one.

Song of Solomon actually is a ringing endorsement of physical pleasure in married sex. The scenes of sexual and emotional love all through this book picture beautifully our third purpose for sex: to enter into the most pleasurable of all human experiences together with the one you love and to whom your life is committed.

Solomon's marriage to the Schulamite maiden probably occurred early in His reign before he was led into gross immorality and idolatry by his 1000 wives and concubines (1 Kings 11:1-8) [Though he already had 140 when the book was written (6:8)]. There is speculation that many of his marriages, initially, were politically motivated, and the Schulamite in Song of Solomon was his true love.

Solomon's perspective on his wedding night

In chapter 4, Solomon describes his emotions during his first sexual experience with his bride. In verses 1-11, he describes her body as he undresses her, using some terms that definitely are from another era. How would your wife like for you to say her hair resembles "a flock of goats" (vs. 1)? Or "Your neck is like the tower of David, built for an armory, on which hang a thousand bucklers, all shields of mighty men" (vs. 4)?

But all men who have experienced God's love poured out through them to a woman can identify with vs. 9-11:

> *"You have ravished my heart,*
> *My sister, my spouse;*
> *You have ravished my heart*
> *With one look from your eyes....*
> *How fair is your love*
> *My sister, my spouse;*
> *How much better than wine is your love,*
> *And the scent of your perfume than all spices!*
> *Your lips, O my spouse*
> *Drip as the honeycomb;*
> *Honey and milk are under your tongue;*
> *And the fragrance of your garments*
> *Is like the fragrance of Lebanon."*

As Solomon caresses his wife in preparation for intercourse, he describes this virgin bride with some of the most beautiful and erotic language of the book, if the reader can read with insight and imagination.

> *"A garden enclosed*
> *Is my sister, my spouse,*
> *A spring shut up,*
> *A fountain sealed.*
> *Your plants are an orchard of pomegranates*
> *With pleasant fruits,*
> *Fragrant henna with spikenard,*
> *Spikenard and saffron,*
> *Calamus and cinnamon,*
> *With all trees of frankincense,*
> *Myrrh and aloes,*
> *With all the chief spices-*
> *A fountain of gardens,*
> *A well of living waters,*
> *And streams from Lebanon." (vs. 12-15)*

The Shulamite is now ready for the consummation of the marriage, and cries out in eagerness:

> *"Awake, O north wind,*
> *And come, O south!*
> *Blow upon my garden,*
> *That its spices may flow out.*
> *Let my beloved come to his garden*
> *And eat its pleasant fruits." (vs. 16)*

At this point, the marriage is consummated. Notice as the Schulamite gave herself sexually to Solomon, she changed terminology from "my garden," to "his garden." She was inviting Solomon to possess her sexually, to take her fully, a physical expression of God's purpose for woman; to give herself completely to her man. Solomon, basking in the afterglow of his love for his bride, expresses his understanding of having taken her by saying in 5:1:

> *I have come to my garden, my sister, my spouse;*
> *I have gathered my myrrh with my spice;*
> *I have eaten my honeycomb with my honey;*
> *I have drunk my wine with my milk."*

There are other scenes in the book equally as descriptive; The Schulamite's description of Solomon (5:10-16), and their sexual relationship (6:2,3; 7:9b,10), and Solomon's further description of the Schulamite (7:1-9), among others.

An inexhaustible pleasure

God gave us sex for pleasure, because He loves us, and when properly used, it is an inexhaustible, renewable pleasure. It never gets old. However, as an end in itself, the pleasure can be depleted rather quickly.

Ryan was a college acquaintance from a wealthy Oklahoma oil family. He dated a well-known campus beauty queen, trying every trick he knew to get her to go to bed with him, all to no avail. She told him that sexual intercourse was off-limits unless he married her, giving him just enough sexual foreplay to hook him. She was able to resist going all the way, because she had a master-plan she was following perfectly. Ryan became obsessed with having sex with her.

They finally married, and were divorced inside one year, with the beauty queen receiving what was rumored to be a very substantial settlement. She had achieved her objective.

A mutual friend told me this story. I'll never forget what he said Ryan told him after the divorce. These are not the exact words, but very close;

"We had nothing in common, no reason to be together, but sex. And after a few weeks, sex with her was like scratching a place that didn't itch anymore." He had achieved his objective as well, at great cost to himself.

What a description! "Scratching a place that doesn't itch." Before Ryan married the beauty queen he could not have conceived that sex with her could ever lose its appeal. But it did. I'm sure, after six months, in his eyes, all her beauty had turned to ashes. How can sex remain a renewable pleasure, even into middle- and old-age? That's what God intends, and I want to conclude this chapter with three principles that, if understood and applied, will go a long way to achieving that goal.

A drive, not a need

The humanist approach to sex is to consider it to be a physical need that must be satisfied, like eating or drinking. They say that everybody will indulge in sex, married or unmarried. If we are but animals, the product of evolution, we will naturally act like animals. Sex is something that cannot be avoided because it is a need, and to deprive anyone of that need is not healthy for them, just like depriving them of food or water would be unhealthy. This is the thinking that leads to school-based health clinics at high schools that provide free contraceptives, and even access to abortions without parental knowledge.

The Bible teaches, of course, that we are not simply animals, but that we are created in God's image. Sex is a drive God has placed within us, for specific purposes, that we can, and must, control. Listen to 1 Thessalonians 4:3-8:

"For this is the will of God....that you should abstain from sexual immorality; that each of you should know how to possess his own vessel in sanctification and honor....that no one should take advantage of and defraud his brother in this matter, because the Lord is the avenger of all such, as we also forewarned you and testified. For God

did not call us to uncleanness, but in holiness. Therefore he who rejects this does not reject man, but God, who has also given us His Holy Spirit."

We can see from these verses that God is not some kindly old gentleman with a white beard, who pats us on the head when we sin and says, "there, there." He is an awesome God, in whose presence no one can stand, and who is very serious about His sexual standards. Not only will we naturally reap what we have sown, as we have seen in this chapter, but when we violate those standards, we expose ourselves to the discipline of our loving heavenly Father (Hebrews 12:5-11). He plays hard-ball.

Keeping his body under control was a constant concern of Paul's, because he could see clearly the overriding importance of eternal rewards as compared to fleeting, temporal pleasures. "But I discipline my body and bring it into subjection, lest, when I have preached to others, I myself should become disqualified" (1 Corinthians 9:27). How many Christian leaders have not followed Paul's example, and have given up what they have built over a lifetime for a fleeting moment of sexual pleasure!

God expects us to rule over our bodies in purity, and we can, in the power of the Holy Spirit, because sex is a drive, albeit a strong one. It is not a need.

Not for self-gratification

The second principle that will help to assure that sex will continue to be a vital part of a couple's life together is to understand that sex is not for self-gratification. When we lose sight of God's purpose for sex, it is very easy to fall into this trap. The sex drive turns inward, and expresses itself in lust. Men get involved in pornography and masturbation. Women dress sensually and flirt. It has been said, I believe correctly, that "Men lust, and women lust to be lusted after."

If one has used sex in this way while single, the tendency is to continue, even after marriage, the pattern that has been established. The marriage ceremony doesn't change ingrained habits. Men continue with pornography and masturbation, and women continue to dress sensually to attract other men, and flirt with them. Sex, even with one's spouse, rather than being an experience to be shared unselfishly together, is still turned inward as a means to self-gratification.

This selfish use of God's gift makes continuing physical intimacy with one's spouse very difficult to maintain once the newness has worn off.

Saving through losing

In Chapter 9, I mentioned the spiritual principle the Lord teaches in Matthew 16:24,25, the principle of gaining through losing. It is nowhere more applicable than in the area of sex in marriage, and follows very naturally after the previous principle of sex not being for self-gratification. Jesus said:

> *"If anyone desires to come after Me, let him deny himself, and take up his cross, and follow Me. For whoever desires to save his life will lose it, and whoever loses his life for My sake will find it."*

The way to true fulfillment in the sexual relationship in marriage is to concentrate on *giving pleasure to the one you love,* rather than taking for yourself. To see one's mate as an object to be used for self-gratification is to insure that that fulfillment will not be realized. On the other hand, as you attempt to bless your spouse by giving yourself to him or her with joyful abandon, without concern for your own needs, you will truly "find your life."

In this chapter we have explored the very important topic of God's purpose for sex. As you attempt to obey Him, He will empower you by His Holy Spirit, enabling you to "glorify God in your body."

"Father, I know that our enemy, the Devil, will try to use the area of sex in my life to render me ineffective for You and Your Kingdom. Give me the understanding and the resolve to be able to stand against his attacks, and to keep my "vessel in sanctification and honor" (1 Thessalonians 4:4). Amen"

Questions for discussion

1. Considering the soul-tie that is established through sex, why can it be said that sex <u>before</u> marriage is committing adultery? What will be the effect on the future marriage bond?

2. What is God's purpose for "making out?" What effect do you think it might have on your future marriage? Is recreation one of God's purposes for sex?

3. What do you say to the question, "How many children do you want?" By answering that question, what are some things you are in actuality saying?

4. How does the third purpose for sex, pleasure, differ from the world's perspective on sex for pleasure? How does that practically effect the practice of sex?

---

[1] Along with Kasun's *The War on Population*, there is E. Calvin Beisner, *Man, Economy, and the Environment in Biblical Perspective*, (Moscow, ID: Canon Press, 1994), and *Prospects for Growth: A Biblical View of Population, Resources and the Future* (Crossway, 1990). Julian L. Simon, *The Ultimate Resource* (Princeton, NJ: Princeton University Press, 1981); *The Economics of Population Growth* (Princeton University Press, 1978); *Population Matters: People, Resources, Environment and Immigration* (New Brunswick NJ: Transaction Press, 1990); Max Singer, *Passage to a Human World: The Dynamics of Creating Global Wealth* (Indianapolis, IN: Hudson Institute, 1987); Dixie Lee Ray, *Trashing the Planet* (Washington, DC: Regnery Gateway, 1990).

Chapter 15

Principles of Purity

"But be doers of the word and not hearers only, deceiving yourselves. (H)e who looks into the perfect law of liberty and continues in it, and is not a forgetful hearer but a doer of the word, this one will be blessed in what he does." (James 1:22,25)

Knowing the information in the last three chapters, whole-heartedly agreeing with it, and even having strong convictions about it, is very different from being able, in daily experience, to walk out such convictions. Remaining sexually pure in today's world, when there is absolutely no cultural encouragement to do so, is very difficult, even for the most devout Christian. Yet, keeping our vessels pure by not only giving mental assent to God's sexual standards, but actually obeying them, is the way to blessing. Conversely, disobeying them brings much pain and heartache.

It is not that all is lost for the young person who has engaged in pre-marital sex. There will just be more emotional and spiritual damage that will have to be healed at some point. We are all sinners, but we want to minimize our sin and its effects as much as possible in order to be able to function at maximum capacity in the family business of extending the kingdom of God.

In this chapter, I want to first look at some of the harmful effects of pre-marital sex, and then discuss the powerful progression that occurs when a sexual relationship is begun. Failure to understand this phenomenon is a major reason sincere, Christian, young people stumble in their attempts to remain sexually pure. Finally, I want to propose four biblical principles of purity that, if adopted and followed carefully, will get the next generation of kingdom warriors to the altar without the crippling results of youthful ignorance that render so many would-be warriors ineffective in the battle.

The debilitating effects of pre-marital sex

We have seen that pre-marital sex creates a soul-tie that makes bonding with one's future mate difficult, diluting the one-flesh relationship that God intends for His children in order for them to function at optimum capacity. The more sexual partners one has had, the more ties to hinder marital unity.

We never break God's law without consequences. There are always results, even though it may take some time, maybe even years, for those results to manifest themselves. Multiple soul-ties, while probably the most debilitating effect of pre-marital sex, is not the only result by any means. Guilt is a second inevitable result for a Christian. While a non-Christian can sometimes sin without feeling guilty (his conscience has been seared [1 Timothy 4:2] and he suppresses the truth [Romans 1:18]), a Christian will not be able to break the law of God that is written on his heart (Jeremiah 31:33) and enjoy his sin. He will be miserable as the Holy Spirit convicts him and leads him back to the path of righteousness (Psalm 23:3).

Modern psychology recognizes the enormous problem that guilt presents in our society, and therefore many psychologists attempt to eliminate the problem by eliminating the behavioral standard. They reason that if we can just throw off the old external, "puritanical" taboos, there will be no more guilt, and we can sin with impunity. They fail to understand that all men have the work of the law written on their hearts, and no matter how many times they are told that sin is permissible, they must still either accuse themselves (recognize their guilt) or excuse themselves (suppress the truth) in reference to God's law (Romans 2:14,15). God's law will not go away, but remains the benchmark by which all human conduct is judged. The only remedy for guilt is genuine repentance toward God, and then forgiveness in Jesus Christ.

Another problem with pre-marital sex is the loss of respect that inevitably follows, for oneself as well as one's partner. Tom was a young pastor's son who had grown up in church, attended a Christian high school, and then went away to a Christian college. He met a girl from a similar background during his first semester, and after a whirl-wind romance, tearfully broke the news to his parents at Christmas that she was pregnant. He had been like a kid in a candy store, enjoying dating for the first time, not understanding what we are discussing here. As he examined the possible courses of action with his parents, he was hesitant to consider marriage, because, as he said, "I have lost respect for her." This logically makes no sense, because they were both willing participants, but because she had given in to his advances, he no longer respected her.

No matter how insistent a man may be in the heat of the moment, his ideal bride is still a virgin. And even though a woman is a willing partner in a pre-marital affair, she secretly longs for a man who honors her and does not violate her purity before God.

Premarital sex causes her to lose respect for the man, but also to doubt that she, herself, is worthy of his esteem. "Maybe all I have to offer to a man is my body," she reasons subconsciously. This loss of self-respect, and the feeling of worthlessness that follows, is a tremendous burden that is very difficult to unload.

Lack of trust is another consequence of failing to remain sexually pure. Even when a man or woman eventually marries their sexual partner, there can be nagging questions as to that one's ability to remain faithful. "The marriage fence meant nothing to him before we were married. I wonder if it means anything to him now." When marriage partners must be apart, a lack of trust can be devastating to the intimacy, effectiveness, and satisfaction that God is building into the one-flesh relationships of His children.

Finally, sexual impurity leads to lack of restraint. Countless women have yielded to the temptation to have sexual intercourse fully believing that they would marry the men who were professing undying love for them. After the conquest was accomplished, the men were off to other pastures, eventually marrying women who would not yield to their sexual advances, and who they, therefore, could "respect." The sex drive is so strong that many men will say anything to be able to satisfy it, even deceiving themselves into believing what they are saying in the passion of the moment. The jilted women, now without their virginity, find that having chaste relationships is not so important anymore. The horse is gone, so why keep the barn door locked? What was so significant the first time, now becomes almost casual.

It is not difficult to see that the results of pre-marital sex are almost invariably devastating, and yet our young people continue to be trapped in this snare. They are unknowingly placing tremendous strain on their future marriages, many of which will not survive the problems I have just enumerated. If you are one of those young, single Christians, how can you practically "abstain from sexual immorality," and "possess your vessel in sanctification and honor," and "not in passion of lust" (1 Thessalonians 4:3-5)? To be successful at this task demands measures that those who will not remain pure may consider extreme, but the prize is worth their ridicule.

"Get me to the church on time" - the sexual progression

First, it is absolutely crucial to recognize the tremendous power that God built into the human sex drive. In chapter 13 we discussed the fact that He designed sex to make two people one flesh in order for them to be complete fighting units for the extension of the kingdom of God. Sex is the engine God uses to create the foundation upon which those units are built. Once this motor is started, it is very difficult to shut it off, so it is imperative that it be started only at the proper time.

Imagine a young man on a date with a girl he has just recently met. He finds her very attractive, and as the evening progresses, he discovers they have much in common. She is a great conversationalist, and as they are leaving the movie they have attended, he holds her hand as they walk to the car. His heart races as he touches her skin, and a warm glow spreads over his whole body.

She has been equally as impressed with him. He is very considerate and kind, and yet he seems to be strong, and able to make decisions. She can relax knowing that he will take care of any eventuality. When he takes her hand as they leave the movie, her heart leaps. She finds the touch of his hand to be an almost erotic experience.

As he takes her home, he makes a date to take her to church the next Sunday night. She is thrilled that he wants to see her again.

On Sunday after church, they stop for ice cream, and then go for a walk in the park. Conversation comes easily for both of them, with absolutely no uncomfortable periods of silence. They are both perfectly at ease. When he holds her hand, both notice the level of excitement is considerably lower than it was the first time. The sexual law of diminishing returns is now operative: There must be deeper, more intimate physical contact to receive the same stimulation as the previous sexual encounter produced.

It seems very natural for him to kiss her as he tells her good night at her door. As he drives away and she goes inside, they both are excited that the thrill is back. They both have a sense that their budding romance is alive and well. What they don't recognize is that the sexual progression is also alive, and already the process of making two people one flesh is underway. A light good-night kiss will soon not be sufficient to cause the bells to ring, and the kisses will get longer and more passionate. The motor has been turned on.

If you have ever been involved physically with the opposite sex you know how the story progresses. All relationships proceed in the same manner once there is male-female physical contact. Only the names of the characters and the length of time for the progression to reach its conclusion change. That time frame depends on the resolve of the participants to remain pure, but eventually, assuming one of the lovers does not lose interest and break the other's heart, the relationship will continue down the slippery slide to sexual intercourse. Each further step in the progression more strongly cements the bond that is being formed.

Steps to oneness

In his book, Intimate Behavior,[1] Desmond Morris, a zoologist-anthropologist, and the author of a number of books that chronicle studies of the human species, relates how humans in practically every culture establish intimate relationships. He detects a pattern that is generally observable. Though he is a strong environmentalist, heavily committed to animal rights, who certainly does not have a biblical world view, his observations may be helpful. In our context we would say that the steps in this process are the steps taken as a one-flesh bond is formed. Here are Morris's steps, with my adaptation and inter-pretation added:

Step 1 **Eye to person**. He notices her across a crowded room. "Where Have I been?," he says.

Step 2 **Eye to Eye**. Their eyes meet. There is magic in the air!

Step 3 **Voice to voice**. This is a get-acquainted time as the couple gets to know one another. There are no overt sexual overtones. This step occurs in a group setting.

At this point, little if any bonding has occurred. Either or both parties can stop the relationship because the sexual progression has not begun. There has been no physical sexual contact nor any bonding due solely to romantic, emotional attachment. The relationship can remain stationary here with the two parties remaining as a brother and sister in Christ. However, if both parties desire to take the relationship further, definition is necessary. Who are we? Just friends, or something more? In the plan that I will suggest for selecting a mate, this is where courtship would begin. This will be covered in detail in Chapters 17,18 and 19.

Step 4 **Hand to hand.** "We are a couple." They have decided to continue the progression. This is the first "sexual" contact.

Step 5 **Arm to shoulder.** This is the first signal that "I want to protect you."

Step 6 **Hand to waist.** At this stage vision, deeply held beliefs, values, and life goals are shared. This is an opportunity to know one another rather intimately without sexual pressure.

Some bonding has now occurred, but nothing that cannot be rather easily broken. However, from this point on, the bond firms dramatically. This is the last chance to get out of this relationship without someone being seriously hurt. Hundreds of hours have been spent together, and a determination as to the permanent suitability of the couple for each other can be made. "Do I want to spend the rest of my life with this man/woman?" It's commitment time! If the bonding process continues, the engagement, or "betrothal" now occurs. The couple is assured of each other. If it has been discovered that the couple are not God's choice for one another, the courtship is ended.

Step 7 **Face to face (mouth to mouth).** Kissing occurs for the first time. Much time seems to be spent gazing into each other's eyes. Care must be taken as the motor is now running. The wedding had better be approaching.

Step 8 **Hand to head.** This signifies complete confidence. Who do you allow to touch your head? Only those you trust completely.

Step 9 **Eye to body.** This is not sexual in nature. "I've grown accustomed to the tent in which you live."

If Step 7, kissing, occurs too early in the process, before a permanent commitment, strain on the bond will occur because of the sexual pressures that will be introduced. Many hours should be spent together during the courtship phase of the relationship before this intimate physical contact occurs. The final three steps need no explanation. They occur after the wedding.

<u>Step 10</u> **Hand and mouth to breast.**
<u>Step 11</u> **Hand to genital.**
<u>Step 12</u> **Genital to genital.**

Morris's steps are a graphic picture of the sexual progression in action. God designed the slippery slide to end in intercourse, two people becoming one flesh. For anyone to think that he or she can stop the progression whenever they choose is foolish and naive.

We are concerned in this chapter about the bonding that occurs as a result of physical contact. It is important to note that bonding also occurs without actual physical sex when young people are romantically involved during the dating process as "boyfriend and girlfriend." This is the topic of Chapter 17.

The total package

Sex is not intercourse alone. Sex is the total package, beginning with holding hands. We do not hold hands with members of the same sex. Why? Because even holding hands is sexual in nature. Each step, beginning with holding hands, is designed by God to lead one step nearer the ultimate goal of sexual union.

One can see that sex is not recreational. "Making out" has a specific purpose, not to have a good time, but to continue the bonding process, leading eventually to sexual union within marriage. It is important to see this if sexual purity in obedience to God is the goal. I can hear someone saying, "Andrews, you have gone too far. Do you really believe that holding hands is sexual and should be avoided?" Yes, I do, until the appropriate time. Remember the problems inherent in pre-marital sex discussed at the beginning of the chapter. It is impossible to overemphasize the power of the sex drive when it is unleashed. Whatever starts the sexual engine <u>must</u> be avoided if purity is the goal.

When I taught this material many years ago a married woman came up to me afterwards. "I never thought of it before," she said, "but when I first held hands with my husband it definitely was an erotic experience. I can see that holding hands starts the motor."

Having standards that preclude any sexual contact with members of the opposite sex until a permanent commitment is made may incur the world's temporary ridicule, but that is a small price to pay for sexual purity, for after all, "Whoever therefore wants to be a friend of the world makes himself an enemy of God" (James 4:4).

Sexual progression summary

Before looking at several principles one can follow to remain pure as a single person, I would like to complete this section on the sexual progression with five ideas about the bonding process.

First, the sexual progression is irreversible. Once one has started down the slide, it is very difficult, if not impossible, to climb back up to a previous step. Romantic involvement can be terminated, but a male-female relationship can not be continued at a previous level. God's machinery is too powerful.

Second, proper bonding is gentle and slow if it is to survive. By jumping ahead in the progression too rapidly before the relational foundation is laid, the chances of failure are magnified. A solid, carefully-built one-flesh bond will be the framework for personal intimacy after marriage. Courtship (before step 4) and engagement (before step 7) give definition to the current stage of the progression.

Third, the bonding process is public and exclusive. Both participants are proud of the one with whom they are identified, and they want to "show him/her off." There is no attempt to hide how far the relationship has developed. When a couple is married, everyone knows they are having sex together. If they have not made that public declaration of commitment that is the marriage ceremony, and are sexually involved, they are bearing false witness, which is breaking one of the ten commandments. The process is exclusive in that it is not occurring with more than one person simultaneously.

Fourth, bonding is permanent. If a bond is broken, there will be pain, and there must then be emotional healing. The further down the progression, the firmer the bond, and the greater the emotional damage.

Fifth, the bond must be maintained. Attention, consideration, trust, and mutual respect are all necessary ingredients to maintain a strong one-flesh bond. Both the man and the woman must develop these skills, and the time to begin is as the bond is forming in anticipation of marriage.

We are now ready to look at some very practical biblical principles that, if followed, will go a long way in assuring that a single young person will make it to the altar with virginity intact.

230

The Principle of making no provision

"But put on the Lord Jesus Christ, and make no provision for the flesh, to fulfill its lusts" (Romans 13:14).

The young couple was going for a drive so they could "be alone and just talk." They somehow arrived at a spot with a sweeping view of the twinkling lights of the city stretched beneath them. It was a clear, balmy, starry summer night with a full moon shining brightly overhead. They found themselves suddenly caught up in the intoxication of the sights and smells of the evening and the magnetism of each other's presence. At this point, it would take Herculean resolve to not succumb to such temptation.

Their battle was lost, not in the parked car, but when the young couple left the safety of the presence of other people. The automobile has become a "sex-mobile," allowing young couples with hormones raging to be alone wherever the car can go. It makes "making provision for the lust of the flesh" very, very, easy. The young couple in our example should have gone to Denny's to "just talk" where they could have been "alone" in the restaurant. In the chapter on courtship, we will see how parents can be involved in this process and provide wisdom and protection for their young sons and daughters who often do not have the experience to understand the dangers that lie along the path to the altar.

Any situation that provides opportunity for sexual activity should be avoided by those who are romantically involved. Being alone in the home after parents have retired, traveling from one city to another alone in the car, and any other activity where the couple is alone without strict time frames and specific things to do or places to go should be shunned.

Years ago, precautions like these were a part of our culture. I remember as a youth learning from my parents to never be alone with a girl in her house. The culture taught, "Avoid every appearance of evil." However, today's culture has thrown off all such taboos. Anything goes. As a result, serious Christians will be considered "prudes" as they follow the guidelines in this chapter. We must fear God, and sinning against Him, and not man and his ridicule.

Alcohol - the world's Holy Spirit

Another way to make no provision for the flesh as a young person is to avoid situations where alcohol is available with both boys and girls present. Alcohol allows those who drink it to lose inhibitions and do things they would not ordinarily do. Drinkers feel that this is a good thing in moderation, for they see themselves as friendlier and more outgoing when they have had a few drinks. However, alcohol also breaks down resistance to things sexual in nature. How tragic to wake up in the cold light of day, not only with a hangover, but with the realization that you have been sexually compromised. Like alcohol and gasoline, alcohol, boys, and girls don't mix.

The Bible says, "Be not drunk with wine,...but be filled with the (Holy) Spirit" (Ephesians 5:18). In this verse there is an obvious parallel between wine and the Holy Spirit. When a man is filled with the Spirit, he is able to do things he would not ordinarily be able to do. He also loses inhibitions, and is friendlier, more outgoing, and more concerned with others.

The world does not have the Spirit, but it has a substitute - alcohol, the world's Holy Spirit. In a limited way, alcohol does for the world what the Holy Spirit does for God's people. At every worldly function, alcohol is served in order for the guests to be able to relax and have a good time. Christians don't need a substitute because, "The fruit of the Spirit is ...joy" (Galatians 5:22).

The principle of fleeing

"Flee sexual immorality" (1 Corinthians 6:18).

"Flee also youthful lusts, but pursue righteousness, faith, love, peace with those who call on the Lord out of a pure heart" (2 Timothy 2:22).

As a slave in the household of Potiphar the Egyptian, Joseph was a classic example of how power and rule accrue to those who serve (Genesis 39). Because of his diligence in service, Joseph found favor in his master's sight, and was eventually given responsibility for Potiphar's "house and all that he had," until Potiphar "did not know what he had except for the bread which he ate" (vs. 4,6).

Strong, responsibility-takers are attractive to women, and Potiphar's wife saw that the real ruler in her home was no longer her husband. He had abdicated his responsibility to Joseph, and was not ruling well over his wife. To use the language of Chapter 6, Potiphar was not tending to his African violet. Because she was not being cared for, she found this handsome, young Israelite extremely attractive. One day she propositioned him to have sex with her. After he refused, she began, day by day, to try to break down Joseph's resistance, probably with sexy talk (vs. 10)

Notice it says "he did not heed her, to lie with her or to be with her" (vs. 10). Even though it is tempting to titillate yourself by "just flirting," Joseph refused even that, to the point of avoiding her completely. He was doing his best to "make no provision for the lust of the flesh."

When I taught chemistry in a public high school years ago, I watched as many of the male teachers carried on flirtatious relationships with their female students. It is very flattering to older men when attractive, 18-year-olds have crushes on them, and many play it to the hilt. I saw a fairly young biology teacher leaving after school in his car with one of the girls with whom I knew he had been flirting.

Sandy came up to me after class one day with a camera, gave it to a friend, and said, "Mr. Andrews, can I get my picture with you?" I was not expecting her to sensually press herself up against me as her friend snapped the picture. I was tempted to flirt with her in the weeks that followed, as she certainly gave me every opportunity to do so, but somehow the Lord gave me the grace to refrain. At the end of the year, during year-book signing day, she came up with a page reserved for me to write a long message to her. I wrote, "To Sandy, best wishes for an enjoyable summer, Mr. Andrews."

There came a time when "making no provision" was not enough. Joseph had done everything possible to not place himself in a compromising position, but one day Potiphar's wife grabbed him, and he found it necessary to flee, leaving his "garment" in her hand (vs. 12). He recognized that adultery with her was "great wickedness" and a "sin against God" (vs. 9). Joseph's fear of God, and his desire to please Him led to more than two years in prison because of Potiphar's wife's lie, but eventually to exaltation as the ruler of all of Egypt, second in command to Pharaoh himself.

Sometimes, no matter how careful a young man or woman has been to not be in compromising situations, they may find themselves in a place where to flee is the only recourse. Maybe it's in a car where everyone is doing drugs, or at a party where alcohol is flowing freely, or alone with a boy that you are not sure about. Fleeing will seem to be juvenile, prudish, and foolish to those around you, but this is the time to fear God rather than man. "The fear of the Lord is the beginning of wisdom" (Psalm 111:10), and "The fear of man brings a snare" (Proverbs 29:25).

It's not all her fault

Before we go on to the next principle of purity, let's take a moment to analyze Potiphar's relationship with his wife in light of what we have learned. Every teaching I have ever heard on this passage pictures Potiphar's wife as the villain, and certainly she was no paragon of virtue. However, an understanding of the kingdom of God will give us a slightly different picture.

The woman is the glory of the man (1 Corinthians 11:7), i.e., she reflects his rule in her life, showing his care or neglect by her countenance, speech, and behavior. Potiphar was obviously not providing her with the love and leadership she desperately needed. His primary interest was surely elsewhere, probably in his job as the captain of Pharaoh's guard. He had abdicated his rule over his home so completely that "he did not know what he had except for the bread which he ate" (vs. 6). His wife's advances toward Joseph were undoubtedly out of desperation for the affection Potiphar had long since ceased to give her.

A woman who has an affair is generally seen as an unfaithful seductress, when in actuality, more often than not, she is the ignored, put down, and unappreciated wife of some selfish slob who does not have a clue about how to rule over her with love and leadership.

The principle of setting the mind

"...bringing every thought into captivity to the obedience of Christ" (2 Corinthians 10:5).
"Set your mind on things above, not on things on the earth" (Colossians 3:2).

It has been said, and I believe rightfully so, that the most important sex organ is the mind. For both men and women, sex begins there, and a Godly, pure sex life begins with an ability to control one's thought life. That is why the Bible has so much to say about "setting your mind." Satan is after the minds of God's children, because he knows if he can capture their minds, their bodies will follow, and they will be immobilized as a fighting force.

To remain sexually pure, it is imperative to control what comes into the mind. Movies, books, TV, magazines, etc., unless very carefully screened, are like a sewer, constantly flowing through our minds. One cannot consistently feed the mind on a diet of sewer-water and be healthy. Even if a Christian is able to resist acting out what he has seen, his thoughts cannot be "captive to the obedience of Christ." To think and meditate on noble, just, pure, lovely, virtuous and praiseworthy things (Philippians 4:4) is very difficult to do when a sewer was flowing through the mind just a minute ago.

I am not saying that it is necessary to read only the Bible, or to only go to church, only sing hymns, and never go to the movies. Not every activity in which we are involved can be positive and uplifting spiritually. However, what we do must not be detrimental to our spiritual life. There are three types of activities in regard to moral or spiritual content:

1. Obviously spiritual activities. i.e., worship, Bible study, church attendance, prayer, etc. (can obviously be done to the glory of God).
2. Activities that are not specifically spiritual or religious. i.e., job, athletics, school, some music, dress, hobbies, recreation, etc. (can be done to the glory of God or not, depending on the mind-set of the participant).
3. Spiritually and morally detrimental activities, i.e., pornography, some music, most R-rated movies, books that advocate illicit affairs, etc. (can never be done to the glory of God).

It is not necessary only to do activities from category 1, but by being involved in these things as much as possible, the mind-set that leads to sexual purity can be more easily maintained. Category 2 activities add spice and enjoyment to life, and a kingdom warrior will extend the rule of Jesus Christ into these areas, bringing the activities themselves into the realm of the kingdom of God. The danger to beware of is that these things can become idols, pushing out the motivation to extend the kingdom. Category 3 activities must be avoided completely. It is impossible to maintain the proper mind-set while engaged in them.

Nothing is more important to a kingdom warrior who desires to walk in sexual purity than the principle of setting his mind, for "as he thinks in his heart, so is he" (Proverbs 23:7).

The principle of forgiveness

"(I)f we walk in the light as He is in the light, we have fellowship with one another, and the blood of Jesus Christ His Son cleanses us from all sin. If we say we have no sin, we deceive ourselves, and the truth is not in us. If we confess our sins, He is faithful and just to forgive us our sins and to cleanse us from all unrighteousness" (1 John 1:7-9).

The final section in a chapter on principles of purity has to be on forgiveness, for as Solomon said, "Who can say, 'I have made my heart clean, I am pure from my sin'?" (Proverbs 20:9). No matter how many principles we understand about sexual purity, or how earnestly we attempt to follow them, the measure of purity we attain falls infinitely short of the purity that God demands, the absolute holiness of His person.

However, we are to "Be holy, for I am holy" (1 Peter 1:16), and "cleanse ourselves from all filthiness of the flesh and spirit, perfecting holiness in the fear of God" (2 Corinthians 7:1). How can we do something that God is asking us to do, that we in fact cannot do? How can we be holy when our best efforts fall so short?

The answer lies in the true gospel of Jesus Christ. God has His children on a path to glory and holiness, and arrival at the destination is assured. "Whom He predestined, these He also called, whom He called, these He also justified, and whom He justified these He also glorified" (Romans 8:30). All the verbs are in the Greek aorist tense, which signifies an action completed in the past. To God, your glorification is already accomplished. You can do nothing to thwart His unstoppable plan! You are already dressed in the pure robes of righteousness of Jesus Christ.

On the other hand, when we stumble and fall off the path, God holds us accountable, but He provides us a wonderful avenue of restoration. That avenue of restoration is not pretending that we have no sin by making excuses. It is not hiding from the evaluations of others that we are afraid will be less than perfect, nor is it by blaming our sin on somebody else. Those are characteristics of religious people, like the

Pharisees, who think they have no sin, and who are trying to please God by being good enough.

No, the way of restoration that God has designed is to eagerly embrace our sin, owning responsibility for every last vestige of it that we can find, and then repenting of it, knowing that by walking in the light in this way the experiential power of God's forgiveness is released, allowing His kingdom to grow.

Two truths exist in tension: (1) God has already glorified his children; (2) His children must walk in repentance on the path to glory. May God help us to understand the glorious fullness of His Gospel.

"Father, in order for me to walk in sexual purity, I must first see that I am accepted already in your beloved Son. Without that knowledge, all the other material in this chapter will be of little use. Then Lord, I want to glorify You with my purity of life. Thank You for supplying me with the hope that that will happen. Amen"

Questions for discussion

1. Which of the results of pre-marital sex given in this chapter do you feel to be the most damaging? Which seem to be inconsequential or less serious? Why?

2. What do you plan to do in your relationships with the opposite sex in light of the information on the sexual progression, if anything? Is your strategy realistic and workable?

3. What situations in which you have found yourself in the past warranted avoiding in light of "make no provision?" How could you have avoided them? Is "fleeing" realistic? Why or why not?

4. What are some practical suggestions that would be helpful in learning to "set your mind?" What activities in which you are now engaged are detrimental to your mind-set?

5. How can you reconcile God's sovereign control over us in moving us up the path to glory, and our responsibility to stay on the path by walking in repentance?

---

[1] Desmond Morris, *Intimate Behavior*, (New York: Random House, 1971).

Chapter 16

Communication

During the Gulf War, one of the highest priority targets for United States bombing raids was the Iraqi communications network. The United States military knew that if an enemy's communication capability was disrupted, he would become an ineffective fighting force.

In the same manner, in the great cosmic war in which we are involved, the enemy of our souls knows that if he can disrupt communication between husband and wife, their one-flesh fighting unit will be impotent against him. There is no greater cause for powerlessness among married warriors than a lack of communication with one another.

In Chapter 13 we discussed the fact that the marriage commitment provides the protection necessary for true intimacy to grow from the one-flesh sexual relationship that forms its foundation. Marital intimacy is the complete sharing of oneself with one's spouse, spiritually and emotionally as well as physically. It allows the couple to function at maximum capacity. However, without communication skills, the couple will not achieve the intimacy they were created to experience, and they will be ineffective in the spiritual battle in which they are involved. For most of us, this ability to communicate does not just happen. It is a learned art, requiring skill, sensitivity, and a life-time to master.

What is communication?

First, communication is the <u>giving of oneself to another.</u> In marriage, that giving is complete, in every way, including physical, in order that the one-flesh unit can function at maximum capacity. "This is who I am. You know everything about me. I have hidden nothing from you." It is the opening up of oneself for the total investigation of one's spouse.

We will note in subsequent chapters that, before marriage, transparency in communication between members of the opposite sex must be carefully guarded against. Even praying alone with a boy friend or girl friend can form premature emotional bonds, and even cause Christian young people to be drawn into unwanted physical relationships. Giving of oneself, both physically and emotionally, to a member of the opposite sex must be reserved for marriage.

However, once we are married, walking in the light with brothers or sisters of the same sex, or with other couples, is a vital part of the love we are to have for one another in the Body of Christ. This openness is a very necessary component of God's institution of the church, if it too is to be effective in the battle. Not being genuine, not confessing our faults one to another (James 5:16), and instead pretending we are something we are not, are all ways to fail to communicate truth, and therefore hinder the growth of the Body (Ephesians 4:15,25). Others are always aware of our faults much more clearly than we are, so it is ridiculous for us to feign perfection. Not only do we look foolish, but also the wall of denial that we have built to protect ourselves keeps others out and hinders open communication. It is our pride that keeps us from facing ourselves.

Christians desperately need to be transparent one with another. How can I be built up together with you if you refuse to let me know the real you? I cannot be one in marriage, or in the Body of Christ with someone who will not let me into his or her life. The vulnerability that comes with true communication needs to be protected. That is the function of marriage and the church: to provide the framework of a permanent covenant of protection that binds us together in commitment one to the other. Certainly we do not share ourselves intimately with strangers. We use caution because we know not if this new acquaintance is trustworthy. But we are permanently bound in a one-flesh relationship with our mates, and we are one in Jesus Christ with our brothers and sisters in the church (Ephesians 4:1-4).

However, very practically, before we lower our protective walls and give ourselves to each other, whether mates, or brothers and sisters in the church, we must know that we are loved and accepted. We are commanded to provide that security time and again in the scriptures.

Therefore, in both marriage and church, the second aspect of communication that is absolutely crucial is the <u>receiving of another as he is, without condemnation.</u>

Build up rather than tear down

Receiving others as they are involves edifying them with our tongues, rather than being critical and tearing them down. "Let no corrupt communication proceed out of your mouth, but what is good for necessary edification, that it may impart grace to the hearers" (Ephesians 4:29). We generally take this verse to refer to off-color talk or profanity, and that is certainly a part of the intended meaning. But there is no more "corrupt communication" than negative criticism. Nothing is more destructive to communication than a critical spirit.

For example, Jill is a perfectionist, and wants everything to be just right. I am naturally a last-minute, fly-by-the-seat-of-your-pants kind of a person. This is a fatal combination on those "let's-get-away-alone-so-we-can-communicate" weekends.

I would tend to make last-minute arrangements, everything would not be perfect, and Jill would not be satisfied, always ready to communicate to me her displeasure. I felt like I couldn't do anything right to bless her, and her criticism didn't make me want to try. For a long time, I felt like I was condemned for everything I tried to do. As a result, I didn't want to be vulnerable with Jill and share myself with her. Her critical attitude cut off communication between us.

Over the years I have realized that a lot of my lack of preparation for times alone was, just as Jill suspected, a result of my not caring for my African violet as I should, and I have tried to become a better gardener. On the other hand, she is learning to take the expressions of love that I do give her and be satisfied, even grateful. Gratefulness brings more blessing; dissatisfaction dries it up. We are learning to receive one another without condemnation.

Men as verbal communicators

In marriage, it is crucial that a husband provide special opportunities to communicate with his wife. Weekends away without the kids and other such things, communicate that she is important to him. It may come as a shock to some men, but real, verbal communication with a woman is the way you communicate that, not by wanting to make love to her. If a man has not talked with his wife, and shared himself verbally with her, and yet wants to have sex with her, she will feel like nothing more than a piece of meat. In a long term relationship, a woman's sexual response is inseparably linked to verbal communication.

Men are notoriously poor verbal communicators, because we are not generally as relational as our wives. When I married, I was no exception. When my wife was not as interested in making love as I was, invariably it was because I had not communicated with her. I would pout, or sulk, and attempt to make life miserable for Jill by claming up. That, of course, did not achieve the desired result of making her feel sorry for me, because nothing is more despicable than a pouting man.

Learning to relate verbally on something more than a superficial level is the solution. If Jill feels that we are together spiritually and emotionally, and we have shared our hearts with one another, physical togetherness follows naturally.

A positive experience in the midst of a negative evaluation

There are obviously times when criticism is necessary. If a man has a family, it is mandatory for him to evaluate his wife and children, for that is a part of ruling, and sometimes, of necessity, that evaluation will be negative. However, he must develop the ability to build them up, even in the process of correcting behavior. His love and acceptance of them has nothing to do with their performance, and he must communicate that to them. He is still accepting them as they are, but he doesn't want to see them stay there! The attitude should be, "I believe in you. You can do it. I'm committed to you." An employer who has this attitude with his employees will see a marked improvement in performance, even though he must at times make negative evaluations. Kingdom principles apply in every area, because no part of life is independent of the rule of Jesus Christ.

There is a tremendous difference between a husband who is critical of an overweight wife, and one who helps her to lose weight. There is a great difference between a wife who is critical of her husband's inability to make a living for the family, and one who is satisfied and grateful for what they have, but who helps him with a plan to improve his employment. To be effective communicators, we must learn the trick of edifying, not tearing down, even when it is necessary to adjust or speak hard truth to one another. This will "impart grace to the hearer" (Ephesians 4:29).

Reaping and sowing in communication

A second biblical principle to consider besides "Let no corrupt communication proceed out of your mouth but what is good for necessary edification," is the principle of reaping and sowing. If I am critical of others, and tear them down, the very judgment that I have measured out to them, will return upon my head (Matthew 7:1). On the other hand if I have compassion for others, love them as brothers, am tenderhearted, courteous, do not return evil for evil, or reviling for reviling, but extend to them a blessing, 1 Peter 3:8 and 9 says that I will inherit a blessing myself. I will reap what I sow.

Summary of communication skills

Let's look at a summary of what we have said about communication:

1. Communication is the giving of oneself to another, whether to a member of the opposite sex in marriage in a one-flesh experience, or to the members of the church in a one-body experience, the Body of Christ. Without the principles of transparency, honesty and a willingness to confess faults one to another, the battle-readiness of either institution will be hindered significantly.

2. Communication is the receiving of another person as he/she is, without condemnation. It is important to see that we are all on a path, and that no one has arrived. We are further down the path than we were yesterday; not as far along as we will be tomorrow. I determine to accept and love you, as my wife, my brother, or my sister, where you are today. I want you to know that by what I do, not just by what I say.

3. I want to bless you rather than criticize you. I want to build you up rather than tear you down so you will be edified, our marriage will be a weapon for victory, and the church will be both strengthened and better equipped to batter down the gates of the enemy.

4. When it is necessary for me, in order to see you be all that God intended you to be in His kingdom, to give you a negative evaluation, I want you to know that I love you, that I want you to be a man or a woman of God, and that I will stick with you until that is accomplished. Conversely, if you are in authority over me, and it is necessary for you to give me a negative evaluation, I want to receive the evaluation as from God, and act upon it. If you have no authority in my life, and you are critical of me in some way, I want to ask the question, "Oh Lord, is it true?," and honestly desire to hear the answer.

Conversational basketball

When I was in college, my roommate and I developed a game we called conversational basketball. We played it with anyone, but we particularly enjoyed the game on double dates with girls we did not know. Even though our blind dates did not realize they were playing our little game, we would watch to see how well they would perform. Our motivation was terrible, because we would be critical later of the girls who didn't play our little game very well. However, I learned a great communication skill through it that I have tried both to apply in my own life and to teach to my children. The game went like this:

Upon first meeting the blind date, I would begin to ask her questions about herself, like "Where are you from?," "Why did you decide to come to the University of Oklahoma?," "What is your major?," "Why did you decide on that?," "What are you going to do when you graduate?," etc., trying to find out about her and get her to talk about herself. In other words, I would "throw her the ball."

Are you aware how few people really want to know anything about you and your interests, and how few are willing to actually talk about you, or be interested when you talk? The vast majority of people are really only interested in themselves and their things, and therefore constantly talk only about themselves. These girls were generally no exception. After catching the ball, rather than dribbling it a couple of times and then throwing it back with a question to me about myself, they would dribble it the rest of the evening like a Harlem Globetrotter, going between the legs, and behind the back with amazing dexterity. Every question I would ask would be a new opportunity to show off their ball-handling ability.

After taking them home at the conclusion of the evening, my roommate and I would compare notes, and almost invariably the results were the same: "What does she now know about me?" Absolutely nothing. She did not ask me one question about myself. "What do I know about her?" Absolutely everything, from food preferences, to what she did last summer, all in amazing detail. The girls always had a smashing evening, not because my roommate and I were so suave and debonair, but because we simply talked about them, probably the only boys they had ever met that were willing to do so, at least so extensively.

It was a game to us, and we probably had no more of a genuine interest in them than previous boys did, although once the habit of focusing on others is developed, it is amazing how interesting others can be. "Conversational basketball" has become second nature to me now, and I almost always play from a sincere motivation to get to know another person well.

Some examples of unskilled players

It is amazing how self-centered we are. One of the young men in my fraternity in college could turn absolutely anything that was said into a discussion about himself and his accomplishments. We were all amazed at his skill in being able to get the conversation on himself. He had a nick-name that we didn't call him to his face. We referred to him as old "That's-nothing-guess-what-I've-done Jones." I see the same selfishness in my life; wanting to be sure you know all the accomplishments of myself and my children, always wanting to promote myself and my family, always wanting you to listen to me talk about me and whatever is mine: my children, my ministry, my book, my stroke, my vision, my..., my...., my.... on into infinity. We are truly fallen sinners who need constant renewal in kingdom life.

This self-centeredness is not the method of operation of a good communicator. It is a sure formula for being a boor, and for losing effectiveness for the kingdom of God. People are not influenced, on a personal level, by such pontificators. I have occasionally been with high-profile, well known Christian leaders who did not express a glimmer of interest in anyone else but themselves. They were extremely gifted, knowledgeable, and insightful. Yet because of their lack of interest in others, except as others gave them an audience, they were limited in their personal effectiveness.

I have observed several traits that most poor communicators have in common beyond not asking anything about me or mine. First, they frequently interrupt what I am saying to change the subject. I am left hanging in mid-sentence. Obviously what I was saying was not important and, by logical extension, I am not either. They would not do that with someone they respected. Second, they don't look at me when I am talking. They look out the window, read the paper, or give their attention to their children. They have just been expounding at great length, making an extended pronouncement, and now I have a brief moment finally to say something, and they communicate that what I am saying is unimportant. Third (and this is big), as soon as I get the floor, they look at their watch, as if to say, "Hurry up and finish what you are saying, I have more important things to do." This has happened to me so many times that I have learned that if I am talking to someone and have to look at my watch, I always try to do it while I am talking.

To find a good communicator who is actually interested in me is such a rare thing that when I do I have to be careful to not talk my head off. I know several such people, and spending time with them is a joy, because they make me feel worthwhile. The ball is constantly thrown back and forth, with a mutual sharing of ourselves, our problems, our successes, and our failures. Indeed our lives are open and we are transparent. We receive each other with genuine interest, and without condemnation. The Body of Christ is built up as such lives are shared.

Some conversational all-Americans

I will never forget the first such person I met. I was a freshman in college, and I had a first date with a new friend's sister. I was playing conversational basketball, fully expecting the typical response, when I began to realize that she was skillfully giving of herself, but the majority of the questions were being asked of me. Try as I might, I could not keep the focus of our evening on her. Before the evening was over, though she was not a particularly beautiful girl, she was extremely attractive to me. I tried to date her further, but a senior football player had also found her attractive, and had beaten out this skinny freshman in the game of romance. I was never an all-star in that league.

Just recently I visited a church in another state where a pastor had a very successful outreach to the poor, and had written a number of books on that subject and others as well. I wanted to see how he identified the truly biblically poor, and kept from subsidizing the lazy and rebellious. He was a very busy man, but he gave Jill and me about an hour of his time. He did not seem in the least hurried, but made us feel that we were the most important people in the world to him during that time. He asked me a number of questions about Tree of Life and our ministry, and we left not only with some new information, but also encouraged and built up in the battle.

Becoming good communicators

Ramah has always been somewhat of a steamroller in her relationships with others, and we recognized that trait relatively early in her life. It often seems to go with leadership ability. We began to work with her on giving others space, being quiet, and letting others have the stage. It was extremely hard for her. I can remember one instance in junior high chauffeuring her and the girl who lived next door back home from some activity they had attended. Ramah so totally dominated the conversation in the back seat of the car that I don't believe the girl said more than two words all the way home, about a fifteen minute drive. When we got home, I pointed out to Ramah what she had done. She, as a thirteen or fourteen year-year-old, had been oblivious to it.

We continued to work with her, but it was very difficult for her to recognize when her steamroller was running. She was monopolizing her friends to such a degree that we felt we needed to get her away from them to give them space to develop in their own right, and to spend more time with her ourselves. We decided to withdraw her from our church school and home school her for the second semester of the eighth grade.

Her time alone with her mother that semester was invaluable. They both look back at that time as a milestone in their relationship. We hoped to see the fruit of it in Ramah's relationships with others.

We enrolled her the next year in the large Christian high school that her brothers had attended. I was coaching the boy's basketball team there, and teaching the family living class to the seniors, so I was there all day and able to monitor Ramah's progress. One day, as we drove home from school, she said, "Daddy, I'm so glad you have been working with me on talking about myself and not letting others talk, because Carrie does that all the time and it is so unattractive." We sat in the driveway and talked for several more minutes about being a good conversationalist and being interested in other people. I went in the house with her with rejoicing in my heart, knowing that our training was paying off, and that she was going to learn to be a good communicator.

Three biblical truths to apply to communication

What a man says is indicative of what is in his heart (Matthew 12:34), and if you have identified yourself as a poor conversational basketball player, it could well be because of pride. Your heart is filled with yourself, and you have little room for others. If you are willing to see that now, and repent of it, I want to give you three principles you can work on to become a better conversationalist. If you have not taken care of the root of pride, these suggestions will be mechanical, and not genuine. There are those who understand conversational basketball and try to play it, but who are still not genuinely interested in others, and have not repented of that fact. Others can tell.

247

1. The first principle is found in 1 Peter 5:6.

"Therefore humble yourselves under the mighty hand of God, that He may exalt you in due time."

Humbling myself is a continual process, not something I can do once and forget about. Personally, pride rears its ugly head constantly in my life, and I know I must smash it every time. I must be ruthless with myself, denying myself the luxury of that sweet, delicious experience of exalting myself, knowing from this verse that God will do that at the appropriate time.

I want to take a seat at the foot of the Master's table, and let the Master bid me come to the head of the table in His time (Luke 14:8-11). I don't want to push myself, and force the Master to humble me. My prayer is that if He has to, it will be before that great day when the thoughts and intents of my heart are laid bare for all to see (1 Corinthians 4:5).

When my heart has been humbled before God and those with whom I live, I will be able to "Let another man praise [me], and not [my] own mouth; a stranger and not [my] own lips" (Proverbs 27:2). I am always very impressed with someone who has accomplished something of note, and I discover that fact, not from them, but from someone else. That person has immediate credibility in my eyes, and I am open to hear what he has to say. The fruit of a humble heart is a mouth that deflects praise from oneself, and exalts the Lord and others.

2. The second biblical principle to apply to the area of communication is found in Philippians 2:3,4.

"Let nothing be done through selfish ambition or conceit, but in lowliness of mind let each esteem others better than himself. Let each of you look out not only for his own interests, but also for the interests of others."

This is the positive aspect of the previous truth. Not only am I not to exalt myself. That is hard enough. But now these verses say that I am also to exalt others. I am to esteem, or give honor, regard or deference to others. I am to build them up. I am to regard them as better, more important, and more worthy of a place of honor than I am. Are you able to be open and honest about yourself and your weaknesses with other brothers and sisters in the church? Have you had them pray for you? This is a practical expression of believing that others have something to offer you. How refreshing an attitude like this is when all about us are scrapping and scratching for recognition and honor.

Not long ago a man in our church sought my counsel concerning a difficult situation he was facing at his job. John's boss, who in John's estimation was not entirely competent, was using John's expertise in a certain area, and taking complete credit for it himself. John was irritated to say the least, and wondered what He should do.

We discussed the kingdom principle of establishing the one in authority over you, and the above verses as well. I suggested that he esteem his boss as competent and do everything possible to make him look good to insure his success. John followed my advice, and reported that he had a new joy and peace on the job. Walking in the kingdom "is not food and drink, but righteousness and peace and joy in the Holy Spirit" (Romans 14:17).

Verse 4 says that I am to be interested in the things of others and not just my own things. This is the biblical foundation for conversational basketball. It also means giving of my time to help others. Helping a brother move on my only free day of the week, going to somebody else's son's basketball game, and helping somebody else put in the Formica in his kitchen are all expressions of this truth. It means getting out of myself and being involved with others when I have absolutely nothing to gain. This is "looking out for the things of others."

3. The final principle concerning communication is found in Hebrews 13:1-3.

> "Let brotherly love continue. Do not forget to entertain strangers...., Remember the prisoners as if chained with them, and those who are mistreated, since you yourselves are in the body also."

These verses contain at least two principles that make for good communication. First is the concept of hospitality, both to those who are strangers in need, as well as to those who are well known to you. A warm, open home invites open hearts, and is a wonderful tool with which to build the Lord's church, and thereby to attack the gates of hell! Guests for dinner should be a regular occurrence in the homes of those who are serious about communicating with others, as should house guests in need of temporary shelter.

Second, in these verses we are admonished to remember those in chains, "as if chained with them, and those who are mistreated..." To extend yourself to those who are in bondage to the enemy takes insight. To see the invisible chains that are binding them, and to be willing to help them to be free takes a measure of maturity.

A wonderful example of being willing to help free captives is extending oneself to visitors and new members at church. Invariably, visitors are not looking for the best worship, or the most eloquent preacher, but a place where they will be accepted and cared for, and though they might not know it, where they can be freed from the bondage of the Devil.

The temptation for those of us who have both found a measure of deliverance from the enemy's chains, and who have already been accepted and cared for in the body of Christ, is to think that church is primarily for our enjoyment and comfort. We forget what it was like before we found our place in the Body of Christ. We do not have the empathy we would have if we still remembered the chains, and acted "as if chained with them." We go to church and wait to see who will extend themselves to us, rather than thinking of who might need us to extend ourselves to them. To meet new people, practice a little conversational basketball when visiting with them after church, and then invite them to dinner the next week is the demeanor and behavior of a warrior who is determined to spoil the strong man's house (Matthew 12:29).

What kind of a communicator are you? Are you afraid to share yourself for fear of being hurt? It's time to take the risk. The way to healing is to open your wound to the healing salve of Jesus Christ, first in the person of your mate, and then in His Body, the Church. Are you critical and judgmental of your mate, and of the brothers and sisters with whom you have been placed? The reason for that is that you are critical and judgmental of yourself. It's time to see yourself as one of the precious ones for whom Christ died. He chose you in eternity past from among all of his created ones to call, to justify, and to glorify (Romans 8:30)! He has accepted you in Jesus Christ (Ephesians 1:6). It's time for you to accept yourself.

"Father, show me the true gospel, so I can get out of myself, and focus on extending Your kingdom in the life of my mate, my family, in the church, and in the world. Amen"

Questions for discussions

1. If you are married, do you feel you are able to share yourself totally with your mate? Does he/she agree with you? If not, why not?

2. If you gossip and are critical of others, why do you do that? Do others think you are critical and judgmental? Do you think they are wrong about you?

3. If you are not a good conversational basketball player, what strategies can you devise to help you to reach out to others?

4. Has this chapter and these questions made you feel uncomfortable? Why do you think that is? Do you agree or disagree with what has been said? With what do you disagree?

Part Five
"Selecting a Mate"

Chapter 17

Dating

My teenage years in the 1950's were the most painful of my life. For me, the advent of puberty meant a massive dose of zits. Combine that with a body so skinny that when I got sunburned on my back my chest peeled, and you have a boy who had a lot of free time on weekends. I was a good student, and, surprisingly enough, a fair athlete. But at that age all that really mattered in my high school was social standing, and I had none.

Tulsa Central High, a three-year school, had over 3000 students. It had a very rigid social structure, complete with high school fraternities and sororities. I still remember the names of them all, and the pain I felt at being snubbed by most of the people in them, the people that I thought really "counted."

Dating, of course, was an integral part of the whole social scene. As seventh graders, we all joined Skilley's Dance Studio to learn to dance, and then were encouraged by our parents to begin to pair up. Dances were held in homes on the weekends, with the parents staying discretely in another room while eighth and ninth graders began to learn about sex to slow music in a darkened basement. We were beginning to play out the romantic ideas concerning this adolescent ritual of dating that had been force-fed into our minds since we were toddlers by our culture. I'm sure our well-meaning parents were concerned about us "being popular" when we got to high school. My parents, however, didn't seem to worry about that, and it's a good thing, because I definitely wasn't.

Dating began in earnest in high school, with all the rumors of sexual conquests, girls who "would do it," and those who wouldn't. I had to content myself with athletics and studies, yet I was always longing for the thrill of having a girl friend. Much to my great dismay, the Lord was protecting me.

255

Looking back from a forty year vantage point, I can see clearly the foolishness, even the destructiveness, of much of the social customs of the day. However, the pain I felt then was very real. Dating was the only way I knew to relate to the opposite sex.

Likewise, today many Christians as well know of no other option when it comes to finding a husband or a wife. Until relatively recently the only books on mate selection in Christian bookstores have been on "Christian dating."

I want to try to analyze the process of dating in this chapter, and then propose an alternative in Chapter 18. Remember, we are trying to order our lives as much as possible by the Bible, believing that it has the answers to all the important issues in life, including the right way to get married.

The history of dating and romance

It may be surprising to most to learn that dating - indeed, the whole concept of romance - is a relatively recent phenomenon. It grew out of the aftermath of the Enlightenment in Europe, as men moved away from the Bible as the standard for all of life.

Until the middle of the 17th century, mate selection was a family decision, with the children of both sexes given, at most, veto power over prospective husbands and wives. However, from 1660 to 1800, a dramatic shift occurred. It became customary for children to make their own choices, with parents being left with no more than the right of veto over socially or economically unsuitable candidates.[1]

At the same time there was an inevitable shift of emphasis in motives for marital choices away from family interests toward romantic love. While many still agreed that both physical desire and romantic love were unsafe bases for an enduring marriage, since both were "violent mental disturbances which would inevitably be of only short duration,"[2] for the first time in history, romantic love became a respectable motive for marriage among the propertied classes.

What caused this dramatic shift in the method of mate selection from deference to family to individual autonomy? Why did the motives to marry change from family, economic, social or political considerations to personal romantic feelings? The rising flood of Romance literature reflecting the spirit of the Enlightenment, particularly the romantic novel, was undoubtedly a prominent factor in the cultural change that was occurring.[3]

Some of these writers of the Romantic period proposed that one might appropriately cultivate romantic feelings for a member of the opposite sex who was not one's spouse, whether or not one was married to somebody else. Secret romances, seductions, and doing what the emotions dictated were encouraged by the Romance novels and poems of the day. Even those who held to physical marital faithfulness, saw emotion-only affairs where the parties "fanned the flames of their passions without giving release to physical affection" as permissible, even noble.[4]

With an understanding of this historical background,[5] it is easy to see how our present dating system came into being. The groundwork had been laid by the independent, autonomous spirit of the Romantic period, and with the advent of the automobile in this century, new occasions for couples to be alone together on dates, and, consequently, to become sexually involved, proliferated. Along with this obvious sexual opportunity, dating also encouraged the more subtle and still very damaging practice of multiple emotional romantic attachments.

In the last chapter we dealt with physical involvement, and the resultant one-flesh bond. In this chapter we will discuss how bonds are formed during the dating process apart from actual sexual activity.

Emotional fornication[6]

Unlike the Romanticists, Christians rightfully believe that it is proper and necessary for married couples, after they are married, to have, not only exclusive sexual rights to their spouse, but exclusive emotional rights as well. Jill has the right to believe that I will not be emotionally involved with another woman.

However, we do not hesitate to condone and even encourage romantic, emotional-only attachments before marriage, as long as there is no physical sex. It has been understood that Christian young people will date, even "go steady," and develop romantic emotional feelings for maybe a half dozen members of the opposite sex, before there is any intention of a permanent commitment. It does not seem to matter to us how promiscuous our young people are emotionally. We actively encourage the dating process that makes multiple emotional bonding a natural result, a process we could call "emotional fornication." And generally, somewhere along the way, it's a good bet that the sexual progression will have taken another couple physically further down the slide than they wanted to go.

No one has everything

What are the results of this "emotional fornication?" As we date, we learn that giving one's heart away can be done a number of times. We know what it's like to have been emotionally involved with different types of girlfriends or boyfriends, each one with different strengths and weaknesses. It then becomes very difficult to be satisfied with only one type when it comes time to marry.

For example, Jill had to face the fact that I am just not a poetry-loving, artistic type, though at times I try. If I had been the only man with whom she had ever been involved, it would have been much easier for her to be satisfied with me. Conversely, she is not naturally particularly attentive to me and my needs as are some wives toward their husbands, though her desire is that she would be. Neither of us have all the qualities that we would like to have in order to meet all of our spouse's expectations.

To those who grow up playing the dating game, there is a constant search for the "perfect" mate. It seems that variety truly is the spice of life, even to those who have not been physically promiscuous. Those who date have related to many different types of prospective mates, enjoying the various qualities that each of them bring to the relationship.

Old habits die hard, and often the man (or the woman) who has developed many emotional attachments before marriage will naturally continue to do so afterwards, because his mate doesn't completely satisfy him. She can't compete with that composite woman in his mind who possesses all the wonderful qualities (and none of the bad ones!) of all the women he has ever dated. Dissatisfaction with one's spouse is the first result of the emotional fornication that occurs in the dating process.

The two possible outcomes of dating

The one who does not choose to end a "steady" dating relationship, but whose boyfriend or girlfriend does, often does not find that romantic experience to be as pleasurable in the final analysis as it at first appeared to be. Once the couple has progressed past friendship on to romantic involvement, generally only two things will happen: they will marry, or someone will be hurt. Very, very rarely does the break-up come by mutual consent. If the couple is too young to marry, heartache lies ahead for one of the parties. The breaking of the emotional bond that has formed will be damaging and leave scars that will hinder clean, solid bonding with the future spouses of both parties. Memories of old flames make it difficult to kindle a new fire. Any physical entanglement, of course, deepens the bond, and compounds the problem.

An extended romance where the couple find each other as teen-agers, date all through high school, and eventually marry, is always a possibility. Some do marry their "high school sweet-hearts." However, the sexual progression will inevitably have taken over with even the most well-meaning Christian couple, often forcing them to live a lie and bear false witness as to the state of their one-flesh relationship. They are pretending to be single, while actually being one-flesh, or if they have not had actual intercourse, they are probably involved in physical activities that go along with intercourse. Remember, sex is a total package. Guilt, lack of respect, and lack of trust, as we saw in the last chapter, are very real if the package is opened before the wedding.

Do you belong to me?

A fourth result of dating is often a possessiveness that assumes rights and privileges for dating couples that rightfully belong only to those who are married. As we saw in Chapter 13, 1 Corinthians 7 clearly teaches that a husband and wife have certain rights over each other. "Forsaking all others," as is often repeated in marriage vows, applies to more than just physical relationships, but emotional as well. It is a fruit of the permanent, public commitment before God and the witnesses who were gathered at the wedding. As I mentioned above, Jill and I have a right to expect emotional, as well as physical fidelity and accountability from one another.

However, dating couples often make these same demands upon each other. They demand to know where their "steady" was the previous evening, and where they will be tomorrow. They want to be considered when all plans are made, and even demand "faithfulness" to their dating relationship. They are jealous if their partner talks with, or spends too much time with, a member of the opposite sex.

As you can see, dating a steady boy friend or girl friend, even if sex is not involved, is an attempt to enjoy the fruits of marriage before being ready to take on the responsibilities. Making all plans together, constant consideration of the other's wishes, and being accountable for emotions and actions to someone who loves us, are all facets of the loyalty that comes with being one-flesh together within the marriage commitment. These fruits all grow from the marriage root that includes responsibility for material and emotional provision, faithfulness and care in times of sickness or poverty, and complete identification with that one in every area of life until death do you part! The fruit without that root will turn out to be rotten to the taste!

Practice for divorce

An aspect of the dating syndrome of going steady and then breaking up, and going steady and breaking up *ad infinitum*, is that the ending of emotional attachments gets to be commonplace. What was difficult to do the first time, gets to be, if not easier, at least more familiar, with each occurrence. We learn that emotional bonds are not permanent, because we've had a dozen of them!

Marriage, on the other hand, demands a perseverance in the face of tremendous adversity. When she is rebellious and won't follow his leadership, when he is lazy, selfish and inconsiderate, when emotions have cooled, and when everything that is done seems to be an attempt to be irritating, they are still married. Their vows were for better or for worse, and even when things couldn't get any worse, their commitment still holds.

By capturing us in this crucible of marriage, God burns the dross from our lives. We can't get away. The very best tool He has to burn away our imperfections is our spouse, and the marriage commitment is how he keeps us from running when He turns up the heat.

However, if we have dated, we have practice in getting out of uncomfortable situations: break up and blame the other party. That makes it much easier to get out of an uncomfortable marriage without asking the Lord that unpleasant question: "Oh Lord, is it I? Is it my fault?" All of our dating experiences have been practice for divorce.

Whom do I obey?

Another result of dating is a confusion of authority. Remember from Chapter 5 that most basic of all questions, "Who is in charge?"? That is an important consideration when we examine a dating relationship. How should we answer that question?

Since steady dating is a male-female relationship like marriage with similar emotional commitment, only supposedly to a lesser degree, the temptation is to say, "The boy." However, he has absolutely no authority in the girl's life. Her father is her authority, and will continue to be until he relinquishes that authority in response to the question, "Who gives this woman to be married to this man?"

What if her boyfriend asks her to do something her father has told her not to do? What if her boyfriend does not want her to do something her father wants her to do? Whom should she obey? Obviously, her father, but refusing to submit to a man with whom she has an emotional attachment will be very difficult for her. She will be torn, and the experience will not help her in her future task of submitting to her husband. How much better if her father does not allow other men to be in a position to challenge his authority in her life.

The worst of both worlds

In 1 Corinthians 7, one of Paul's arguments for remaining single is that the single man or woman without emotional attachments will be free to be more single-minded in the pursuit of the Lord. Also, because of the pressures of marital responsibilities and cultural opposition, singleness provides greater freedom to be unhindered in devotion to Jesus Christ.

Dating, for those involved, would appear to be the reverse of Paul's ideal situation. By being single they miss the fulfillment and effectiveness of the one-flesh marriage union, and by being committed to dating they miss the freedom that should be inherent in singleness. Massive amounts of mental energy are spent worrying about the state of any relationships that are currently ongoing, and even more energy is expended by worrying if there is no one at the present time. Can we not trust God for a mate and invest that time and energy for the kingdom?

Why do I want to date?

We have looked at seven results of dating and we have seen that there is not a lot to recommend it. Yet it is the accepted way in our country to relate to the opposite sex, and to find a mate. What motivates our young people to be involved in this madness? Listen to Greg Spencer's excellent analysis of the motivation for young people to become emotionally involved during the dating process:

At the root of emotional fornication are covetousness and impatience. As with sex, we lust after the prize and cannot wait for it, little knowing that the thing we desire is not so much the act itself, but the act in the context of a bond which gives meaning to the act. We lust after "having a boyfriend" because

261

we want the security of knowing we are loved. Yet our lust insures our defeat, creating a grasping, insecure relationship.....

And we are impatient. Since we cannot trust God for the other, we spin intricate webs which we believe will hold our prey.

Covetousness and impatience. We want what married couples have, and we are not willing to wait until God gives it to us at the right time. We live in a culture that encourages instant gratification ("If it feels good, do it," or, "I want that car, and I want it now!"), and short-term vision (we expect the Lord to return tomorrow and rescue us). However, to delay gratification by refusing romantic involvement now, in anticipation of that one supreme romance with the bride or bridegroom God has for you, will strengthen your future marriage immeasurably. By rejecting the short-term pleasure of a boy friend or a girl friend, in confident expectation of the long-term joys of a solid one-flesh bond, you help to build the kingdom of God.

If we are to be warriors in the kingdom, we must continue to learn the ways of God, no matter how radical they may appear to the world, and then not hesitate to implement them in our lives, regardless of the consequences.

"Father, give me the grace to trust You to provide for my every need, including my need to be loved and to belong to someone. Protect me from emotional entanglements that will lessen my interest and involvement in your kingdom, and help me to enter it in my relations with the opposite sex. Amen"

Questions for discussion

1. What is meant in this chapter by the term "emotional fornication?" Do you agree with the concept? Why or why not? Do you think it can occur without physical involvement? How?

2. Nearly all high school students think they are immune from the sexual progression as well as getting hurt by a broken dating relationship? Why do you think that is?

3. Which of the seven results of dating given in the chapter do you feel is the most damaging? Why?

4. The reasons given as to why young people date were covetousness and impatience. Is this a fair analysis? Why do you feel Christians date?

---

[1] Lawrence Stone, *The Family, Sex and Marriage In England 1500-1800* (New York: Harper & Row, 1977), p. 183.

[2] *Ibid.*

[3] By the end of the 18th century, these books, many of them written by women, had so proliferated in England that it was said that "four thousand and seventy-three novels are now in the press from the pens of young ladies of fashion." Many recognized the problems attendant to this paradigm shift, and warned that "women of little experience are apt to mistake the urgency of bodily wants (male lust) with the violence of delicate passion (the emotion described in the romance novels)." Some even observed that "people would never fall in love if they had not heard of love talked about," believing that romantic love was a product of learned cultural expectation. Stone, *Family, Sex and Marriage*, p. 190.

[4] Jonathan Lindvall, "Youthful Romance: Scriptural Patterns," *Gentle Spirit Magazine*, February, 1993.

[5] This period, at the conclusion of the 18th and the beginning of the 19th centuries, draws its name, the "Romantic" period, from a philosophical movement that penetrated all of European life, not just mate selection. The emphasis was on passion rather than logic, and impulsiveness and spontaneity over self-discipline. All movements have influential leaders, opinion-shapers, and Romanticism was no exception. Jean Jacques Rousseau was one of those. He was a philosopher and author on the continent whose writings, opposing political tyranny and acclaiming the virtues of emotion rather than reason, greatly influenced the English writers of the Romantic period, such as William Wordsworth, Lord Byron, John Keats, William Hazlitt and Samuel Coleridge. Rousseau's writings, extolling the perfectability of man, also helped to fuel the French Revolution as well as other revolutionary

socialist movements of the 19th and 20th centuries. For a complete discussion of the Romantic Period, see M. H. Abrams, ed., *The Norton Anthology of English Literature* (New York and London: W. W. Norton and Company, 1986), p. 1-19.

[6] For many of the ideas in the remainder of the chapter I am indebted to Greg Spencer, the author of an unpublished manuscript entitled "Emotional Fornication," copyright 1986 in Eugene, Oregon, and also the above-referenced Jonathan Lindvall in "Youthful Romance: Scriptural Patterns."

Chapter 18

Courtship - An alternative

As you read the last chapter I hope dating took a pretty damaging hit in your mind. There is a chance that you or someone you've known has been able to navigate dating's treacherous waters without any known harm, but you are an exception. Wisdom does not use the exception to make the rule. I'm convinced the vast majority of adults, from a mature perspective, will admit that dating was a less than ideal way to relate to the opposite sex, and to find a spouse.

If my arguments in the last chapter were effective, what you are now saying is, "O.K., I'm convinced that dating is not the way to go, but what can you offer to take its place? I hope you are not suggesting arranged marriages!"

It is very true that you can't beat something with nothing, and if we are going to recover Godly mate selection, there must be an alternative to dating that is practical in the twentieth century. I believe the Bible, as always, has the answer for us. However, we must put on our kingdom spectacles as we read the Bible, or we won't see the answer!

First, let me say, in case anyone missed it, our modern dating system is not in the Bible. That doesn't necessarily mean we can't practice it. Airplane rides, computers, and industrial corporations are not in the Bible either. The Amish have withdrawn from society with a fortress mentality because they only want to do things specifically mentioned in the Bible. They are considered to be nothing more than a curious oddity, a quaint tourist attraction. As God's people, we must not withdraw from the world, but we must have a dominion mentality if we want to see the reign of Jesus Christ extended in it.

Dating does, however, violate the Biblical principles that we have developed over the last few chapters, so it is necessary to find an alternative if we want to order our lives by the Bible. Even though the

Bible does not have a section entitled "Mate Selection," we can mine some principles from it that will guide us as we attempt to develop a workable method for today. Whatever we come up with must be aligned with those principles in order to be valid. My claim is not that what you are about to read is "the Biblical method;" only a method that is biblically consistent.

Old Testament mate selection

In the Old Testament, the most obvious pattern of mate selection is that the parents, or parental representatives, arranged the marriage. In Genesis 24 Abraham sent his trusted servant back to Abraham's original home to find a wife for his son Isaac among his kinsmen. Abraham did not go himself because he was probably too old to make the trip (vs. 1). He delegated his authority to his servant. After finding Rebekah, and then recounting the miraculous manner in which God led him to her, the servant asked Rebekah's father Bethuel and her brother Laban to allow him to take her back to be Isaac's wife (vs. 48,49). They recognized the Lord's hand in the venture and agreed (vs. 50,51).

Notice that Isaac and Rebekah were not involved in this transaction. They were comfortable with their fathers' (and father's delegated representative's) decisions. The emphasis in the Bible is on loving whomever God has provided through His representative authority, the father. When the servant brought Rebekah back to Isaac, the Bible says that he "took Rebekah and she became his wife, and he loved her."

There is an indication that the girl had right of refusal in the Biblical system of arranged marriages. Bethuel and Laban asked Rebekah if she would go with the servant (vs. 58). There is some confusion as to whether the question concerned the fact of going at all or the time of the departure. If Rebekah had a say as to the time of departure (a comparatively insignificant issue), she surely would have a say as to whether she would go at all. Abraham also seemed to anticipate a possible refusal by whomever the servant might find ["And if the woman is not willing to follow you, then you will be released from this oath" (vs. 8)].

In this example we see the respective authorities in the lives of the young people arranging the marriage, with the right of refusal given to the daughter, and by implication, the son. This particular son and daughter, Isaac and Rebekah, trusted that God was at work in His kingdom through His authority structure.

Other Old Testament examples

Jacob followed his father Isaac's specific instructions to marry one of Laban's daughters (Genesis 28:1,2). Isaac evidently had the authority to instruct his son to marry whomever he chose for him. Jacob could choose, but the choice must be one of Laban's daughters if he wanted to please his father. And, thinking from a kingdom perspective, if he pleased his father, he would please God. As a matter of fact, because of Laban's trickery, Jacob married both daughters, first Leah, and then Rachel, who was the daughter he really wanted to marry. Laban, as the father of the girls, had complete authority to give his daughters in marriage or not. Jacob honored the authority of the father even though Laban was deceitful and dishonest. Laban could demand that Jacob meet whatever conditions, or qualifications, he desired. Even when Laban did not keep his word after Jacob faithfully served him for seven years, Jacob honored Laban's revised demands, and served another seven years.

God rewarded Jacob's willingness to submit to kingdom authority, even when it was misused, by eventually prospering Jacob mightily at Laban's expense.

Another example can be found in Genesis 21, in which Ishmael, the child born of Abraham's unbelief, and the father of the Arab nations, came to adulthood. He was an archer, dwelling in the wilderness. He had been sent away from his father Abraham, and, therefore, grew up under the authority of his mother, Hagar. In verse 21, she "took a wife for him, from the land of Egypt." Hagar found a wife for Ishmael.

In Moses's instructions to the Israelites concerning relations with the Canaanites, he said, "You shall not give your daughter to their son, or take their daughter for your son" (Deuteronomy 7:3), implying the father, as God's representative, had control over the marriage partners of both sons and daughters.

An exception to this pattern is Esau, Jacob's twin brother. Esau was a rebel from birth (Romans 9:5-13), and he deliberately went against his parents wishes and married two Canaanite women who caused his parents great grief (Genesis 26:34,35). After Jacob had stolen his blessing, Esau watched as Jacob obeyed his father's specific instructions not to marry a Canaanite. In a belated and inadequate attempt at repentance, Esau tried to please his father by marrying a non-Canaanite for his third wife, a daughter of Ishmael (Genesis 28:6-9).

What can we learn from these examples? Looking through the kingdom lens, we can see that in each instance, except for the rebel Esau, the one in authority in the family had power to give or not give a son or daughter in marriage, with the daughter (and by implication, the son), having the right of refusal.

However, not every biblical account is prescriptive. Just because a character in the Bible, even a Godly character, did a certain thing historically does not necessarily mean that God wants us to do the same thing (such as Jacob's two wives). Such accounts are descriptive in nature. God's people all make mistakes, and the Bible does not attempt to hide them. To find real kingdom principles upon which we can erect biblical prescriptive models we are on more solid ground when a Prophet, such as Moses, gives specific instruction, as in the Deuteronomy passage above. We can know that this is God's will. However, the other passages do give us a general idea about how God's people conducted themselves. In this, we can see a general pattern.

This all occurred a long time ago. Does the New Testament have a more "modern" approach to selecting a mate? Are there specific instructions we can follow? Let's see how God's people attacked the problem 1700 years later.

New Testament teaching on mate selection

Apart from the teaching on not being unequally yoked together with unbelievers (2 Corinthians 6:14), there is little in the Bible about how marriage partners were selected in New Testament times. However, there is one, a very interesting passage in 1 Corinthians 7.

Because of the difficult times that the church was then experiencing, Paul instructed the Corinthians to remain as they were with regard to marriage (vs. 26, 27). A paraphrase of these two verses would be, "If you are single, remain so, but obviously, even though these are tough times, if you are married, remain married." He then goes into a rather lengthy discourse on why being single is preferred during those difficult times. Then in verses 36 to 39 he says:

"But if any man thinks he is behaving improperly toward his virgin, if she is past the flower of her youth, and thus it must be, let him do what he wishes; he does not sin; let them marry. Nevertheless, he who stands steadfast in his heart, having no necessity, but has power over his own will, and has so determined in his heart that he

will keep his virgin, does well. So then he who gives her in marriage does well, but he who does not give her in marriage does better."

In the margin of the New King James Bible, an alternate rendering of the Greek word for virgin, *parthenos,* is virgin daughter, showing that it simply means an unmarried woman. The Greek word gives us no hint as to whether the man mentioned in the passage is her father or her fiancee. That must be determined by the text.

Most modern translations, such as the New King James Bible, assume that the man spoken of is the fiancee, because according to our present custom, the father has little, if any, say as to whom his daughter will marry, and certainly no say as to whether or not she will marry at all. She generally marries whomever she can find that she wants to marry. The translators let their presuppositions and today's customs determine their translation of the text. Today, all decisions are generally made by the young couple, with the respective fathers simply footing the bills. Therefore, the modern translators reason that certainly Paul, in this passage, must be instructing the prospective groom on the decision to marry or not to marry. They relegate a "virgin daughter" interpretation to an alternate rendering in the margin.

Let's look at the passage in question through our kingdom lens, remembering that in the kingdom of God, the delegation of authority and the responsibility for a daughter is given to the father, not to a prospective groom.

1. "But if any man thinks he is behaving improperly toward his virgin." We assume that, because in verses 8 and 9 Paul instructed the unmarried who are burning with passion to go ahead and marry, "behaving improperly" means behaving improperly sexually. In other words, we assume that he is saying the same thing here that he said in verses 8 and 9. However, he used much stronger wording in the earlier verses; why was he more discrete in his language here? Why does he use "behaving improperly," rather than "burn with passion" again? This is because Paul is talking about two different things. Here he is referring to the father, in his unique set of family circumstances, behaving improperly by denying his daughter the opportunity to wed. Paul is giving each man the opportunity to evaluate his kingdom and to make the best decision for those under his authority, even though it goes against the main thrust of Paul's message in this chapter.

2. "[I]f she is past the flower of her youth" Indicates that the daughter is no longer a young girl, but now a mature woman, fully ready for marriage.

3. "[A]nd thus it must be, let him do what he wishes; he does not sin; let them marry." Paul indicates that the father has complete control over his individual situation. Paul's instructions are to be implemented by each individual man in his own family. They are not absolute rules that must be applied in every situation. Each man has leeway as to the application of Paul's teaching in his particular situation that only he, not Paul, fully understands. This is what Paul means in verse 25 when he says, "Now concerning virgins: I have no commandment from the Lord ("no inviolate absolutes that you must follow"), yet I give judgment as one whom the Lord in His mercy has made trustworthy" ("I have a teaching from the Lord that is true. It's up to you to apply it properly").

Let me digress to give an example of how truth must be applied individually in every situation. At Tree of Life we teach that children are a blessing from God, and that having lots of them, if they are properly trained, is not a curse, but a joy. As a result, we have some very large families by today's standards, and we attract families with a similar vision. We recognize that birth control was popularized by Margaret Sanger and Planned Parenthood, and we preach that the church has capitulated to the population controllers by not preaching the Bible's message that large families are the result of the blessing of God (Psalm 128). However, we do not tell our men what they should do personally. We have no "bedroom patrol," insuring that our couples are getting pregnant regularly. It is up to them, as the authorities in their families, how they apply the truth that is taught.

In fact, one of our men, with five children, had a vasectomy after hearing, understanding, and believing the biblical teaching I have just outlined. He was being considered for the office of elder, and several couples felt he should not be considered, because he "went against the teaching of the church." The church recognized that what a man does in his kingdom is his call in an area like birth control, where the scriptures give no "commandment from the Lord" (vs. 25). Only he knows the circumstances and conditions in his family, the feelings of his wife, and all the other factors that affect his decision. He has served faithfully as an elder for four years.

4. "Nevertheless, he who stands steadfast in his heart, having no necessity, but has power over his own will, and has so determined in his heart that he will keep his virgin, does well." Some in the church, maybe even most, have received Paul's teaching and are applying it. Because of the situation, they will keep their daughters and not give them in marriage at the present time (there are no circumstances that would prohibit them from doing so). It is a decision that Paul recognizes the father has the power to make, and commends him for making it.

5. "So then he who gives her in marriage does well, but he who does not give her in marriage does better." This passage removes all doubt as to whether or not the man that Paul is referring to is the father. Whoever the man is, he has the power to "give" the virgin in marriage (In the previous sentence, he had the power to "keep" her). The fiancee can't "give" her; he does not have her yet. Besides, the fiancee wants to "take" her! The Greek word is *gamizo* and means "to give in marriage." The only man who can "keep" or "give" the virgin in question is the father.

The father who gives his virgin daughter away, after evaluating all the attendant circumstances and doing what he deems best, does a permissible thing, but the father who has the faith and the vision to apply Paul's teaching, in light of present circumstances, and "keeps" his virgin daughter does even better. In the same way, the man who has a vasectomy or uses birth control does a permissible thing; he is not sinning. But the man who has the faith and the vision to let God send as many children as He desires does better.

Summary of biblical teaching on mate selection

What have we learned from these passages? The father, if he is living or has not in some way disqualified himself by deserting his family (Abraham deserting Ishmael), has complete authority over his son or daughter with regard to whom they marry, or even if they marry. He is the king in his family kingdom, which is a subset of the kingdom of God. The daughter, however, and by implication the son, have the right of refusal. The son would seem to have some latitude, within parameters, to choose himself (Jacob). All the examples portray the daughters as being given and taken, not the sons. This would imply that the woman becomes a part of the man's new family. There are certainly other scriptures that apply, and other conclusions that can be drawn, but these are enough to give us a foundation for a biblical program of mate selection.

A BIBLICAL COURTSHIP MODEL

A Father's responsibility...

The first thing to put in place in any biblical model of mate selection, is the father's consistent involvement. With all the authority the father has, there comes much responsibility.

I realize that many will read this who have no father or husband in the home. Your road to recovering biblical mate selection will be a more difficult one to travel, but not impossible. It is difficult for a woman to take the role a man should play in the home, but with the help of the elders in your church, it can be done. Hagar had to do this, and the Bible implies that she assumed that authority role over Ishmael. May God give you his wisdom, courage, and perseverance.

...for his sons

A father should realize when his sons are young that he has the awesome task of training them to be Godly men with a vision for the kingdom of God. He should train them in the character traits we will cover in the next chapter, and inculcate in them the vision of one day being husbands and fathers. They should be protected with moral fences until they have adopted the family standards and vision for themselves. They are ready to marry when the father knows that his standards and his vision belong to them, and they are mature enough, in his estimation, to take on the responsibilities of a family.

They should be trained never to try to capture a girl's heart until the proper time. They should learn from their father not to develop romantic relationships until they have permission from both him and the girl's father. They should be taught by their father to treat all girls as sisters in the Lord (1 Timothy 5:2). Their father must be readily involved in every aspect of their lives.

God has built in to every boy a desire to be like his daddy, the image of God in his life, and if we don't quench that desire in some way, it will assure that Godly fathers will produce Godly sons. We will cover that topic in detail in the unit on children.

...and for his daughters

A father's responsibility for his daughters is somewhat different. His wife will train them to be Godly young women, with gentle and quiet spirits, and in the character traits covered in the next chapter. She will be their "older woman." He will give oversight by encouraging his wife, and being sure that she is communicating what he desires that his daughters should be learning. The father's main responsibility for his daughters is protection.

Protecting teen-ager daughters is not easy. The father's job is to present them to their future husbands as chaste virgins, having protected them both physically and emotionally from giving themselves away to some previous man. Girls are always eager to give their hearts away. That is the way they were made by God, the way they find fulfillment, but often they do not have the maturity to delay gratification until the proper time.

Remember, girls are not long-term visionaries like their brothers. Because she is a relational, emotional, creature-of-the-moment, a girl is easy prey for a boy who is able to communicate with her, romance her, and who attempts to capture her heart. A father's job is to insure that that does not happen. Rather than teach her how to resist a boy's advances, and try to encourage her not to give her heart away, a father should never let her be in a situation where that is a possibility. A girl should be taught at a very early age that her father will protect her as she grows up, and that a part of that protection is to be sure she marries the right boy.

A girl who is constantly allowed to be in romantic situations where there is temptation, and who has been trained by her parents to say "no, no, no" to boys, will find it hard to suddenly say "yes, yes, yes" on her wedding night. On the other hand, a girl who has been protected by her father from ever having to resist a boy's advances, will be able to eagerly give herself to her husband after marriage.

What structure will allow this kind of protection by the father? Rather than the current dating-engagement-marriage progression let me propose a friendship-courtship-engagement-marriage model.

"Let's just be friends"

As we saw in the passage in 1 Timothy 5:2, Paul is encouraging Timothy, a young man, to treat all young women as sisters. That is an extremely profound statement, and the rule of the day in the courtship model we are developing.

Jason and Ramah, my younger son and only daughter, are currently in their mid- and early-twenties respectively, four years apart in age. When they were children, Ramah had an amazing ability to get her normally even-tempered brother's goat. Jason would retaliate in some inappropriate way just as Jill or I appeared on the scene. Of course, Jason would get in trouble as Ramah looked on innocently. However, even in the midst of all the squabbles, Ramah would say, when talking about her two brothers, "Adam is so sweet to me, but Jason is so much fun to play with!" Even then she was developing a brother-sister relationship with her brother that today is in full bloom.

While Adam is married with a third child on the way, Jason and Ramah remain single. They illustrate for me, as I write this, what Paul meant in his instructions to Timothy. I love for them to be together, for I know Jason is telling his sister the very things I would be telling her, but from the point of view of a young man her age. As her older brother, he is encouraging her in the ways of the kingdom, helping her to keep that vision ever before her. Unlike when they were children, they are now "pursuing the things that make for peace, and the things by which one may edify another (Romans 14:19)."

Anything that would not be done with a sister, that encourages the development of a romantic relationship, is off limits in our new model. This would obviously include, holding hands, kissing, etc. Romantic relationships are exclusive, turned inward, with the focus on each other. Friendships are inclusive, turned outward, with the focus on friends, activities, and ideas of mutual interest. Jason and Ramah, for instance, do things with each other's friends, are both basketball players and work out together regularly, and are able to talk with each other about, as Jill says, "'portant things."

This does not mean that two friends are never alone together. Certainly a brother and sister often are. But the focus must be on the mutuality that binds them together, not on their relationship with each other.

Currently Ramah has a friend, a boy who went to another high school, whom she knew very slightly. However, they went to the same college, both played basketball there, and have become good friends. They call each other when they are home, and have spent a good bit of time together. He has recently had a new experience with the Lord, and is eagerly sharing that with Ramah. As Ramah's dad, I've got to be evaluating what is happening in my daughter's life, and my evaluation is that this is a healthy friendship.

Friendships are easy in high school and college, because young people are all around you. The trick there is to keep them all just that; friendships, until it is time for marriage. The temptation is to allow them to slip into the old romantic, dating mode.

When a young man reaches his twenties, he generally becomes ready to begin to think about marriage. He recognizes the need for a helpmate to share and complete his life. Unfortunately, the immediate availability of marriage candidates is somewhat less, and it is a bit harder to meet people in group settings. Hopefully by this time he has a degree of maturity and commitment to the courtship model. It is the father's job to evaluate that progress. If his father perceives that maturity, a son could be encouraged to call an eligible girl whom he has just met, and whom he would have no way of getting to know in a group setting, and ask her for a date. Having a "date," with the purpose of simply getting to know someone purely on a friendship basis, with marriage as a goal, is entirely different from "dating," with the purpose of having a boy friend or girl friend and pursuing romance.

The father's role of protector demands that he be abreast of where his sons and daughters are at all times, not only geographically, but in their relationships, and, if necessary, erect fences that his children cannot cross.

When Ramah was a sophomore in high school, a boy one year older than she began to show an interest in her. She returned his interest, and he began to come to see Ramah at our home relatively regularly. I took him aside one day to be sure he knew the rules. I told him that Ramah did not date, nor would she have a boy friend. I did not care if he came to see her at our home as often as he pleased, or if he was with Ramah in group situations. However, he was not to kiss her, or to hold her hand, or to in any way be her boy friend. I asked him if he understood the rules. He swallowed hard, said he did, and still wanted to be Ramah's friend. I allowed them to go to several special functions together over the next two years, always with another couple. I always knew where they were, and what they were doing. This young man was meticulous in his obedience to my rules, always honoring me by doing exactly what I asked him to do. He and Ramah remain good friends to this day, and nothing more.

In the father's role of vision-giver He must continually keep before his sons and daughters the long-term vision of the prize of a successful, fulfilling, fruitful marriage, to enable them to forgo short-term pleasure.

Courtship - the next step

From a wide circle of friends, inevitably a young man will begin to sense a stirring in his heart toward a young woman. I believe that this is the divine order, in keeping with the roles of the man being the aggressor and the woman the responder. When he senses that he would like to be more than a friend to a young woman, and he is ready for marriage, his first confidante is his father. "Am I ready to pursue a serious relationship with marriage as the result?" "Is this young lady an appropriate candidate for a wife for me?" "What do you see that I don't see that could be a problem?" These are questions that the young man should discuss with his father. At this point there is no emotional attachment, no romantic bond. They are able to discuss the relationship in an objective manner with no vested interest in the resultant decision.

The initial contact could also be made by the father. Perhaps he meets a girl suitable to be a wife for his son. He may encourage his son to call her and get to know her. Either way, the father is in a position to encourage the relationship or to end it.

Contact with the girl's father

If Dad gives the green light the next step is to contact the girl's father. He is in authority over his daughter and must be apprised of any interest in her. This is not a request to marry his daughter, but to enter into a courtship phase in the relationship; a period of time for serious investigation by all parties (the girl, the boy, and both fathers) as to whether this young couple are God's choices for each other.

It's a good bet that one of the fathers will still be in the old dating mode. If courtship is new to the girl's father, he should be impressed that anyone is asking him anything. He has not been protecting his daughter, and the fact that the young man is honoring his position of authority will help to establish him in his role as protector of his daughter.

If the boy has been given free rein by his dad to date, it will be a shock to him when he finds that it is necessary to come through the father to have a relationship that is more than friendship with the daughter. This will happen either when he asks the girl for a date, and she tells him that he will have to talk to her dad, or when she shares the family courtship vision with him. At any rate, he will discover soon enough that the father is the door to the daughter, and he must come through the door; he can't jump the fence.

One example of protection for a daughter

A young man expressed an interest in Ramah during her sophomore year in college. They had been friends for two years, but nothing more. Toward the end of the year, he began to hang around with her more, and want to be with her alone. She told him about our no-dating rules, but, not wanting to scare him off, she was not too specific. Something about talking with me, etc. In conversations on the phone, I could detect an independence in Ramah I didn't like, particularly when she talked about this young man. Sensing danger, I hopped on a plane for a quick trip to investigate first hand, and to meet the young man, and be sure Ramah's vision had not been clouded by her new friend.

Ramah had, indeed, lost a portion of the vision during her three months away from home. When those all about you are dating, having boy friends, and sharing their latest romantic experiences, it is very difficult for a 20 year-old to march to a different drummer. After a two hour lunch, Ramah was renewed, and I could sense that my daughter was at least part-way back.

Let me say here that sending a girl away to college, out from under a father's direct supervision, is a very dangerous thing, no matter how solid she may be spiritually, no matter how much she agrees with her father's role in her life, and no matter how committed she is to her father's vision. Girls are responders, and they will respond to the right young man. Fathers must train daughters when they are very young to hide nothing from them, to always walk in the light with them. They must be confident of this, or they should not let their daughter leave their direct supervision.

I met with the young man for several hours the next day, going over very carefully the courtship system, and the qualities I am looking for in the man to whom I will give my daughter (These are in the next chapter). He was not particularly responsive, though very polite. He assured me he would honor my request pertaining to no physical contact with Ramah. It was near the end of the year, and I felt Ramah would be safe, at least until school was out, and she was.

However, as the next school year approached, after several conversations with the young man on the phone over the summer, I knew that spiritually he was not going the way I wanted Ramah's husband to go. Even though he was a Christian from a solid Christian family, he struggled with our vision of the kingdom of God, and, as he said to Ramah after my visit to campus, "I don't want a relationship with your dad; I want a relationship with you!" Too bad. To get to Ramah, you come through me.

When time came to go back to school the next fall, I did not believe I could send Ramah back and be assured she would not develop a romantic, emotional tie with this young man. I knew that she was not fully mine in this area, and that he did not buy my program. So, I broke the sad news to her that she would not be going back. It was a very, very difficult decision for me to make. I coached Ramah's basketball team for two years in high school, and there has been nothing in this life that has given me more pleasure than being involved in basketball with her. However, I knew I couldn't send her back. Jill agreed with my decision, but could not have made it herself. Sometimes a father will have to make a hard decision like that even when he stands alone.

We called the school and withdrew her, and I called her incredulous basketball coach and tried, relatively unsuccessfully, to explain why Ramah was not coming back.

Through all this Ramah had a wonderful attitude, I believe really knowing in her heart that it was the right move. Even though she was very disappointed, she resigned herself to the fact that she had just lost her last two years in college, and her basketball career as well, at least for now.

At the end of the summer, Jill and I were at our cabin in Colorado, where I was working on this book. Ramah came out for a few days with Adam and his family after her summer job was over. She had resigned herself to not returning to school, and her attitude was excellent; no moping or sulking. One day Jill asked her if she wanted to talk. She said she did, and then related to Jill how she had seen that she had been a fool; throwing away her college and her basketball for a boy that probably wasn't right for her anyway. She told Jill how she had submitted everything to me except boys, and she had withheld that, and it had cost her dearly. There was no attempt to get Jill to try to change my mind; just a matter-of-fact recounting of what she had realized.

That night, as Jill related to me what had happened, Ramah came into the bedroom, and climbed up on the bed with us. Jill asked her to tell me what she had seen. As she told me the story, I realized my girl was back, this time, all the way. She had been home all summer, was back in the family and the church, and her vision was restored. In addition, I could see that now I had her heart, even in the area of her future husband!

When I told her that there was no reason now that she could not go back to school, she was elated. She only had a couple of pairs of jeans and a few T-shirts with her, but we called the college and discovered she could still enroll late, and even though the coach had given away most of her scholarship to other girls, she was thrilled to have her back. As we drove to Denver to put her on a flight to school, Ramah was experiencing the freedom of having given everything to the Lord. She was almost euphoric. "I can't believe how you hold on to something that seems so important and you think you will die if you lose it. Then when you finally surrender, and let it go there is such joy. You can't understand why you held on so tightly. I feel so free!"

When she arrived, she saw the boy immediately and apologized to him for leading him on, and not letting him know up front that pleasing me was her number one task. He said, "OK," and walked away. He had another serious girl friend in three weeks.

Ramah has thanked me several times for protecting her. As a matter of fact, after about two months at school, she told me on the phone, "I don't have a very good record of finding boys myself. I've given that to you. When are you going to find me a husband?" I told her that I took that responsibility seriously, and that I was working on it.

Establishing a courtship relationship

If the young man in the previous example had responded eagerly to our time together, and if he had not balked at the knowledge that I would be evaluating him as to his qualifications to marry my daughter, and if he and Ramah were both ready for marriage at that time, and if I knew of nothing that would disqualify him (for instance, if he were not a Christian), I would have allowed him and Ramah to enter into a courtship relationship, as indeed they had desired to do.

What does this mean? Courtship is a time, based on a previous friendship, rather than a romance, when two people are consciously seeing if they are God's choice for each other. Courtship is moving from Step 3 to Step 4 in our sexual progression in Chapter 15. They are now a couple, and while kissing is not allowed, holding hands is, because that is the basic statement that says, "we are a couple."

Courtship provides formal definition, so everyone knows where the relationship is. There are no surprises. Evaluation is occurring: the couple evaluating each other, and asking the question "Is he/she right for me?," the girl's father asking, "Is he right for my daughter?," and the boy's father asking, "Is she right for my son?" The first two of these evaluations that I am about to mention are much more crucial than the last two.

First, during this time, the young man must decide if God has indeed placed *agape* love in his heart for this girl. Is he willing to love her in the manner described in Chapter 7? That love will be the basis for the marriage, and if at any time during the courtship he realizes that he does not, or that he cannot, he must call off the courtship.

Second, the girl's father must decide if this is the young man to whom he will entrust his daughter. After the wedding it is too late; he has no more say. She is his no longer. Now is the time to be sure. The qualifications that will be covered in the next chapter must be met to his satisfaction. If he is fooled, and this young man does not take his daughter in the direction of the kingdom of God, he has lost one of his weapons of war, a part of his heritage, and his influence down through the ages because his grandchildren may not be raised as kingdom men and women. His daughter must follow her husband, and her father cannot meddle with the course his son-in-law sets after the wedding. His future is now her future, for better or for worse. The father must know that it will be for better, as far as the pursuit of the kingdom is concerned.

Third, if the young man has been well-trained by his father, and has adopted his father's vision for the kingdom of God, and is a mature man of God, his father need have no fear. If those things are not true of his son as yet, the son is not ready for courtship, but should still be in the friendship stage. However, if he is ready for marriage, and if God has placed *agape* love in his heart for the girl, his love and leadership are all that is necessary, for he will set the direction for the family. She will follow. The father only must know that his prospective daughter-in-law is willing to give herself unreservedly to his son, and to be a biblical wife, as described in Chapters 9-11.

The final evaluation is that of the girl for the boy. In many ways, this is the least important, because she will probably respond to the agape love of a qualified young man. However, there are factors that may cause her not to respond. Once the young man has gained her father's approval, he must win her heart. His manners, social skills, and interests may not disqualify him with the father, but may disqualify him with the daughter. She has the right of refusal.

During courtship

From the outside, courtship may look a lot like the old dating game, but that is only a surface similarity. Yes, there will be time alone as the couple gets to know each other well. But unlike dating, they know that they are contemplating marriage, and the restrictions on physical contact still hold. The couple is still conscious of the fact that they have no ownership of the other, and they must continue to guard their hearts. There is no commitment at this point.

The fathers must give constant oversight, because the temptation to slide into "steady dating" with all its ramifications will be enormous. They should not allow the couple to spend long hours alone in isolated situations; let the alone times be at Denny's. The girl's father should continue to hold the young man accountable as to time and location when the young people are together. Both should be reminded continually to guard their hearts. Waiting to form an emotional bond will be difficult, but the eventual realization that much more pleasurable! The goal of sexual and emotional purity is worth the wait.

It is very important to see that courtship is not a time when the couple gets ready for marriage by finishing their education, getting financially secure, or maturing in the character qualities that each father is seeking in the one who marries his son or daughter. The purpose of courtship is <u>evaluation</u>, not <u>preparation</u>, and upon entering courtship, both young people should be ready for marriage. Preparation for marriage occurs from childhood to maturity under the watchful eyes of mother (preparing her daughters) and father (preparing his sons).

Certainly there will be some minor adjustments as the young man attempts to meet the girl's father's qualifications. However, if he has not learned honesty, integrity, submission to authority, etc. by now it is foolish to think he will learn it during the courtship period. By the same token, a girl who has been raised as a Christian feminist will not suddenly be changed into a woman who desires to follow the biblical pattern for a wife as covered in Chapters 9-11. Changes will occur during the friendship period, as each is learning about the other, but it is not the job of the respective fathers to teach or change somebody else's son or daughter. That is intruding in another man's kingdom.

Engagement!

When in the courtship period the young man is sure that this is the girl God has for him, he should go to his father and be sure that he concurs, and gives his blessing. Together they should determine an acceptable time for the wedding. After he has acquired his own father's blessing, it is time to seek the approval of the girl's father. Maybe the young man already has an idea of what his answer will be; maybe not. It is assumed that they have been communicating. Periodically, the young man may have asked her father for evaluations as to his ability to meet his qualifications, so he is probably already aware of where he stands. They have developed a relationship.

It is a big moment when the young man, after many months of friendship and courtship with the girl with whom he now desires to spend the rest of his life, asks her father for her hand in marriage. This is her father's last chance to put a stop to this relationship that has so steadily progressed to this point. Maybe he will have some requirements as to timing, but the young man knew what qualifications the father sought in a suitor, and now, according to her father's evaluation, he has demonstrated them. The answer is yes! Her father has given his blessing!

That was the big hurdle. Now, if he has won her heart, and he knows he has, they will be engaged. She has waited for this moment for her whole life, and she gives him an unqualified yes. They seal the engagement with their first kiss.

If her answer is no, he still has her father's approval, and he can proceed to try to win her heart. God has made men out of boys who would not take no for an answer.

The engagement period should be only long enough to prepare for the wedding. Both were ready for marriage or their fathers would not have allowed them to enter courtship. If there is school to finish, or some other circumstances that are such that the couple cannot marry now, the relationship should remain in the friendship phase. Extended engagements only lead to physical pressures, because both now know that they are committed to each other for life.

Courtship summary

We have done our very best to follow the principles that we were able to distill from the Bible for our courtship model, from the perspective of the kingdom of God. The fathers of both the young man and the young woman have absolute authority in the whole courtship process. They carry God's delegated authority in their families. To obey them is to obey God. To please them is to please God. To yield to them is to yield to God.

We have constructed a model where both of the young people are protected, both physically and emotionally, as they investigate God's plan for their futures, and then learn to love and respond to each other. They are not forced to marry against their will, but are given the right of refusal.

Father power

As fathers, we have not understood the kingdom of God. We have not realized that we have authority over our children's marriage choices. Not long ago I met with a father whose daughter was married for only three months. On the honeymoon she discovered that her new husband was a sexual pervert. As I met with her father after his daughter had obtained an annulment, his words were, "I never thought he was right for her, but what could I do?" A lot. He could have put a stop to the wedding, for one thing. But he didn't know he could do anything but pay for it. He is a ruler, ordained by God, who doesn't know he has a kingdom.

It is time for fathers to take back the ground they have abdicated, and restore again a Godly method of mate selection in our land.

"Father, help me, as a father to give my children the leadership and protection they so desperately need to find the right husband or wife that will make their marriage a glory to You. Help me as a young person to submit to Your authority in Your kingdom as expressed by my father. Help me to trust him as I do you. Amen."

Questions for discussion

1. What factors can you see that would militate against you as a father (or your father) protecting your sons and daughters (or you) in the manner described in this chapter? What would you have to do to overcome those obstacles?

2. Which of the ideas proposed in this chapter are the most difficult for you to accept personally? Why? Are they consistent with the Bible?

3. What advantage can you see to following this courtship model? What disadvantages?

4. What do you think would be the reaction of your friends if you and your family adopted this model? Would their reaction matter to you? Why or why not?

Chapter 19

Preparation for marriage

The courtship model that we saw in the last chapter is just that; a model to follow. There are no perfect situations. We are sinners living in an imperfect world, and as much as we strive to attain the ideal, there will always be short-comings. The temptation, because I have not perfectly trained and protected my sons and daughters, is to give up and say, "What's the use? I've already blown it. Why should I even try?" We must understand that the discrepancy between what we do and the ideal is covered by the grace of God. We cannot quit trying to do it God's way just because we have failed in the past. We must repent of our failures, not make excuses for them. If we have opportunity with other children, we can do better, but only if we have been able to face our mistakes and learn from them.

Changing from a dating pattern to courtship, in mid-stream, with teen-agers, is not easy. If they have not grown up with the idea of courtship, there will probably be resistance. The strength of your leadership will be tested. It is much easier if you have taught the concepts to your children when they were very young.

In this chapter I want to begin with a record of my failures in the area of courtship. I have discovered over the years that people don't learn from my successes nearly as much as they do from my failures. To tell only of success exposes pride, and is not reality. There will be failures, because courtship is not an exact science. To share failures is an encouragement to those who have been failures as well.

Then I want to take a look at the lists of qualifications I have used to get my son and daughter ready for marriage. There are other lists that are equally as good and may express better for you what you are after in your children. These are only my lists. I encourage you to make your own that express your desires for your children. I also use them to evaluate potential suitors for my daughter, and prospective wives for my son.

Examples of personal failures and an analysis of the causes

The successful example of protecting Ramah, that I related in the last chapter, came as a result of learning the hard way, from three failures.

Failure #1

The first one was with my oldest son, Adam. When my children entered their teen years, we understood nothing about courtship. We arrived at the conclusion that there must be an alternative to dating, not because of any study of the Bible, but because of an unfortunate experience Adam had in high school. He established an emotional tie with a girl who set out to catch him, did so, and then promptly dropped him. We saw the game she played, and the damage it did to our son. Not knowing anything but that dating was not good, we determined to do it differently with our other two children.

Fortunately, and not because of any help we gave him, Adam recovered without significant long-term damage, and, by the grace of God, met Missy, his wife, his first year at college. Very soon he knew that she was the one God had for him. Neither of them, again by the grace of God, ever went through the dating syndrome while at college. Their struggle was with the sexual progression, and "making it to the church on time" (The wedding was three days after they graduated). They made it, one more time, purely by the grace of God.

Failure #2

Jill and I still didn't know much about courtship when Jason started college a year behind Adam, except that dating was not the way to go. That ignorance of the principles discussed in the last chapter paved the way for failure #2. Jason bought into the "no dating" vision in high school, and had not dated, much to the consternation of the girls in his class. He continued that policy in college, even though he met an attractive Christian girl on the first day of school his freshman year. They got to know one another immediately, as they were both in a very time-consuming extra-curricular program, and were naturally together quite often. After a couple of months of friendship, and after a mutual attraction was obvious, Jason said to her, "You're probably wondering why I don't ask you out. I don't believe in dating, but if you are still available when we are seniors, I would like to pursue a serious relationship with you then."

They continued their friendship for three years. Jason never looked at her as anything but a good friend. Her parents had no problems with dating, so she dated other boys regularly throughout their first three years in school, always knowing Jason was there, patiently waiting for the right time.

He met her parents, and was with them regularly over that time, both at school and at their home, so they had opportunity to get to know him well. Jill and I also were with them, and they even took a vacation to the Northwest and stayed in our home. Our time with them was always very pleasant.

We would ask Jason on occasion, "How's your girl friend?" He would invariably answer, "I don't have a girl friend." He was very carefully guarding his heart.

During the summer before his senior year, one year before he would be ready to marry, Jason determined it was time to investigate entering into a courtship relationship with his friend, though we were not calling it that at the time. He knew that she responded to him, as they had had many talks over the years about every issue imaginable, particularly God's order in the home. She had grown up as the apple of her father's eye, the oldest of three children. She was a very bright, aggressive girl, extremely talented, who had been taught by her father that she could do anything a man can do, and should. Marriage, family, and children were never emphasized to her, so as a result, she had become somewhat of a Christian feminist on the campus, always being sure that women were given proper opportunities and recognition. Her recognition and acceptance at home came from her performance.

We were aware of this, but Jason's input over the years, while they were in the friendship stage of their relationship, had gradually changed her views to more closely correspond to the biblical view of a woman's role, at least when Jason was with her. She believed the Bible, and wanted to follow its teachings. However, when she went home for the summer, or for Christmas vacation, she returned to her old perspective. Jason assured us that the caution we felt was needless; once they were married, and she was with him all the time, she would be fine. Knowing Jason's strength and vision, we believed that to be true.

When Jason approached her father, he asked him if he could "pursue a serious relationship with [his] daughter." He did not know to use the term "courtship," but he thought the terminology he used was self-explanatory. He had been friends with the man's daughter for three years, had spent massive amounts of time with her, had gotten to know her parents well, and they were entering their senior year. Could the intent of his question possibly be obscure? Of course, looking back we can see why he misunderstood; he didn't want to think about his daughter getting married. At any rate, when he said, "Go for it!," Jason took that as permission to "pursue a serious relationship with your daughter," just as he had requested.

At that time, after guarding his heart for three years, fully believing he had her father's permission to court her, and assuming that if the father had any problems with him he would have told him at that time, Jason gave her his heart, and she gave hers to him, at least, so it seemed. I can see, looking back, that it was too early; we did not understand that courtship is still evaluative; the proper time to give one's heart and form emotional bonds is after the engagement, and not before.

Two young people, both very much in love, with graduation approaching, and both fathers seemingly agreeable to the match, means a wedding in the near future, does it not? Jason and I planned when that would occur, he got a ring, and went to ask the father for his daughter's hand.

We all were incredulous when he said "no." Our feelings went from shock, to disbelief, to anger. His claim was that he didn't have a clue that Jason was pursuing his daughter as a possible wife, partly because there was no physical relationship between them. He and his wife felt that there must be something wrong with Jason sexually because he had not kissed their daughter!

To say "no" is perfectly within the father's realm of authority. As I told him in a letter, I have no problem with his rejection of my son as a husband for his daughter. He has his own list of qualifications that a young man must meet to be his son-in-law, and whatever they are is entirely up to him. It is the fact that he did not direct Jason when he came to ask permission to "pursue a serious relationship with your daughter." He did not express reservations, or even tell Jason what his qualifications were. In fact, he did not even give any indication to his daughter that Jason was in any way unacceptable. He waited to do so until they gave their hearts to one another. He locked the barn door too late.

I appreciate the fact that he did not want want his daughter marrying a man with a different vision for his daughter than his own, and I agree with that wholeheartedly. My great mistake was in not communicating with him early on, discovering and understanding his vision for his daughter, and realizing the fact that Jason's vision for a wife that corresponds to Proverbs 31 was irreconcilable with his. If I had done so, we fathers could have stopped the relationship at the friendship stage. I have accepted full responsibility for not protecting my son from giving away his heart prematurely, and for allowing him to invest four years in a hopeless cause. Jason and the girl no longer communicate.

Jason is doing fine. He is 25 years old, in graduate school in architecture, and has a full life. However, I know that he has experienced emotional pain after being with her for seven years. Our best attempt at doing it right ended in what would appear to be failure. However, Jason says that he is experiencing the supernatural joy of the Lord, is a firm believer in the sovereignty of God, and knows that God has someone better for him in the future. We know that this seeming failure has been God's protection for Jason, and the source of much maturity for us all.

Failure #3

Failure #3 was a courtship experience with Ramah just after she graduated from high school. We were gradually learning from our experiences with Adam and Jason, and our present courtship model was taking shape. However, failure #3 let us know that there was more to be learned.

Ramah had been complaining that there would never be anyone for her to marry, because no one except the boys in our church would ever be willing to jump through the hoops in order to meet my qualifications. She already knew these boys well, and they were all just brothers to her. There was no romantic interest, either on her part or theirs.

About that time, a new family with four boys came into our church. The oldest, a tall, thin, handsome basketball player, was Ramah's age, and she perked up immediately. Was the Lord answering her prayers? We had them over for dinner, and Ramah and the boy took an immediate liking to each other. He called me the next day and asked me what he would have to do to get to know Ramah. I gave him the standard "no dating, no physical contact, come by the house, group activities only, you are just friends" line, which he said he would be happy to abide by. Over the next few weeks, he was a rather constant fixture at our home, and his family settled easily into the church life. They seemed to fit very well, responded to the messages, and immediately made a number of friends. The boy and Ramah continued to hit it off famously.

With August approaching, they were each preparing to start their freshman years at different colleges, and Ramah and the boy both wanted something more than just friendship. I should have told them, "No, just 'cool it,' and we will take a look at the situation again next summer." Instead, I sat down with the boy and his dad and explained my new perspective on courtship; that it was the next step past friendship, with the purpose of evaluating whether the interested parties want to marry one another. There would be no boy-friend, girl-friend stage. If he wasn't interested in investigating the possibility of marriage, then friends they would continue to be.

The boy's dad and mom had married while in college, so the fact that he was still in school was not a factor to him. After some thought, he told me, with his father's approval, that he wanted to enter into a courtship relationship with Ramah. I gave him my list of qualifications for Ramah's husband, told him that I would be evaluating him based on that list, and agreed to the arrangement. Ramah was ecstatic.

During that school year they carried on a relationship by phone and letter, seeing each other only at Christmas. Their relationship continued over the next summer, but there began to be some problems. He was finding Ramah a bit stronger-willed than he had anticipated, and he seemed to resent my place in her life, feeling he had to compete with me in some way for leadership with her. His father began to experience some trouble in the church with our positions on certain issues. At the heart of the problem was a different perspective on the authority of the kingdom of God. This, of course, was at the heart of the young man's problems with me. He was following his father's leadership, as he should.

Jill suspected, from some things that Ramah had said, that there had been some physical contact more than holding hands. The young man got together with me about that time and confessed to kissing

Ramah and repented. At this point I should have called the courtship off. I should have seen that his problems with me and my authority in Ramah's life were hindering his ability to respect and obey me. Instead, I told him it would take some time for me to have confidence in him again, but that I forgave him.

From that time on, even though Ramah had been an eager participant in the physical expressions of affection, she began to lose respect for him, primarily because of his resistance to me and what I was teaching. Also, even though she had certainly never resisted his advances, she recognized his lack of strength and leadership because of his failure to honor and obey my standards of physical conduct. His lack of respect for authority was being exposed, though I did not see it clearly.

He sensed he was losing Ramah, but he continued to resist me and my teaching. At Christmas, he got together with me and called off the courtship because he knew Ramah was no longer with him. She was relieved.

I later discovered that there had been physical contact past holding hands again after his previous repentance. He sent me a letter repenting of that again. He and his family have since left the church. I remain very good friends with his father, and love him dearly, and have a sincere affection for the boy, but we have different visions of the kingdom of God.

This experience was a very painful one for us all, but I learned some very valuable lessons from my many mistakes. First, the decision to enter courtship belongs to fathers, and they must not give in to pressure from their sons and daughters. I should have resisted the pressure from Ramah and the boy, and kept the relationship at the friendship level. They were going away to different schools and could not even be together. I gave in to her, because I wanted it to work; I really liked the boy and his family, and it seemed so right, like something the Lord would do. I discovered that surface appearances are not reliable indicators.

Second, I realized that courtship is not preparation, but evaluation. I could tell relatively early that the boy did not meet several of the qualifications that I demanded. Because his folks were in the church and experiencing some difficulty, I didn't want to make more waves than necessary by calling off the courtship. I wanted it to work, so I told myself, "He has great potential," and expected that with time he would come around.

291

Third, I trusted him with my daughter, and he was not ready for that responsibility. I misread him terribly. He had no fear of me, and violated my trust and my daughter. Because of my experience with the previous boy in high school who had obeyed me to the letter, I thought this young man, a part of our church, surely could be trusted to do as I had instructed him. He could not. He did not think what I told him to do was important enough to do it.

Ramah's fault lay in not telling me the first time the boy did more than hold her hand. She was deceitful, and did not walk in the light with her father. I do not fault her for responding to him physically. She is a woman, and women are all responders to those for whom they care. She did genuinely care for this boy. It was totally my fault for allowing her to be in a situation where the fences of protection were not honored. However, not telling me was a very serious violation of the necessary transparent relationship that she must have with her father. When Adam and Eve sinned in the garden, the Bible says "Adam and Eve hid themselves from the presence of the Lord among the trees of the garden" (Genesis 3:8). They did not continue in their transparent relationship with God. I believe Ramah has learned from her experience to always walk in the light with her father, with absolutely no secret shadows, and then with her husband when she marries.

I share these three experiences only because I know they may be helpful to other fathers who are struggling with how to protect their sons and daughters as they try to shepherd them past the potential dangers of the years that lead up to marriage. I have learned a great deal from these failures. I believe others will as well. As God's people, we must recover Godly methods of finding mates for our children, so that they can enter marriage unscathed, and maximize their potential as kingdom warriors.

Qualifications to attain

Whenever we think about qualifications for marriage, we generally think about the qualifications of the ones that we will marry. "What am I looking for in a husband or wife?" Certainly that is a legitimate question for a young person, and his or her father, to ask. However, first, and more basic, is the question, "What kind of a person do I need to be before I marry?"

A father should have a goal in mind when he begins the process of training his children when they are less than one year old (We will cover that in a subsequent chapter). The goal should be the biblical qualities that he desires to see in their lives. If he has had this goal before him, and has been diligent at his task, he will be rewarded with sons and daughters who have attained to his standards. Mates for these children will be provided by other fathers with similar biblical standards. In this way, two can walk together in marriage, because they are agreed (Amos 3:3).

The following qualities are my standards that I have used for the preparation of my own children, and am currently using for evaluation of potential spouses for them.

Standards for young men

1. A desire to seek first the kingdom of God (Matthew 6:33). This means for a young man to have a clear understanding of what is meant by "the kingdom." This concept is not "full-time Christian work," nor is it just becoming a "born-again" Christian from the world's perspective; rather, it is coming under the delegated authority of Jesus Christ and His law-word in every area of life. Seeking the kingdom also means knowing how to apply the Bible, the law of the kingdom, in every area of responsibility where he has been given authority, including his family. Interests, talents, and gifts determine the occupational area where one invests his life for the kingdom.

When my sons were in college, they were active in an evangelical Christian student group on campus. Because the organization did not understand or preach the kingdom, its leaders did not see academic studies as primary. As one staff member told Adam, "Working for _____ Christian organization is more important than good grades." Adam was the president of the group his junior year, but did not let it interfere with his studies.

They recruited many of their students to go into "full-time Christian work," and join their staff upon graduation. Jason had planned to go to graduate school in architecture for years, and after experiencing this group's recruiting and attempted guilt trips, asked me if I thought his life could count for the kingdom of God as much in architecture as in "professional Christianity." I assured him that after considering his gifts and abilities, he should do the desire of his heart (Psalm 37:4). He should build the most beautiful buildings possible for the glory of God. Both of my sons are in graduate school today; Adam in history to be a college professor, and Jason in architecture. They are pursuing their areas of interest.

Any suitor for Ramah needs to demonstrate to my satisfaction that he understands this truth, and has given his life to extending the kingdom, no matter what occupational field he enters. Nominal Christians, who want to attend church on Sunday and live the rest of the week for themselves, need not apply.

2. A sacrificial, unconditional love for his prospective bride (Ephesians 5:25-33). My sons and I have discussed the material in Chapter 7 for years, and I would not give my blessing to a marriage for one of them if I was not convinced that he loved his young woman in that way. Because we saw this kind of love in Jason's heart for the girl in the earlier example, we were able to give that relationship our blessing. He must recognize the difference between her needs and her wants, and between blessing her and pleasing her. The same evaluation and conclusion applies to any young man who is courting my daughter. Often the difference between "I love you," and "I love me and want you" is cloudy in a boy's thinking. It is up to the girl's father to discern the difference. That was the situation in the example of Ramah's friend in the last chapter; he had another girl friend within three weeks.

3. An ability to lead his wife with strong, firm, decision-making (1 Timothy 3:4,5). This is covered very thoroughly in Chapter 8. If a young man is not naturally strong, if he runs from confrontation, and if he is afraid of the disapproval of others, it is sometimes very difficult for him to lead in the home, particularly if he has a naturally non-compliant, strong-willed wife. Unless there is a willingness to see himself honestly, repent of those weaknesses, and be willing to change, lack of leadership will plague him all his life.

No quality is more important than this one, because ruling in the kingdom means leadership. Again, because of Jason's strength, we knew that no matter how much pressure his friend would exert after they were married, his life-course was set, and he would make the day-to-day decisions that he felt were best for his family.

Ramah is a very strong-willed woman, probably the strongest natural leader of my three children. She would always be the one who led the charge through the neighborhood as a little girl. She needs a man who is willing to confront her, and who cannot be intimidated by her verbal arguments. She longs to meet a strong man who can confidently love her and handle her like this, and then lead her into his vision for the kingdom. This is one of the qualities I desire the most in Ramah's husband. She will not respect a man who does not have it.

4. <u>Sexual purity (1 Corinthians 6:18,19; 9:27)</u>. He must understand and agree with the material in Chapters 12-15, and be committed to keeping his vessel in purity. He must understand the power and importance of sex in the plan of God. If he has been indiscreet in the past, he must have repented of that sin, and desire to walk in purity from this time forward. An inability to keep his vessel under control is a cause for disqualification.

5. <u>Respect for others, particularly parents and those in authority (Ephesians 6:1-3)</u> I have taught my children to submit to legitimate authority wherever they find it. We will cover this in great detail in the chapter on child training. It is enough to say here that a man cannot exercise proper authority in the home unless he has first learned to submit to authority himself. A young man who does not yield to his parents and other authority, and seek to please them, will be a poor candidate for a husband. A lack of respect for me and my authority in Ramah's life was at the heart of the difficulty in Ramah's courtship experience related above.

6. <u>Unselfish attitude toward others (Philippians 2:3,4)</u>. These last four qualities, #5-8, will be covered in detail in the child training chapter. This one, #6, was also discussed in Chapter 16. Interest in others, in actions and conversation, is indicative of a man's willingness to be concerned about his wife's welfare, and to be willing to lay down his life for her. Self-centered men make poor husbands.

7. <u>Willingness to admit wrongdoing and to be accountable for his own actions (1 John 1:7)</u>. A man is not ready for marriage until he is willing to look at himself and admit his own faults, walking in honesty and complete transparency with his wife, not hiding anything past or present. No difficulty is too hard to overcome if both husband and wife understand this principle. Until marriage, children must walk in this kind of openness and honesty with their parents, not hiding anything, but initiating repentance even before sin is discovered.

8. <u>Diligence in all things (Colossians 3:23)</u>. This means cultivating the habit of doing everything as well as possible, including studies, jobs, and whatever other responsibilities the young man might have. Is the young man maximizing his abilities? If he is a hard worker, there will always be employment, and he will be able to support his family.

One can see that an important part of ruling in the kingdom is evaluation, both of our own sons and those who would marry our daughters. We must not shrink from the task, even though most young people do not like to be evaluated. These are the qualifications I have used in training my own sons, and the list I am using to evaluate my daughter's potential suitors.

Standards for young women

Let me say that the list by which I will evaluate potential wives for my son is much shorter. There are only two qualifications on it.

Of course, I would love for her to have an understanding of the kingdom, to be sexually pure, to respect authority, to esteem others, to be willing to admit wrongdoing, and to be diligent in all things. I will do my best to see that Jill and I train our daughter in all those areas. But those are not requirements for my daughter-in-law like they are for my son-in-law. No, there are only two requirements on the list.

1. She must be the one for whom God has placed *agape* love in my son's heart. Sometimes God desires to *save* a girl from her previous situation by using the love of her husband to do so. As I explained in Chapter 7, his *agape* love is the strongest force in the universe and God can use that love to redeem her from a life of sin, rebellion, selfishness, unwillingness to repent, and laziness. She may have none of the qualities in the previous list, and yet, for some mysterious reason, God places that "love without reason," *agape* love, in my son's heart for her. Who am I to argue with God in order to save my son from the difficulties that will surely come in their relationship as he "saves" her?

He must know the troubles that lie ahead. He must be ready for the pain of "salvation" as he gradually sees her redemption accomplished. "Salvation" is not free to the "savior." But if he is aware of what will ensue, and still loves her, who am I to say "no?"

Remember, marriage is not for our enjoyment, but for the extension of the kingdom of God. The eternal Bridegroom suffered great pain as His *agape* love sent Him to the cross to redeem His bride, and He calls us as men to follow His divine example as the Son of Man. Just as He accepted His bride in all her sinfulness, "just as she is," in order to save her, we must do the same with ours.

2. She must be willing to give my son her life without reservation. Is not this the only qualification that Jesus has for His bride, the church? Does she have to shape herself up first before He will accept her? Of course not, for He says, "Come, just as you are, and I will dress you in My robes of righteousness" (Philippians 3:9; Revelation 7:9). Her only

qualification is that He has chosen her (John 15:16), and decided to love her and give His life for her (Ephesians 5:2,25). She has responded, and become His. He is her head, and she has given herself unreservedly to Him in response to His love.

Yes, a young man must be qualified to be my daughter's bridegroom, just as Jesus had to qualify to be our Bridegroom, our Savior. It was necessary that He live a perfect life, and meet all the qualifications of His heavenly Father. But, praise God, we did not have to qualify to be His bride! Nor does my son's bride need to qualify. God will be at work in her heart by His Holy Spirit to cause her to respond to his love, just as He was at work in our hearts to cause us to respond to the Lover of our souls. That response will be an unreserved giving of herself to him.

What does that mean? As she takes his name, she takes his identity, just as the name of Jesus is upon those who are identified with Him (Revelation 3:12; 22:6). She will not attempt to find meaning and fulfillment independent of him, in a life of her own apart from him, for as his helpmate, her fulfillment is in him, just as we find our meaning in all of life in Jesus Christ (Philippians 1:21). She adopts his vision for their future, becoming a co-laborer with him in his calling, just as we are co-laborers together with Christ (2 Corinthians 6:1). She attempts to please him in all she says and does, just as we attempt to please the Lord in everything (2 Timothy 2:3,4). She loses her life in his, just as we are called to lose our life in the life of our Heavenly Bridegroom (Mark 8:35).

Is she willing to give herself to my son in this manner? If so, she will "find her life." All other qualifications one might have for a wife are immaterial if she is ready to give him the treasure of her life.

Marriage, as a living picture of Christ's relationship to His bride, the church, corresponds much more than we have realized. The parallels abound, and as we restore an understanding of this kingdom covenant relationship, the family will be a powerful force to see "His kingdom come, His will be done, on the earth as it is in heaven."

"Father, give me, as a father, the grace to evaluate those in my kingdom diligently, and to faithfully protect my sons and daughters from the enemy as he tries to sow seeds of autonomy in their lives. Help me to assist them in discovering the one with whom they will spend their lives. Keep the vision of the kingdom before me, and before them. Amen."

Questions for discussion

1. Do you feel that all the standards for a man to meet before he can marry mentioned in this chapter are legitimate requirements? Which ones do you feel are not necessary? Why?

2. Which of the character qualities do you feel have been developed, at least to a reasonable extent, in your life? In which areas do you feel that there is work to be done? Can you think of a strategy to develop that weak area?

3. Do you think the requirement for a bride to give herself unreservedly to her husband is unreasonable? What do you think the Bible teaches? (i.e., Ephesians 5:22-24).

4. How do you think you could know the difference between "I love you," and, "I love me and want you?"

Part Six
"Building a Heritage"

Chapter 20

"Train Up a Child"

In many ways, my mother and father were first generation Christians. There were other Christians here and there in both families, but my parents were the first to take Christianity very seriously, and pass that attitude on. They grasped very firmly the flag of the gospel of Jesus Christ for the Andrews posterity that would follow.

They were not sophisticated in their understanding of their faith, and did little more than plant that flag, and say, "Here we stand. This is what we believe. We will not be moved." But I learned from them a love for the Lord, a reverence for the Word of God, and obedience to Godly authority.

They ran a tight ship, demanded obedience from me as an only child, and erected fences that got me through fraternity life on a secular state campus relatively unscathed. When my faith became personal for me in college, all the training I had received as a child formed a foundation upon which I have built for the last 38 years. I picked up the flag and saw a mountain ahead of me, with a path leading upward. The Lord said, "Put My flag on the very top."

As a second generation Christian, I have taken the flag up the path toward the summit, which represents that day when "He delivers the kingdom to God the Father, when He puts an end to all rule and all authority and power" (1 Corinthians 15:24). This book records a great deal of that journey.

Along the way I have gotten a clearer view of the flag, because it has unfurled more completely as it has flown in the wind; a wind that has often blown stiffly in my face. I didn't always like the wind at the time because it seemingly held me back, but I see now that without the wind, I would never have seen as clearly the flag I am carrying, because it would have hung limp. I have discovered that it is the flag of a much fuller, richer gospel than my parents ever dreamed. It is the flag of a

301

gospel that is "able to save to the uttermost those who come to God through Him" (Hebrews 7:25), and to redeem whole civilizations as well (Isaiah 2:2-9).

I have also gotten a clearer view of the summit as I've progressed up the path. The kingdom of God, I've seen, is not just a different way of saying all those who believe in Jesus Christ, but it is the sphere of authority where Jesus rules by His law, the kingdom "which shall not pass away,... the one which shall not be destroyed" (Daniel 7:14).

One day, the flag that my parents planted near the base of the hill, will be given up by Jill and me, at the apex of our journey, still short of the summit. My three children will pick it up and carry it further. They are third generation Christians, now with a heritage behind them. They have watched as Jill and I have stumbled on the path, even fallen down, but always gotten up, flag intact, to continue again. They have listened, and learned with us. As a result, their salvation is much more complete than was their parent's at the same age. They have less excess baggage to unload as they progress up the path. They are beginning their journey much further up the mountain than Jill and I did.

The fourth generation Andrews are beginning to arrive. Adam and Missy have two children with a third on the way. I watch as they train them, and marvel at the knowledge, the wisdom and insight that they have. They understand more about the kingdom than I did at forty-five. The fourth generation will go still further up the path. This is how "the earth will be filled with the knowledge of the glory of the Lord, as the waters cover the sea" (Habakkuk 2:14).

Satan's deception

Someone may be saying, "You have been lucky. Your children have not rejected the faith of their parents. Whether or not children stay on the path in today's world is purely a crap-shoot. I'm afraid to have children for fear they will rebel, and be nothing but trouble."

Tragically, this is the attitude of many Christian parents. They feel that the destiny of their children is purely up to chance, a sort of "luck of the draw." Satan has tricked us with misinformation like this, and cut off the major source of power to extend the kingdom of God into the next generation, our children. We are not to be "ignorant of his devices" (2 Corinthians 2:11), so let me tell you how he has deceived us.

First, he has had the church fail to emphasize family, and not teach the material in this book. It is "too hard," or "too controversial." If there is nothing we can really do to effect how our children ultimately turn out anyway, we might as well not deal with these issues that divide us.

As a result of this kind of thinking, our emphasis has been outward and superficial. We have gone out to save the world and left our children in the care of youth group leaders who are no more mature than those they lead, sometimes less. Parents have thought that the church would do their job for them, and the church has not succeeded, because God never intended the church to train children. Youth group leaders should be abolished and replaced by fathers, who together provide a corporate experience for their sons and daughters (and other young people in the church without Christian fathers). Youth group cannot replace the parents' training of their own children, but it has given fathers the erroneous idea that training is occurring.

Our evangelism has produced many first generation Christians, but in the process our children have often been lost to the cause of Jesus Christ, so we have a net "no gain." We actually have a net loss, because our children were possible *second generation Christians!* They have more potential to carry the flag further, with probably less baggage to unload along the path, than the new converts from our evangelistic campaigns. By focusing almost exclusively on evangelism, we have lost our heritage. We must secure our posterity, and then take them with us to reach the world. Satan gains ground when we have to start over again every generation with first generation Christians.

Satan's second ploy is to get the church to focus on the short term rather than the long term. We are like a speculative investor who is always looking for the quick fortune, and neglects to regularly, systematically save for the future until it is too late. It is much more fun to look at prophecy charts, and speculate on the nearness of the Lord's return based on the latest world event, than it is diligently, day in and day out, to do the dirty work of bringing up our children "in the training and admonition of the Lord" (Ephesians 6:4). Our sub-conscious thinking is "I won't need to do this child training thing and get too deeply into what the Bible says about it. My children won't have time to grow up anyway because the Lord will return first."

Satan's third deception, based on the short-term thinking mentioned above, is that he has clouded the minds of church leaders as to the meaning of Ephesians 4:11,12: "He gave some as apostles, prophets, evangelists, and some pastors and teachers, for the equipping of the saints for the work of the ministry..." They have not seen that "equipping the saints for the work of the ministry" includes the primary ministry of training children, for well trained children form a foundation for the rest of a man's ministry (1 Timothy 3:4,5). The church has developed little theology of the family to assist him in training his children.

In these last chapters, I'm going to cover biblical child training principles. The destiny of your children depends on the faithful application of these truths. "Train up a child in the way he should go, and when he is old (a mature adult), he will not depart from it" (Proverbs 22:6). Here we have God's promise that if He has placed in your heart the desire and ability to follow His plan of child training, you will succeed. It is not up to chance.

What does it mean to "train" my children?

"Behold, children are a heritage from the Lord, The fruit of the womb is His reward. Like arrows in the hand of a warrior, So are the children of one's youth. Happy is the man who has his quiver full of them; They shall not be ashamed, But shall speak with their enemies in the gate. (Psalm 127:3-5).

First of all, training children involves seeing them in the context of Psalm 127, as weapons of war in the great cosmic battle that is being fought at this very minute between God and the Devil. Without this understanding, we see that trained, well-behaved children make our lives as parents more pleasant, allow us to be proud of them (and proud of ourselves for being such good parents!), and keep us from having to be embarrassed by their behavior. However, in these verses, God has a much greater purpose for our children. They are said to be a heritage, or a gift, that is passed down to the father from the Lord, a gift that is to be used in battle.

In verse 3, the "is His" is in italics in the New King James Bible, signifying that it is not in the original language, but is inserted by the translators for clarification. I believe the "His" should not be capitalized, because the reference is, I believe, to the father, not to the Lord. Children are a heritage, even a reward, to fathers. In other words, they are much to be prized. Why? Because they are the means by which a father can continue to live and extend his influence down through the ages. What do I mean?

Let me give an example from my own life. My father was a man of impeccable character, but of few words. You found out about my dad by watching him, not by listening to him. When he did talk, I was all ears. These are some of the pearls he dropped:

"Always do your share and a little bit more."

"You have to trust people. You will get taken advantage of occasionally, but that is better than being suspicious of everyone."

"Son, never cheat on your income tax. God may be the only one who sees, but He does."

"Always do the right thing, even when it's hard."

These words of wisdom have become a part of my life so that I do not even associate them any longer with my father. They have been worked into the fabric of my being so that they are now mine.

I have now passed these maxims on to my children, along with many others (I'm a much bigger talker than my dad was!), and through these words my dad lives in the lives of grandchildren he never met. His influence has been extended far past his lifetime.

In Psalm 127, this heritage, this reward, is considered in the context of war. My children, properly trained, are going to be the means by which I put some serious hurt on the Devil! They are said to be arrows, weapons of war in the hand of a warrior. I am that mighty warrior, eager to inflict as much damage on the kingdom of darkness as I can! My ultimate effectiveness will be determined by how much effective firepower I have, how many arrows are in my quiver, and how battle-ready each arrow is. The arrows represent not only my physical children, but children in the faith as well.

Preparing to release my arrows

A warrior is sure that his weapons are in excellent condition, because he knows that in the battle, they must be ready to perform for him. My arrows must be sharp and straight, ready to be launched at the heart of the Devil. It does not matter how carefully an arrow is aimed, if it is not sharp and straight, it will be ineffective. We have eighteen to twenty years to sharpen and straighten our arrows as we do the difficult, time-consuming, thankless, and often heartbreaking job of training our children.

If we have been faithful to do so, sometime during that period they will be ready for battle, different children at different times. We can take them from our quivers, put them in our bows and begin to point them at the Devil's heart, as we inculcate into them the vision for the kingdom of God, the vision that will determine the course of their lives. If we have properly exercised the authority of the kingdom with them and ruled over them well, our vision will become their vision. When we release them as they leave home, they will extend our influence into the generations to come, far beyond our short lifetimes!

In order to be equipped to train our children effectively there are at least four major areas that must be addressed: the role of the parents in the training process; the condition of the child to be trained; the necessity to control the child; and finally, the inculcation of the family standards and vision.[1] I will cover the first two areas in this chapter, and the last two in the last three chapters of the book.

Parent power

The first thing a parent must realize is that he or she is in absolute authority over the child. "Children, obey your parents *in all things,* for this is well pleasing to the Lord" (Colossians 3:20). There can be only one will in the home, the will of Jesus Christ, as determined by the father, and faithfully carried out by the mother in his absence. God has delegated His authority in His kingdom in this way. When the father speaks to the child, either directly, or through the mother, Jesus Christ (who always does the will of his Father), is speaking straight from His throne.

Child training cannot be effective until this is realized. The most basic issue in the family is "who is in charge?" At this stage in this book, I know that that statement is redundant, but we can't begin discussing child training without saying it again. God has given parents the authority to force their children to comply with their will for the purpose of training them.

It is important for parents to see that training their children is not optional. God has delegated to them this awesome responsibility (Deuteronomy 6:6,7; Ephesians 6:4), and will hold them accountable for how they do the task. It is not possible to tell the Lord, when He presents you with a child, "I decline the job of training this child."

Listen to the Lord's statement concerning the prophet Eli:

> *"For I have told him that I will judge his house forever for the iniquity which he knows (the sins of his sons), because his sons made themselves vile, and <u>he did not restrain them</u> (1 Samuel 3:13).*

The first step is seeing clearly the responsibility God has given to parents, and the absolute authority God has given them to carry it out.

No little angels

One of the hardest things for parents to grasp, particularly mothers, is the sinfulness of their children. They know it intellectually in theory, but when it comes to practical application, they forget. I often hear, "He wouldn't do that," when a child sins or misbehaves. Yes, Mom. Yes, Dad. He would.

Mothers are especially blind to their children's sin and are adept at covering or making excuses for them. At Tree of Life we have had a cooperative home school for a number of years. The mothers have shared the teaching load, and, therefore, teach other children besides their own in certain subjects. As an impartial bystander with no children in the school, I have watched mothers be particularly tough on other people's children, and then let their own get away with identical behavior. In addition, they rarely respond well to others' criticism of their children. Mothers are like momma bears, protecting their cubs, often refusing to see when their children have their hands in the honey jar.

Some years ago, I observed a young child, probably about six, exhibiting some inappropriate behavior at church. His mother was in another part of the building, so I found her, and told her what I had just seen her son doing. Her answer was, "Oh, he wouldn't do that."

I replied, "You don't understand. I saw him do it with my own eyes."

"Well, I know he doesn't do that," she said. "I'll go ask him."

I was incredulously shaking my head as she went to find him. She asked him if he had done what I said he had done, and, of course, he answered "No."

She returned and said these very words. "He said he didn't do it. I knew he wouldn't do that." With this mind set, child training is impossible. Parents like this woman had better prepare for some very difficult times during their child's teen years.

Making excuses for our children is another way we miss opportunities to train them. I was talking to a mother in the church parking lot while her little girl swung on the gate at the entrance. As we talked, the mother told her to stop at least four times with absolutely no effect on the child. Without even realizing what she was saying, and not missing a beat in our conversation, the mother said, "She's really tired." The girl continued to swing until her mother gathered her up and they left. Children do get tired, but once they are old enough to understand and mind, tired is no excuse for disobedience. The habit of making excuses for her child's disobedience was so ingrained in the mother that she didn't even realize that she had done so.

Discerning between our job, and God's job

Until we see that our child's heart is "deceitful above all things, and desperately wicked" (Jeremiah 17:9), we will not be effective in our child training efforts. For the sake of that precious little child that we love so much, we must agree with Jesus about his heart. "For out of the heart proceed evil thoughts, murders, adulteries, fornications, thefts, false witness, blasphemies" (Matthew 15:19). It's hard to believe that all that could be in the heart of that beautiful child, but the Bible says it is, and God has given us the responsibility to train that child to overcome these sinful tendencies, and exhibit the character of Jesus Christ.

Some feel that if their children just get born again everything will be fine. God will then change them. This is where we must have a clear understanding of what is His job, and what is our job.

Parents send their children to summer camps and youth retreats, in the hope that they will have an experience with the Lord and everything will then be all right. The experience they may have with the Lord there can be very genuine, and is necessary in order for our children to experience new life. That is God's job. Try as we might as parents we cannot make such new life happen. The more we try, the more religious we become, and the more we turn off our children. We can only pray that God Himself, in His divine sovereignty, will touch our children, and cause them to be born again (John 1:12,13).

But just because a child has been born again, that does not mean that his character has been changed. It may help to make him more receptive to his parents' training, but building character into a child is a job that has been given by God to parents (Ephesians 6:4, Deuteronomy 6:6,7). Giving life is God's job; building character is the father's. We must clearly understand this division of labor. If fathers do not do their job, it will remain for the Lord to do it when the children are adults. The character lessons are much harder to learn then, and the degree of success is generally smaller. We will suggest some character traits to build into children, and how to do it, in Chapter 22.

What do you do with a rebellious child who challenges your every directive, and makes life miserable for everyone? That's the topic of Chapter 21.

"Father, give me a vision for the purpose of training my children. Show me what to do, and give me grace to always do it, to the best of my ability. Help me to push past the difficult times with them, and to not grow weary in well-doing. Thank you for your promise that, if I do my job, you'll do yours. Amen."

Questions for discussion

1. Which of the three deceptions used by Satan has been the most effective in your life? If you have not fallen for any of these, how has he diverted you focus away from the proper view of your posterity?

2. What heritage did you receive from your parents that you have been able to pass on to your children? What have you learned that they didn't know that will be of benefit to your posterity?

3. Do you agree with the concept of absolute parental authority over children (I'm not referring to abusive situations, but to normal, loving situations)? Why or why not? Do you have trouble seeing yourself in that role? If so, why?

4. In what ways does your child demonstrate that he or she is "deceitful and desperately wicked?" In what ways have you seen yourself making excuses or covering for them?

---

[1] This four point outline for training children, along with many of the ideas that I will relate, I owe to J. Richard Fugate, *What the Bible says about Child Training*, (Tempe, Arizona: Alethia, 1980). I cannot recommend this book highly enough. Fugate's book has become such a part of my life, it would be impossible to credit him with everything I have learned from it during the faithful application of its principles for the past fourteen years. To him, a personal friend, go my heartfelt thanks.

Chapter 21

Controlling the Child

We have seen that we, as parents, directly represent the King of kings, and speak to our children with His authority. He has entrusted us with their lives for but a brief time, and then we must give them back to Him, our time as stewards over them completed. We must never grasp and attempt to hold on to them, for they do not belong to us. God has placed them in our care for a very specific task; getting them ready to join in the family business of extending God's kingdom. Everything we do in their lives has this as its ultimate goal.

Our work is cut out for us, considering the effects of the fall in our children's hearts. We would be powerless to do this job on our own, but the Holy Spirit has been sent to us to give us all we need to accomplish the task; insight to know what to do, wisdom to know how to do it, and grace to actually get it done. He will be our Comforter when we have temporary set-backs, and He will encourage us to persevere until our assignment is complete. Praise God, Jesus has not left us as orphans, to do the job alone (John 14:16-18).

What is control?

Controlling the child is the first step in child training, and the sooner we begin, the better. Every year that passes without bringing a child under control will make it that much harder to train him, so it is crucial to understand just what controlling a child means, so we can get started.

Listen to Richard Fugate's definition:

> "Control is the force, or pressure, by which you exercise your right of parental rule - the right to set the standards for, to direct the actions of, and to administer justice to, your children.

As a parent, you have the responsibility and legitimate right to exert pressure on your children."[1]

In other words, a parent can tell little Johnnie what he can or cannot do, where he will or will not go, and then by exerting legitimate pressure, insure that Johnnie does exactly as he is told.

I don't need to tell you that this kind of obedience does not just naturally happen. Children do not have a built-in desire to do as their parents request, or the maturity to do what is best for themselves. Left to themselves, they would play in the freeway, eat ice cream and cake every meal, and never brush their teeth or take a bath. They need invisible fences that limit their options and protect them from danger. Fences bring freedom, for now the child is able to play to his heart's content within the boundaries his parents have erected for him. He feels safe and secure. He knows in his heart that he is not mature enough to run his own life. So, if his parents don't do so, he is frustrated, unhappy and insecure.

However, because of sin, children resist the imposition of their parents' will upon their own. They are unaware that the new restrictions will ultimately bring freedom. They only know that their will is being crossed. They must learn, through the exercise of force, to obey what their parents say.

Pitfalls to avoid

Parents do not have to be perfect parents to control their children. They do not have to earn their children's respect or qualify in any way to make them obey. They are kings and queens in their homes, ruling as representatives of Jesus Christ.

They must not fall for any of the tricks that children pull in an attempt to get their parents to back off from their demands. "I hate you," "You are a meannie," and "You don't love me," are old standards that must be seen for what they are: manipulations by the child in an attempt to relieve pressure and get his own way.

Parents must not be motivated by a desire for their children to love them, or by a desire to please their children. With this as a primary concern controlling them is impossible. Parents must win every battle of the wills until the child yields to the parents' will. They must see that this is the ultimate expression of love; forcing the child to yield to authority. Without learning this most basic lesson in all the universe, the child will be lost to the purpose of God. A soldier is useless in battle unless he can follow orders.

God has given to parents the assignment of teaching this most basic lesson, because it is most easily learned when we are very young. The child knows in his heart that the unyielding pressure that is being applied is an expression of love, and he will respond eventually. It is every child's subconscious desire to be under the authority of parents who love him enough to stick with him and win the battle of the wills. If the child wins, he will lose respect for his parents. The very thing the parents wanted by giving in to him, his love, will be lost. There will be no room in his heart for his parents, because it is filled with himself.

Once a child is under control, and not before, he is in a position to learn from the parents the family values and standards. The reason so many young people have rejected their parents' life-style is not because they made a studied evaluation of it and then decided to reject it. It is because they were never controlled as children, and they interpreted that lack of control as rejection. They lived a sort of "uneasy truce" with their parents until they left home, and then rejected all they were taught. Listen to this description:

"Counselors who work with runaway youth have isolated a consistent attitude in many of these youths. They have found that these youths usually believe that their parents did not love them because the parents would neither restrain nor direct them. They felt rejected because their parents did not care enough about them to protect them from themselves. These parents rejected their parental responsibilities, and thereby the youths felt rejected. Delinquent parents produced delinquent youth."[2]

Getting ready for war

Once a parent decides to face the challenge to control his child, he must be prepared for conflict. Can you see that conflict is easier to handle with a one-year-old than a teen-ager? The earlier you start the better.

Often the first indication of resistance to parental authority occurs on the changing table. When the child begins to kick and resist having his diaper changed, it is time to begin to exert pressure. Tell the child "no," firmly, while holding him still for a moment. When he is released, if he continues to resist, tap him lightly on the upper thigh with a small switch, concurrently with another "no," holding him still again. Repeat if necessary. Very soon he will understand the association between his resistance, the "no," and the pain that follows disobedience. This begins the process of controlling your child.

After the child has mastered "no," and is mobile, he must learn the commands "stop" and "come." How may times have you seen a mother running after a fleeing two-year-old, or shouting at a resistant child to "come here!" Control means that the child obeys with the first command given in a normal tone of voice.

The biblical method of exerting the pressure to insure that the child obeys will be explained in detail later in the chapter, but let me say here that children will do exactly what you want them to, if you make them. If you would like to count to ten, scream and holler, or use another signal to communicate that now you are serious and really mean it, you can do that. Or, you can make them obey at the first command, given in a normal voice. It's up to you.

A finite number of conflicts

There will be times when it seems to the mother as though the whole day is filled with conflict. She may feel she can't stand another confrontation. When those times occur, she must remember to look at each instance as another opportunity to bring that child under control for the kingdom of God. She will have only a finite number of opportunities to do so while the child is under her stewardship, and they must not be wasted. There are also a finite number of battles that the parents must win before the child gives up, and the parents win the war. The number varies with every child. Strong-willed children wage more battles; compliant ones, fewer. "And let us not grow weary while doing good, for in due season we shall reap if we do not lose heart" (Galatians 6:9). The next battle may be the last one before he realizes that his parents love him enough for him to trust them with his life.

After Adam came, Jill and I thought we were perfect parents. He was very compliant from the start, always seeming to want to please us, and indeed, most of the pressure we ever exerted on him was because of attitudinal problems.

Then came Jason, and our view of ourselves as perfect parents was exploded. He was strong-willed and stubborn, and looked for ways to get away with resisting our authority. Once, after being potty-trained for some time, he began to wet his pants. There were no changes in his life, no new pressures to warrant a relapse, and his response to our reprimands was, "I don't know when it's coming." We took him to the doctor to see if that indeed could be the case. He examined him carefully, and, as he told us there was absolutely nothing wrong with Jason, he smiled as if to say, "He's got you buffaloed." We realized that wetting his pants was one way Jason had been able to resist our authority without consequences. Pressure was applied, and the problem was solved.

God will give you insight, as he did us in this instance, to see what is occurring. If you don't "see," you can't act. How many Christian parents do you know that are oblivious to their children as they are disrespectful to them, resist them, or even hit at them? It is impossible to rule if you do not see the rebellion in your kingdom.

Is it too late?

What if your child is a teen-ager who is still resistant to your will? What should you do? If you have decided to bring your child under control, and you are ready for the battle that will ensue, let me suggest the following procedure. Sit down with your son or daughter, and explain to them that God has placed you, as the father, in a position of rulership in your home. You want to repent to them for not ruling well and giving them the leadership that they have needed in the past, and ask them to forgive you. Explain to them that, from now on, by the grace of God, you are going to love them enough to provide that leadership. You expect them to obey what you tell them to do. Then tell them what the consequences will be for disobedience. (We will cover that shortly). Then expect the battle to begin.

If you are still able to physically control your child, or if the child submits to your discipline, there is still hope. If the child will not submit to your discipline, and is too big to control, he cannot remain under your roof. There must be but one will in the family, or there will be no peace in the home. You cannot compromise your leadership by tolerating rebellion. Along with the provision that you supply as the head of your home comes mandatory obedience to your rules. No obedience, no provision. As I said in Chapter 5, this view of ruling may seem harsh, but it is the way the kingdom of God functions.

The nineteen-year-old daughter of one of our elders felt that her father was too controlling, and began to strongly resist his authority in her life. At a men's meeting, he shared what was occurring in his family, repented of his failure to see and deal with his daughter's rebellion when she was young, and then stepped down as an elder, based on the qualifications for elders in 1 Timothy 3:4,5.

His daughter moved out, and was estranged from her family for almost two years. Her father would not allow her to partake of the benefits of the family without submitting to its authority structure. The parents were broken-hearted as they watched their daughter dive headlong into the world.

Finally, she called her father in tears and said, "I know the requirements, and I want to come home." He was very skeptical, making it very clear to her that to come home meant submitting to his demands. She knew, and she yielded. That has been some three years ago now. He has been restored as an elder, and his daughter, after standing before the church and repenting in tears (there were no dry eyes in the building!), is now a vibrant, functioning member of her family and the church.

By following kingdom principles, this father's daughter was restored. As my father told me years ago, "Always do the right thing, even if it's hard."

Rebellion - the enemy of control

What is it that makes controlling a child so difficult? It is the same thing that makes us want to slip off our shoes and wriggle our toes on the lawn with the sign that says, "Don't walk on the grass." The same urge causes us to look for a pebble when we see an empty house with the sign, "Don't throw rocks at the windows." That urge can be masked by respectability, like, "I have to be my own boss. It's too hard for me to work for someone else," or "I can't seem to find a church where I can fit in." These are all symptoms of the same root problem that manifests itself in a child by making him difficult to control. It is called rebellion.

Satan rebelled against God. He did not like God ruling over him. Adam rebelled against God. He did not like God telling him what he could and could not eat. And we, as Adam's descendants, having inherited his nature, rebel against God and His delegated authority. For, as they say in the South, "I ain't takin' nothin' off nobody."

Our children are simply demonstrating the unsophisticated version of that same natural, inborn tendency. We are all sinners; therefore rebellion proceeds naturally from our hearts. God has given parents the initial task of confronting that rebellion in their children, breaking it, bringing those children under control, and causing them to be soft and malleable under the hand of God.

He has given us a specific method for this, which, if properly used, will guarantee results. But first we need to be able to recognize rebellion when we see it. It's not always easy.

Recognizing rebellion

There are two kinds of rebellion; active and passive. Active rebellion is more commonly associated with boys and is easy to spot. Grocery store lanes are filled with examples. The child who says "no!" to his mother, hits at her, kicks at her, belligerently refuses to do as he is told, screams when she comes to get him, defiantly tells her to go away, throws a temper tantrum, sulks, pouts, argues, talks back, refuses to listen, refuses to answer, walks away while being talked to, etc. You get the picture. Children with these characteristics are all actively rebellious children.

When the child reaches teen years the symptoms are a little more subtle, but not much. They include acting "cool," bored, disrespectful to parents and other adults, deliberately disobedient, putting others down, having trouble with teachers at school, not wanting to be with parents, and following the world's pattern for teen-agers (which is rebellion) in terms of dress and music. Those are all signals that the young person is actively rebellious, has exerted his will against that of his parents, and is not willing to let them rule over him.

Children are designed by God to model themselves after their parents, which can be a serious problem if one or both parents is still in rebellion themselves. If the children see that their father is resistant to authority at work, at church, or to the civil government, or that the mother functions autonomously from her husband and does her own thing, it will be very hard to address the rebellion in the children effectively.

If you see yourself in that category and want to see the rebellion in your children broken, face yourself and repent to God and the one whose authority you have resisted. If your children are older, tell them what you have done. Tell them that you didn't have the benefit of parents who broke your rebellion when you were young, and that it has created much difficulty for you in your adulthood. By the grace of God, you love them too much to make them go through what you have had to go through.

317

Passive rebellion

Passive rebellion is much more difficult to spot, and parents must be vigilant not to miss it. If rebellion is not recognized when the child is young, then it is shocking when suddenly it appears as he or she enters the teen or adult years. Often the comment is, "They were too strict with her, and when she had a chance she rebelled." No, that's not the problem. The rebellion did not suddenly appear because the child now had the freedom to rebel. It was there all along, but it was of the passive variety. Rather than being too strict, the parents were too lenient. They did not recognize the passive rebellion and confront it when the child was young. Now it has come to the surface as active rebellion for all to see.

A family, very involved in Tree of Life, had two children who spent the majority of their grade school and junior high years in our cooperative home school. Both mother and father are first generation Christians, so without a Christian background it was often difficult for them to recognize rebellion in the lives of their children, though they desperately wanted to be good parents. The boy was the focus of most of the attention from the father, because his rebellion was, as is generally the case with boys, of the active variety.

The girl, on the other hand, was very polite, quiet and docile, and even had a gift of serving others. However, some of us could recognize passive rebellion in her, particularly when it came to her studies. It was difficult for her parents to see. When she reached high school, they moved about 45 minutes away, and though they continued to come to church, they enrolled their children in public school.

A few months ago, after a brief confrontation with her mother, the girl told her that she was pregnant. As the girl told my wife, "At school everyone had a boy friend, and I felt left out." The father of the unborn child is very violently anti-Christian. The girl has just recently run away from home for the second time. The story is yet to be finished.

I share the bare outline of what has occurred not to embarrass the parents, but to illustrate two extremely important truths. First, the girl is a classic case of passive rebellion. She told her parents what they wanted to hear, while all the time living a lie. Second, the father's actions illustrate beautifully the proper way to handle this situation.

He stood before the church the Sunday after his daughter had run away the first time and told us in detail what had happened. Then he accepted full responsibility for not seeing and dealing with his daughter's rebellion. There was no attempt to blame the public school, the boy who had gotten her pregnant, or even his daughter. He was in authority, it happened on his watch, and he took the blame. The church responded with a mighty outpouring of affection and prayer for the whole family. When one accepts responsibility in this manner, the church wants to cover that one with love in a way it cannot when others are blamed. No one said, "It's not your fault," because we knew it was. Yet, we also knew that only the sovereign grace of God separates the rest of the fathers in the church from the same experience.

Because the father was quick to accept blame for rebellion in his family, there have already been some very positive results. I will not go into detail concerning what the father is doing specifically, but let me say he is very proactive in his approach to saving his daughter, following carefully the principles of the kingdom. He is demonstrating a new soberness, a new maturity about the things of the Lord, and new wisdom and insight he has never had before. He is suddenly seeing other areas in his kingdom that are awry, and he is addressing them. In short, he has become a man of God.

His son, now 15 years old, has seen the firmness and resolve with which his father is dealing with his older sister. Any tendency toward some similar defiance of his father has, I am sure, been reconsidered.

Some guidelines to follow

If this true story put the fear in you, it was designed to do just that. Ignoring passive rebellion in a child is very dangerous, as you can see. It is so hard to recognize because there is often external obedience, but internal resistance. The child is sitting down on the outside, but standing up on the inside. There are several indicators that will tip you off that passive rebellion has invaded your kingdom.

The first indicator is when your child **obeys, but in his own time.** You have asked him to wash the car, and his response was a cheery, "O.K., Dad." However, two hours later, the car is not washed. When you ask him again, it's, "Oh, I forgot. I'll get right to it." Thirty minutes later, when you notice the car is still unwashed it's "I was just going to do that." If you did not keep on him, the car would not get washed. He didn't say, in defiance, "I won't do it." He knew better, but the end result is the same. He has controlled two and one-half hours of time in which he refused to do as you asked him. That is passive rebellion.

There are actually two symptoms of rebellion here that need to be identified. Not only did this child obey in his own time, but he used the age-old excuse, "**I forgot.**" Occasionally forgetting instructions is understandable. We all forget. But consistently forgetting means that your instructions have not become important enough to him for him to remember them. He has counted your authority over him as irrelevant. He needs to have you impress upon him the importance of remembering to obey that authority.

If the time frame for the completion of the task is not important, that should be spelled out when the instructions are given. If your desire was that he get the job done immediately, he has been passively rebellious.

The third symptom of passive rebellion to authority is that the child **obeys, but in his own way.** If you want your child to clean up his room, you should make him very aware of the standard that you will accept for a clean room. Anything short of that standard is not cleaning the room, but disobeying you. The child must learn to obey you the way you desire, not the way he would choose. You set the standard as the authority, not he.

Rebellion, then revolution

Parents must resist the temptation to feel bad and to blame themselves about the inevitable conflict that occurs during the controlling phase of child training. When conflict occurs, that means that the parents are simply doing their job. The alternative is to allow rebellion to grow unchallenged, often with the result of the complete overthrow of parental authority in the life of the child.

A huge majority of today's young people have been allowed to establish their own will as ruler in their lives, many times actually taking over the rule of the whole family, as well. They are the center of attention, controlling everyone around them with their demands and their temper tantrums. Their cowed parents attempt to pacify them by acquiescing to every demand, and by giving them piles of material things in an unsuccessful attempt to make them happy. Their rebellion has turned to revolution, and the revolution is complete. Parental authority has been overthrown.[3]

These are the children who struggle with all authority when they become young adults, because they will not allow anyone to cross their will. In today's society, they can go for a long time without having their will crossed. If it did not happen at home, it probably won't happen at public school, where the fear of that paddle that once hung on the wall in the principal's office has been removed. The counselors at the public school want to understand the environment from which these children come, and make contracts with them about their behavior as long as they are not too disruptive, rather than confront their rebellion. Even the criminal justice system refuses to see the root problem of rebellion in their hearts. With social workers, suspended sentences, parole, and community service, their rebellion remains untouched.

If a child's rebellion is not broken, he will struggle all his life, even if he makes it to adulthood without serious problems. A rebellious man will have difficulties with employers, with church leadership, and even with ruling in his own home. For, as we saw in Chapter 5, in order to exercise authority well, one must first know how to submit to it. A rebellious woman will always struggle with submitting to her husband. Do you see that we are doing our children no favors by yielding to them, rather than forcing them to yield to us? We are actually contributing to their destruction.

Improper methods to deal with rebellion[4]

Anytime you sniff that your child is resisting your right to rule in his life, be it active or passive rebellion, you must confront it. The Bible has a very specific method for this. However, before we see what that is, I want to look at some common methods the world uses to control children. None of them address the issue of rebellion. Therefore, for all practical purposes, they are essentially worthless.

The first of these is **negotiation**. When a parent has lost the right to rule in a child's life, he is forced to negotiate with the child in order to reach some sort of a compromise when their two wills clash. Of course, if the child refuses to compromise, the parent is helpless. Even at my daughter's Christian high school, a young English teacher was teaching her students how to "negotiate" with their parents.

The second improper method to attempt to control children is **bribery**. "If you will clean up your room, I'll give you a cookie." There is nothing wrong with blessing a child after the fact, for a job well done, but the command of the parent, not some reward, is incentive enough to do the job.

Third is the threat of **taking away something the child likes,** such as TV privileges or getting to go outside and play. These can be legitimate punishment for disobedience that is not rebellion (we will cover that in the next chapter), but it should not be used as a threat in an attempt to get the child to do what was commanded. The expressed will of the parent must be sufficient.

The fourth method is to use **manipulation** to get the child to feel guilty ("What you are doing is hurting mommie's feelings") or to redirect his attention to avoid confrontation. Parents can use their superior mental powers to control their children in this way, but their rebellion remains untouched.

Another false idea is expressed by this statement: "You can't confront everything. You have to pick your spots." If that is the method of operation of the parents, the child is always willing to gamble that this spot will be one the parents won't pick. He will chance it even if his odds are one in ten. Before he finally yields to his parents will, he must believe that <u>every</u> act of rebellion will be challenged.

The biblical cure for rebellion - fear

In Psalm 2, the kings of the earth who have set themselves in rebellion against God, and His anointed King, Jesus Christ, are told to "Serve the Lord with fear, and rejoice with trembling,... lest He be angry, and you perish in the way." Revelation 14:7 says, "Fear God and give glory to Him, for the hour of His judgment has come." The fear of God's wrath in judgment would seem to be a strong motivation for ceasing to rebel against His authority.

The fear of God is also said to be cleansing (Psalm 19:9), to cause one to hate evil (Proverbs 8:13), to be the beginning of wisdom (Proverbs 9:10), and to be a fountain of life (Proverbs 14:27). Those things are all desirable for our children, but impossible if they are in rebellion against God's authority.

The fear of God and His judgment must become real to our children through His delegated authority. No wonder that, as a nation, we have lost our fear of eternal judgment; there is little reason today to fear temporal judgment through God's institutions. Parents don't spank, governments don't execute, and churches don't excommunicate, each of those sanctions being an expression of God's judgment. We must restore the fear of God in our families.

Chastisement - the biblical method to deal with rebellion

Fifty years ago, it was common practice for all families, Christian and non-Christian alike, to spank their children in order to control them. It was also accepted practice in public schools, all the way through high school. Though I never had to visit the principal's office, I heard the stories told by those who had, and I can remember the fear that gripped my heart when I even considered the possibility of such a visit. Of course, man has devised a "better way" of dealing with rebellion, and has rejected God's way. We are reaping the results today of at least thirty years of that "better way."

In the Bible, spanking is called chastening, or chastisement. It is the imposition of legitimate, Godly force to impose the will of the parent upon the child when the child is in rebellion against it.

There are those, even Christians, who say that spanking (chastening) is child abuse. They say that it is barbaric and teaches a child to handle problems by hitting. Some even say that the verses I'm going to quote are not to be taken literally, but figuratively.

Remember, our epistemology is the revealed law in the Word of God. There is room for different interpretations, but we must not twist (or misread or manipulate) the Bible to allow for our own prejudices. As you read the following verses, ask yourself if they were meant to be taken literally or figuratively. Do you really believe that we are to live our lives by the Bible?

In chapter 12, the author of Hebrews is discussing how the circumstances the readers are enduring are really the chastening of the Lord, and how God's discipline, even His scourging (whipping), is evidence that he loves us and that we are His sons. He then moves to an example the readers can understand, the chastening an earthly father gives to his sons.

> "If you endure chastening, God deals with you as with sons, for what son is there whom a father does not chasten? But if you are without chastening, of which all have become partakers, then you are illegitimate and not sons. Furthermore, we have had human fathers who corrected us, and we paid them respect. Shall we not much more readily be in subjection to the Father of spirits and live? For they indeed for a few days chastened us as seemed best to them, but He for our profit, that we may be partakers of His holiness. Now no chastening seems to be joyful for the present, but grievous; nevertheless, afterward it yields the peaceable fruit of righteousness to those who have been trained by it" (Hebrews 12:7-11).

The author is equating the chastising of the Lord, as seen in the circumstances in which the readers found themselves, with something they could understand, the physical chastening of their earthly fathers. Let's look at some details in these verses.

323

First, all sons were spanked. That's a given, and if you were not spanked, it was a sign that you were illegitimate, i.e., the father did not care enough to train you. **Second**, chastisement produced respect for, or fear of, the father. **Third**, spanking was at the father's discretion ("as seemed best to him"). **Fourth**, chastisement is painful when it is inflicted, but produces righteousness "to those who have been trained by it." Spanking was the way children were trained. The motivation for chastisement was love. Spanking was even proof of love, for if there was no spanking, there was no love ["For whom the Lord loves, He chastens, and scourges (whips) every son whom He receives (Hebrews 12:6)].

Parents who say that they love their children too much to spank them really love only themselves. They want to spare themselves the conflict that will result when their children's rebellion is properly confronted and dealt with. They are willing to sacrifice their children for their own comfort. "Chasten your son while there is hope, and do not set your heart on his destruction" (Proverbs 19:18). They certainly don't understand, but by refusing to properly chastise their children they are literally setting their heart on their destruction.

Other verses in Proverbs that seem to me rather hard to interpret figuratively are: "He who spares his rod, hates his son, but he who loves him disciplines him promptly" (Proverbs 13:24). "Foolishness is bound up in the heart of a child, but the rod of correction will drive it far from him" (Proverbs 22:15). "Do not withhold correction from a child, for if you beat him with a rod, he will not die" (Though he may sound like he is dying!). "You shall beat him with a rod and deliver his soul from hell" (Proverbs 23:13,14).

From these verses, we can see that the proper instrument to use for spanking is a "rod." This is a flexible branch from a tree; what we called a "switch" when I was a child. It needs to be the proper size for the particular child; nothing more than a twig for the baby who is resisting on the changing table, and a good sized branch for the rebellious 14 year-old boy. Belts are for holding up your pants, and hands are for loving and nurturing. The rod is the symbol of authority in the family, and the proper instrument to use for chastisement. It should strike fear in the heart of the child.

Typical mistakes

The use of the rod has been abused, and God's enemies have used those mistakes to discredit its use altogether. We don't need to cease the use of the rod; just use it correctly, and it will be the path to life for our children! Here are the most common mistakes.

1. Using the rod in anger. Never, ever use the rod in anger. You must remember that chastisement is for the benefit of the child, not to "get back" at him for what he has done to you. His training is a project that you have been given to complete, and the use of the rod is a part of that project. There should be no anger whatsoever as one uses the rod, but rather regret that its use is necessary, and compassion for the child. You should communicate to the child that you are committed to training him for as long as it takes, and you will do this every time he disobeys.

The major reason spanking is done in anger is because parents use the rod as a last resort, after nothing else they have tried has controlled the child. They finally blow up, see red, and whale the child for all they are worth. If they had spanked him at the first hint of rebellion against authority, before they were even slightly irritated, they could have done it properly. Putting off spanking until the last resort means you are more interested in your own comfort than in training the child. Spanking becomes a way to relieve the pressure the child has exerted on the parent, rather than being used to exert pressure on the child. Spanking should be a regular, daily part of life for a child, like eating, until he has learned to control himself.

2. Spanking too lightly. This is particularly pertinent for mothers. If the anticipation of the rod does not bring fear to the child, either you are not spanking hard enough, or the rod is not large enough. Spanking through diapers is notoriously ineffective.

3. Verbally abusing the child during chastisement. Everything that comes from a parents mouth during chastisement should be positive and uplifting. The child should be loved, encouraged, built up, told that you believe he can obey, and given a vision for living a life in submission to authority. Then he should be spanked so firmly that he does not want to be spanked again. This approach will break the stubborn, rebellious will, and build up and encourage the spirit.

One of Satan's biggest tricks is to tell us that we should control our children with our tongues, rather than the rod. He tells us that the rod is abusive. In actuality, controlling a child only with the tongue will invariably degenerate into verbal negatives when the child does not obey, as at times he certainly will not. These angry accusations, put-downs, demeaning remarks, unfavorable comparisons with siblings, etc., represent verbal child abuse, and lead to a broken spirit, and leave the rebellious will untouched. The rod, on the other hand, combined with verbal encouragement, breaks the rebellious will, and feeds and builds up the spirit. Satan has tricked us into doing just the opposite of what we should be doing.

4. Spanking for punishment. Chastisement is used only for rebellion. Punishment because of a broken standard due to immaturity, childishness, a poor decision, or some reason other than rebellion, should not be the rod. The punishment should correspond to the transgression. The rod is used exclusively when it has been determined that the parent's will has been deliberately defied.

A proper way of chastisement

The mechanics of administering the rod can vary. The method outlined below has been developed over the last ten years at Tree of Life cooperative home school. The fathers delegated to me the authority to discipline their children as their representative while the children were at school. All the young fathers in the church use some variation of this method, with outstanding results.

1. Opportunity for admission of guilt and confrontation. When it has been determined that a child has defied authority, he is asked questions that encourage the admission of that fact. "What did you do?" ("I was disrespectful and told you to 'shut-up'"). Lying, or trying to blame somebody else ("I was talking to my doll, not to you," or, "I meant to say 'shut the door,'" or, "Billy told me to say it"), is, in itself, an indication of rebellion. You don't have to make him tell the truth, just give him an opportunity to confess. Let him know that you know he is lying, and confront him with exactly what he has done. "You have been disrespectful to me. We don't do that in the Andrews family, because God tells you to honor your parents. My job is to see that you obey Him."

Never ask the child, "Why did you do that?" That only gives him an opportunity to make an excuse. The issue is not, "Why," but that he did indeed rebel.

2. Reading appropriate scripture. Read the verses in Proverbs listed above to reinforce the fact that God is the one who commands you to spank him. You can make appropriate comments after each verse, i.e., "It was a foolish thing to call me a 'do-do head,' wasn't it?" (Proverbs

22:15). It is not necessary to read the verses each time, but it is a good reminder occasionally that God is behind this. After the verses comes the pronouncement, "In view of these verses, I have no choice but to spank you."

3. Application of the rod. If the child is young, have him lie over your lap while you are seated. If he is too big for that, have him bend over while grasping a chair or desk. About four to six swats applied very firmly to the buttocks are sufficient. You are not trying to get the child to cry. Extremely rebellious teen-agers will not cry. Young children will sob their hearts out. You are being obedient to God, and inflicting pain to break rebellion. The swats need to be strong enough so that this is not a pleasant experience for the child.

4. Prayer. After the spanking, take the child in your arms (make him put his arms around your neck if you are seated), and pray for him, asking God to break the rebellion in his heart, and to show him the importance of learning not to lie, cheat, defy his mother, etc. Ask God to love and encourage him.

5. The charge. After the prayer, hold the child at arm's length, look him in the eye (make him look you in the eye as well), and tell him that he's going to become a man of God, and that you are going to stick with him until he does. Tell him that you love him, and you are going to try to be consistent and to spank him every time he defies you or his mother. Then excuse him to go.

The rod is the God-ordained way to break rebellion. There is no other. Isolation by sending the child to his room, or to a "time-out chair," is not God's way. That only gives the child an opportunity to be alone to seethe in his rebellion against authority, and to build a case against his "mean" parents. The rod, on the other hand, is like God's "magic wand" when used properly and consistently. Different children come under control over different lengths of time, but ultimately faithful parents will see the desired results.

The father should do the disciplining if he is home. If he is not, the mother should handle the chastisement. This means that she must establish her own authority relationship with the children. They should be very aware that she carries their father's authority, and that he will affirm completely the decisions she has made in his absence. He must back her totally. This is assuming, of course, that she fully supports his leadership and does not undermine his child training policy.

The consistency in the implementation of a policy like this to address rebellion is absolutely critical. There will be times when conscientious parents will wonder if the effort involved to be consistent is worth the energy and time that is necessary. That's when we must have a long-term vision of those children as mighty men and women of God, extending our influence for the kingdom into the next generation.

An example of the effectiveness of "God's magic wand"

In the early days of our school, when the principles I have related in this chapter were still fairly new to us, a single mother who had been a prostitute became a Christian and came into the church. She had a very big, physically mature sixth-grade son who had been expelled from his grade school as incorrigible. We decided to take him into our school and do everything we could to help the mother, who was helpless to do anything with him.

On his first day, I told the teacher to be on the look-out for defiance, and to bring him down to the office at the first sign of rebellion.

I didn't have long to wait. Within the hour Tim brought a glaring, defiant Billy into my office. He sat down and I went through the above procedure with him. When we got to the step where he was to lie over my knees, he refused. Tim and I grabbed him and forced him, kicking, fighting, and swearing, into position. Tim tried to hold him as I administered the swats. He was large and hard to hold in place, and a couple of the blows landed on Tim's arm, but we finally got it done.

Before I prayed, I told him to put his arms around my neck so I could hug him. He refused. I motioned to Tim, and we went through the whole struggle again. At first Billy again refused the request to put his arms around my neck, but when I motioned to Tim to grab him for a third spanking, he very reluctantly placed his arms on my shoulders so I could hug him. I prayed for Billy, told him that we loved him and were going to stick with him, and that we would spank him every time he was rebellious. Tim took him back to class, as defiant as ever. Tim and I were exhausted.

The next day Billy and Tim were back. The same story was repeated, only this time he put his arms around my neck on the first request. There was no swearing, but he still did not submit to the spanking willingly. Force was necessary, and the glare remained, but there seemed to be less resistance.

That week, Billy and Tim were back at least two more times, and each time there was less fighting back than the day before. On Friday, the glare was gone, he actually hugged my neck as I prayed, and as he and Tim left my office, I will never forget what occurred. Billy stopped at the door, turned around, looked me in the eye, and said, "I love you," and left.

I would like to be able to report long-term victory for Billy and his mother. However, this occurred toward the end of the school year, and before the next school year began, Billy and his mother had left the church.

No one had loved Billy enough to fight through all the resistance to demand that he obey. My prayer is that he remembers that we did, and that he has come to know over the years that God does, too.

"Father, give me the vision to see that chastisement is an expression of my love for my children. Give me the perseverance not to allow them to wear me down, and the vision to see the glorious result; kingdom warriors whose lives are a glory and honor to you. Amen."

Questions for discussion

1. What manipulations does your child use to attempt to remove your pressure to control him? Have you fallen for it? Can you see what your rationale was to give in to him?

2. Is your child passive or active in his rebellion? What are the symptoms of his rebellion?

3. If you have used the rod in the past, did you find that you have fallen into any of the methods listed as "improper?" Which ones? Do you agree that that method should not be used? Why or why not?

4. If you have not used the rod consistently in the past, do you agree with the main thesis of this chapter that you should be? Why or why not?

---

[1] J. Richard Fugate, *What the Bible says about Child Training*, (Tempe, Arizona: Alethia, 1980), p. 95.

[2] *Ibid.*, p. 100.

[3] *Ibid.*, p. 120.

[4] *Ibid.*, p. 122.

Chapter 22

Teaching Kingdom Principles

One particularly gifted young athlete played for several years on the little league baseball team that I coached. He had a mother and father who were both lawyers. At least one of them came to most of the games. He was a very emotional boy, and it was necessary to establish with him at the beginning of the first year that I would be doing the decision-making for the team. After that, except for several crying episodes when he didn't get his own way, the boy caused no problems. However, because of his emotional instability, he was not reaching his very considerable athletic potential.

In discussing his situation with his father, who wanted his son to excel, I encouraged him to work on his son's confidence along with his athletic skills. If he did so, I felt he had the potential to be a very good baseball player. His response was typical of the half dozen or so fathers who told me basically the same thing over the eight years that I coached: "You talk to him. He won't listen to a thing I say."

What a tragedy when a father knows his son's baseball coach has more influence with his boy than he does. That dad did not know that he had the right and the responsibility to not only make his son listen to him, but also to make him do what he told him to do. Not being able to help him learn the game of baseball was relatively insignificant, but I knew at the time that he would not be of much help to his son in the game of life either. The boy was the best athlete on the team, and was good at any sport he tried. Yet by the time he reached high school, he was into drugs and heavy metal music instead of sports, and didn't even attempt to go out for any of the school's athletic teams. The last time I saw him, he was about 22, and was just starting to try to get his life back together.

Control as the basis for teaching

This young man had never been forced to do anything he didn't want to do. His parents had never crossed him, and as a result, when it was time for his father to teach him, he did not respect his father enough to listen and learn. It is a fact of life that we are very seldom willing to learn from anyone we do not respect. Children do not respect parents who have not ruled over them. Oh, they may "love" them, or get to a point that they no longer give them trouble. But they will consider their parents to be essentially irrelevant, and they will learn the basic issues of life from someone else whom they respect.

During the control phase of child training, very little teaching is necessary or even advisable. Nothing is more frustrating than to see a grown man or woman trying to get little Johnnie to do something, like brush his teeth, by reasoning with him. Explaining to a five year old about the long-term effects of tooth decay is ludicrous. The issue is that the parent wants Johnnie to brush his teeth every night before he goes to bed. Johnnie does not need to know or understand why, nor does he really even care. He simply must obey.

Even with an older child who refuses to obey until he gets an explanation, no explanations should be given, because he is still in rebellion. The divine order is, "Obey first, and then, if you are still interested, I'll tell you why (John 7:17)." Most questions from children are simply attempts to evade the obligation of obedience, not an indication of a sincere desire to understand.

However, once rebellion is broken, it is mandatory that older children begin to know why certain standards are expected. If the parents have ruled well, the child's mind is open to absorb and assimilate the family standards. Then they should be given reasons why "the Andrews do this." "This is why you are expected to do it as well. You are an Andrews."

Pride of family identity is a good thing, and will help the child to withstand pressures that would tear him away from loyalty to the family and its vision. However, if a father continually answers, in response to the non-rebellious child's questioning, "Because I told you so," he will eventually lose that child's respect. That son or daughter will be vulnerable to being captured by wolves that want to split him or her away from the protection his family provides.

If the child is ready to obey, then the question is genuine and should be answered. If there is no good answer, the parent should rescind the command.

Overlap of controlling and teaching

There is no distinct time when controlling ends and teaching begins. When the child is very young, child training is all control. When he is a late-teen, and not rebellious, it is all teaching. During the intervening years, controlling hopefully is becoming less and less necessary as the child learns submission to parental authority, and teaching becomes more and more possible.

Teaching does not occur only at formal times during the family devotions, although that is a good time for instruction. The best times for the children to learn are as they face daily life with their parents. Each decision, each crisis, each victory, and each defeat, is an opportunity for the child to watch his parents, and learn Godly character as they provide "show and tell" for him. If they are at day-care, or being kept by others, this will be much more difficult, but not impossible. You can see that teaching occurs constantly, even when the child is very young. But the bulk of it will be communicated as the child reaches a level of maturity and freedom from rebellion.

Biblical character standards

Once rebellion is broken, what character qualities should parents attempt to build into their children? With no goal, children of parents who have controlled them will learn, more or less by osmosis, the character of their parents. If the parents have not controlled their children, the children will absorb the character of the peer group with which they identify, and the leaders whom they admire. Since parenting is not an exact science, both of these options are operative, in varying degrees, in the lives of most children.

Therefore, it is wise for parents to have a goal in mind for the character development of their sons and daughters. I covered these characteristics briefly in the chapter on courtship as qualifications for marriage; I want to go into more detail here as we look at these attributes as character qualities to be built into children by parents.

Just as it is difficult for a rebellious parent to teach a child not to be rebellious, it is also very hard to inculcate the following character qualities in a child when the parents do not possess them themselves. Learning new tricks if you are an old dog is not easy, but not impossible.

At Tree of Life we refer to the acronym **READ** as a basis for our teaching of character. Respect for authority, Esteem others as better than yourself, Admit when you are wrong, and Diligence in all things are all biblical character traits. Let's look at each of these attributes.

1. Respect for authority (Ephesians 6:1-3). First, as I have already said, whatever command the parent gives, the child must obey. To obey and honor parents, as mentioned in these verses, are the only commands specifically given to children in the Bible. "Obey" addresses external actions, while "honor" speaks to the heart attitude.

One of the fruits of the Reformation in Europe was that the commands in the Bible for children to honor and respect parents were seen to apply to all adults, as indeed the Bible teaches (Leviticus 19:32; Proverbs 16:31). However, many children in today's society are overly familiar with adults, treating them as they would other children their own age. They ignore the command to have a submissive attitude toward their elders (1 Peter 5:5). We must help our children to properly respect adults.

An excellent way to teach this is to insist that children call adults by "Mr.," and "Mrs.," rather than by first names. This indicates respect, and immediately sets the adult apart from the child's friends. Not understanding the principle involved, many adults will say, "Call me (their first name)." A parent can then explain that using "Mr." and "Mrs." and the last name, is being done for the child's sake, to help him to learn to show respect for adults.

To speak to an adult by name ("Hi, Mr. _____") when spoken to, and even to speak first, shows a measure of honor and regard, rather than just the perfunctory, "Hi," with no name attached. Speaking to adults at all is more than some rebellious children can do, and calling adults by name, while looking them straight in the eye, is a mark of respect. Any child whose parents have helped him master all three of these habits: always speak to adults (preferably first), call them by name as Mr. or Mrs., and look them in the eye will demonstrate the respect for authority that is a vital part of the kingdom of God.

A very common way that a child shows lack of respect for adults is by interrupting adult conversations. This is often done by pulling continuously on Mother's arm while saying "Mommie, Mommie, Mommie, Mommie, Mommie," repeatedly until Mommie gives the child her undivided attention. The child has demanded priority over the adult with whom her mother was speaking, and in essence has said, "Me first! I'm more important than you are!" The tragedy is that most parents are oblivious to this very prevalent way of showing disrespect to adults, and will generally acknowledge the child immediately, even doing so when their adult friend is in mid-sentence.

A child who has something to say to parents who are engaged in conversation should be trained to come and stand quietly beside his parent, making sure that his parent sees him. At an appropriate time after the other party has completed a thought, the parent can say, "Excuse me one moment," and turn and acknowledge the child, who has been waiting patiently. After answering the child's question, the adult conversation can be resumed. The child's concern has been addressed, but at the parents discretion, not the child's.

When adults are engaged in conversation in the presence of children, for instance, at dinner, the children should not dominate or dictate the direction of the conversation. The way another generation expressed this thought was, "Children should be seen and not heard." It is not that children should not speak at all, but that they should not think that they have equal status around the dinner table with the adults. Many children, if not taught respect by their parents, will actually dominate the conversation, making it impossible for the parents and guests to have an adult discussion.

Children should be taught to sit quietly and respond enthusiastically when spoken to, or when an adult shows an interest in them or their activities. They should be spirited **responders,** and not **initiators,** when adults are present.

This practice of teaching our children respect for authority goes against the flow of our society, whose attitude is reflected by the bumper sticker from the 1970's still occasionally seen, "Question Authority." On the contrary, the Bible says to:

> *"...be subject to the governing authorities. For there is no authority except from God, and the authorities that exist are appointed by God. Therefore whoever resists the authority resists the ordinance of God, and those who resist will bring judgment on themselves"* *(Romans 13:1,2)*

This does not mean that children *obey* all adults: only those to whom their parents have delegated that authority, such as teachers. However, there should be a deference given to adults by children because of their age and experience.

When Ramah was in high school she had some difficulty with the concept of respecting a position of authority, whether or not she respected the particular person in that position. One of her teachers was in his first year, just out of college, only a few years older than the students. Ramah's class was filled with strong-willed girls, and they literally made life miserable for this young teacher throughout the first semester.

I found out what was occurring sometime early in the second semester, and confronted Ramah. She readily admitted what she had done, and agreed to apologize to the teacher. I told her that at the end of the school year I would ask him not only if Ramah had behaved herself in class, but if she had been a positive blessing to him during the second semester. Did he actually enjoy having Ramah in class? Did she literally brighten up his day? If he could not give me an enthusiastic "Yes!," there would be no basketball all summer. Ramah swallowed hard, and changed her behavior.

When I got together with that teacher on the last day of school, and asked him the big question, he broke into a grin, and told me that he couldn't believe the change in her, and yes, she had become an unqualified blessing.

Respecting authority is something our children can do. Learning to respect all authority is foundational for our children's future.

2. **Esteem others** (Philippians 2:3,4). Because we are naturally self-centered, as we saw in the chapter on communication, we all want to talk about ourselves, and brag about our own accomplishments. Children, of course, become masters at thinking only of themselves, and if parents don't address this issue, they will be exactly the same way as adults.

One of the men at Tree of Life has a young son who, as a freshman, got considerable playing time on his high school basketball team, a team good enough to play in the state tournament. His father has been working with him on esteeming others in word and deed. I was recently discussing prospects for next year's team with the boy. Rather than telling me how he undoubtedly will start (which he will) and be the star, he told me what a good player another boy from the church is going to be. He raved about this boy, who played last year on the junior varsity team as a sophomore, and about the great contribution he will make to the team. He did not once mention himself. His father was thrilled to hear that his training was bearing fruit.

Parents should be aware of their children's degree of development in this crucial area, and make building up others rather than themselves top priority in the teaching phase of their training. "Let another man praise you, and not your own mouth" (Proverbs 27:2), should be a verse that every child should commit to memory. Nothing hinders one's ability to communicate the gospel of the kingdom more than bragging about one's self and being unwilling to be interested in another. Once a child is ready to listen to your teaching as a parent, this truth needs to be worked into his life.

3. **Admit to wrongdoing** (1 John 1:7). To refuse to be accountable for our actions, even to the point of lying to cover and hide from our wrongdoing, is common to the human race. Parents must realize that their child, whom they love so very much, is a born liar. We all must learn to tell the truth.

This character quality should be built into children when they are young, or parents will not be able to trust what they say when they are too old to constantly be with them. Without the confidence that your child will not lie to you, you are helpless to really know what is happening in your child's life. A situation that will cause permanent damage may be threatening the child, who is blinded by emotion, or who is not mature enough to see the danger at hand. If your child has not been taught to always tell the truth to his parents, hiding nothing, you are helpless to intervene to save your child.

When the children were little and bed-time arrived, Jill and I would tell them to go get their 'jamas on, brush their teeth, and hop in bed. Then we would come up, pray with them, and love them good night. It was a regular ritual, and they had learned that no stalling was allowed. Bed-time was not a hassle.

When Ramah was a child she was an inveterate liar. She would lie when it would be better for her if she told the truth. One night, when I came up to pray with her, I noticed that her breath was not fresh when I kissed her. I asked her if she had brushed her teeth. Her bright, immediate answer was, "Yes, Daddy."

I said, "Let me ask you one more time, 'Did you brush your teeth?'"

The "Yes, Daddy," was more hesitant this time.

I told her that I had smelled breath that had not come from a mouth full of freshly brushed teeth, and I was going to spank her, not only for deliberately disobeying me by not brushing her teeth, but for lying to me as well. After spanking her, and loving her, she assured me that she had learned her lesson, and now she would obey me and always tell the truth. I sent her back into the bathroom to brush her teeth.

When she returned, and I kissed her, I definitely smelled toothpaste on Ramah's breath, but sensed something still was not right. I asked her if she had now brushed her teeth. "Yes Daddy," was the reply.

I went to the bathroom and came back, holding a bone-dry toothbrush. She knew she was caught, but when I said, "I'm going to ask you one more time, 'Did you brush your teeth?,'" she still replied, this time very hesitantly,

"Yes, Daddy."

After the second spanking, I sent her back to the bathroom, waited a moment, and followed her, just in time to see her running water on her toothbrush without brushing her teeth! I'm not sure if even the third spanking that evening convinced Ramah then that it would have been much easier for her to have just brushed her teeth! We are truly sons and daughters of Adam and Eve, who hid from God after they sinned, and did their very best to avoid accountability.

One summer on a camping trip we saw that we were making progress in the battle to break Ramah of her deep-seated habit of lying. We had all finished dinner except for Ramah, who was having a great deal of difficulty with her broccoli, not one of her favorite foods. We told her that the four of us were going to go for a walk, and she could come as soon as she finished her broccoli. We left the camper, and soon Ramah joined us, proclaiming that, yes, she had indeed finished her broccoli.

In the middle of the night Ramah climbed in our bed, woke up Jill, and said she couldn't sleep because she had lied to us. She had thrown her broccoli in the garbage. We rejoiced that she was beginning to learn the lesson of admitting wrongdoing.

Being willing to be accountable for one's own actions and not covering up mistakes or deliberate wrongdoing is a difficult lesson that we continue to learn over a lifetime. It is one of the primary ingredients of successful leadership. We can give our children a tremendous boost in life if we will be relentless in our attempts to build this character quality into their lives.

4. **Diligence in all things** (Colossians 3:23). A child who has learned to be a hard worker will be an adult in demand as an employee. This is a biblical character quality that is in short supply in the world, but one that is universally appreciated.

There are many opportunities to teach diligence to children. Daily chores are obviously an excellent way. Children should be given responsibilities as soon as they are old enough to do them. Many parents have devised helpful charts and checklists to monitor a child's progress in the completion of their jobs.

The weekly allowance should not be given as an inducement to get the child to do his chores. What if he decides he doesn't care if he gets an allowance? Does he then get out of having to do chores? No. He does chores because the parents demand it of him and he obeys. His weekly allowance is a blessing from his father. It is an example of free grace given to him because he is a family member, just as God's grace is free to His family members. In the world we work for wages, because the world does not function by grace. The family does.

Another excellent way to teach diligence is with school-work. The attitude of doing the very best that the child can do, rather than making a particular grade, should be emphasized. Different children have different intellectual capacities, but hard work and diligence is a goal that is attainable for all children.

Application

A child should clearly understand that these standards are expected of him. They are not unattainable. They can be achieved. The goal is that the child will be able to apply them himself to specific instances. Until he can, the parent will have to make the application for him. There should be no misunderstanding as to what is expected.

For instance, "When Mr. and Mrs. Smith come over for dinner, I want you to call them by name, and sit quietly during dinner unless you are spoken to" (An example of #1). As the child gets older, and he becomes more familiar with the standards, he will be able to make the application himself.

It is not necessary that the child agree with the standard, or the specific application of it. Many times he will not. It is only important that he understand what is expected of him.

What if the standard is broken?

These four standards of conduct are basic biblical ones that all children should be taught to meet. There will be others that individual parents will want to teach their children. They are the authorities in their children's lives, and can train them in the objectives that they feel are important. If they are Godly objectives, principles defining those objectives can be found in the Bible.

What if a standard is broken, as they invariably will be? The following is a suggested procedure:[1]

Step 1. The first step is for the parent to **evaluate** the cause for the disobedience. Parents are given the task of judging their children's words, deeds and attitudes. Was it childish forgetfulness? If the child is old enough to remember, he should be held accountable to remember. Was it misunderstanding or not thinking? The rebuke that follows in Step 2 will clarify what is expected in the future. Was it deliberate rebellion? Then the child should be chastised.

Step 2. **Rebuke** is the declaration that the child's behavior broke a standard. If it has been determined that the child is not to be held accountable, because he did not know of the standard, confession is not necessary. The rebuke establishes the standard for future reference. But if he is to be held accountable (i.e., he should have known better), after the rebuke, the child should acknowledge his guilt, be forgiven by the parent, and receive the appropriate punishment. If he refuses to acknowledge guilt (i.e., he refuses to accept your evaluation as the parent, or makes excuses, or blames someone else), then he should be chastised and pay the penalty for the broken standard as well. He is not submitted to your rule.

Step 3. **Forgiveness** follows acknowledgment of guilt, and restores the child to full fellowship with his parents. It is important that the parent demonstrate that the child is forgiven in some demonstrable way; a hug, or a kiss is appropriate. The child needs assurance that he is forgiven. The offense is not brought up again by the parent as a weapon against the child in the future. Forgive and forget is the rule after the child genuinely acknowledges his guilt.

Step 4. The **punishment** must fit the offense. Chastisement is only for rebellion. There are many times when a parent will know that the child was not deliberately defying his authority, yet a standard has been broken and punishment is in order.

Examples of broken standards

When I coached basketball, if any of my players got a technical foul for arguing with a referee, they had to sit out the next game. The standard of not arguing with referees demonstrated the first character quality, respect for authority. Although due to the emotion of the moment, breaking the standard demanded appropriate punishment. I knew the player was not deliberately defying me as the coach by arguing with the referee.

An example of breaking the second standard, esteeming others, is the teen-age habit of putting others down verbally, ignoring or making fun of them. An appropriate punishment would be some penalty in the social area, such as not letting the child be with his friends for a period of time. Continued behavior like this cannot be tolerated and should be handled as rebellion. This behavior is difficult to spot, because children are generally on their best behavior when parents are around. That's why it is important to handle this fault before the child gets old enough to be sophisticated enough to hide his sin from the parent.

Always blaming others is a part of childhood, and sadly, a majority of adults have never learned to be personally accountable for their actions. A failure to admit wrongdoing and yield to the parent's evaluation is rebellion, and should be handled with the rod. In the tooth brushing incident with Ramah, she didn't brush her teeth as she knew to do. It is conceivable that she could have legitimately forgotten. I would have accepted that excuse once. However, when she was caught, she chose to lie and not accept responsibility for her disobedience. That was rebellion.

The fourth character trait is diligence. It is difficult to learn to work hard, and easy to procrastinate when there is a job to do. The penalty for failure to complete a reasonable task could be added work before being free to play. If Johnnie was to stack the wood after he cleaned up his room, and Dad comes home and finds Johnnie playing in the yard with the wood still not stacked, Dad might have Johnnie not only stack the wood, but wash the car as well. Continued failure adequately to perform jobs that are reasonable means that Johnnie has set his will against his dad's will. That is rebellion, and the rod is in order.

Divine assistance

Discerning when disobedience is resistance to the parent's authority, and therefore is rebellion, and when it is disobedience for some other reason, demands divine help. God is eager to give it. Let me give you an example of the kind of thing God will do.

One of the men in the church was following the courtship procedure outlined in the previous chapters with his daughter. No dating, no physical contact, just friends, etc. She had a special friend who had agreed to the father's demands, but found it hard to comply. They both liked each other very much, and looked for ways to be together alone. One night, after a basketball game, when her father thought his daughter was with some other girls, she ended up alone with the boy in his car. They had seen the father leave, thought they were free to be alone, and proceeded to go park under the stars to "just talk."

The father, for some reason he still does not understand, came back to the school, just in time to see his daughter leaving alone with the boy. He followed them at a distance, and pulled up beside them just as the boy began to kiss his daughter. You can imagine the reaction! God had supernaturally helped a father who was trying to do his best to protect and train his daughter. He will come to the aid of all parents who want to do the same.

"Father, give me the wisdom to know how to build Your character into Your children whom You have entrusted to me for a time. I cannot do it without Your supernatural help. Amen"

Questions for discussion

1. Do you agree that it is difficult to open yourself up to learn from someone you don't respect? Why is that? If children do not adopt their parents lifestyle, whose will they adopt? In your experience, do they eventually return to their parent's way of life?

2. Which of the four character traits has been the most difficult for you to learn? What other qualities do you think are important that are not covered by these four?

3. How have you as a parent dealt with broken standards in the past? Have you distinguished between rebellion and other causes for the disobedience? In dealing with broken standards when rebellion is not involved, what do you see is good about this procedure? What, if anything, does not appear to be workable?

4. How do your children generally respond to your training? Has it been successful? Why, or why not?

---

[1] J. Richard Fugate, *What the Bible says about Child Training*, (Tempe, Arizona: Alethia, 1980), p. 218, 219. Fugate's treatment of the procedure for teaching standards is excellent, and very detailed. I am summarizing only briefly. I recommend that his book be read in its entirety.

Chapter 23

Nurturing Our Kingdom Posterity

At this point, some parents may feel that I have painted a picture of stern policemen trying to hold juvenile delinquents in check, rather than one of parents enjoying warm relationships with their children. Training children is not easy, and there are times when parents do feel like cops. The effects of sin in our lives and the lives of our children are indeed all-pervasive. But the rewards for faithfulness in performing our parenting task are so satisfying that they make all the effort and energy necessary to bring those precious little ones to adulthood worthwhile.

The same infrastructure that undergirds God's training of His children, His unfathomable love, undergirds child training. Since as fathers (and mothers) we are identified with, and patterned after, our Heavenly Father (Ephesians 3:14,15), God has put in the heart of every parent that same love. This love is the foundation for child training, and without it all techniques and methods, lists and goals, are, as Paul says, "sounding brass or a clanging cymbal;" i.e., worthless.

It is not necessary constantly to tell your child that you love him. Love, or the lack thereof, is communicated in a thousand little ways that either corroborate or refute what is professed. The old saying, "What you do speaks so loudly I can't hear what you are saying," certainly applies here. Children know whether or not they are more important to their parents than their parents' desires and activities, and, if they are, they will view strict discipline as a natural result of that love. Without it, child training, no matter how carefully done, is an exercise in futility, and often is harsh and demeaning.

One weekend when I was in college, I made an unscheduled trip home. My parents were not expecting me, and as I came into the house unannounced by way of the back door, my dad was standing in the den with his back toward me. He heard the door open, and turned to see who was there. This occurred almost forty years ago, but I can still see my father's face as clearly as if it were only yesterday. As he turned and saw me, his only son, standing before him, his face, so indelibly imprinted upon my mind, said more than all the "I love you's," he had a hard time saying. It said more than all the expensive gifts that my parents were able to buy for me. It was as though someone had turned on an electric switch, and his face came alive with the incandescent light of love and joy. I knew my father loved me with all his heart. He could not have convinced me otherwise if he had tried.

In this final chapter I want to give parents some ways to very practically let that love that God has put in all parent's hearts for their children shine through. The love is there, though it may be shut off by sin. Parents may harbor bitterness toward their own parents, their mates, or toward other primary people in their lives. This harbored root of bitterness, unless it is faced honestly, repented of, and forsaken, will often show up in an unrelated area, such as an inability to really love one's children. Parents' personal emotional needs prevent the free flow of love to their children. Finally, we will look at the latent power in the family to extend the kingdom of God.

Time equals love

Little children have a hard time understanding that missing a dance recital or a little league game in order to close a big sale or attend an evening committee meeting, will sometimes be necessary. Although it does not mean that they are not as important to their parent as those other activities, to a child's mind, having his mother and father present at important functions means that they love him, and that he is the top priority with them. To him, all time with Daddy and Mommy is "quality time," and the more the better.

My parents were always on the front row for everything I did as a child, from athletic events to school plays. I know it must have often been boring for them, because I rarely excelled at what I did, particularly in high school. I was a very small fish in an extremely large pond (there were about 1000 in my graduating class), but they were always there to watch me sit on the bench at basketball games, and play a bit part in the school play. When I was in college, they often made the

250 mile round-trip to Norman, Oklahoma for the three-game baseball weekend home series in hopes that I, a seldom-used relief pitcher, would get in the game. They were always supportive, always building me up, always encouraging me to do the best that I could do.

Jill's mother, on the other hand, as a young widow, didn't see the importance of participating with her daughter in her school activities. After a hard day of working to support her three children, there probably wasn't energy left to do so. But Jill remembers vividly the hurt of her mother not seeming to consider her activities to be important.

Jill and I have attempted to share our children's lives with them as much as possible. We have attended countless ball games, ballet, piano, violin and gymnastics recitals. We have been to a full range of school plays and other various and sundry dramatic productions. We have been to five graduations and anticipate going to three more. I have coached all three of my children on four separate athletic teams for a total of eleven years, and taught them all in school as well.

Just as my parents communicated to me that I was top priority in their lives, we have tried to do the same with our children. For they are our heritage, and in their lives is deposited all that we are. We were there for all the significant events in their lives, and, as a result, they have a sense that their accomplishments are a continuation of a family heritage. The Andrews heritage that we have attempted to pass on is one of Godliness, of excellence, of a maximization of ability, and of dominion for the kingdom of God. The joy of watching Adam already pass that same heritage along to his children is indescribable.

Understanding terms

Before we consider other ways to nurture children besides being at as many of their activities as possible, let me discuss the meaning of four words that are very often misunderstood. Those words are **compassion, leniency, firmness, and harshness.** Satan would like nothing better than to confuse God's warriors about the meanings of these terms, thereby handicapping us as we attempt to train the next generation.

Many times in the New Testament Jesus was said to be "moved with compassion" as he saw some individual, or group of individuals, experiencing difficulty. The word *compassion* comes from two root words that mean "to suffer together." To have compassion, then, is to have the ability to participate in the sufferings of another, with the urge to help.[1]

The difficulty in child training does not come from too much compassion for our children. How can we "suffer together," or empathize, with them too much? To suffer with our children as they experience the painful process of becoming men and women of God is to follow in the steps of the One who so empathized and identified with us that He bore our sins for our eternal salvation. Our children will know that we understand the pain that they are experiencing. We cannot have too much compassion for our children.

The problem comes as well-meaning parents not only empathize with the pain and pressure that their children are facing, but when they go one step farther by attempting to alleviate that pressure. At the first sign of discomfort the "compassionate" parent says "there, there," and often removes the pressure or lowers the standard that is causing the pressure, causing the child to continue on his course unchanged.

God uses the pressures that come into our lives to change us, and His standards must not be lowered. To do so is to confuse compassion with *leniency*, and does our children a terrible disservice. At my daughter's Christian high school, the teachers were fond of "extending grace," and giving the students "a second chance." As a result, many students were poorly prepared for college. They had not learned that accountability, with its resultant sanctions, is a fact of the kingdom because compassion was confused with leniency.

Firmness and harshness are equally as misunderstood. One of the aforementioned teachers said to me, "Why are you so hard on Ramah?" I tried to explain that I was hard on her because I expected her to do her very best at whatever she attempted. Her tendency in high school was not toward doing that. The bolts of Godliness and excellence need continual tightening, and until Ramah was mature enough to tighten those bolts herself, it remained my job.

At one point Ramah said to me, "What's wrong with B's, Daddy?"

"Nothing," I said, "if that's the best you can do. But you can make A's." Ramah went through high school with my size 11's squarely in her back. Her resultant grades were good enough to help defray college expenses. Now that she is in college diligence in her studies continues to be an area where she must constantly remind herself to focus, because it doesn't come naturally to her. However, she is now mature enough to do that herself, with occasional reminders from me. Firmness is demanding the maximization of potential, and I want to be *firm* with love and tenderness.

On the other hand, I <u>never</u> want to be *harsh* with my children. I don't want to raise my voice, to be angry, or to be unreasonable; only demanding. I want to keep the edge of displeasure out of my voice, while I demand that they maximize every bit of ability God has given them, in every area of their lives, for the glory of God.

Satan has often tricked parents into being lenient and harsh, with tragic results; we must learn to be compassionate and firm.

Blessing our children

Our Heavenly Father loves to bless His obedient children (Deuteronomy 28:1-14). As we seek to please Him in all we do, the blessings of God are said to "come upon" and "overtake" us (vs. 2).

When our children were little, Jill and I taught them that on shopping trips they were not to beg for things. As a matter of fact, begging meant that they would certainly not get what they wanted. On a trip to the sporting goods store when the boys were about 5 and 6, I saw them gazing longingly at the footballs. They as yet did not have a football, and I could tell that they were now old enough to really want one. They did not say a word, however, for fear that a request would be construed as begging. After they had left the store with their mother, I bought a football and secretly smuggled it home to surprise them. My joy in giving it to them far surpassed the considerable joy they experienced in receiving it.

When we are conditioned to respond to our children, rather than being the initiators toward them, we have a tendency to wait until they press us before we give them what will bring them joy. Since God's Fatherhood is our pattern, as our children are obedient to us and yield to our authority in their lives, we need to aggressively look for ways to shower them with blessings.

Always "yes," unless there is a reason

Ruling means blessing those over whom one rules, actively looking for ways to bring them joy. An excellent way to do this, that I mentioned briefly in Chapter 6, and that I have tried to follow with my children as we have trained them, is to always say "yes" to their requests unless there is a reason to say "no." If we delight ourselves in our Heavenly Father, He takes pleasure in giving us the desires of our hearts (Psalm 37:4). Can we do less with our children? If they have yielded to our leadership in their lives, and delight to please us in what they do, can we not attempt, whenever possible, to make them happy?

However, it is important to see that parents must not shirk from saying "no" when it is necessary to do so for the long-term well-being of the child. Young people often cannot see the dangers inherent in a certain activity or course of action because of their lack of experience. Until children marry, parents still carry the authority and the responsibility, if necessary, to make final decisions to avoid disastrous results. There may often be violent disagreement, and the parents may even be wrong in their decision, but God can be trusted to achieve His sovereign will through them. When parents know that their children are going to do what they say, they will be very careful in what they tell them to do.

Many parents use exactly the opposite approach. Their immediate response is always to say "no" to all their children's requests. Typically the children will then begin to beg and cajole their parents until they finally get them to give in and say "yes." This teaches the child that his parents' decisions are never really final, and if he can exert enough pressure on them, he will eventually get his way. His desire is not really to please his parents, but himself. [The examples in Scripture that would seem to corroborate this approach (the persistent widow in Luke 18, and our Lord's injunction to keep on asking, seeking and knocking in Matthew 7), are designed to teach persistence in prayer, not manipulation and badgering].

Children should learn how to appeal to their parents about a decision made with which they do not agree, without challenging their parent's right to make the decision. Parents should allow such an appeal as long as their authority is not challenged. If it is, they must stand firm. They cannot surrender their right to rule. However, it is possible that there is information of which the parent is not aware that will affect their decision. Maybe there is a perspective the parents have not considered. After all the information is in and all appeals have been made, if the answer is still "no," the child must know that God is ultimately in charge, and that by yielding in his heart to his parent's will, he is yielding to God. The parent must never be too proud to change his mind, or to admit that he was wrong. If the child believes his parent is doing his very best to make the right decision, and really has his best interest at heart, pleasing the parent will not be burdensome. The yoke of the father's leadership will truly be easy, and the burden to obey him will be light.

Children are for God

There are many reasons for parents to train their children diligently. Well-trained children are easier to raise, they are more enjoyable, and they make people think we are good parents. These are all reasons to train our children for us. If they are trained when they are young and their rebellion against authority is broken, they will have a much better chance at success whatever they do. That is a reason to train our children diligently for them. But by far the most important reason to train our children is so that they might be able to maximize all the potential that God has placed in them; to be the very best that they can be at everything they do; and then to join with Him in the family business of extending His kingdom over all the earth. That is training them for God. All other reasons pale into insignificance in comparison.

Untrained children who are still living their lives unto themselves cannot be effective for the kingdom of God. As we saw in Chapter 20, children are as arrows in the hand of a mighty warrior, and they must be straightened and carefully pointed in order to be efficient.

Jonathan Edwards was a great Puritan preacher and one of the leaders of the Great Awakening in the Eighteenth Century. He and his wife Sarah had eleven children, all of whom lived to adulthood (an unusual blessing in an era of infant mortality). Edwards' posterity is an example of the impact on the battle that straightened and properly pointed arrows can make. Biographer Elisabeth Dodds says:

"Their eleven children have been a gift to American cultural history. In 1900 a reporter tracked down 1400 descendants of Jonathan and Sarah Edwards. He found that they included 13 college presidents, 65 professors, two graduate school deans, 100 lawyers, 66 physicians, 80 holders of public office, including three senators and three

governors of states. Members of this clan had written 135 published books, and the women were repeatedly described as "great readers" or "highly intelligent." These people seem also to have had a talent for making money: their numbers included a roster of bankers and industrialists. Of course there were platoons of missionaries. The report asserted: 'The family has cost the country nothing in pauperism, in crime, in hospital or asylum service: on the contrary, it represents the highest usefulness.' "[2]

What a heritage! The influence of Jonathan Edwards has been powerfully felt in America for 250 years. By the grace of God, we will have a similar heritage. Do you see that having well-trained children is not enough? Without a vision of the task of defeating God's enemies and extending the rule of Jesus Christ over the earth, we simply are admiring the sharp, straight arrows in our quivers. Arrows were not made to be admired, but released in battle!

Some simple arithmetic
What would happen if parents began to see children not only as blessings from God to be enjoyed, but also as weapons of war to be deployed? What if they determined to have as many children as God, who really does open and shut the womb, would send them?

There are roughly 250 million people in the United States, some 50% of whom claim to have had a born-again experience. That number obviously is very inflated, but we could safely say that 10%, or 25 million, are genuine Christians. Let's assume that these believers make up 10 million Christian families who have a desire to please God, and respond to the message conveyed in this book, the message of the family being a weapon that God can use to answer the prayer of His Son, "Thy kingdom come, Thy will be done, on the earth as it is in heaven."

If these 10 million families begin to understand our task, and give themselves to it, their families will begin to increase in size as they see that children are weapons of war, and it is foolish to be underarmed in battle. If each family had six children over the next thirty years - a huge family now, but an average sized one only two generations ago - there would then be 60 million Christians in America. I am assuming that they would follow biblical child-training methods as outlined in this book, and would therefore be able to claim the promise that if they train up their children in the way they should go, when they are old they will not depart from it (Proverbs 22:6).

Assuming those 60 million believers all marry other Christians, and have an average of six children, in another thirty years there would be 180 million Christians in America (30 million Christian families, six children per family).

After one more thirty year period there would be 540 million Christians. Assuming the rest of the population continues to abort their babies and have small families (simply reproducing themselves), Christians would make up 70% of the population in America, 540 million Christians compared to 225 million non-believers!

An amazing vision

Do you have any idea what would happen if 70% of the population were Christians who want to be obedient to the law of God? Christians would be in the majority in every area of national life; government, education, the media, medicine, business, science, the arts, etc. Our national life would be changed dramatically as God would become, in our experience, what He is in fact; the King over all other kings, and the Lord of all other lords.

Notice I am not proposing some utopian society based on the inherent goodness of man and achieved by human effort, but a society based on Christianity. I am saying that all civilizations are based on someone's religion, someone's law, someone's moral code, and that our civilization, western civilization, sprang from the Gospel of Jesus Christ. It is under attack today for that very reason. Any law will do today, except God's law. If Christians again become a majority, God's law would very naturally again become the law of the land; not superimposed from the top down, but demanded from the bottom up!

We are at war with the enemy of our souls who does not care if we stay in our pews, sing hymns, and share precious verses. However, if we begin to have the audacious idea that Jesus Christ rightfully rules over every area of life according to His law, and then attempt to establish that rule as His ambassadors, all hell will break loose. We are already seeing that happen today as the church begins to awaken to its task. God's enemies are almost frantic in their vitriolic denunciations of "Christian fundamentalists," and "right-wing fanatics," because they intuitively know that they cannot stop the inexorable, irresistible force of the gospel! The gates of hell will not stop the advance of the Lord's church!

Answering objections and excuses

Whenever the concept of letting God plan the family and send as many children as He desires is discussed, there is generally a good bit of uneasiness. Let's look at what I believe are the four main reasons for this.

First, because of the propaganda campaign carried on by the media, many people today genuinely think that the world is overpopulated and that resources are scarce. They think that the concept of 765 million people in the United States in the previous illustration is unthinkable. That objection was covered in Chapter 3, with a bibliography for further study given in the footnote in Chapter 14. Satan has used "pop" science (i.e., pseudo-science) as a tool to fool us. Many Christians have not taken the time to research the issue fully, but have believed what they have read in the newspaper, not realizing the media is simply pushing an anti-Christian agenda. Really, research is not necessary to be convinced of the fallacy of the media's propaganda. A car trip through the states in the Western half of our country is sufficient. The vast stretches of empty land are mind-boggling.

Second, many Christians are afraid that God will send them twenty children if they don't do anything to keep from getting pregnant. They feel that sex always results in babies, and how in the world will they support all those kids?

We must see that God really does send babies! That is not just a nice way of saying we make babies ourselves. He opens and shuts the womb, and when He sends a child to a family, it is not by mistake. He must know that they are able to take care of it, or He would not have sent it. We often do not see, or understand, how that will happen. The circumstances seem impossible. But we are not God! That is the problem. We want to be!

In God's inscrutable plan, we cannot know what He is doing as He weaves our lives and circumstances together to make the beautiful tapestry that is human history. We can only know that He loves us with an incomprehensible love that does not allow anything into our lives but those things He desires to be there. Let Him be God.

Third, the most prevalent reason for not having more children is undoubtedly the inconvenience they inevitably bring with them. Raising children is time-consuming, difficult, and severely limits one's activities. The thinking goes like this: "Parenting is a full-time job with the one child I have now. I can imagine what it would be like with six!" Or, "No way will I have more than two children. How could you ever ride herd on any more?"

The problem is that observations are made, and conclusions drawn, based on untrained children! I would not want to have even one rebellious child, much less six. But by applying biblical principles of child training consistently, all children become the unqualified blessing the scriptures portray (Psalm 128). Trained children are the key. The older children become producers rather than consumers in the family, and actually are a help with the work that must be done.

Obviously, children take time to train; time to control, time to teach, time to nurture. There obviously will be less time for personal and private pursuits. But it is important to realize that we are at war, and in wartime it is not business-as-usual. We do not have the luxury of doing exactly what we want. "No one engaged in warfare entangles himself with the affairs of this life, that he may please him who enlisted him as a soldier" (2 Timothy 2:4). When we came to Jesus Christ we might not have realized that along with having our sins forgiven, and receiving eternal life, we were getting drafted into a cosmic war, but we were. We are now soldiers, commissioned to arm ourselves with our posterity. Our convenience is not something extremely high on the priority list of our Commander-in-Chief.

Fourth, many married couples are gripped by the fear that they will be failures as parents. They have seen too many of their friends who have very unattractive children, or they know that their parents failed with them, and are afraid that they will follow in their parent's footsteps.

This would be a valid complaint, if we had been left on our own, to do the best job we could do. But we have not been left alone. We have been left with three tremendous resources upon which to draw for help: the Holy Spirit to empower us (John 16:7), the church to equip us (Ephesians 4:11,12), and the Bible to instruct us (Psalm 119:105). We must trust the One who dwells within us and is greater than the devil (1 John 4:4). Then we must find a church that emphasizes child training and that will equip us for this ministry, a place where other parents are struggling as well to raise warriors for the kingdom of God. Finally we must reject theories, or feelings, or the latest child training techniques, and remember that the Word of God is our guide. If we will do these things, we can conquer whatever difficulties come, and raise a generation of mighty warriors!

These objections are representative of the response many have to the concept of letting God plan the family. If one or more of them is your response, know that God is patient with us as we learn new things. God's desire is not to condemn you, but to lovingly and gently bring you into the fullness of His plan.

When children are young, changing dirty diapers, cleaning up throw-up, and wiping snotty noses seems to be an interminable process. It is very difficult to keep in mind the vision of the end result. If you are struggling with the daily drudgery of parenting, and feeling sorry for yourself as others, even some Christians, are "enjoying the good life," and living for themselves while you are having babies, ask God to renew your mind. Ask Him to give you a picture of the power and authority your children will exercise in His Name in the cosmic battle in which you are training them to fight. Ask Him to show you the truth of the fact that your children are a reward for you. Know for sure that your time for enjoyment will come!

Another family's posterity

As we were learning about the importance of heritage several years ago at Tree of Life, one of our elders, Doug Steiner, found a rather detailed copy of his family tree, reproduced in Figure 3 below. It traces the lineage of Daniel Steiner, who lived from 1746 to 1811. He is represented by the trunk of this tree. Doug's grandfather, who lived at the beginning of the 20th century, is a part of the last generation on the tree, and is depicted by a twig way out on the extremity of the diagram, in the upper right hand corner.

356

Figure 3

357

Doug decided to do some pruning on his family tree. What if each of his ancestors had only had four children, a large family by today's standards? Figure 4 represents what the new Steiner family tree would resemble.

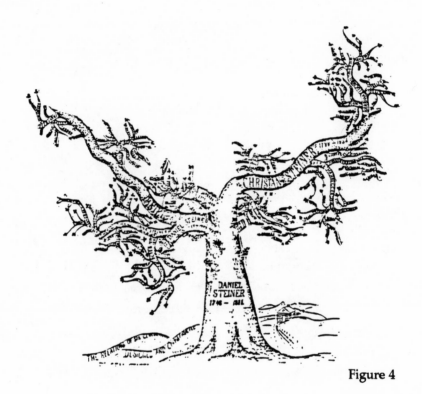

Figure 4

Needless to say, neither Doug, who is a church elder, nor his father, who was a medical missionary to India, nor his grandfather, would ever have lived to make the contributions they have made to the furtherance of the gospel. As you can see, a huge portion of Daniel Steiner's posterity would never have lived to bear the image of God and to take dominion over the earth, as God commissioned us to do in Genesis 1:26-28. We are all sacrificing the potential power of our descendants for the extension of the kingdom of God as we limit the size of our families.

We are winning!

Several years ago I stumbled upon one of the most amazing magazine articles I have ever read. It appeared in the November, 1990 issue of *Mission Frontiers* magazine, and was entitled, "The Diminishing Task!" The Lausanne Statistics Task Force, headed up by David Barrett, Ph.D., the author of *World Christian Encyclopedia*, arrived at the following figures to show that over the years there has been a constantly decreasing number of non-Christians per committed Christian in the world.

Column 1	Column 2	Column 3	Column 4
DATE	Non-Christians	Committed Christians	Non-Christians / Com. Christians
100 A.D.	180	0.5	360
1000 A.D.	220	1	220
1500 A.D.	344	5	69
1900 A.D.	1062	40	27
1950 A.D.	1650	80	21
1980 A.D.	3025	275	11
1989 A.D.	3438	500	7
	(In millions)	(In millions)	Col. 2 / Col. 3

A "non-Christian" is someone who doesn't consider himself to be a Christian. This number does not include people who DO consider themselves to be Christians and who have the Bible in their language but may not truly know or believe in the God of the Bible.

A "committed Christian" means people who have read, believe and obey the Bible.

The specific numbers here are correct within a small percentage of error, except for the earlier centuries. But the overall trend is what is unarguable, despite most gloomy statements to the contrary. Whereas in 1000 A.D. there were 220 non-Christians in the world for every committed Christian, today the ratio is 7 non-Christians for every committed Christian. Both groups are growing, but the Christians are growing at a faster rate.[3]

Upon some reflection, this is not hard to see. On the Day of Pentecost there were 120 people in the upper room, the total number of Christians in the world; the total fruit of the ministry of Jesus Christ. Today, there are 500 million disciples, and one-third of the world's population names His Name.

This relentless march to victory is in spite of the impotence of the church in America, in spite of its retreat to wait for the Lord's return over the last 100 years, in spite of its unwillingness to compete with evolutionary humanism in the marketplace of ideas. But most of all, this trend that we see in the world is in spite of the church's tacit denial of the power of generational Christianity. It has done this by failing to emphasize the family as a weapon for victory, and without actively resisting the Planned Parenthood agenda of birth control and small families. We have hopped in bed with the enemy.

In spite of all this we are still winning! Think what will happen when we see the potential that resides in our posterity, when the church all over our land begins to trumpet the message that the family is indeed God's weapon for victory. The kingdom of God will not be denied, for "the earth will be filled with the knowledge of the glory of the LORD, as the waters cover the sea" (Habbakuk 2:14).

"Father, may I see my children as weapons of war, to be raised for You and Your great eternal purpose of bringing all creation under the rule of Jesus Christ, that You might be all in all."

Questions for discussion

1. Did (Do) you feel you were (are) top priority with your parents? Why or why not? Do you think they were or were not involved in your activities?

2. Give some examples of leniency and compassion, harshness and firmness from your own experience, either as a child or a parent.

3. What are some ways you can aggressively bless your children?

4. How do you feel about letting God plan your family? Do you think it is a biblical concept?

---

[1] *Webster's New World Dictionary,* (Cleveland and New York: World, 1959).

[2] Elisabeth S. Dodds, "My Dear Companion," *Christian History,* Volume IV, No. 4, p. 16.

[3] "The Diminishing Task," *Mission Frontiers,* November, 1990, p. 18.

Appendix

The Applicability of the Word of God

After reading this book, you will have a pretty good idea of what kind of person I am. You might not have learned about the foods I like to eat, or what I do for recreation, but you will certainly know what I think about all the issues discussed on the preceeding pages. Assuming my actions are consistent with my words, and you read my words carefully, you will also know how I act in the context of my family. That's because my words spring from what I am, though not always perfectly or consistently.

In the same way, the Word of God, perfectly and consistently, springs from what He is. It is a revelation of His character. When the Bible says, "You shall not bear false witness against your neighbor" (Exodus 20:16), it is because God Himself does not lie. When Paul says, "Whatever you do, do it heartily..." (Colossians 3:23), he is telling us that God's character includes diligence, rather than slothfulness. The Gospels picture for us the life of a man, Jesus Christ, who, in word and deed, was the perfect embodiment of God's character (Hebrews 1:3).

Bearing in mind that the Bible is an expression of the character of God, let's look at three very important questions that must be answered before we can practically apply the Bible to our lives. "What is the time-frame to which the Bible applies?" "How much of the Bible applies to us as Christians?" and "To whom does the Bible apply?"

1. To what time-frame does the Bible apply?

There are those who say, "The Bible was written long ago to an ancient, agrarian people, in a patriarchal society completely different from ours. Times have changed. The Bible cannot be taken literally, and then applied literally to situations today, including the family."

Our society is indeed a great deal different from that of both the Old and New Testaments, and many of the differences are improvements that have been brought about because the Bible has been applied literally. The just treatment of women, and the religious and political freedom we enjoy in America, are direct results of the application of the Bible to society. Individual liberty that springs from Christianity has fostered the creativity and entrepreneurship that has produced most of the world's scientific and technical advances. Moslem, Hindu, and Buddhist countries produce little in the way of technical advances because their religions don't teach industry, personal development, and free enterprise to the extent that Christianity does.

Times, then, have changed, but men have not. We continue to come into the world as sinners, just as men always have. We still need to be redeemed so that we may then live lives that produce the fruit of that redemption, just as Abraham, Rachel, Moses, and Peter did. Aren't the problems they experienced timeless? Men still have trouble leading their families into righteousness and not surrendering that leadership to their wives, just as Abraham did several times with his wife Sarah. Women, like Rachel, still manipulate their husbands to get their own way. We can identify with the rage of Moses that drove him to murder an Egyptian, and the cowardice of Peter on the night of Jesus' crucifixion. Yes, the sinfulness of human nature is unabated by time.

If man has not changed, maybe God Himself has changed His mind about certain behaviors and attitudes, and therefore also toward the conduct of His children. This would certainly mean that we could not be sure of the validity of any particular portion of scripture that seems unreasonable in today's culture. For instance, God speaks strongly against adultery in the Bible (Deuteronomy 22:21-25; Leviticus 20:10). Some would consider that to be too restrictive in today's sexually liberated society, where a "meaningful relationship" is all that is important in order to become sexually involved.

The Bible teaches, however, that God has not changed. Psalm 102:26,27 teaches that the earth will "grow old like a garment," but the Lord will remain the same. Hebrews 1:10-12 repeats the same theme of a dying earth but a transcendent God who actually brings about the decay of His creation from without, but does not change Himself. James says there is "no variation or shadow of turning" with God (James 1:17), and Malachi, several hundred years earlier, said the same thing. "For I am the LORD, I do not change..." (Malachi 3:6). It is clear that God is the same God today that He was in both the Old and New Testaments; neither His character nor His will have evolved. He has not been surprised by the latest trends in public or private morality, and He has not changed His mind or altered His standards. He does not trick us or hide Himself from us, and we can trust that what He said in the Bible he continues to say today.

Certainly our culture is far different than the culture in which Jesus and Paul lived, and as the Bible is applied today there will be an obvious necessity to interpret spiritual truth based on that difference. But how we relate to one another, to God and God's moral standards, is timeless. Therefore, God's word applies to all time frames.

2. How much of the Bible applies?

It is a common practice in evangelical circles today to discount the Old Testament when it speaks in a way that is uncomfortable or incomprehensible. "Oh, that's Old Testament," often means, "I'm not going to pay any attention to that part of God's Word because I don't like it or understand it, so I'm going to revert to human law as my basis of authority." Some teach that there is no continuity between the Old and New Testaments, and unless an Old Testament command is repeated in the New Testament, that particular Old Testament law is invalid for today. The Old Testament becomes sort of a "Word of God, Emeritus," or, like the retired army officer, the "Word of God, (ret.)." If this is our attitude, over 3/4 of the Bible becomes out-dated and is not practically authoritative for us as God's people today.

In the Old Testament, having sex with animals (bestiality) is said to be a perversion, an abomination, is accursed, and the guilty party is to be put to death (Exodus 22:19; Leviticus 18:23; 20:15,16). I would say God feels pretty strongly about that, wouldn't you? Remember, His character and His will have not changed. However, bestiality is not mentioned in the New Testament, so to be consistent, the one who says all Old Testament laws must be repeated in the New to be valid, must say that bestiality is acceptable to God today; nothing in the New Testament forbids it.

Jesus' view of the Old Testament

To discount the Old Testament is to contradict the words of Jesus in Matthew 5:17-19;

"Do not think that I came to destroy the Law or the Prophets. I did not come to destroy but to fulfill. For assuredly, I say to you, till

heaven and earth pass away, not one jot or one tittle will by no means pass from the law till all is fulfilled. Whoever therefore breaks one of the least of these commandments, and teaches men so, shall be called least in the kingdom of heaven; but whoever does and teaches them, he shall be called great in the kingdom of heaven."

These three verses represent some of the most crucial in the Bible as to our understanding of the binding character of the Old Testament, so I'm going to spend some time analyzing them.

What does Jesus mean when He says that He has come to *fulfill* the Law and the Prophets? Does that mean, as some teach, that Jesus lived in obedience to the Old Testament perfectly, and fulfilled it once-for-all, so it no longer applies to us? The Greek word translated here as *fulfill* appears also in Colossians 1:25 as Paul relates his commission from God to *fulfill* the gospel, or to preach it fully,[1] but certainly not to bring it to an end. In Matthew 5, Jesus is correcting the misconceptions of the Old Testament that had been taught as rabbinical traditions by the Pharisees. He is "preaching the law of God fully," or confirming it, not twisting it as the Pharisees had done. Neither is He completing or adding to an incomplete Old Testament, for the Holy Spirit-inspired Psalmist says that the law, in his own day, was "perfect, complete" (Ps 19:7f).

For example, in verses 27 and 28, Jesus reaffirms the Old Testament principle of a sexually pure thought-life, found in Proverbs 6:25 and Exodus 20:17, while the Pharisees in their teaching dealt only with the physical act of adultery. They had taken Deuteronomy 24:1 as an excuse to divorce their wives for any frivolous reason whatever, so Jesus corrected them in verses 31 and 32 with the proper interpretation of that Old Testament verse, explaining that the only cause for divorce given in that scripture was sexual immorality ("uncleanness").

The Pharisees taught that you were to "love your neighbor and hate your enemy" (vs. 43, 44), but the Old Testament nowhere teaches hatred for personal enemies, and even gives specific instructions not to abhor the Edomites nor the Egyptians (Deuteronomy 23:7), two peoples who were antagonistic to the Jews. Jesus corrects that false teaching in verses 44-48.

Rather than abrogating the Old Testament law, or in any way adding to it or changing it, Jesus is confirming it; he is re-establishing its true meaning to His disciples who had undoubtedly been influenced by current rabbinical teaching.

In verse 18, Jesus is underscoring the teaching of verse 17; not one tiny bit of the Old Testament law will become invalid until heaven and earth pass away! This is an idiomatic way of saying "never." Jesus could not be more emphatic. The word translated *fulfilled* here is a different word than in verse 17. The meaning of the phrase is simply that none of God's law will be set aside until all things "come to pass" i.e., until the end of the world. If we discount what God says in His Old Testament law about anything, even what might be considered the least of His commandments, and influence others to do the same, Jesus says that that will effect our standing in the kingdom of God adversely (vs. 19). This verse certainly militates against any understanding of the word "fulfill" in verse 17 to mean any kind of setting aside of the Old Testament law. Do you see how important it is to use the whole Bible as our authority source? It is really foolish, and I might add, dangerous, to think that just because a principle is "Old Testament truth," it is not for today. That position contradicts the very words of our Lord. By using another source of information for our standard besides the whole Bible, we are forsaking the map that leads us to the hidden treasure of kingdom life.

Paul's view of the Old Testament

The Apostle Paul echoes Jesus' view of the Old Testament. In 2 Timothy 3:16,17 Paul says: "All Scripture is given by inspiration of God, and is profitable for doctrine, for reproof, for correction, for instruction in righteousness, that the man of God may be complete, thoroughly equipped for every good work."

The "Scripture" Paul refers to here, of course, is the Old Testament, because the New Testament as yet had not been canonized as "Scripture." Notice Paul says that the entire Old Testament, which was the Scripture of his day, was inspired, or, as that word means, God-breathed, and was profitable for more than just doctrine, but for instruction in righteousness; i.e., to tell you how to live. The date of this epistle is sometime in 67 A.D., well after the Day of Pentecost and the advent of the New Covenant. If the Old Testament was now obsolete, Paul would certainly not have advocated its continual use as the instrument to equip men of God for "every good work."

David says, in reference to the law of God, "The entirety of Your word is truth, and every one of Your righteous judgments endures forever" (Psalm 119:160), and God, speaking through Moses in

Deuteronomy 12:32 says, "Whatever I command you, be careful to do it; you shall not add to it nor take away from it."

The testimony of the Bible, then, is that all its truths remain applicable today, even those of the Old Testament; there is continuity between Old and New.

Ceremonial law vs. moral law

However, it is important to distinguish between the ceremonial aspects of God's Old Testament law, and the moral applications and sanctions of that law. The redemptive, sacrificial system contained in the Levitical ceremonial ordinances was a temporary shadow, or type, of the permanent sacrifice that was to come, Jesus Christ (Hebrews 9:23; 10:1). The whole book of Hebrews was written to demonstrate that the purpose of that sacrificial system had been completed. While the truths the temporary system taught were eternal, the reality had come in Jesus Christ. There was no longer any need for the shadow.

Other ritualistic observances in the Old Testament, such as dietary laws, feast days and the Sabbath, are specifically set aside in the New Testament (Colossians 2:16,17). While continuing to keep them is often a healthy and wise thing to do, it cannot be said that they continue to carry the weight of law in the New Covenant.

The dietary laws pictured God's desire to keep Israel physically separate from the pagan nations around them, their worship, their women, and their way of life (Deuteronomy 7). Today, the people of God are spiritual Israel, those who have faith in Jesus Christ (Galatians 3:7,9,29; 6:16), the land we are asked to occupy is not Canaan but the whole world (Matthew 28:18-20), and we are not to isolate ourselves from unbelievers (John 17:18), but to shine among them as light, and influence them as salt (Matthew 5:13-16).

The feasts of the Old Testament picture various aspects of the ministry of Jesus, and the Sabbath is representative of the rest we, as believers, have entered in Him. Hebrews 4:9-11 refers to a "rest for the people of God." That does not refer to entering heaven when we die as some say, but to a rest entered by faith in Jesus Christ. That means we have ceased from all labors to gain right standing with God through works. Now we come to Him on the basis of faith alone.

The ceremonial laws, then, are "out of gear," teaching truths that are eternal, but that were simply types of the reality that came in the New Covenant in Jesus Christ.

The moral laws are a different story. They include general and specific ethical statements, like the prohibition of adultery, murder, theft, bribery, perjury, sexual sins, slander, arson, etc. These laws all need to be interpreted in light of today's culture, but they must be assumed to remain valid today unless they have been rendered inoperative by the death of Christ, or have been specifically set aside by the New Testament.

This science of interpretation is called *hermeneutics*, which simply means trying to determine what a passage of Scripture means. Biblical hermeneutics is not easy, but if our epistemology is right, i.e., if we believe that the whole Bible is our authority source, we can arrive at truth as we trust the Holy Spirit to guide us (John 16:13). Remember, God has not changed as to how He feels about ethics; what once was sin remains sin; and God's method of dealing with that sin through His delegated authorities (family, church and civil government), remains the same today.

A class of moral law found in the Old Testament is the case law. The case law is a particular application of a more general moral law. For instance, wearing clothing of the opposite sex reflects God's attitude toward sexual perversion, and is said to be an abomination to God (Deuteronomy 22:5), and building a railing around a house's flatroof was mandatory to keep guests from falling off and killing themselves (Deuteronomy 22:8). These case laws are applicable today in that the principle taught can be applied even if the specifics no longer apply. We don't generally have flat roofs on our homes that need safety rails, but back-yard swimming pools do need fences around them. This principle is the basis for our property liability laws today.

The moral law of God as expressed in both the Old and New Testaments remains in full force today, along with their sanctions for civil crimes. Expressing the eternal will of God, it serves as a mirror to show us how we deviate from the character of God in our lives. For an unbeliever, the law shows him his need for a savior, and the absolute lunacy of trying to please God by being good enough. James says that even if you keep the whole law (the Old Testament), and yet offend in only one point, you are as guilty as if you had broken them all (James 2:10). For the Christian, the law shows us God's standard for our lives, and drives us to grateful repentance for the discrepancy between that standard and our conduct. David loved the law of God (Psalm 119:97), because it allowed him to acknowledge his sin before God with a broken and contrite heart, and turn from it (Psalm 51, 139).

3. To whom does the Bible apply?

The Old Testament law was given originally for the nation Israel (Exodus 20:22), but Deuteronomy 4:6-8 makes it clear that Israel was to be an example to the surrounding nations, particularly in the wisdom and understanding of their statutes and judgments. Was God only the God of the Jews, or does He have a claim over all nations? The Bible teaches that the earth belongs to Him, along with every thing that is in it. (Psalm 24:1), the kings of the earth should serve the Lord with fear (Psalm 2:11), for the whole world will be judged by Him (Psalm 9:8).

The question is, what will be the standard by which God judges? Will God have a different set of laws to judge the Spanish than He does the Chinese? Will the Moslems and Hindus be judged by a different standard than the Christians?

God sent Jonah to preach to the wicked citizens of Ninevah and to call them to repentance. The Bible says they turned from their evil ways and repented in sackcloth and ashes. Jonah, as a Jewish prophet of Jehovah God, didn't preach a special standard for the Ninevites, but the only law he knew to preach, the law of Moses. The result was that God's judgment was stayed, based on their repentance from breaking that Mosaic law. God held pagan Ninevah accountable to keep His eternal law as recorded in the books of Moses in the Bible.

In Isaiah 2:2-4, the Church is pictured as a mountain that grows until it becomes the chief of mountains, with all the nations of the world streaming to it to learn how to live. The church, by following God's blueprints in the Bible in every area of life, will have demonstrated to the world the excellency of the ways of God by serving as a "living epistle," a model of Biblical truth. As a result the pagan nations of the earth will come to the church and say, "Teach us God's ways. We can see from your lives the legitimacy of your claim that His ways work." This passage goes on to say that the law of God will flow forth from the church and form the basis of God's judgment "between the nations."

Matthew 4:4 speaks of man living by the words of God, not just the Jews, and Proverbs 14:34 says that righteousness (certainly based on God's revealed standard) exalts any nation. Obviously, the law of God is applicable to all peoples and all nations, not just Israel.

To summarize, we have seen that the law of God contained in the whole Bible is applicable to all people in every age. Proper hermeneutics must be used, i.e., the whole Bible applies unless an Old

Testament law is specifically set aside in the New Testament, or is a ceremonial law that is satisfied or completed by the ministry of Jesus Christ in the New Covenant. This is the epistemology that must be used when we come to the Scriptures if we are to be consistent.

Righteousness by faith

Let me make one thing clear so there can be no misunderstanding. The Bible teaches clearly from cover to cover that righteousness does not come from keeping the law of God, but by faith alone. God's law for Christians is not a means to gain standing with our Heavenly Father nor a way to cause Him to love us more. His love for His church is not conditioned on our performance, but is a powerful, irresistible love, that, when we experience it, causes us to respond with, "Oh Lord, what can I do to please you?" His law gives the answer to that question. Obedience to the Law of God is not legalism, but the glad response of a sinner who has experienced a genuine conversion. It is a response that is not burdensome but truly a joy; one that springs, not from an attempt to gain favor with God, but from one who knows the security of right standing with Him by faith (1 John 4:19; John 14:21; Psalm 119:24, 77, 92, 143, 174).

The Jews misunderstood this truth and tried to establish their own righteousness by the works of the law (Romans 9:30 - 10:4), even though the wonderful message of righteousness by faith had been established by Abraham (Romans 4:1-4).

Blessings by obedience

Righteousness, then, does not come by obedience to the law, but blessing does. God loves to reward His obedient children from His vast storehouse of blessings, both spiritual and material. Even non-Christians who follow the principles of the Law of God will experience the promised blessings of Deuteronomy 28:1-14. Here God lays out for the Jews, and, if the law applies to all nations, everyone else as well, the results of obedience. This principle, blessing based on obedience to God's law, is as inviolate as the law of gravity, and is universally true. A non-Christian who even unknowingly keeps God's precepts during his lifetime will experience temporal blessing, but without faith in Jesus Christ he will spend eternity in the lake of fire, according to Revelation 20:15. Conversely, disobedience to the law of God will bring the cursings mentioned in Deuteronomy 28:15-68 to those who are God's people as well as to pagans. Paul was simply reiterating this eternal principle when he wrote in Galatians 6:7, "Do not be deceived, God is not mocked; for whatever a man sows, that he will also reap." Earthly blessing follows obedience; righteousness in God's eyes follows faith in Jesus Christ.

This book has laid out biblical principles for family living that will be successful if followed, whether the family members are Christians or not. Certainly the empowerment of the Holy Spirit gives Christians a tremendous advantage.

---

[1] W.E. Vine, *Expository Dictionary of New Testament Words*, (Old Tappan, New Jersey: Fleming H. Revel Company, 1966), Vol. II, p. 135.

To order additional copies
of this book or
for volume discounts
please call 1-800-247-6553